√ B ε T

W9-BZG-417

The Land of Contrasts

The American Culture

NEIL HARRIS—General Editor

THE LAND OF CONTRASTS

1880-1901

Edited,
with Introduction and Notes by

Neil Harris

George Braziller   New York

Wingate College Library

Copyright © 1970 by Neil Harris

Published simultaneously
in Canada by
Doubleday Canada, Limited.
All rights reserved.
For information address the publisher:
George Braziller, Inc.
One Park Avenue
New York, N. Y. 10016

Standard Book Number:
        0-8076-0550-6, Cloth edition;
        0-8076-0549-2, Paper edition
Library of Congress Catalog Card Number: 71-104962
Book Design by Jennie Bush
Second Printing
Printed in the United States of America

089230

Acknowledgments

For their aid in preparing this volume I wish to thank Emily Faber, Silke-Marie Garrels, James L. Merriner, Richard J. McCarthy, and the staff of the Houghton Library, Harvard University.

Acknowledgment is gratefully made to the following:

The Bobbs-Merrill Company for permission to reprint portions of Herbert Quick, *One Man's Life*.

The Bowdoin College Museum of Art, Brunswick, Maine, for permission to reproduce "Athens" by John La Farge, and "Venice" by Kenyon Cox.

The Library of Congress, Washington, D. C., for permission to reproduce "The Arts" and "The Sciences" by Kenyon Cox, "Peace" and "War" by Gari Melchers, "Good Administration" and "Corrupt Legislation" by Elihu Vedder, and "The Mantle of the Law" by Frederick Diehlman.

Preface

"Do not tell me only of the magnitude of your industry and commerce," wrote Matthew Arnold during his visit to the United States in the 1890's; "of the beneficence of your institutions, your freedom, your equality: of the great and growing number of your churches and schools, libraries and newspapers; tell me also if your civilization—which is the grand name you give to all this development—tell me if your civilization is *interesting*."

The various volumes that comprise THE AMERICAN CULTURE series attempt to answer Matthew Arnold's demand. The term "culture," of course, is a critical modern concept. For many historians, as for many laymen, the word has held a limited meaning: the high arts of painting, sculpture, literature, music, architecture; their expression, patronage, and consumption. But in America, where physical mobility and ethnic diversity have been so crucial, this conception of culture is restricting. The "interesting" in our civilization is omitted if we confine ourselves to the formal arts.

The editors of THE AMERICAN CULTURE, therefore, have cast a wider net. They have searched for fresh materials to reconstruct the color and variety of our cultural heritage, spanning a period of more than three hundred years. Forgotten institutions, buried artifacts, and outgrown experiences are included in these books, along with some of the sights and sounds that reflected the changing character of American life.

The raw data alone, however fascinating, are not sufficient for the task of cultural reconstruction. Each editor has organized his material around definitions and assumptions which he explores in the volume introductions. These introductions are essays in their own right; they can be read along with the documents, or they can stand as independent explorations into social history. No one editor presents the same kind of approach; commitments and emphases vary from volume to volume. Together, however, these volumes represent a unified effort to restore to historical study the texture of life as it was lived, without sacrificing theoretical rigor or informed scholarship.

NEIL HARRIS

Contents

Illustrations

Introduction

NEIL HARRIS

Historians are more comfortable with description than with definition. Social scientists have criticized our carelessness in employing models and our reluctance to discuss them. Apparently we prefer the shelter of details to the exposure of abstractions.

But definition can create its own pitfalls. The term culture offers one such instance. Almost every contemporary usage of the word, descriptive as well as normative, has invited criticism, opposition, and sometimes abuse. At one time a verb meaning to cultivate or nourish, culture was applied to almost every experience from gardening to education. Passage to the noun form, however, has involved continuous controversy. In the late nineteenth century the word frequently referred to a condition or state of achievement; social critics in England and America vied with one another to determine just which individuals were "cultured" and which civilizations had created a "culture." In our own times its more frequent use, at least among scholars, has been as a category of investigation: all societies have cultures, it is a matter of determining just which values, institutions, and activities can be sheltered within the concept. This greater tolerance, however, has not produced greater agreement. For once scholars have decided just which elements to put into a culture, they then translate their pragmatic judgments into rigorous and sometimes mutually exclusive definitions of the word itself.

These definitions lie strewn around like discarded favors, soiled through controversy but still appealing. Occasionally they are anthologized and re-examined. When inadequacies and contradictions appear, new offerings replace the old. But they suffer the fate of their predecessors, unable to include all the relevant and exclude the irrelevant social data.

Such controversies, however confusing, have not reduced the popularity of the word. Anthropologists, sociologists, journalists, historians, all continue to employ it frequently and productively. For the attempt to describe a culture, whatever the dilemmas of precise definition, involves a search for unities which link human beliefs, habits, and organizations. Connections and relationships enrich our understanding of isolated pieces of information by placing them within a context. In the absence of a concept of culture, however provisional or arbitrary, most artifacts and institutions appear unintelligible, and their study seems eccentric. Students of human society, challenged continually by new information and unfamiliar objects, seek to retrieve lost intentions and associations. A concept of culture permits the creation of unities, and its use will continue, even if the word is embroiled on a battlefield of its own.

Cultural historians then, trying to join specific objects with social generalizations, commonly offer complex explanations for simple problems. Critical observers are often struck by the contrasts. Some scholars are exempted from charges of pedantry. Anthropologists, for example, dealing with unfamiliar social orders, are not ridiculed for their patient study of word names, myths, and magic. The romance of the mysterious permits unfamiliar objects and exotic experiences to undergo study for their own sake. Historians and sociologists, however, studying social systems that are more comprehensible, produce some amusement and even contempt. Bantu myths and Ashanti dances are one thing; baseball, restaurants, and masonic lodges are another. Everyone claims to understand the basis for baseball and lodges; no special learning seems necessary to place them in a larger setting. They have achieved location because of their familiarity. Using social science techniques to explain the familiar seems like swatting a mosquito with a laser beam: the power of the weapon is out of proportion to the size of the quarry.

The widespread suspicion of these techniques expresses a prejudice of our times. Modern men, certain of their superiority to more "primitive" societies, tolerate technical vocabularies when used to describe these "less sophisticated" peoples. Movement from the simple to the complex obviously requires translation and the construction of special categories.

But to use these terms for our recent ancestors or even ourselves, can be threatening. Modernity seems a less distinctive and less progressive achievement when it can be subjected to the categories used to decipher "primitivism."

One way to lessen prejudice against scrutiny of the familiar is to demonstrate, as generations of social anthropologists have done, the complexities of primitive societies. "Every civilization tends to overestimate the objective orientation of its thought," Lévi-Strauss reminds us. Such assumptions have led to contempt for the intellectual activities of less advanced peoples.

By diluting our patronizing attitudes toward aboriginal man, anthropological techniques can seem more appropriate for modern societies.

Another means of demonstrating the value of cultural history is to assemble some fragments from our past and suggest how they relate to more complex generalizations. Until social details have been worked into acceptable arguments, the task of describing them will be reserved, as it has been for so long, to the antiquarian and anecdotalist. It is the rescue of these rituals and materials which the cultural historian should aim for.

The following selections, then, are offered as clues to such a reconstruction. The most trivial objects contain hints of a larger reality. No one anthology can record every significant detail, and perhaps some distortion is inevitable. But this book is meant to suggest at least a few of the ways by which men try to match form with content, and more particularly, to argue that the changing shape of the physical environment in the late nineteenth century produced novel tries at understanding the national community. Since artifacts and ideas inhabit the same universe, the way they influence each other forms a legitimate subject for discussion.

II

To justify the presentation of cultural data is one thing; to defend its periodization is another. In many ways spatial definitions are easier to accept than temporal ones. Barriers of land and water help to identify the frontiers of the anthropologist's study. But historians must seize on more subjective evaluations, and often rather arbitrarily select events as objective correlatives to historical insights and suspicions. Wars, Presidential terms, party changes, and economic depressions are among the popular boundary stones.

However arbitrarily chosen, two major events do act as natural borders on the 'eighties and 'nineties. They indicate, if not a perfectly unified period, at least the passage from one age to another. The last fifth of America's nineteenth century opened and closed with acts of violence. Twenty years apart, two American Presidents were publicly murdered; the difference between the two assassinations suggests the differences between two eras.

Making his way along a Washington railroad platform on Saturday morning, July 2, 1881, President James Garfield was fatally shot by a small, strange-looking man, Charles J. Guiteau. Only the second time in American history that a President had been cut down, the event touched off waves of shock and anger. During the long summer months while Garfield's life slowly ebbed because his physicians could neither locate nor remove the bullet, the assassin was universally ridiculed. In the lengthy trial the following winter, Guiteau was found guilty and hanged. Despite the testimony of eminent physicians concerning his deranged state, the court insisted on statutory punishment. Compassion did not extend to the killer of a President.

But with all its outrageousness, Guiteau's deed touched off no general reign of terror or search for villains. Even if not legally insane, Guiteau was eccentric enough to be considered an anomaly. He was simply too absurd for society to accept responsibility for the crime or assume a collective guilt. The major political effect of the murder was to renew interest in civil-service reform, though this accomplishment, historians have suggested, was more symbolic than real.

There were, moreover, special domestic, even nostalgic associations attached to the murderer which diluted public fears and bewilderment. Guiteau was a relic from an older, more innocent era of enthusiasm and reform, a perverted legacy of the early republic. His father, Luther, businessman and banker, had been a devout believer in the doctrines of John Humphrey Noyes, a perfectionist contemporary of Emerson and Thoreau. Like his father, Charles Guiteau was converted by Noyes's mystical writings and his promise of freedom from sin. In 1860 Guiteau joined the famous Oneida Community in New York. But Biblical communism, complex marriages, and compulsory introspectiveness did not suit the young man, and he left the faithful after some bitter quarrels and an exchange of threats.

Once out of Oneida, Guiteau's problems only deepened. Enduring the anxiety-ridden lot of the young man on the make in post-bellum America, he moved from job to job and city to city, lecturing, studying law, publishing exotic religious tracts, a migrant in search of celebrity and fortune. His total lack of success nourished compensatory delusions of importance. An unattached man, an enthusiast for new causes, a self-educated oracle of minority opinions, Guiteau's wanderings might have been more acceptable in an earlier America. He was born too late. By 1880 he was a misfit, an outcast, a remnant of the years when New Harmony, Nashoba, Oberlin, and Brook Farm had unleashed their ferment of reforms.

But if distorted, Guiteau's associations remained recognizable. In 1880 the Civil War was still a green memory. Ralph Waldo Emerson, Wendell Phillips, Harriet Beecher Stowe, and James Russell Lowell were all alive; William Lloyd Garrison had died only one year before. Certainly the old enthusiasms had cooled in time, for reconstruction had put a bitter end on many dreams. Darwin and Spencer were more influential names than Lincoln, and utopian communities had stopped multiplying. But the Grand Army of the Republic protected its shrines, and New England reformers continued to testify to earlier commitments. The great crusades of the past left many survivors.

Recognizable also was the setting for the deed. However, pragmatically chosen by the assassin, the railroad station was symbolically appropriate as an ambiguous figure of progress. Careers like Guiteau's were in large part stimulated and doomed by the railroad networks. During the previous three decades the railroad companies had encouraged speculation and get-rich schemes. The success of their promoters inspired many a young man to dreams of fame and prosperity. Guiteau's ambitions were formed in an atmosphere of heady expansion and geographical mobility.

But the railroads also emphasized efficiency and organization. One hundred thousand miles of track were transforming the country into a more disciplined national state, hostile to the pretensions of self-styled eccentrics. In 1881 the transformation was still incomplete, but Guiteau's mad act occurred in the precincts of this agency of change, the herald of America's first industrial revolution.

Twenty years later, almost to the month, another Presidential assassination rocked the nation. On September 6, 1901, at the Pan-American Exposition in Buffalo, a self-proclaimed anarchist named Leon Czolgosz shot William McKinley. The channeled and controlled anger which had succeeded the earlier crime now became an outburst of fear and anxiety. Laws were proposed limiting the activities of political radicals, angry patriots decried the dangers of unlimited immigration, newspaper editors thundered against unnamed terrors subverting society, mobs wrecked immigrant newspapers and attacked foreigners on the streets.

The two assassinations differed in many ways. Czolgosz apparently had little to do with native traditions of radicalism. Though American-born, he was associated with the millions of aliens now entering the country from Southern and Eastern Europe, distant in appearance, religion, and deportment from middle-class Protestant ideals. His deed reflected a world-wide political movement. Czars, kings, emperors, and presidents were being attacked everywhere. Since 1880, Haymarket, Homestead, and Pullman had shaken America's confidence in her ability to maintain a united society. The insulation, the absurdity, even the semi-comfortable eccentricity of Czolgosz's background had disappeared.

Czolgosz's crime took place at one of those great festivals Americans had been organizing since the Philadelphia Centennial in 1876. In 1893,

1901, and 1904, Chicago, Buffalo, and St. Louis all held pageants of national greatness, celebrating human progress and scientific control. If the railway station was an appropriate setting for Guiteau's deed, electricity and the new world of instantaneous communications formed an apt stage for Czolgosz's. The Pan-American Exposition, paying lip service to hemispheric solidarity, was actually glorifying the electric light and power which had transformed America into a more cohesive and self-conscious society in less than twenty years. The distance between the two murders was the distance between the age of steam and the age of electricity, between a relatively isolated, insular America and an involved world power, between a nation still unaware of its unparalleled wealth and a people suddenly conscious of the riches—and divisions—within its midst.

III

If any one term summed up the cultural life of this era, it was self-consciousness. The rate of physical change had always been remarkable in the United States; from the seventeenth century on, observers recorded their astonishment at its pace. But in the late nineteenth century, as the tempo increased, so did the instruments for charting—and directing—this change. Edison's electric light bulb, offering a new, steady glare of illumination, contrasted in its harsh clarity with the romantic flickerings of the older gaslight. The light bulb promoted and symbolized the new self-consciousness conditioning American life in the 'eighties and 'nineties. If progress meant loss of the picturesque, this was a price many were prepared to pay. The cultural life of this era was the product of social anxiety and general curiosity, of a restless, sometimes desperate desire to learn the habits, the thoughts, the working patterns, and dreams of others in the community. These decades witnessed the sudden discovery of pluralities—of class, age, nationality, condition—which made up the American community. The fiction, the newspapers, the amusements, and the education of a people reflected this desire to know more, to collect data and savor the experience of learning.

Technology was crucial in serving this national curiosity. A series of innovations nourished demands for communications and possibilities for self-expression at the same time. The typewriter and the telephone, both novelties at the 1876 Centennial in Philadelphia, playthings fondled by visiting royalty and gawked at by curious crowds, revolutionized in twenty years the pace at which Americans gathered and retrieved information. Between 1880 and 1900 the number of telephones in the United

States increased from less than fifty thousand to almost one and a half millions. The West coast remained out of reach, but New Yorkers could speak to Chicagoans across one thousand miles of space. The paper work on which the great corporations depended was controlled by a new breed of female secretaries, graduates of typing schools which the manufacturers happily established. An inner sanctum of the American male was penetrated by the women who were temporarily confused with the instruments bringing them jobs and security. "Here I sit with my typewriter on my knee," quipped vaudevillians, and the audiences roared, delighted by the novel confusion of sex and machinery.

Other devices were equally revolutionary. Mergenthaler's linotype and Edison's mimeograph intensified the flow of written information; the influence of the new mass newspapers and popular magazines was multiplied by the sextuple printing press. But the power of the word itself began to diminish alongside the appeal of the picture. It was no accident that the late nineteenth century became a favorite period for color symbolism. Lewis Mumford's *Brown Decades*, Mark Twain's *Gilded Age,* and Thomas Beer's *Mauve Decade* all labeled the last third of the century. And contemporaries were fond of tinted imagery themselves. Silverites and Greenbackers fought gold conspiracies; yellow journalism and the Yellow Peril became popular phrases; *The Red Badge of Courage* thrust a young writer into immortality (not to forget "The Black Riders" and "The Blue Hotel"); *The Purple Cow* became a literary battle cry, while The White City fulfilled an architectural dream.

To men accustomed to the Red Scare, Black Power, Green Berets, and the Blue Eagle, the 'eighties and 'nineties do not seem exceptional in their imagery. But if not exceptional, they were anticipatory. For the 'eighties and 'nineties were a visual age, the first time that the picture, the print, the cartoon, and the photograph had been produced on so large a scale. Newspapers and popular magazines, exploiting halftone pictures and rotogravure, transformed their traditional appearance. And electricity's many marvels dazzled the eye. American cities had become visually exhilarating. "Theatres, restaurants, stores are outlined in incandescent lamps," the Englishman William Archer wrote, describing New York in the 1890's. "The huge electric trolleys came sailing along in an endless stream, profusely jeweled with electricity; and down the thickly gemmed vista of every cross street one can see the elevated trains, like luminous winged serpents, skimming through the air." The garishness of the city might appall others, Archer admitted, but for the first time, electricity had divorced light from smoke and heat. The eye could take in this brilliant illumination, undistracted by ancient and unpleasant by-products.

But the camera was perhaps most important of all. To the millions for whom words had been difficult and alien instruments of communication, the photograph promised release from ignorance. Daguerrotypes, calotypes, tintypes, and finally photographs had been available for decades, but the development of the dry-plate process and the appearance of the pocket camera expanded the picture's use, and encouraged men to record their own experiences graphically. They no longer had to rely on the vagaries of memory, the imprecision of anecdote, or the intervention of a professional artist. George Eastman's famous slogan, "You Push the Button, We Do the Rest," helped make Kodak a part of the vernacular.

The spread of photography only increased the demand for other visual diversions. Where once Thomas Nast had reigned supreme and solitary in the world of cartooning, *Judge, Puck, Life,* and *Harper's* now published the work of artists like J. A. Wales, Frederick Opper, M. A. Woolf, and Charles Dana Gibson. Daily newspapers began employing political cartoonists regularly; Outcault's Yellow Kid initiated the reign of the comic strip, while George Luks, John Sloan, William Glackens, and Robert Henri—future painters all—sketched for the mass periodicals. The taste for cheap pictures was so great that a *North American Review* writer called his an age of "over-illustration" and blamed on it the absence of a sound literature. America's want of great writers, Charles Congdon concluded in 1884, may be attributed in part "to the intellectual indolence that a habit of indulgence in mere picture-gazing" originated and confirmed. In 1884 the real expansion still lay ahead, with motion pictures a decade away.

The growth of visual communication trained readers and consumers in a new kind of symbolic shorthand. Compressed images, trademarks, seals, and signs began to penetrate the American consciousness as intensely as the stained-glass iconography of Christian belief had dominated a pre-Gutenberg world. Ivory Soap, Quaker Oats, Sapolio, and Hire's Root Beer were among the pioneers in this new sensory education. Advertising agencies like Lord & Thomas and the J. Walter Thompson Company grew in size and wealth, and helped bring Frederic Remington, Maxfield Parrish, and Will Bradley into publicity work. "When the history of advertising is written," one journal noted in 1896, "the present will be known as the 'picture period.'" Clever copywriters did their best to match the ingenuity of the illustrators, and the visual trademarks were matched in compressive power by the new slogans, still another form of abbreviated information serving to personalize the vast array of consumer goods.

The information explosion was not visual alone. The phonograph preserved sound as the photograph did sight. For some, including Thomas Edison and Edward Bellamy, this was one of the most dramatic inventions of the entire era. Recordings seemed a promising substitute for the printed page, a time-saver essential in this hurried society. Utopian novelists, who flourished in the 'eighties and 'nineties, employed the device in spectacular settings. Their exaggerated predictions remind us of the optimism with which late nineteenth-century Americans viewed mechanical advances. Workers now complained increasingly about the speed-ups, physical dangers, and unemployment they blamed on machinery. Some utopians, moreover, did fear the monotony of a mechanized universe. But these groups were isolated in their criticism. Conservative opposition to machine changes, the tradition of Carlyle, Ruskin, and William Morris, had less support in the United States than in England. Each new device seemed to promise relief from basic social and demographic problems. The electric trolley was hailed as a democratic successor to the more imperious and noisy steam railroad, a means of equalizing conditions in city and country. "The brain racking rout of steam," cried the *Independent,* the cause of so much nervous exhaustion, was yielding to the new power of electricity, morally and physically "the superior force." And the automobile was proclaimed by no less a prophet than Ray Stannard Baker as a solution to dirty roads and traffic jams. Our crowded streets, Baker predicted confidently in *McClure's* in 1899, "will be almost as quiet as a country lane," with the coming of the auto; "all the crash of horses' hoofs and the rumble of steel tires will be gone."

Not all the new marvels were heroic achievements. Some were simply conveniences. In the 'eighties and 'nineties the cash register, the time clock, the fountain pen, and the adding machine appeared, to facilitate the measuring and dissemination of information. Even the modern computer was prefigured in Herman Hollerith's electric punch card system, which was compiling population statistics for the Eleventh Census in 1890. There were sound reasons for Eugene White to complain about "The Plague of Statistics," in the *Atlantic Monthly* in 1901. We have grown so dependent on numerical expression, White warned, that numbers have become both ends and means. "No longer do we appeal to the emotions, no longer do men sway men with truth of words. Facts, and the exact expression of them, are what we seem to desire. Would we convince the average American? It is best done by figures."

Long-standing efforts to comprehend and control data were thus immensely strengthened; industries sprang up to satisfy the curious. E. W.

Scripps and William Randolph Hearst, Joseph Pulitzer and Edward Bok, Frank Leslie and Cyrus Curtis struggled to translate the passion for information into money, and succeeded in doing so. Circulation growth made them rich.

Before the 1880's most American magazines had been relatively small operations, aimed at specialized, often elite audiences, disseminating opinions on crucial public issues. As such they carried little advertising. Until 1882 *Harper's Monthly* refused all advertisements but those of its own publisher. But starting in the late 'eighties a whole series of new periodicals—*Cosmopolitan, Munsey's Magazine, McClure's, The Ladies Home Journal*—were aimed at mass audiences. With low prices and hundreds of ads for bicycles, pianos, cosmetics, and typewriters their circulation burst the older limits. Cyrus Curtis and Frank Munsey admitted that their success rested on the willingness of businessmen to expand their advertising budgets. *The Ladies Home Journal,* Curtis conceded, was published primarily to give manufacturers a chance to tell American women about their products. The huge advertising sections, along with the increase in scientific and journalistic articles, fed readers' demands for more information about the world they lived in. A corps of magazinists, not the short story writers Edgar Allan Poe had in mind when he coined the term fifty years earlier, but journalists who could cover stories anywhere, arose to meet the need. Men like Julian Ralph, Poultney Bigelow, Stephen Bonsal, and James Creelman turned out an endless supply of articles, featuring everything from military campaigns to distant cities.

Newspapers, seeking to exploit the magazine taste by publishing their own Sunday supplements, shared the benefits of the information explosion. Their advertising revenues were increased by the enormous new department stores, eager to centralize their publicity as they had already centralized their retailing. By 1900 the two thousand dailies in the country had a combined readership of more than fifteen millions.

The accelerating ability of journalists, photographers, and gossip columnists to push open formerly closed doors irritated some people. Louis D. Brandeis and Samuel Warren published their famous "Right to Privacy" article in the 1890 *Harvard Law Review*. Contending that recent innovations, "instantaneous photographs and newspaper enterprise" had "invaded the sacred precincts of private and domestic life," Brandeis and Warren outlined legal principles which could protect the individual's privacy. "The intensity and complexity of life, attendant upon advancing civilization, have rendered necessary some retreat from the world," the authors warned; solitude and privacy had become more, not less essential. Yet journalistic assaults continued, and would end only by destroying all "robustness of thought and delicacy of feeling."

Many Americans besides Brandeis and Warren complained about the pervasive publicity. One man's right to remain invisible was as unquestionable as another man's wish to know what he was being private about, *Harper's* insisted in 1891. But the desire for information was not confined to the private lives of prominent men and women, nor did it rest solely on improved methods of communication. The physical marvels of the age required description also: the first skyscrapers, the great Brooklyn Bridge, the huge railway stations, the new municipal subways. Their construction and completion was celebrated in a rhetoric mingling technical details with praise for national ingenuity.

Increasing travel facilities and rapid urbanization made it easier, moreover, for many Americans to gain firsthand knowledge of this new environment of steel and electricity. Hundreds of thousands made pilgrimages to the great fairs, forming throngs whose respect for the complex scientific exhibits impressed observers. Everywhere in Chicago, the French visitor Paul Bourget reported, he saw "the serious attention of minds imperfectly grasping new ideas." In the "gaze of those rustics" who had come to the Columbian Exposition "there was less pride than curiosity— or shall I call it the awakening of a dormant mind, first learning how to comprehend?"

Other Americans, temporarily sated with urban life and its concentration of men and buildings, made their way to the spaciousness of the Far West, attracted by the writings of Theodore Roosevelt, Owen Wister, and John Muir. The chivalric code of the cowboy and the challenges of the strenuous life contrasted with the dangers of "over-civilization." Outing, fishing, and hunting clubs, summer camps, rodeos, conservation societies, all evidenced this fascination with wildness which would develop more fully in the first decade of the next century.

The appearance of the first travelers' checks in 1891, devised by the General Agent of the American Express Company, testified to this increased movement, just as the development of the first Travelers' Aid Society some years later, pointed to some of its hazards. European excursions remained the goal of the wealthy and upper middle classes, but more Americans now spent vacations discovering their own country. For those who could not make the trip themselves, magazinists like Charles Dudley Warner and Julian Ralph described the glories of Yosemite, the Grand Canyon, the Yellowstone, as well as the burgeoning young cities springing up nearby: Denver, Omaha, Salt Lake City. Many Easterners, anxious about the nation's future and skeptical about the possibilities of unlimited progress, took refreshment in Warner's words. It is good, he wrote, "to see men who believe in something heartily and without reserve, even if it is only in themselves. There is a tonic in this challenge of all time and history." Frederick Jackson Turner provided a pedigree for Western enthusiasm, and travel agents helped increase the tourists.

The discovery of local color—which included New England and the Old South, as well as the Far West—serviced fiction as well as facts. Sarah Orne Jewett, Ellen Glasgow, Joel Chandler Harris, Bret Harte, Hamlin Garland sketched the dialects, assumptions, and prejudices of their regions, just as the isolation which had protected regional peculiarity was being continually broken down.

But discovery of local color was not the most important result of self-consciousness and social curiosity. The proliferation of inventions and the growth of population had combined to create novel occupations and living patterns. The great collective institutions which today are taken for granted—hospitals, libraries, museums, universities, department stores, labor unions, giant hotels—either were born or underwent considerable growth during these decades. And Americans wanted to know more about them.

Statistics reveal at least the dimensions of this harvest of institutions. In 1904 the Bureau of the Census compiled a list of more than sixteen hundred hospitals and dispensaries functioning throughout the United States. They included establishments of every size and competence, ranging from poor country dispensaries which treated several hundred patients annually, to the great municipal centers which took in tens of thousands. But the most startling feature of the report was its revelation of recent growth. Of the total number of hospitals only 367, less than twenty-five per cent, had been founded before 1880. In only two decades the expansion had occurred. More and more Americans were visiting, convalescing, and dying in hospitals; more and more were involved in their foundation and supervision. The size of these new and largely unfamiliar enterprises, their courtesies and perils, their tables of organization and rules of procedure became subjects of interest and fascination. Journalists set out to rescue these institutions from popular ignorance and fear. Roosevelt Hospital, A. B. Ward told the readers of *Scribner's*, is a quiet, old-fashioned place, with corridors bordering on lawns and gardens. "The air is like that of the country, too; but then, ventilation is a fine art at Roosevelt." And so was the food. St. John's Hospital in Brooklyn was run by religious sisters, gentle and compassionate. Ward life there was usually friendly. On discharge "the place holds so many associations, dark and fair, that something very like a regret seizes you. . . . And you have dismissed from your mind the repulsive picture of the Hospital which was formed there." The patient's experience became archetypal, requiring narration and explanation. The public demand for information was really a request for reassurance, and journalists treated it as such.

What was true of hospitals was true, with fewer forebodings, of restaurants, hotels, department stores, and factories. The executive skills required to feed, clothe, house, and educate millions simultaneously were products of ingenuity and improvisation. Such human victories served to symbolize, in periodical literature, the larger accomplishments of nineteenth-century civilization. After outlining the complicated duties and heavy responsibilities of the modern hotel manager, Jesse Lynch Williams told his readers not to be surprised that the steward of a great hotel received the same salary as a Supreme Court Justice, $10,000. The manager, after all, had to supervise "the workings of all this many cog-wheeled machine and take note on the action of its various parts," from cooking to carpentry and plumbing. The metaphors of the hotel and the restaurant recur in the writings of Edward Bellamy and William Dean Howells, both of whom experimented with utopian themes. Howells set *A Traveller from Altruria,* that harsh satire on American egotism and materialism, in a great resort hotel, while Bellamy took many pages to detail the eating and shopping habits of the Bostonians in *Looking Backward.* Even Henry James, returning to America in 1904, felt compelled to note what he called the "hotel spirit," the public display of thousands within gilded labyrinths. "Here was a social order in positively stable equilibrium," noted James in *The American Scene.* "Here was a world whose relation to its form and medium was practically imperturbable; here was a conception of publicity *as* the vital medium organized with the authority with which the American genius for organization, put on its mettle, alone could organize it." The American hotel then, was both a social and an aesthetic ideal, "a synonym for civilization, for the capture of conceived manners themselves." The Waldorf Astoria, the Royal Poinsietta, San Francisco's Palace, and the Palmer House were public shrines. Outside, a hurried, noisy, turbulent world; inside, a controlled environment which promised peace, luxury, and ordered human contacts.

But the hotel, the hospital, the department store, and the other great collectivities posed difficulties. They might bring respite from daily dis-

Wingate College Library

orders, but they could be expensive and even dangerous. Precision and standardization were necessary to satisfy rising public expectations, yet precision itself demanded a level of planning which curtailed spontaneity and individualism. When efforts were made to subdue the entire environment to the order of hotel life, serious problems ensued.

Examining one effort to discipline the living habits of a factory force, Pullman, Illinois, Richard Ely responded with mingled admiration and concern. "What might have been taken for a wealthy suburban town is given up to busy workers, who literally earn their bread in the sweat of their brow," wrote Ely. "Unity of design and an unexpected variety charm us." But healthy amusement required planning, and planning on this scale meant control. Ely compared George Pullman's philanthropy to Bismarck's; the Illinois experiment was actually a "benevolent well-wishing feudalism." Touring the much more squalid iron centers of western Pennsylvania, Charles D. Spahr offered a similar observation. If "all that I saw while with the managers of the Carnegie works might be described under the title of 'Triumphant Democracy,'" he noted, "nearly all that I saw while with the men might be described under the title of 'Feudalism Restored.'" Careful management might produce only paternalism and political apathy; neglect, however, yielded ugliness and frustration. Were weeds better than Carnegie's American Beauty rose? The problem had cultural as well as political implications.

Whether or not solutions were at hand, more information appeared. The new collectivities, the new social roles—casualties as well as beneficiaries of industrialization and urbanization—invited investigation. But casual observation was no longer possible; no one could retain his own identity and claim to understand this world of new relationships and systems. A new cultural strategy was needed. It became an age of disguise. Reporters, novelists, sociologists, and economists became tramps, workmen, department store clerks, and urban transients, piecing together the experiences of the hidden or submerged, revealing whole subcultures of deviance and poverty. Nelly Bly made her first newspaper coup by impersonating a lunatic and exposing the horrors of Blackwell's Island; Josiah Flynt lived with tramps; Lillian Pettengill became a domestic servant; Owen Kildare described the ordeals of city bums; Walter Wyckoff worked on the road as an unskilled laborer. Their published reminiscences provoked enormous interest.

Never before had Americans confronted differences so directly, not temporary, peripheral differences, but permanent, pervasive distinctions. The policeman's uniform, the banker's dress, the shopping counter, the city streets were changed for Wyckoff's laborer and Annie MacLean's clerk. These familiar signs were now symbols of an alien power, a repressive force. For some, aesthetic absorption in poverty no longer seemed enough.

Public interest, however, guaranteed neither improvement nor reform. The responses, both of the investigators and their audiences, indicated varieties of confusion. The expansion of cultural information, in fact, was leading to a greater formalism in American life, an increasing consciousness of boundaries, barriers, divisions, which rapidly resulted in aesthetic and even legal formulation.

At first glance, this paradox might seem forced. For decades nationalists had been insisting that the genius of American culture lay in its boundlessness, its inclusiveness, its refusal to submit to the categories promoted by class-ridden European societies. An abundance of information had been the hope and prophecy of ante-bellum artists. We are yet to know, wrote Emerson, "the value of our incomparable materials," still to discover "in the barbarism and materialism of the times, another carnival of the same gods" we admire in Homer. "Banks and tariffs, the newspaper and caucus, Methodism and Unitarianism," as well as "our fisheries, our Negroes and Indians," these had remained unsung. The heart of the vernacular tradition seemed to lie in its capacity to exalt the humble and dignify the ordinary. Whoever broadened the national attention, alerted it to its subcultures, its institutions, its varieties, nourished old ideals and fulfilled ancient dreams.

And some reforms followed the exposures. The degradation of factory labor, the fatigue of urban clerks, the filth of city slums pressured both the legislature and the judiciary. Annie MacLean's department store girls benefitted from the Consumers' Leagues her article encouraged; housing laws and tenement codes resulted from the indignant reports of Jacob Riis.

Even intellectuals shared in this questioning of older assumptions. The era's most creative minds engaged in what Morton White had termed a "revolt against formalism," a disinclination to accept the traditional borders of scholarly disciplines. Their desire to "come to grips with reality" was fulfilled in a series of epic works of cultural reassessment. John Dewey, Thorstein Veblen, William James, Oliver Wendell Holmes all opposed compartmentalized thinking.

Economic reforms and intellectual integration, however, proved less influential than the growth of cultural separatism. Increasing knowledge demanded ordering and mediators. Guides who could provide reassurance and advice were welcomed. The result of this expansion of information was not therefore a richer experience but one more carefully programmed, better organized, more secure. With ordinary men bewildered by the options at their disposal, intermediaries stepped in.

Sometimes the aid came quickly and cheaply. Social propriety was always a matter of concern in a mobile society, but now emotional response seemed just as prob! 'matic. Letter writers began appealing to newspaper and magazine columnists for advice on their marriages, their love lives, their personal dilemmas and hopes. "Ruth Ashmore" began a "Side Talks with Girls" in the *Ladies Home Journal* which yielded more than ten thousand letters a year. In 1896 "Dorothy Dix" founded her famous column of advice in the *New Orleans Picayune,* and two years later "Beatrice Fairfax" followed the pattern in the *New York Journal.* Bewildered wives, mothers, daughters, and sweethearts turned to gossip columnists as specialists, where they would once have relied on the more generalized knowledge of ministers, friends, or novelists.

Some advice was more expensive. Most home builders, Edith Wharton and Ogden Codman, Jr. complained in 1897, confined the architect's task to elevation and floor-plans; room decoration was left to upholsterers. Because upholsterers lacked "the preliminary training necessary for architectural work," it was inevitable that they sacrifice form to color "and composition to detail." Interior decorators who "understood the fundamental principles of their art," who could restore scientific method to room planning, were indispensable. The amateurish, ad hoc orientation of previous generations had become inappropriate in an age of specialists; the wealth, the variety, the complexity of American life demanded training as well as experience. As with interior decoration so municipal sanitation, library science, sports training, school administration, and advertising also required the services of experts.

Hundreds of new organizations in the late century staked out their claims to public recognition. Economists, political scientists, accountants, lawyers, mechanical engineers all formed national associations in the 'eighties to publish periodicals, lobby for special privileges, and define standards of competence. All began to develop cultures of their own, disseminating values, propelling myths, channeling ambitions, and glorifying heroes. *E Pluribus Unum* had been the motto of a pre-professional age; community opinion was now a poor substitute for the specialist on many subjects, and when experts and the public clashed, professionals claimed victory.

Cultural divisions caused by professionalization, however, seemed less striking than the new consciousness of class and ethnic differences. Photographs, cartoons, books, and pamphlets were continually reasserting diversity, without celebrating it. The 'eighties and 'nineties were decades of angry suspicion. Catholics, Jews, Negroes, farmers, workers, millionaires, all were perceived by other members of society as dangerous enemies to collective security. Hundreds of books, thousands of articles bewailed the growth of social hostilities. The American Protective Association campaigned to reduce Catholic influence in politics and education; patrician New Englanders organized to limit immigration to favored races; Southern mobs terrorized black men with rope and fire; Californians discovered an Oriental menace. Cataclysm and disaster became popular themes, the "Volcano Under the City," a common fear. In Ignatius Donnelly's famous dystopia of 1889, *Caesar's Column,* the contrasts of class and wealth reached an unbearable intensity. The rulers of America were surrounded with all that luxury and art could provide, "the very profligacy and abandon of unbounded wealth." But only a thin "crust of earth separated all this splendor from that burning hell of misery beneath it. And if the molten mass of harrow should break its limitations and overflow the earth! Already it seemed to me . . . I could hear the volcanic explosions; I could see the sordid flood of wrath and hunger pouring through these halls; cataracts of misery bursting through every door and window, and sweeping away all this splendor into never-ending blackness and ruin." Orgies of bloody violence and the end of civilization seemed near at hand.

From fears produced by self-consciousness, many groups in America began to turn in on themselves, to withdraw from indiscriminate participation in American life, to drift toward sharper cultural self-definition. No other era witnessed the formation of so many clubs, societies, lodges, and fraternal organizations. The Gilded Age was more properly a Guilded Age, an era of association for protection.

None moved more rapidly to disengage than the wealthy and leisured. The photograph, the newspaper, and the realistic novel seemed dangerous, disseminating information that threatened their integrity as a group and challenged their taste as individuals. Publicity which exposed the contrasts of American life propelled the rich toward the construction of their own society, governed by elaborate rules and subtle distinctions. The wealth piled up by industrial expansion was released in expenditure, the creation of art collections and great homes, the purchase of yachts and foreign alliances. Sherry's and Delmonico's, Newport and Long Branch, Palm Beach and Monterey became landmarks in this search for private amusement. Industrial families from the hinterlands joined older eastern clans in creating a new social extravagance. "Strange to narrate," the *Independent* reported in 1902, "in our free, democratic United States, almost within a decade, there has sprung up an exclusive social caste as valid at certain European courts as an hereditary titled aristocracy—a powerful class of fashionable multi-millionaires who at their present ratio of ascendancy bid fair in time well nigh to patronize royalty itself."

The life style of the rich received continual attention. The photographs which survive of the great mansions in Chicago, New York, and San Francisco perpetuate their mixture of opulence and anxiety, the fear that a single space might be empty or a moment of time unencumbered with social obligations. The leopard skins atop the Persian rugs atop the hardwood floors, the walls covered with enormous paintings and mirrors, the huge stacks of crystal and china, the indiscriminate mingling of rococo, classic, Moorish, and Gothic—as if exclusive selection of any was a limitation on all—became the hallmarks of leisured life in the late nineteenth century. Profusion and extravagance demonstrated membership in an elite.

But the new instruments of publicity made expenditure dangerous. In the early years of the republic European visitors had noted the caution of the American rich, their aversion to display, their fear of offending the sensibilities of the lower and middle classes whose political power they respected. Prudence apparently deserted the nabobs of the 'eighties and 'nineties, however, and the fright they received turned them inward. The growth of private preparatory schools, with their careful imitation of English manners and Spartan morals, was one sign. Contact with immigrant children in urban public-school systems could thereby be avoided, and some contrasts reduced. Along with the schools came the first country clubs, proudly consuming immense acreages for the benefit of golfers, proclaiming free communion with nature and restricted communion with men.

Housing as well as education and amusements required protection and isolation. In St. Louis the Private Place idea, originated by Julius Pitzman shortly after the Civil War, grew in popularity until the clusters of fine homes—protected from the outside by locked gates facing landscaped squares and ovals—numbered in the hundreds. In Tuxedo Park, New York, Pierre Lorillard III constructed an entire secluded community, with cottages, private roads, separate sewage system, and a keeper's lodge. Travel might cause the rich some problems but the new private railroad cars, the yachts, and the first-class sections of trans-Atlantic liners promised to solve them. Visitors to California might take the California Limited, its owners advertised, "the only train to California . . . that does *not* carry second-class sleepers and second-class passengers."

Experts now provided the certification necessary to limit participation in this culture. The *Social Register,* published in the 'eighties for the first time, permitted hosts to give parties or parents to plan alliances without fearing impostors. Tiffany's established a department of blazoning, marshaling, and designing of arms for those who could trace their ancestors back far enough. Society queens employed advisers like Ward McAllister, to keep their standards rigorous.

On forays out of their enclosures, however, the wealthy abandoned their dreams of separatism in favor of cultural intervention. The same executive skills and single-minded purposes that produced fortunes in industry and finance, proved invaluable in protecting infant symphony orchestras and museums. Contributing to armories and National Guard regiments was one method of furthering social control; construction of cultural fortresses was another. Refinement, deference, and social peace might flourish if Americans cherished the arts.

This benevolence, however, frequently caused resentment. Critics charged Henry Lee Higginson, the architect of the Boston Symphony Orchestra, with monopolistic and authoritarian practices. The founders of the Metropolitan Opera House, upset they could not purchase boxes in the old Academy of Music, were pilloried as vulgar swells. We are still in the early stages of the war on poverty, the *Atlantic Monthly* complained in 1878, but workers have begun to regard "works of art and instruments of high culture, with all the possessions and surroundings of people of wealth and refinement, as causes and symbols of the laborer's poverty and degradation, and therefore as things to be hated." As much as the caste barriers constructed by the rich were disliked, their attempts to cross over the line and compensate philanthropically for their ecomonic aggressions seemed even more dangerous. Assimilation of their ideals might corrupt the masses, and institutions of culture could easily become agencies of oligarchy and aristocracy. Voluntary isolation, after all, had advantages as well as dangers; it kept the group identifiable and reduced its power to manipulate the rest of society.

A similar ambiguity surrounded the response to immigrant culture. Aroused by what they viewed as challenges to traditional Americanism, patriotic societies, almost without number, sprang up to preserve ethnic purity. The Daughters of the American Revolution, the Society of Colonial Wars, the Order of Founders and Patriots, the Mayflower Descendants, all were established within twenty years. Descendants of early immigrants, like the Dutch and the Huguenots, and those claiming ancestry from the peerage of England formed their own groups. These organizations did not testify to increased wealth, for many of their members were only marginally successful in the competitive arenas of the business world; unlike their ancestors they shunned hand to hand fighting. They were rather islands of security in a society grown so diverse, that national traditions in government, religion, race, even language, seemed threatened. If only immigrants thought, looked, and spoke like other Americans, social problems would disappear. But since immigrants persisted in remaining different, the solution seemed to lie in legislation. Immigration restriction lay only a few years ahead.

But while some feared immigrant distinctiveness, others wished to preserve it. The question of cultural assimilation could be answered only when the value of homogeneity itself had been established. Visitors to the ghettos could not quite decide whether the coming assimilation was a political boon or a cultural danger. When John Corbin's immigrant theatres turned into the standardized world of the vaudeville circuits, described by Edwin Royle, had there been a net gain or loss? Henry James, visiting the Bowery Theater in the early twentieth century, considered the question. The immigrant audience was watching the complicated machinery of an American farce, confronting national culture. "Were they going to rise to it, or rather fall to it—to *our* instinct, as distinguished from their own, for picturing life. Were they to take our lesson, submissively, in order to get with it our smarter traps and tricks, our superior Yankee machinery. . . . Or would it be their dim intellectual resistance, a vague stir in them of some unwitting heritage—of the finer irony" to withstand this effort at corruption and react, above "our offered mechanic bribes, on our ingrained intellectual platitude?" James was not optimistic about the outcome.

The problem of cultural separatism was more severe for another American group, the blacks, and they were not permitted to make their own choice. Here the stereotype was to be supported by terror rather than bribes. The fables of Joel Chandler Harris, the minstrel blackface, the Sambo and Bones routines set up cultural boundaries which Negroes were not allowed to pass. Legal segregation, in schools, transport, and amusements, was reinforced by the lynch mob, Ida Wells's "Red Menace." Reality was filtered through the stereotype, and when Negroes challenged the stereotype's accuracy, they paid a heavy price. The closer blacks came to participation in white culture, the more forcibly they were reminded of their differences.

In some ways, this experience also held true for the American female. The legatees of decades of protest, women were now demanding the right to full participation in political and economic life. Innovations like the bicycle and the typewriter aided this quest, the one bringing release from constrictions of dress, the other promising an end to economic dependence. The position of the genteel spinster, unable to perform remunerative labor and doomed to exist on the sufferance of parents was capsuled in the most famous sensation of the age, the Lizzie Borden trial. Whether or not the girl was guilty of parricide, the tensions governing her life were those of an entire class.

But the trial could also be taken as a warning. Women were entitled to respect and deference only so long as they remained within their sheltered enclaves and preserved the ideals of home and family. Attempts to break out would reduce them to the level of men, and either release female appetites for violence and competition, or deny them their special needs. Lizzie was charged with murdering for money, in effect for independence. The prosecutor in the Borden case trod gently on the sensibilities of his jury, reminding them the defendant was a lady, "no ordinary criminal" to be quickly disposed of. "You have been educated to believe, you are proud to recognize your loyalty, your fealty to the sex," he went on. But the sex also possessed "cunning and deftness," it could, under certain conditions, outdo the male in ferocity. What layers of guilt were probed by the trial, what chords touched off by the image of the avenging female who had stepped out of her station to commit a crime of horror?

Opponents of feminism warned that psychological satisfaction and political power were mutually exclusive for women. The Republic of the Future, which Anna Bowman Dodd created, demonstrated the dangers of technological progress and sexual equality. Once more cultural assimilation was chimerical. "Woman has placed herself by the side of man, as his coequal in labor and vocation, only to make the real distance between them the greater. She has gained her independence at the expense of her strongest appeal to man, her power as mistress, wife and mother." Separatism was a preservative, contrasts made for unity. The subculture guaranteed the survival of the larger whole.

Most of all, perhaps, it was the status of the child which demonstrated the era's insistence on carefully defined diversity. There was no greater hope for the future, wrote Charlotte Perkins Gilman in 1903, than "this new thought about the children," a recognition of "children as a class, as citizens with rights to be guaranteed only by the state." Child life was now described as a psychic universe of its own, with stages and progressions, fantasies and dreams, anxieties and dramas. The popularity of Froebel's kindergarten movement and the increased importance given play showed the interest in juvenile culture; the development of professional child study and the new definition of adolescence, both sponsored by G. Stanley Hall, added scholarly support. Few doubted that the young possessed special virtues and peculiar needs. Child labor laws, the growth of juvenile courts, the appearance of Junior Republics, the increase in children's fiction, all were attempts to preserve the world of the young. Like women, children were vital symbols of innocence, social instruments of redemption whose purity might liberate the social order from its larger corruptions.

But like women also, like the immigrants and the blacks, the innocence of the young was to be programmed, their choices limited. The true purpose of learning the juvenile's vocabulary was not to leaven the adult world, but control the child's. The difference between etiquette books like Eliza Lavin's, and Julia Dewey's primer on school-room manners, was only one of degree. The right to be different was not, after all, the right to be eccentric, for difference was meant to strengthen the comunity's confidence in its overall standards. "Should you like to be thought odd or queer?" asks Julia Dewey's teacher; "No ma'am," is the approved response.

Literature contained its own divisions. Realism and naturalism met determined resistance by critics and clergymen who divided writing up into rigid categories. Unlike the newspaper page and the muckraking article, accepted fiction was not open, in Henry James's words, to even the "appearances of extreme intimacy." Genteel editors like Hamilton Wright Mabie insisted that "the order of the world is moral in every fibre." Against attacks like Clarence Darrow's assault on traditional art, they argued, in Mabie's words, that "idealism is wrought into the very fibre of the race, and is as indestructible as the imagination in which it has its roots." An artist's work was "as much a matter of his character as of his genius." Such doctrines, vulgarized by censors like Anthony Comstock and evangelical preachers like De Witt Talmage, harried the efforts of many young writers and forced some, like Dreiser, to postpone publication of important books. What was not banned or postponed, was often mutilated by the authors themselves, to conform with the conventions which ordered their art.

Forcefully spurning Theodore Roosevelt's theory of patriotism, Henry James, again, noted in the late 'nineties that "we may have been great fools to develop the post office, to invent the newspaper and the railway; but the harm is done—it will be our children who will see it; we have created a Frankenstein monster at whom our simplicity can only gape." Increased communication was a monster because it intensified a sense of difference even while it expanded consciousness. Stereotypes, segregations, and controls followed revelations more easily than tolerance and reforms. Social curiosity had its penalties along with its rewards.

IV

The discovery of varying life styles within the community then, did not release the investigators from responsibility. Forebodings about class war, anxiety about the battle of the sexes, distress over generational antagonism, concern for the processes of ethnic assimilation, and sheer exasperation at controlling so heterogeneous a population thrust social critics into action. Some despaired and panicked; but others outlined the intervention necessary to avoid catastrophe. The interveners might be sociocrats like Lester Ward's trained experts; they might be social workers or John Dewey's new teachers, university academicians or Veblen's engineers. All would appear on stage in the era which followed. But massive intervention and structural change still seemed radical to most Americans. Perhaps the arts, more traditional instruments of social control, might succeed in restoring unity.

One difficulty was that many artists did not seem interested in meeting social needs. The appeals of expatriation and absenteeism grew in the 'eighties and 'nineties. Henry James, John Singer Sargent, Harold Frederic, Bret Harte, Henry Harland, Marion Crawford, and others were living abroad, apparently abandoning the effort to come to terms with American civilization. William Dean Howells bravely tried to deny the problem; pointing to Shelley and Byron, to Kipling and Heine, Turgenev and Ibsen, he insisted that literary absenteeism was neither an American vice nor an American virtue. "It is an expression and a proof of the modern sense which enlarges one's country to the bounds of civilization," the "result of chances and preferences which mean nothing nationally calamitous or discreditable." Public anxiety about artistic exile, however, was real and could not be quieted.

Those who remained at home, moreover, particularly the visual artists, seemed willfully to have ignored the details of American industrial life. A few of the architects engaged in a novel task. Chicago's office-buildings, exclaimed Paul Bourget, were "a new sort of art—an art of democracy made by the masses and for the masses, an art of science where the invariability of natural laws gives to the most unbridled daring the calmness of geometrical figures." But Americans were not as conscious as foreign visitors of their own artistic innovations. They tolerantly accepted artistic indifference to the new urban landscape. Complaining about the quest for prettiness among American painters, Samuel Isham, in his 1905 history of the art, argued that a posterity curious about turn-of-century America would discover little in paint and canvas. Europe's artists, in "an infinity of pictures" would yield future historians "the very age and body of the time." But American painters concentrated on idyllic landscapes and fashionable clients. All they sought were ideal alternatives, a poetry which softened the prose of daily life, rather than described it.

Nonetheless, homogenized unity, a concentration on ideals instead of realities, became an increasing preoccupation for some artists. The first true school of American muralists grew up in the 'eighties and 'nineties, bent on covering the walls of state-houses, museums, and court houses with calls to patriotism and virtue. The depersonalized art which Kenyon Cox, Frank Millet, and Will Low produced was matched by a series of patriotic monuments, often but not exclusively devoted to the memory of Civil War heroes. One journal insisted a "monument mania" had swept the country leaving behind it arches, mausoleums, equestrian statues, and commemorative tablets. This official art, complemented by elaborate ceremonies of dedication and remembrance, was presented as a material basis for nationality, a check to the country's cultural contrasts in a defined and ritualized religion of patriotism. The Sons of the American Revolution commissioned a statue of Nathan Hale to stand in Central Park; not to be outdone, the Daughters of the American Revolution supported a memorial for Mary Washington, the President's mother; the Society of Colonial Wars unveiled a monument at Louisbourg. Inspired by the frenzy, Mark Twain even proposed a monument to Adam, as a tourist lure for Elmira, New York. Historical sites like Mount Vernon were restored, battlefields marked, military parks created, manuscript collections indexed. Flag worship became the order of the day. And, of course, a giant public subscription raised the famous pedestal for Bartholdi's colossal Statue of Liberty, the era's most grandiose effort to capture American ideals in stone and bronze.

Another possible source of unity lay in the sheer exhilaration of consumption. The thousands of pages of advertising in magazines and newspapers promised material rewards for self-control and hard work, and a constant stream of consumer products aroused awe and ambition. The rituals of buying and selling, however, were becoming more mechanized. Instead of purchasing from peddlers and salesmen, rural Americans were now ordering from the enormous mail-order catalogues of Montgomery Ward and Sears, Roebuck. Chain stores, department stores, brand names replaced more personal transactions; the first cafeterias and automatic vending machines, both products of the 1890's, were precursors of things to come. In this increasingly quantified environment, whose efficiencies seemed only to increase contrasts of wealth and ethnicity, occasions for demonstrating the presence of a collective vocabulary and some kind of social discipline had become more necessary. Ceremony could play a new and important role.

In no area was the value of ceremony more apparent than in sports. The 'eighties and 'nineties developed many athletic novelties. Intercollegiate football gained enormous popularity; baseball consolidated its role as the national pastime; basketball and volleyball were invented; cycling and roller skating became the rage. Historians have often connected the growth of sports to the period's psychic strains. The themes of strenuosity, competitiveness, and individual assertion against the environment were carried through by the athletic contest no less than the jingoism of the Spanish-American War or the rhetoric of political leaders.

But while the exhilaration of combat was an important source for this interest in athletics, the rituals attached to these spectacles were perhaps as important. The rites of spectatorship were as exciting, and probably more influential, than the rules of play. Codes of sportsmanship became as necessary to the fans as to the players. The ability to subordinate intense desires to win or to channel intercollegiate and inter-urban jealousies into a regularized code of behavior, indicated the possibilities of self-restraint in a divided society. Referees, umpires, and judges frequently became targets for the abuse of frustrated fans, but anger was temporary and rarely interfered with the progress of the match.

For while winning and losing were the immediate goals, the continuity of leagues, series, and associations made individual results only temporary, and less fundamental than the rituals associated with the events. The difference between games and rituals, Lévi-Strauss points out, is that games must end in divisions between winners and losers; rituals, however, end in equilibrium, uniting their participants into a community. Games were necessary in this industrial society which disciplined aggressive instincts and desires for self-assertion, but the rituals which accompanied them and restored a sense of oneness to embattled groups were just as important.

It was appropriate then, that the last years of the century witnessed an effusion of books on sportsmanship by coaches, managers, educators, and players, as well as the creation of annual events which structured and channeled competition. This was the era of the World Series, the Tournament of Roses, the Army-Navy Game, the Davis Cup, the Kentucky Derby, the International Olympics, each with its intricate attachment of rituals and associations. Efforts were made to group champions together, to make equals out of competitors, as in the All-America teams which first appeared in 1889. Sporting rules grew more elaborate and strategies more scientific. Corbett's victory over Sullivan at New Orleans in 1892 and the successful incumbency of coaches like Amos Alonzo Stagg and Walter Camp symbolized the direction of the future.

The enticement of art and the rites of spectatorship were occasionally combined, and perhaps nowhere so effectively as in the Columbian Exposition of 1893 which became for many Americans the great promise of social unity. In the swamps of Chicago's lake shore workers created a park almost overnight, and architects filled it with stately white palaces. The separate states, nations, and sexes had their own buildings in this festival supposedly celebrating Columbus' voyage, but actually proclaiming the New World's maturity to the Old. The spectacle of planned magnificence enchanted the millions of visitors, whose good behavior seemed itself a tribute to democracy and social order. The technical marvels and the wonders of modern science seemed less astonishing than American ability to reconstruct "with Aladdin-like magic" the outlines of an artistic environment. It appeared as a vigorous refutation to the charge that America was only a universe of materialists, a spiritually exhausted refuge for philistines and money-grubbers. "Say not, 'Greece is no more,' " crowed the poet Richard Watson Gilder. "Her white-winged soul sinks on the New World's breast./ Ah! happy West—/ Greece flowers anew, and all her temples soar!"

But in retrospect, one can see that this temporary community of such unexpected splendor raised its own problems. Stylistically, its neo-classicism and traditionalism seemed an insult to native traditions of design which desperately required recognition and nurture. Louis Sullivan and Frank Lloyd Wright would look back with revulsion to the Fair's influence. But more important still was the ethic of the Exposition itself. It seemed to argue that America could create a beautiful environment by an act of will, that no fundamental reordering of political, economic, and social life was necessary to fulfill the dream of an alabaster city. Lavish patronage and artistic cooperation seemed sufficient. The fact that Chicago's squalor lay only a few miles away demonstrated that art could flourish in unhealthy soil.

To social critics therefore, the Fair's achievement seemed miraculous, and disturbing. Could these giant stage-sets actually convince spectators that their society was equitable and unselfish—the actual intention. Then they spelled a danger. For the relationship between American society and the White City was not organic, it was dialectical. The Fair's unity was one of facade, its order the result of artifice. Its virtue lay as an alternative, not an achievement.

It was this attitude William Dean Howells took in employing the persona of a visitor from Altruria—a Utopian society practicing equality—to record his reactions to the Fair. Howells' stance toward his own society was as complicated as a reader might wish, and his ambivalences were retained in the Altrurian letters. Thus, despite his suspicions of wealth, Howells could insist that Chicago millionaires had as "luminous a sense of the true relations of the arts and the interests" as any impartial observer might desire; despite his promotion of realism he praised those academic (and idealizing) artists who sacrificed their time and money to create imperishable beauty. Even as an Altrurian satirist, Howells softened when he could. Life in Howells' pages, Henry James once remarked, is "never too hard," and "passions and perversities never too sharp, not to allow, on the part of his people, of such an exercise of friendly wit about each other as may well, when one considers it, minimize shocks and strains."

But whatever his limitations, Howells understood the character of choices. The Court of Honor required a society which denied the demands of egotism, but the Midway Plaisance next to it idealized competition and struggle. The one was beautiful, symmetrical, unified; the other mobile, energetic, picturesque, and Howells mistrusted the picturesque. In another Altrurian Letter, this time describing New York, he noted that a street of tenement houses "is always more picturesque than a street of brownstone residences," but is also less comfortable. "In a picture it would be most pleasingly effective," Howells added of a tenement neighborhood. "But to be in it, and not have the distance, is to inhale the stenches of the neglected street, and to catch that yet fouler and dreadfuller poverty-smell which breathes from the open doorways. . . . It is to see the work-worn look of the mothers, the squalor of the babes, the haggish ugliness of the old women, the slovenly frowziness of the young girls." New York, like the Midway, seemed governed by accident and exigency, its inhabitants meeting rarely, and then only in moments of tragedy or catastrophe. Strolling along a New York street in Howells' novel A Hazard of New Fortunes, Basil March is startled by a young woman running away from a policeman, and cries out the author's revulsion from a society of contrasts. "Can that poor wretch and the radiant girl we left yonder really belong to the same system of things? How incredible each makes the other seem!"

The rituals, the patriotism, the environmental planning then, supplied a basis for unity, but only a provisional one. The contrasts of American life were too strong to be healed by art or entertainment. Howells had concluded that aesthetic diversity demanded too high a price in misery and injustice to preserve it, though a few, like Andrew Carnegie, comfortably blessed the heterogeneity. "The difference between the palace of the millionaire and the cottage of the laborer" measured the progress of the race, Carnegie insisted. "Much better this great irregularity than universal squalor."

Others brooded about what might happen when boundaries no longer restrained the human contrasts, when stereotypes and genteel conventions could not contain demands for recognition. "How will it be with the kingdoms and with kings," asked Edwin Markham in his 1899 poem, "With those who shaped him to the thing he is/ When this dumb terror shall reply to God/ After the silence of the centuries?" The gulfs which lay between America's classes and subcultures at the end of the century mocked efforts to proclaim Americanism, but if the barrier were removed, what would replace them? The sanitized millennium of Edward Bellamy? The dream landscape of the White City? The skyscrapered vitalism of Louis Sullivan? Or the violent nightmare of Ignatius Donnelly? The social explorers of the 'eighties and 'nineties could only turn up the skeletons at the feast; a later generation would have to move beyond recognition to reform.

PART ONE

OVERVIEW

1. A Traveler's Report

James F. Muirhead was a Scotsman, born in 1853, who studied at the University of Leipzig in the eighteen-seventies. While in Leipzig he became associated with Karl Baedecker's publishing firm, then producing the most famous travel guide series in history. In the early eighteen-nineties Baedecker sent Muirhead to America in order to prepare a handbook to the United States. Europeans expected that the Columbian Exposition of 1893 would attract many foreign visitors, and if the habit endured American guidebooks could possess a ready and a permanent market.

Muirhead made the trip and produced an excellent handbook. Many of his observations were too personal and subjective to be included within it, however, so he published his opinions in a separate volume of reminiscence several years later. Fascinated by the variety of American social life, particularly the dominant roles of women and children, the popularity of intercollegiate sports, and the pretensions of high society, Muirhead caught vividly many of the discrepancies the national community contained. Amused as well as startled by some of the contrasts he unearthed, Muirhead managed to avoid the clichés and stereotypes that marred so many commentaries on the American scene, and produced an incisive testament to the energies of the nineties.

The Land of Contrasts

JAMES F. MUIRHEAD

When I first thought of writing about the United States at all, I soon came to the conclusion that no title could better than the above express the general impression left on my mind by my experiences in the Great Republic. It may well be that a long list of inconsistencies might be made out for any country, just as for any individual; but so far as my knowledge goes the United States stands out as preëminently the "Land of Contrasts"—the land of stark, staring, and stimulating inconsistency; at once the home of enlightenment and the happy hunting ground of the charlatan and the quack; a land in which nothing happens but the unexpected; the home of Hyperion, but no less the haunt of the satyr; always the land of promise, but not invariably the land of performance; a land which may be bounded by the aurora borealis, but which has also undeniable acquaintance with the flames of the bottomless pit; a land which is laved at once by the rivers of Paradise and the leaden waters of Acheron.

If I proceed to enumerate a few of the actual contrasts that struck me, in matters both weighty and trivial, it is not merely as an exercise in antithesis, but because I hope it will show how easy it would be to pass an entirely and even ridiculously untrue judgment upon the United States by having an eye only for one series of the startling opposites. It would show in a very concrete way one of the most fertile sources of those unfair international judgments which led the French Academician Joüy to the statement: *"Plus on réfléchit et plus on observe, plus on se convainct de la fausseté de la plupart de ces jugements portés sur un nation entière par quelques ecrivains et adoptés sans examen par les autres."* The Americans themselves can hardly take umbrage at the label, if Mr. Howells truly represents them when he makes one of the characters in "A Traveller from Altruria" assert that they pride themselves even on the size of their inconsistencies. The extraordinary clashes that occur in the United States are doubtless largely due to the extraordinary mixture of youth and age in the character of the country. If ever an old head was set upon young shoulders,

James F. Muirhead, *The Land of Contrasts. A Briton's View of His American Kin* (Boston, New York, London, 1898), pp. 7–23.

it was in this case of the United States—this "Strange New World, thet yit was never young." While it is easy, in a study of the United States, to see the essential truth of the analogy between the youth of an individual and the youth of a State, we must also remember that America was in many respects born full-grown, like Athena from the brain of Zeus, and coördinates in the most extraordinary way the shrewdness of the sage with the naïveté of the child. Those who criticise the United States, because with the experience of all the ages behind her, she is in some points vastly defective as compared with the nations of Europe, are as much mistaken as those who look to her for the fresh ingenuousness of youth unmarred by any trace of age's weakness. It is simply inevitable that she should share the vices as well as the virtues of both. Mr. Freeman has well pointed out how natural it is that a colony should rush ahead of the mother country in some things and lag behind it in others; and that just as you have to go to French Canada if you want to see Old France, so, for many things, if you wish to see Old England you must go to New England.

Thus America may easily be abreast or ahead of us in such matters as the latest applications of electricity, while retaining in its legal uses certain cumbersome devices that we have long since discarded. Americans still have "Courts of Oyer and Terminer" and still insist on the unanimity of the jury, though their judges wear no robes and their counsel apply to the cuspidor as often as to the code. So, too, the extension of municipal powers accomplished in Great Britain still seems a formidable innovation in the United States.

The general feeling of power and scope is probably another fruitful source of the inconsistencies of American life. Emerson has well said that consistency is the hobgoblin of little minds; and no doubt the largeness, the illimitable outlook, of the national mind of the United States makes it disregard surface discrepancies that would grate horribly on a more conventional community. The confident belief that all will come out right in the end, and that harmony can be attained when time is taken to consider it, carries one triumphantly over the roughest places of inconsistency. It is easy to drink our champagne from tin cans, when we know that it is merely a sense of hurry that prevents us fetching the chased silver goblets waiting for our use.

This, I fancy, is the explanation of one series of contrasts which strikes an Englishman at once. America claims to be the land of liberty *par excellence,* and in a wholesale way this may be true in spite of the gap between the noble sentiments of the Declaration of Independence and the actual treatment of the negro and the Chinaman. But in what may be called the retail traffic of life the American puts up with innumerable restrictions of his personal liberty. Max O'Rell has expatiated with scarcely an exaggeration on the wondrous sight of a powerful millionaire standing meekly at the door of a hotel dining-room until the consequential head-waiter (very possibly a coloured gentleman) condescends to point out to him the seat he may occupy. So, too, such petty officials as policemen and railway conductors are generally treated rather as the masters than as the servants of the public. The ordinary American citizen accepts a long delay on the railway or an interminable "wait" at the theatre as a direct visitation of Providence, against which it would be useless folly to direct cat-calls, grumbles, or letters to *The Times*. Americans invented the slang word "kicker," but so far as I could see their vocabulary is here miles ahead of their practice; they dream noble deeds, but do not do them; Englishmen "kick" much better, without having a name for it. The right of the individual to do as he will is respected to such an extent that an entire company will put up with inconvenience rather than infringe it. A coal-carter will calmly keep a tramway-car waiting several minutes until he finishes his unloading . . .

The old Puritan spirit of interference with individual liberty sometimes crops out in America in a way that would be impossible in this country. An inscription in one of the large mills at Lawrence, Mass., informs the employees (or did so some years ago) that "regular attendance at some place of worship and a proper observance of the Sabbath will be expected of every person employed." So, too, the young women of certain districts impose on their admirers such restrictions in the use of liquor and tobacco that any less patient animal than the native American would infallibly kick over the traces.

In spite of their acknowledged nervous energy and excitability, Americans often show a good deal of a quality that rivals the phlegm of the Dutch. Their above-mentioned patience during railway or other delays is an instance of this. . . . Boston men of business, after being whisked by the electric car from their suburban residences to the city at the rate of twelve miles an hour, sit stoically still while the congested traffic makes the car take twenty minutes to pass the most crowded section of Washington Street—a walk of barely five minutes.

❋   ❋   ❋

Even in the matter of what Mr. Ambassador Bayard has styled "that form of Socialism, Protection," it seems to me that we can find traces of this contradictory tendency. Americans consider their country as emphatically the land of protection, and attribute most of their prosperity to their inhospitable customs barriers. This may be so; but where else in the world will you find such a volume and expanse of free trade as in these same United States? We find here a huge section of the world's surface, 3,000 miles long and 1,500 miles wide, occupied by about fifty practically independent States, containing seventy millions of inhabitants, producing a very large proportion of all the necessities and many of the luxuries of life, and all enjoying the freest of free trade with each other. Few of these States are as small as Great Britain, and many of them are immensely larger. Collectively they contain nearly half the railway mileage of the globe, besides an incomparable series of inland waterways. Over all these is continually passing an immense amount of goods. The San Francisco *News Letter*, a well-known weekly journal, points out that of the 1,400,-000,000 tons of goods carried for 100 miles or upwards on the railways of the world in 1895, no less than 800,000,000 were carried in the United States. Even if we add the 140,000,000 carried by sea-going ships, there remains a balance of 60,000,000 tons in favor of the United States as against the rest of the world. It is, perhaps, impossible to ascertain whether or not the actual value of the goods carried would be in the same proportion; but it seems probable that the value of the 800,000,000 tons of the home trade of America must considerably exceed that of the *free* portion of the trade of the British Empire, *i.e.*, practically the whole of its import trade and that portion of its export trade carried on with free-trade countries or colonies. The internal commerce of the United States makes it the most wonderful market on the globe; and Brother Jonathan, the rampant Protectionist, stands convicted as the greatest Cobdenite of them all!

We are all, it is said, apt to "slip up" on our strongest points. Perhaps this is why one of the leading writers of the American democracy is able to assert that "there is no country in the world where the separation of the classes is so absolute as ours," and to quote a Russian revolutionist, who lived in exile all over Europe and nowhere found such want of sympathy between the rich and poor as in America. If this were true it would certainly form a startling contrast to the general kindheartedness of the American. But I fancy it rather points to the condition of greater relative equality. Our Russian friend was accustomed to the patronising kindness of the superior to the inferior, of the master to the servant. It is easy, on an empyrean rock, to be "kind" to the mortals toiling helplessly down below. It costs little, to use Mr. Bellamy's parable, for those securely seated on top of the coach to subscribe for salve to alleviate the chafed wounds of those who drag it. In America there is less need and less use of this patronising kindness; there is less kindness from class to class simply because the conscious realisation of "class" is non-existent in thousands of cases where it would be to the fore in Europe. As for the first statement quoted at the head of this paragraph, I find it very hard of belief. It is true that there are exclusive *circles,* to which, for instance, Buffalo Bill would not have the entrée, but the principle of exclusion is on the whole analogous to that by which we select our intimate personal friends. No man in America, who is personally fitted to adorn it, need feel that he is *automatically* shut out (as he might well be in England) from a really congenial social sphere.

Another of America's strong points is its sense of practical comfort and convenience. It is scarcely open to denial that the laying of too great stress on material comfort is one of the rocks ahead which the American vessel will need careful steering to avoid; and it is certain that Americans lead us in countless little points of household comfort and labour-saving ingenuity. But here, too, the exception that proves the rule is not too coy for our discovery. The terrible roads and the atrociously kept streets are amongst the most vociferous instances of this. It is one of the inexplicable mysteries of American civilisation that a young municipality,—or even, sometimes, an old one,—with a million dollars to spend, will choose to spend it in erecting a most unnecessarily gorgeous town-hall rather than in making the street in front of it passable for the ordinarily shod pedestrian. In New York itself the hilarious stockbroker returning at night to his palace often finds the pavement between his house and his carriage more difficult to negotiate than even the hole for his latch-key; and I have more than once been absolutely compelled to make a detour from Broadway in order to find a crossing where the icy slush would not come over the tops of my boots. The American taste for luxury sometimes insists on gratification even at the expense of the ordinary decencies of life. It was an American who said, "Give me the luxuries of life and I will not ask for the necessities"; and there is more truth in this epigram, as characteristic of the American point of view, than its author intended or would, perhaps, allow. In private life this is seen in the preference shown for diamond earrings and Paris toilettes over neat and effective household service. The contrast between the slatternly, unkempt maid-servant who opens the door to you and the general luxury of the house itself is sometimes of the most startling, not to say appalling, description. It is not a sufficient answer to say that good servants are not so easily obtained in America as in England. This is true; but a slight rearrangement of expenditure would secure much better service than is now seen. To the English eye the cart in this matter often seems put before the horse; and the combination of excellent waiting with a modest table equipage is frequent enough in the United States to prove its perfect feasibility.

In American hotels we are often overwhelmed with "all the discomforts that money can procure," while unable to obtain some of those things which we have been brought up to believe among the prime necessaries of existence. It is significant that in the printed directions governing the use of the electric bell in one's bedroom, I never found an instance in which the harmless necessary bath could be ordered with fewer than nine pressures of the button, while the fragrant cocktail or some other equally fascinating but dangerous luxury might often be summoned by three or four. The most elaborate dinner, served in the most gorgeous china, is sometimes spoiled by the Draconian regulation that it must be devoured between the unholy hours of twelve and two, or have all its courses brought on the table at once. Though the Americans invent the most delicate forms of machinery, their hoop-iron knives, silver plated for facility in cleaning, are hardly calculated to tackle anything harder than butter, and compel the beef-eater to return to the tearing methods of his remotest ancestors. The waiter sometimes rivals the hotel clerk himself in the splendour of his attire, but this does not render more appetising the spectacle of his thumb in the soup. The furniture of your bedroom would not have disgraced the Tuileries in their palmiest days, but, alas, you are parboiled by a diabolic chevreau-de-frise of steam-pipes which refuse to be turned off, and insist on accompanying your troubled slumbers by an intermittent series of bubbles, squeaks, and hisses. The mirror opposite which you brush your hair is enshrined in the heaviest of gilt frames and is large enough for a Brobdignagian, but the basin in which you wash your hands is little larger than a sugar-bowl; and when you emerge from your nine-times-summoned bath you find you have to dry your sacred person with six little towels, none larger than a snuff-taker's handkerchief. There is no carafe of water in the room; and after countless experiments you are reduced to the blood-curdling belief that the American tourist brushes his teeth with ice-water, the musical tinkling of which in the corridors is the most characteristic sound of the American caravanserai.

If there is anything the Americans pride themselves on—and justly—it is their handsome treatment of woman. You will not meet five Americans without hearing ten times that a lone woman can traverse the length and breadth of the United States without fear of insult; every traveller reports that the United States is the Paradise of women. Special entrances are reserved for them at hotels, so that they need not risk contamination with the tobacco-defiled floors of the public office; they are not expected to join the patient file of room-seekers before the hotel clerk's desk, but wait comfortably in the reception-room while an employee secures their number and key. There is no recorded instance of the justifiable homicide of an American girl in her theatre hat. Man meekly submits to be the hewer of wood, the drawer of water, and the beast of burden for the superior sex. But even this gorgeous medal has its reverse side. Few things provided for a class well able to pay for comfort are more uncomfortable and indecent than the arrangements for ladies on board the sleeping cars. Their dressing accommodation is of the most limited description; their berths are not segregated at one end of the car, but are scattered above and below those of the male passengers; it is considered *tolerable* that they should lie with the legs of a strange, disrobing man dangling within a foot of their noses.

Another curious contrast to the practical, material, matter-of-fact side of the American is his intense interest in the supernatural, the spiritualistic, the superstitious. Boston, of all places in the world, is perhaps, the happiest hunting ground for the spiritualist medium, the faith healer, and the mind curer. You will find there the most advanced emancipation from theological superstition combined in the most extraordinary way with a more than half belief in the incoherences of a spiritualistic séance. The Boston Christian Scientists have just erected a handsome stone church, with chime of bells, organ, and choir of the most approved ecclesiastical cut; and, greatest marvel of all, have actually had to return a surplus of $50,000 (£10,000) that was subscribed for its building. There are two pulpits, one occupied by a man who expounds the Bible, while in the other a woman responds with the grandiloquent platitudes of Mrs. Eddy. In other parts of the country this desire to pry into the Book of Fate assumes grosser forms. Mr. Bryce tells us that Western newspapers devote a special column to the advertisements of astrologers and soothsayers, and assures us that this profession is as much recognised in the California of to-day as in the Greece of Homer.

It seems to me that I have met in America the nearest approaches to my ideals of a *Bayard sans peur et sans reproche*; and it is in this same America that I have met flagrant examples of the being wittily described as *sans père et sans proche*—utterly without the responsibility of background and entirely unacquainted with the obligation of *noblesse*. The superficial observer in the United States might conceivably imagine the characteristic national trait to be self-sufficiency or vanity (this mistake *has*, I believe, been made), and his opinion might be strengthened should he find, as I did, in an arithmetic published at Richmond during the late Civil War, such a modest example as the following: "If one Confederate soldier can whip seven Yankees, how many Confederate soldiers will it take to whip forty-nine Yankees?" America has been likened to a self-made man, hugging her conditions because she has made them, and considering them divine because they have grown up with the country. Another observer might quite as easily come to the conclusion that diffidence and self-distrust are the true American characteristics. Certainly Americans often show a saving consciousness of their faults, and lash themselves with biting satire. There are even Americans whose very attitude is an apology—wholly unnecessary—for the Great Republic, and who seem to despise any native product until it has received the hall-mark of London or of Paris. In the new world that has produced the new book, of the exquisite delicacy and insight of which Mr. Henry James and Mr. Howells may be taken as typical exponents, it seems to me that there are more than the usual proportion of critics who prefer to it what Colonel Higginson has well called "the brutalities of Haggard and the garlic-flavors of Kipling." While, perhaps, the characteristic charm of the American girl is her thorough-going individuality and the undaunted courage of her opinions, which leads her to say frankly, if she think so, that Martin Tupper is a greater poet than Shakespeare, yet I have, on the other hand, met a young American matron who confessed to me with bated breath that she and her sister, for the first time in their lives, had gone unescorted to a concert the night before last, and, *mirabile dictu,* no harm had come of it! It is in America that I have over and over again heard language to which the calling a spade a spade would seem the most delicate allusiveness; but it is also in America that I have summoned a blush to the cheek of conscious sixty-six by an incautious though innocent reference to the temperature of my morning tub. In that country I have seen the devotion of Sir Walter Raleigh to his queen rivalled again and again by the ordinary American man to the ordinary American woman (if there be an *ordinary* American woman), and in the same country I have myself been scoffed at and made game of because I opened the window of a railway carriage for a girl in whose delicate veins flowed a few drops of coloured blood. In Washington I met Miss Susan B. Anthony, and realised, to some extent at least, all she stands for. In Boston and other places I find there is actually an organised opposition to the extension of the franchise to women. I have hailed with delight the democratic spirit displayed in the greeting of my friend and myself by the porter of a hotel as "You fellows," and then had the cup of pleasure dashed from my lips by being told by the same porter that "the other *gentleman* would attend to my baggage!" I have been parboiled with salamanders who seemed to find no inconvenience in a room-temperature of eighty degrees, and have been nigh frozen to death in open-air drives in which the same individuals seemed perfectly comfortable. Men appear at the theatre in orthodox evening dress, while the tall and exasperating hats of the ladies who accompany them would seem to indicate a theory of street toilette. From New York to Buffalo I am whisked through the air at the rate of fifty or sixty miles an hour; in California I travelled on a train on which the engineer shot rabbits from the locomotive, and the fireman picked them up in time to jump on the baggage-car at the rear end of the train. At Santa Barbara I visited an old mission church and convent which vied in quaint picturesqueness with anything in Europe; but, alas! the old monk who showed us round, though wearing the regulation gown and knotted cord, had replaced his sandals by elastic-sided boots and covered his tonsure with a common chummy.

Few things in the United States are more pleasing than the widespread habits of kindness to animals (most American whips are, as far as punishment to the horse is concerned, a mere farce). Yet no American seems to have any scruple about adding an extra hundred weight or two to an already villainously overloaded horse-car; and I have seen a score of American ladies sit serenely watching the frantic straining of two poor animals to get a derailed car on to the track again, when I knew that in "brutal" Old England every one of them would have been out on the side-walk to lighten the load.

In England that admirable body of men popularly known as Quakers are indissolubly associated in the public mind with a pristine simplicity of life and conversation. My amazement, therefore, may easily be imagined, when I found that an entertainment given by a young member of the Society of Friends in one of the great cities of the Eastern States turned out to be the most elaborate and beautiful private ball I ever attended, with about eight hundred guests dressed in the height of fashion, while the daily papers (if I remember rightly) estimated its expense as reaching a total of some thousands of pounds. Here the natural expansive liberality of the American man proved stronger than the traditional limitations of a religious society. But the opposite art of cheese-paring is by no means unknown in the United States. Perhaps not even canny Scotland can parallel the record of certain districts in New England, which actually elected their parish paupers to the State Legislature to keep them off the rates. Let the opponents of paid members of the House of Commons take notice!

Amid the little band of tourists in whose company I happened to enter the Yosemite Valley was a San Francisco youth with a delightful baritone voice, who entertained the guests in the hotel parlour at Wawona by a good-natured series of songs. No one in the room except myself seemed to find it in the least incongruous or funny that he sandwiched "Nearer, my God, to Thee" between "The man who broke the bank at Monte Carlo" and "Her golden hair was hanging down her back," or that he jumped at once from the pathetic solemnity of "I know that my Redeemer liveth" to the jingle of "Little Annie Rooney." The name Wawona reminds me how American weather plays its part in the game of contrasts. When we visited the Grove of Big Trees near Wawona on May 21, it was in the midst of a driving snow-storm, with the thermometer standing at 36 degrees Fahrenheit. Next day, as we drove into Raymond, less than forty miles to the west, the sun was beating down on our backs, and the thermometer marked 80 degrees in the shade.

There is probably no country in the world where, at times, letters of introduction are more fully honoured than in the United States. The recipient does not content himself with inviting you to call or even to dinner. He invites you to make his house your home; he invites all his friends to meet you; he leaves his business to show you the lions of the town or to drive you about the country; he puts you up at his club; he sends you off provided with letters to ten other men like himself, only more so. On the other hand, there is probably no country in the world where a letter of introduction from a man quite entitled to give it could be wholly ignored as it sometimes is in the United States. The writer has had experience of both results. No more fundamental contrast can well be imagined than that between the noisy, rough, crude, and callous street-life of some Western towns and the quiet, reticence, delicacy, spirituality, and refinement of many of the adjacent interiors.

The table manners of the less-educated American classes are hardly of the best, but where but in America will you find eleven hundred charity school boys sit down daily to dinner, each with his own table napkin, as they do at Girard College, Philadelphia? And where except at that same institute will you find a man leaving millions for a charity, with the stipulation that no parson of any creed shall ever be allowed to enter its precincts?

In concluding this chapter, let me say that its object, as indeed the object of this whole book, will have been achieved if it convinces a few Britons of the futility of generalising on the complex organism of American society from inductions that would not justify an opinion about the habits of a piece of protoplasm.

PART TWO

CONTRASTS

2. Communications

The spread of telephones, typewriters, and phonographs heightened American notions of speed and verisimilitude, particularly with regard to news. Although the flow of public information dramatically increased in the 'eighties and 'nineties, citizens clamored for more. Great metropolitan newspapers streamlined their appearance and techniques to satisfy this appetite, and encouraged their reporters to obtain news that was fresher than any competitor could deliver.

Seeking to indicate the marvels of the future, therefore, Edward Bellamy (1850–1898) naturally turned to communications. A lawyer and sometime journalist himself in Springfield, Massachusetts, Bellamy was most famous for his utopian romance, *Looking Backward*, published in 1888. Enormous sales popularized Bellamy's notions of state capitalism, an economic structure which would abolish poverty and competition. Nationalist Clubs were formed throughout America to work for the realization of his ideas. Readers were equally fascinated, however, by the technological marvels Bellamy contrived, and "With the Eyes Shut" was only one of several short stories he wrote to celebrate the future wonders of machinery.

Bellamy's journalistic career was secondary to his other achievements; a group of professional reporters in the late 'nineties made news gathering a conspicuous profession. Covering wars in South Africa, the Middle East, and Cuba for their aggressive editors, Richard Harding Davis, Stephen Crane, Julian Ralph, and James Creelman—to name just a few—dramatically increased the circulations of their newspapers and magazines. Some objected to their methods and sensationalism, and to the political effects their stories had. News coverage was not always benevolent. But James Creelman, who defended these techniques, was one of the most prolific and daring of these correspondents; he helped lead a famous charge which took a fort in Cuba, and he captured the flag for his newspaper, William Randolph Hearst's *New York Journal*. His defense of yellow journalism was that of a participant in its creation.

With the Eyes Shut

EDWARD BELLAMY

Railroad rides are naturally tiresome to persons who cannot read on the cars, and, being one of those unfortunates, I resigned myself, on taking my seat in the train, to several hours of tedium, alleviated only by such cat-naps as I might achieve. Partly on account of my infirmity, though more on account of a taste for rural quiet and retirement, my railroad journeys are few and far between. Strange as the statement may seem in days like these, it had actually been five years since I had been on an express train of a trunk line. Now, as every one knows, the improvements in the conveniences of the best equipped trains have in that period been very great, and for a considerable time I found myself amply entertained in taking note first of one ingenious device and then of another, and wondering what would come next. At the end of the first hour, however, I was pleased to find that I was growing comfortably drowsy, and proceeded to compose myself for a nap, which I hoped might last to my destination.

Presently I was touched on the shoulder, and a train boy asked me if I would not like something to read. I replied, rather petulantly, that I could not read on the cars, and only wanted to be let alone.

"Beg pardon, sir," the train boy replied, "but I'll give you a book you can read with your eyes shut. Guess you haven't taken this line lately," he added, as I looked up offended at what seemed impertinence. "We've been furnishing the new-fashioned phonographed books and magazines on this train for six months now, and passengers have got so they won't have anything else."

Probably this piece of information ought to have astonished me more than it did, but I had read enough about the wonders of the phonograph to be prepared in a vague sort of way for almost anything which might be related to it, and for the rest, after the air-brakes, the steam heat, the electric lights and annunciators, the vestibuled cars, and other delightful novelties I had just been admiring, almost anything seemed likely in the way of railway conveniences. Accordingly, when the boy proceeded to

Edward Bellamy "With the Eyes Shut," *The Blindman's World* (Boston and New York, 1898), pp. 335–365.

rattle off a list of the latest novels, I stopped him with the name of one which I had heard favorable mention of, and told him I would try that.

He was good enough to commend my choice. "That's a good one," he said. "It's all the rage. Half the train's on it this trip. Where'll you begin?"

"Where? Why, at the beginning. Where else?" I replied.

"All right. Didn't know but you might have partly read it. Put you on at any chapter or page, you know. Put you on at first chapter with next batch in five minutes, soon as the batch that's on now gets through."

He unlocked a little box at the side of my seat, collected the price of three hours' reading at five cents an hour, and went on down the aisle. Presently I heard the tinkle of a bell from the box which he had unlocked. Following the example of others around me, I took from it a sort of two-pronged fork with the tines spread in the similitude of a chicken's wish-bone. This contrivance, which was attached to the side of the car by a cord, I proceeded to apply to my ears, as I saw the others doing.

For the next three hours I scarcely altered my position, so completely was I enthralled by my novel experience. Few persons can fail to have made the observation that if the tones of the human voice did not have a charm for us in themselves apart from the ideas they convey, conversation to a great extent would soon be given up, so little is the real intellectual interest of the topics with which it is chiefly concerned. When, then, the sympathetic influence of the voice is lent to the enhancement of matter of high intrinsic interest, it is not strange that the attention should be en-chained. A good story is highly entertaining even when we have to get at it by the roundabout means of spelling out the signs that stand for the words, and imagining them uttered, and then imagining what they would mean if uttered. What, then, shall be said of the delight of sitting at one's ease, with closed eyes, listening to the same story poured into one's ears in the strong, sweet, musical tones of a perfect mistress of the art of story-telling, and of the expression and excitation by means of the voice of every emotion?

When, at the conclusion of the story, the train boy came to lock up the box, I could not refrain from expressing my satisfaction in strong terms. In reply he volunteered the information that next month the cars for day trips on that line would be further fitted up with phonographic guide-books of the country the train passed through, so connected by clock-work with the running gear of the cars that the guide-book would call attention to every object in the landscape, and furnish the pertinent information— statistical, topographical, biographical, historical, romantic, or legendary, as it might be—just at the time the train had reached the most favorable point of view. It was believed that this arrangement (for which, as it would work automatically and require little attendance, being used or not, according to pleasure, by the passenger, there would be no charge) would do much to attract travel to the road. His explanation was interrupted by the announcement in loud, clear, and deliberate tones, which no one could have had any excuse for misunderstanding, that the train was now approaching the city of my destination. As I looked around in amazement to discover what manner of brakeman this might be whom I had understood, the train boy said, with a grin, "That's our new phonographic annunciator."

Hamage had written me that he would be at the station, but something had evidently prevented him from keeping the appointment, and as it was late, I went at once to a hotel and to bed. I was tired and slept heavily; once or twice I woke up, after dreaming there were people in my room talking to me, but quickly dropped off to sleep again. Finally I awoke, and did not so soon fall asleep. Presently I found myself sitting up in bed with half a dozen extraordinary sensations contending for right of way along my backbone. What had startled me was the voice of a young woman, who could not have been standing more than ten feet from my bed. If the tones of her voice were any guide, she was not only a young woman, but a very charming one.

"My dear sir," she had said, "you may possibly be interested in knowing that it now stands just a quarter of three."

For a few moments I thought—well, I will not undertake the impossible task of telling what extraordinary conjectures occurred to me by way of accounting for the presence of this young woman in my room before the true explanation of the matter occurred to me. For, of course, when my experience that afternoon on the train flashed through my mind, I guessed at once that the solution of the mystery was in all probability merely a phonographic device for announcing the hour. Nevertheless, so thrilling and lifelike in effect were the tones of the voice I had heard that I confess I had not the nerve to light the gas to investigate till I had indued my more essential garments. Of course I found no lady in the room, but only a clock. I had not particularly noticed it on going to bed, because it looked like any other clock, and so now it continued to behave until the hands pointed to three. Then, instead of leaving me to infer the time from the arbitrary symbolism of three strokes on a bell, the same voice which had before electrified me informed me, in tones which would have lent a charm to the driest of statistical details, what the hour was. I had never before been impressed with any particular interest attaching to the hour of three in the morning, but as I heard it announced in those low, rich, thrilling contralto tones, it appeared fairly to coruscate with previously latent suggestions of romance and poetry, which, if somewhat vague, were very pleasing. Turning out the gas that I might the more easily imagine the bewitching presence which the voice suggested, I went back to bed, and lay awake there until morning, enjoying the society of my bodiless companion and the delicious shock of her quarter-hourly remarks. To make the illusion more complete and the more unsuggestive of the mechanical explanation which I knew of course was the real one, the phrase in which the announcement of the hour was made was never twice the same.

Right was Solomon when he said that there was nothing new under the sun. Sardanapalus or Semiramis herself would not have been at all startled to hear a human voice proclaim the hour. The phonographic clock had but replaced the slave whose business, standing by the noiseless water-clock, it was to keep tale of the moments as they dropped, ages before they had been taught to tick.

In the morning, on descending, I went first to the clerk's office to inquire for letters, thinking Hamage, who knew I would go to that hotel if any, might have addressed me there. The clerk handed me a small oblong box. I suppose I stared at it in a rather helpless way, for presently he said: "I beg your pardon, but I see you are a stranger. If you will permit me, I will show you how to read your letter."

I gave him the box, from which he took a device of spindles and cylinders, and placed it deftly within another small box which stood on the desk. Attached to this was one of the two-pronged ear-trumpets I already knew the use of. As I placed it in position, the clerk touched a spring in the box, which set some sort of motor going, and at once the familiar tones of Dick Hamage's voice expressed his regret that an accident had prevented his meeting me the night before, and informed me that he would be at the hotel by the time I had breakfasted.

The letter ended, the obliging clerk removed the cylinders from the box on the desk, replaced them in what they had come in, and returned it to me.

"Isn't it rather tantalizing," said I, "to receive one of these letters when there is no little machine like this at hand to make it speak?"

"It doesn't often happen," replied the clerk, "that anybody is caught without his indispensable, or at least where he cannot borrow one."

"His indispensable!" I exclaimed. "What may that be?"

In reply the clerk directed my attention to a little box, not wholly unlike a case for a binocular glass, which, now that he spoke of it, I saw was carried, slung at the side, by every person in sight.

"We call it the indispensable because it is indispensable, as, no doubt, you will soon find for yourself."

In the breakfast-room a number of ladies and gentlemen were engaged as they sat at table in reading, or rather listening to, their morning's correspondence. A greater or smaller pile of little boxes lay beside their plates, and one after another they took from each its cylinders, placed them in their indispensables, and held the latter to their ears. The expression of the face in reading is so largely affected by the necessary fixity of the eyes that intelligence is absorbed from the printed or written page with scarcely a change in countenance, which when communicated by the voice evokes a responsive play of features. I had never been struck so forcibly by this obvious reflection as I was in observing the expression of the faces of these people as they listened to their correspondents. Disappointment, pleased surprise, chagrin, disgust, indignation, and amusement were alternately so legible on their faces that it was prefectly easy for one to be sure in most cases what the tenor at least of the letter was. It occurred to me that while in the old time the pleasure of receiving letters had been so far balanced by this drudgery of writing them as to keep correspondence within some bounds, nothing less than freight trains could suffice for the mail service in these days, when to write was but to speak, and to listen was to read.

After I had given my order, the waiter brought a curious-looking oblong case, with an ear-trumpet attached, and, placing it before me, went away. I foresaw that I should have to ask a good many questions before I got through, and, if I did not mean to be a bore, I had best ask as few as necessary. I determined to find out what this trap was without assistance. The words "Daily Morning Herald" sufficiently indicated that it was a newspaper. I suspected that a certain big knob, if pushed, would set it going. But, for all I knew, it might start in the middle of the advertisements. I looked closer. There were a number of printed slips upon the face of the machine, arranged about a circle like the numbers on a dial. They were evidently the headings of news articles. In the middle of the circle was a little pointer, like the hand of a clock, moving on a pivot. I pushed this pointer around to a certain caption, and then, with the air of being perfectly familiar with the machine, I put the pronged trumpet to my ears and pressed the big knob. Precisely! It worked like a charm; so much like a charm, indeed, that I should certainly have allowed my breakfast to cool had I been obliged to choose between that and my newspaper. The inventor of the apparatus had, however, provided against so painful a dilemma by a simple attachment to the trumpet, which held it securely in position upon the shoulders behind the head, while the hands were left free for knife and fork. Having slyly noted the manner in which my neighbors had effected the adjustments, I imitated their example with a careless air, and presently, like them, was absorbing physical and mental aliment simultaneously.

While I was thus delightfully engaged, I was not less delightfully interrupted by Hamage, who, having arrived at the hotel, and learned that I was in the breakfast-room, came in and sat down beside me. After telling him how much I admired the new sort of newspapers, I offered one criticism, which was that there seemed to be no way by which one could skip dull paragraphs or uninteresting details.

"The invention would, indeed, be very far from a success," he said, "if there were no such provision, but there is."

He made me put on the trumpet again, and, having set the machine going, told me to press on a certain knob, at first gently, afterward as hard as I pleased. I did so, and found that the effect of the "skipper," as he called the knob, was to quicken the utterance of the phonograph in proportion to the pressure to at least tenfold the usual rate of speed, while at any moment, if a word of interest caught the ear, the ordinary rate of delivery was resumed, and by another adjustment the machine could be made to go back and repeat as much as desired.

When I told Hamage of my experience of the night before with the talking clock in my room, he laughed uproariously.

"I am very glad you mentioned this just now," he said, when he had quieted himself. "We have a couple of hours before the train goes out to my place, and I'll take you through Orton's establishment, where they make a specialty of these talking clocks. I have a number of them in my house, and, as I don't want to have you scared to death in the night-watches, you had better get some notion of what clocks nowadays are expected to do."

Orton's, where we found ourselves half an hour later, proved to be a very extensive establishment, the firm making a specialty of horological novelties, and particularly of the new phonographic time-pieces. The manager, who was a personal friend of Hamage's, and proved very obliging, said that the latter were fast driving the old-fashioned striking clocks out of use.

"And no wonder," he exclaimed; "the old-fashioned striker was an unmitigated nuisance. Let alone the brutality of announcing the hour to a refined household by four, eight, or ten rude bangs, without introduction or apology, this method of announcement was not even tolerably intelligible. Unless you happened to be attentive at the moment the din began, you could never be sure of your count of strokes so as to be positive whether it was eight, nine, ten, or eleven. As to the half and quarter strokes, they were wholly useless unless you chanced to know what was the last hour struck. And then, too, I should like to ask you why, in the name of common sense, it should take twelve times as long to tell you it is twelve o'clock as it does to tell you it is one."

The manager laughed as heartily as Hamage had done on learning of my scare of the night before.

"It was lucky for you," he said, "that the clock in your room happened to be a simple time announcer, otherwise you might easily have been startled half out of your wits." I became myself quite of the same opinion by the time he had shown us something of his assortment of clocks. The mere announcing of the hours and quarters of hours was the simplest of the functions of these wonderful and yet simple instruments. There were few of them which were not arranged to "improve the time," as the old-fashioned prayer-meeting phrase was. People's ideas differing widely as to what constitutes improvement of time, the clocks varied accordingly in the nature of the edification they provided. There were religious and sectarian clocks, moral clocks, philosophical clocks, free-thinking and infidel clocks, literary and poetical clocks, educational clocks, frivolous and bacchanalian clocks. In the religious clock department were to be found Catholic, Presbyterian, Methodist, Episcopal, and Baptist time-pieces, which, in connection with the announcement of the hour and quarter, repeated some tenet of the sect with a proof text. There were also Talmage clocks, and Spurgeon clocks, and Storrs clocks, and Brooks clocks, which respectively marked the flight of time by phrases taken from the sermons of these eminent divines, and repeated in precisely the voice and accents of the original delivery. In startling proximity to the religious department I was shown the skeptical clocks. So near were they, indeed, that when, as I stood there, the various time-pieces announced the hour of ten, the war of opinions that followed was calculated to unsettle the firmest convictions. The observations of an Ingersoll which stood near me were particularly startling. The effect of an actual wrangle was the greater from the fact that all these individual clocks were surmounted by effigies of the authors of the sentiments they repeated.

I was glad to escape from this turmoil to the calmer atmosphere of the philosophical and literary clock department. For persons with a taste for antique moralizing, the sayings of Plato, Epictetus, and Marcus Aurelius had here, so to speak, been set to time. Modern wisdom was represented by a row of clocks surmounted by the heads of famous maxim-makers, from Rochefoucauld to Josh Billings. As for the literary clocks, their number and variety were endless. All the great authors were represented. Of the Dickens clocks alone there were half a dozen, with selections from his greatest stories. When I suggested that, captivating as such clocks must be, one might in time grow weary of hearing the same sentiments reiterated, the manager pointed out that the phonographic cylinders were removable, and could be replaced by other sayings by the same author or on the same theme at any time. If one tired of an author altogether, he could have the head unscrewed from the top of the clock and that of some other celebrity substituted, with a brand-new repertory.

"I can imagine," I said, "that these talking clocks must be a great resource for invalids especially, and for those who cannot sleep at night. But, on the other hand, how is it when people want or need to sleep? Is not one of them quite too interesting a companion at such a time?"

"Those who are used to it," replied the manager, "are no more disturbed by the talking clock than we used to be by the striking clock. However, to avoid all possible inconvenience to invalids, this little lever is provided, which at a touch will throw the phonograph out of gear or back again. It is customary when we put a talking or singing clock into a bedroom to put in an electric connection, so that by pressing a button at the head of the bed a person, without raising the head from the pillow, can start or stop the phonographic gear, as well as ascertain the time, on the repeater principle as applied to watches."

Hamage now said that we had only time to catch the train, but our conductor insisted that we should stop to see a novelty of phonographic invention, which, although not exactly in their line, had been sent them for exhibition by the inventor. It was a device for meeting the criticism frequently made upon the churches of a lack of attention and cordiality in welcoming strangers. It was to be placed in the lobby of the church, and had an arm extending like a pump-handle. Any stranger on taking this and moving it up and down would be welcomed in the pastor's own voice, and continue to be welcomed as long as he kept up the motion. While this welcome would be limited to general remarks of regard and esteem, ample provision was made for strangers who desired to be more particularly inquired into. A number of small buttons on the front of the contrivance bore respectively the words, "Male," "Female," "Married," "Unmarried," "Widow," "Children," "No Children," etc., etc. By pressing one of these buttons corresponding to his or her condition, the stranger would be addressed in terms probably quite as accurately adapted to his or her condition and needs as would be any inquiries a preoccupied clergyman would be likely to make under similar circumstances. I could readily see the necessity of some such substitute for the pastor, when I was informed that every prominent clergyman was now in the habit of supplying at least a dozen or two pulpits simultaneously, appearing by turns in one of them personally, and by phonograph in the others.

The inventor of the contrivance for welcoming strangers was, it appeared, applying the same idea to machines for discharging many other of the more perfunctory obligations of social intercourse. One being made for the convenience of the President of the United States at public receptions was provided with forty-two buttons for the different States, and others for the prinicipal cities of the Union, so that a caller, by proper manipulation, might, while shaking a handle, be addressed in regard to his home interests with an exactness of information as remarkable as that of the traveling statesmen who rise from the gazetteer to astonish the inhabitants of Wayback Crossing with the precise figures of their town valuation and birth rate, while the engine is taking in water.

We had by this time spent so much time that on finally starting for the railroad station we had to walk quite briskly. As we were hurrying along the street, my attention was arrested by a musical sound, distinct though not loud, proceeding apparently from the indispensable which Hamage, like everybody else I had seen, wore at his side. Stopping abruptly, he stepped aside from the throng, and, lifting the indispensable quickly to his ear, touched something, and exclaiming, "Oh, yes, to be sure!" dropped the instrument to his side.

Then he said to me: "I am reminded that I promised my wife to bring home some story-books for the children when I was in town to-day. The store is only a few steps down the street." As we went along, he explained to me that nobody any longer pretended to charge his mind with the recollection of duties or engagements of any sort. Everybody depended upon his indispensable to remind him in time of all undertakings and responsibilities. This service it was able to render by virtue of a simple enough adjustment of a phonographic cylinder charged with the necessary word or phrase to the clockwork in the indispensable, so that at any time fixed upon in setting the arrangement an alarm would sound, and, the indispensable being raised to the ear, the phonograph would deliver its message, which at any subsequent time might be called up and repeated. To all persons charged with weighty responsibilities depending upon accuracy of memory for their correct discharge, this feature of the indispensable rendered it, according to Hamage, and indeed quite obviously, an indispensable truly. To the railroad engineer it served the purpose not only of a time-piece, for the works of the indispensable include a watch, but to its ever vigilant alarm he could intrust his running orders, and, while his mind was wholly concentrated upon present duties, rest secure that he would be reminded at just the proper time of trains which he must avoid and switches he must make. To the indispensable of the business man the reminder attachment was not less necessary. Provided with that, his notes need never go to protest through carelessness, nor, however absorbed, was he in danger of forgetting an appointment.

Thanks to these portable memories it was, moreover, now possible for a wife to intrust to her husband the most complex messages to the dress-maker. All she had to do was to whisper the communication into her husband's indispensable while he was at breakfast, and set the alarm at an hour when he would be in the city.

"And in like manner, I suppose," suggested I, "if she wishes him to return at a certain hour from the club or the lodge, she can depend on his indispensable to remind him of his domestic duties at the proper moment, and in terms and tones which will make the total repudiation of connubial allegiance the only alternative of obedience. It is a very clever invention, and I don't wonder that it is popular with the ladies; but does it not occur to you that the inventor, if a man, was slightly inconsiderate? The rule of the American wife has hitherto been a despotism which could be tempered by a bad memory. Apparently, it is to be no longer tempered at all."

Hamage laughed, but his mirth was evidently a little forced, and I inferred that the reflection I had suggested had called up certain reminiscences not wholly exhilarating. Being fortunate, however, in the possession of a mercurial temperament, he presently rallied, and continued his praises of the artificial memory provided by the indispensable. In spite of the criticism which I had made upon it, I confess I was not a little moved by his description of its advantages to absent-minded men, of whom I am chief. Think of the gain alike in serenity and force of intellect enjoyed by the man who sits down to work absolutely free from that accursed cloud on the mind of things he has got to remember to do, and can only avoid totally forgetting by wasting tenfold the time required finally to do them in making sure by frequent rehearsals that he has not forgotten them! The only way that one of these trivialities ever sticks to the mind is by wearing a sore spot in it which heals slowly. If a man does not forget it, it is for the same reason that he remembers a grain of sand in his eye. I am conscious that my own mind is full of cicatrices of remembered things, and long ere this it would have been peppered with them like a colander, had I not a good while ago, in self-defense, absolutely refused to be held accountable for forgetting anything not connected with my regular business.

While firmly believing my course in this matter to have been justifiable and necessary, I have not been insensible to the domestic odium which it has brought upon me, and could but welcome a device which promised to enable me to regain the esteem of my family while retaining the use of my mind for professional purposes.

As the most convenient conceivable receptacle of hasty memoranda of ideas and suggestions, the indispensable also most strongly commended itself to me as a man who lives by writing. How convenient when a flash of inspiration comes to one in the night-time, instead of taking cold and waking the family in order to save it for posterity, just to whisper it into the ear of an indispensable at one's bedside, and be able to know it in the morning for the rubbish such untimely conceptions usually are! How often, likewise, would such a machine save in all their first vividness suggestive fancies, anticipated details, and other notions worth preserving, which occur to one in the full flow of composition, but are irrelevant to what is at the moment in hand! I determined that I must have an indispensable.

The bookstore, when we arrived there, proved to be the most extraordinary sort of bookstore I had ever entered, there not being a book in it. Instead of books, the shelves and counters were occupied with rows of small boxes.

"Almost all books now, you see, are phonographed," said Hamage.

"The change seems to be a popular one," I said, "to judge by the crowd of book-buyers." For the counters were, indeed, thronged with customers as I had never seen those of a bookstore before.

"The people at those counters are not purchasers, but borrowers," Hamage replied; and then he explained that whereas the old-fashioned printed book, being handled by the reader, was damaged by use, and therefore had either to be purchased outright or borrowed at high rates of hire, the phonograph of a book being not handled, but merely revolved in a machine, was but little injured by use, and therefore phonographed books could be lent out for an infinitesimal price. Everybody had at home a phonograph box of standard size and adjustments, to which all phonographic cylinders were gauged. I suggested that the phonograph, at any rate, could scarcely have replaced picture-books. But here, it seemed, I was mistaken, for it appeared that illustrations were adapted to phonographed books by the simple plan of arranging them in a continuous panorama, which by a connecting gear was made to unroll behind the glass front of the phonograph case as the course of the narrative demanded.

"But, bless my soul!" I exclaimed, "everybody surely is not content to borrow their books? They must want to have books of their own, to keep in their libraries."

"Of course," said Hamage. "What I said about borrowing books applies only to current literature of the ephemeral sort. Everybody wants books of permanent value in his library. Over yonder is the department of the establishment set apart for book-buyers."

The counter which he indicated being less crowded than those of the borrowing department, I expressed a desire to examine some of the phono-graphed books. As we were waiting for attendance, I observed that some of the customers seemed very particular about their purchases, and insisted upon testing several phonographs bearing the same title before making a selection. As the phonographs seemed exact counterparts in appearance, I did not understand this till Hamage explained that differences as to style and quality of elocution left quite as great a range of choice in phono-graphed books as varieties in type, paper, and binding did in printed ones. This I presently found to be the case when the clerk, under Hamage's direction, began waiting on me. In succession I tried half a dozen editions of Tennyson by as many different elocutionists, and by the time I had heard

"Where Claribel low lieth"

rendered by a soprano, a contralto, a bass, and a baritone, each with the full effect of its quality and the personal equation besides, I was quite ready to admit that selecting phonographed books for one's library was as much more difficult as it was incomparably more fascinating than suiting one's self with printed editions. Indeed, Hamage admitted that nowadays nobody with any taste for literature—if the word may for convenience be retained—thought of contenting himself with less than half a dozen ren-derings of the great poets and dramatists.

"By the way," he said to the clerk, "won't you just let my friend try the Booth-Barrett Company's 'Othello'? It is, you understand," he added to me, "the exact phonographic reproduction of the play as actually rendered by the company."

Upon his suggestion, the attendant had taken down a phonograph case and placed it on the counter. The front was an imitation of a theatre with the curtain down. As I placed the transmitter to my ears, the clerk touched a spring and the curtain rolled up, displaying a perfect picture of the stage in the opening scene. Simultaneously the action of the play began, as if the pictured men upon the stage were talking. Here was no question of losing half that was said and guessing the rest. Not a word, not a syllable, not a whispered aside of the actors, was lost; and as the play proceeded the pictures changed, showing every important change of attitude on the part of the actors. Of course the figures, being pictures, did not move, but their presentation in so many successive attitudes presented the effect of movement, and made it quite possible to imagine that the voices in my ears were really theirs. I am exceedingly fond of the drama, but the amount of effort and physical inconvenience necessary to witness a play has rendered my indulgence in this pleasure infrequent. Others might not have agreed with me, but I confess that none of the ingenious applications of the phonograph which I had seen seemed to be so well worth while as this.

Hamage had left me to make his purchases, and found me on his return still sitting spellbound.

"Come, come," he said, laughing, "I have Shakespeare complete at home, and you shall sit up all night, if you choose, hearing plays. But come along now, I want to take you upstairs before we go."

He had several bundles. One, he told me, was a new novel for his wife, with some fairy stories for the children,—all, of course, phonographs. Besides, he had bought an indispensable for his little boy.

"There is no class," he said, "whose burdens the phonograph has done so much to lighten as parents. Mothers no longer have to make themselves hoarse telling the children stories on rainy days to keep them out of mischief. It is only necessary to plant the most roguish lad before a phonograph of some nursery classic, to be sure of his whereabouts and his behavior till the machine runs down, when another set of cylinders can be introduced, and the entertainment carried on. As for the babies, Patti sings mine to sleep at bedtime, and, if they wake up in the night, she is never too drowsy to do it over again. When the children grow too big to be longer tied to their mother's apron-strings, they still remain, thanks to the children's indispensable, though out of her sight, within sound of her voice. Whatever charges or instructions she desires them not to forget, whatever hours or duties she would have them be sure to remember, she depends on the indispensable to remind them of."

At this I cried out, "It is all very well for the mothers," I said, "but the lot of the orphan must seem enviable to a boy compelled to wear about such an instrument of his own subjugation. If boys were what they were in my day, the rate at which their indispensables would get unaccountably lost or broken would be alarming."

Hamage laughed, and admitted that the one he was carrying home was the fourth he had bought for his boy within a month. He agreed with me that it was hard to see how a boy was to get his growth under quite so much government; but his wife, and indeed the ladies generally, insisted that the application of the phonograph to family government was the greatest invention of the age.

Then I asked a question which had repeatedly occurred to me that day,—What had become of the printers?

"Naturally," replied Hamage, "they have had a rather hard time of it. Some classes of books, however, are still printed, and probably will continue to be for some time, although reading, as well as printing, is getting to be an increasingly rare accomplishment."

"Do you mean that your schools do not teach reading and writing?" I exclaimed.

"Oh, yes, they are still taught; but as the pupils need them little after leaving school,—or even in school, for that matter, all their text-books being phonographic,—they usually keep the acquirements about as long as a college graduate does his Greek. There is a strong movement already on foot to drop reading and writing entirely from the school course, but probably a compromise will be made for the present by substituting a shorthand or phonetic system, based upon the direct interpretation of the sound-waves themselves. This is, of course, the only logical method for the visual interpretation of sound. Students and men of research, however, will always need to understand how to read print, as much of the old literature will probably never repay phonographing."

"But," I said, "I notice that you still use printed phrases, as superscriptions, titles, and so forth."

"So we do," replied Hamage, "but phonographic substitutes could be easily devised in these cases, and no doubt will soon have to be supplied in deference to the growing number of those who cannot read."

"Did I understand you," I asked, "that the text-books in your schools even are phonographs?"

"Certainly," replied Hamage; "our children are taught by phonographs, recite to phonographs, and are examined by phonographs."

"Bless my soul!" I ejaculated.

"By all means," replied Hamage; "but there is really nothing to be astonished at. People learn and remember by impressions of sound instead of sight, that is all. The printer is, by the way, not the only artisan whose occupation phonography has destroyed. Since the disuse of print, opticians have mostly gone to the poor-house. The sense of sight was indeed terribly overburdened previous to the introduction of the phonograph, and, now that the sense of hearing is beginning to assume its proper share of work, it would be strange if an improvement in the condition of the people's eyes were not noticeable. Physiologists, moreover, promise us not only an improved vision, but a generally improved physique, especially in respect to bodily carriage, now that reading, writing, and study no longer involves, as formerly, the sedentary attitude with twisted spine and stooping shoulders. The phonograph has at last made it possible to expand the mind without cramping the body."

"It is a striking comment on the revolution wrought by the general introduction of the phonograph," I observed, "that whereas the misfortune of blindness used formerly to be the infirmity which most completely cut a man off from the world of books, which remained open to the deaf, the case is now precisely reversed."

"Yes," said Hamage, "it is certainly a curious reversal, but not so complete as you fancy. By the new improvements in the intensifier, it is expected to enable all, except the stone-deaf, to enjoy the phonograph, even when connected, as on railroad trains, with a common telephonic wire. The stone-deaf will of course be dependent upon printed books prepared for their benefit, as raised-letter books used to be for the blind."

As we entered the elevator to ascend to the upper floors of the establishment, Hamage explained that he wanted me to see, before I left, the process of phonographing books, which was the modern substitute for printing them. Of course, he said, the phonographs of dramatic works were taken at the theatres during the representations of plays, and those of public orations and sermons are either similarly obtained, or, if a revised version is desired, the orator re-delivers his address in the improved form to a phonograph; but the great mass of publications were phonographed by professional elocutionists employed by the large publishing houses, of which this was one. He was acquainted with one of these elocutionists, and was taking me to his room.

We were so fortunate as to find him disengaged. Something, he said, had broken about the machinery, and he was idle while it was being repaired. His work-room was an odd kind of place. It was shaped something like the interior of a rather short egg. His place was on a sort of pulpit in the middle of the small end, while at the opposite end, directly before him, and for some distance along the sides towards the middle, were arranged tiers of phonographs. These were his audience, but by no means all of it. By telephonic communication he was able to address simultaneously other congregations of phonographs in other chambers at any distance. He said that in one instance, where the demand for a popular book was very great, he had charged five thousand phonographs at once with it.

I suggested that the saving of printers, pressmen, bookbinders, and costly machinery, together with the comparative indestructibility of phonographed as compared with printed books, must make them very cheap.

"They would be," said Hamage, "if popular elocutionists, such as Playwell here, did not charge so like fun for their services. The public has taken it into its head that he is the only first-class elocutionist, and won't buy anybody else's work. Consequently the authors stipulate that he shall interpret their productions, and the publishers, between the public and the authors, are at his mercy."

Playwell laughed. "I must make my hay while the sun shines," he said. "Some other elocutionist will be the fashion next year, and then I shall only get hack-work to do. Besides, there is really a great deal more work in my business than people will believe. For example, after I get an author's copy"—

"Written?" I interjected.

"Sometimes it is written phonetically, but most authors dictate to a phonograph. Well, when I get it, I take it home and study it, perhaps a couple of days, perhaps a couple of weeks, sometimes, if it is really an important work, a month or two, in order to get into sympathy with the ideas, and decide on the proper style of rendering. All this is hard work, and has to be paid for."

At this point our conversation was broken off by Hamage, who declared that, if we were to catch the last train out of town before noon, we had no time to lose.

Of the trip out to Hamage's place I recall nothing. I was, in fact, aroused from a sound nap by the stopping of the train and the bustle of the departing passengers. Hamage had disappeared. As I groped about, gathering up my belongings, and vaguely wondering what had become of my companion, he rushed into the car, and, grasping my hand, gave me an enthusiastic welcome. I opened my mouth to demand what sort of a joke this belated greeting might be intended for, but, on second thought, I concluded not to raise the point. The fact is, when I came to observe that the time was not noon, but late in the evening, and that the train was the one I had left home on, and that I had not even changed my seat in the car since then, it occurred to me that Hamage might not understand allusions to the forenoon we had spent together. Later that same evening, however, the consternation of my host and hostess at my frequent and violent explosions of apparently causeless hilarity left me no choice but to make a clean breast of my preposterous experience. The moral they drew from it was the charming one that, if I would but oftener come to see them, a railroad trip would not so upset my wits.

Familiar Glimpses of Yellow Journalism

JAMES CREELMAN

It has been said by those calm students of human events who were untroubled by the cries of oppressed Cuba, that the war between the United States and Spain was the work of "yellow newspapers"—that form of American journalistic energy which is not content merely to print a daily record of history, but seeks to take part in events as an active and sometimes decisive agent.

That was a saying of high reproach when the armed struggle began and when Continental Europe frowned upon the American cause. "Yellow journalism" was blood guilty. It had broken the peace of the world. Its editors were enemies of society and its correspondents ministers of passion and disorder. Its lying clamors had aroused the credulous mob, overthrown the dignified policies of government, and dishonored international law.

But when the results of that conflict justified the instrumentalities which produced it, when the world accepted the emancipation of Cuba from the bloody rule of Spain as a glorious step in the progress of mankind,—then the part played by the newspapers was forgotten, and "yellow journalism" was left to sing its own praises; and its voice was long and loud and sometimes tiresome.

James Creelman, *On the Great Highway. The Wanderings and Adventures of a Special Correspondent* (Boston, 1901), pp. 174–193.

Little politicians arose and, with their hands on their hearts, acknowledged that they had done the thing and were willing to have it known of men. Heroes of a three months' war, who had faced the perils of tinned beef, bared their brows for the laurels of a grateful nation. The party in power at Washington solemnly thanked God that it had had the wisdom and courage to strike a blow for human liberty. The government's press censors in Cuba and the Philippines were instructed to suppress the attempts of indignant "yellow journalism" to call attention to its own deeds.

And yet no true history of the war which banished Spain from the western hemisphere and released the Philippine archipelago from her tyranny, can be written without an acknowledgment that whatever of justice and freedom and progress was accomplished by the Spanish-American war was due to the enterprise and tenacity of "yellow journalists," many of whom lie in unremembered graves.

As one of the multitude who served in that crusade of "yellow journalism," and shared in the common calumny, I can bear witness to the martyrdom of men who suffered all but death—and some, even death itself—in those days of darkness.

It may be that a desire to sell their newspapers influenced some of the "yellow editors," just as a desire to gain votes inspired some of the political orators. But that was not the chief motive; for if ever any human agency was thrilled by the consciousness of its moral responsibility, it was "yellow journalism" in the never-to-be-forgotten months before the outbreak of hostilities, when the masterful Spanish minister at Washington seemed to have the influence of every government in the world behind him in his effort to hide the truth and strangle the voice of humanity.

How little they know of "yellow journalism" who denounce it! How swift they are to condemn its shrieking headlines, its exaggerated pictures, its coarse buffoonery, its intrusions upon private life, and its occasional inaccuracies! But how slow they are to see the steadfast guardianship of public interests which it maintains! How blind to its unfearing warfare against rascality, its detection and prosecution of crime, its costly searchings for knowledge throughout the earth, its exposures of humbug, its endless funds for the quick relief of distress!

Some time before the destruction of the battleship *Maine* in the harbor of Havana, the *New York Journal* sent Frederic Remington, the distinguished artist, to Cuba. He was instructed to remain there until the war began; for "yellow journalism" was alert and had an eye for the future.

Presently Mr. Remington sent this telegram from Havana:—

"W. R. HEARST, *New York Journal*, N.Y.

"Everything is quiet. There is no trouble here. There will be no war. I wish to return.

"REMINGTON."

This was the reply:—

"REMINGTON, HAVANA:

"Please remain. You furnish the pictures, and I'll furnish the war.

"W. R. HEARST."

The proprietor of the *Journal* was as good as his word, and to-day the gilded arms of Spain, torn from the front of the palace in Santiago de Cuba hang in his office in Printing House Square, a lump of melted silver, taken from the smoking deck of the shattered Spanish flagship, serves as his paper weight, and the bullet-pierced headquarters flag of the Eastern army of Cuba—gratefully presented to him in the field by General Garcia —adorns his wall.

The incident which did more to arouse the sentimental opposition of the American people to Spain than anything which happened prior to the destruction of the *Maine,* was the rescue of the beautiful Evangelina Cisneros from a Havana prison by the *Journal's* gallant correspondent, Karl Decker. There is nothing in fiction more romantic than this feat of "yellow journalism." And the events which led up to it are worth telling.

One sultry day in August, 1897, the proprietor of the *Journal* was lolling in his editorial chair. Public interest in Cuba was weak. The Spanish minister at Washington had drugged the country with cunningly compounded statements. The government was indifferent. The weather was too hot for serious agitation. Every experienced editor will tell you that it is hard to arouse the popular conscience in August. Perspiring man refuses to allow himself to be worked into a moral rage. The proletariat of liberty was in a hole. The most tremendous headlines failed to stir the crowd.

An attendant entered the room with a telegram, which Mr. Hearst read languidly:—

"HAVANA.

"Evangelina Cisneros, pretty girl of seventeen years, related to President of Cuban Republic, is to be imprisoned for twenty years on African coast, for having taken part in uprising Cuban political prisoners on Isle of Pines."

He read it over a second time and was about to cast it on his desk—

but no! He stared at the little slip of paper and whistled softly. Then he slapped his knee and laughed.

"Sam!" he cried.

A tall, shaven, keen-eyed editor entered from the next room.

"We've got Spain, now!" exclaimed Mr. Hearst, displaying the message from Cuba. "Telegraph to our correspondent in Havana to wire every detail of this case. Get up a petition to the Queen Regent of Spain for this girl's pardon. Enlist the women of America. Have them sign the petition. Wake up our correspondents all over the country. Have distinguished women sign first. Cable the petitions and the names to the Queen Regent. Notify our minister in Madrid. We can make a national issue of this case. It will do more to open the eyes of the country than a thousand editorials or political speeches. The Spanish minister can attack our correspondents, but we'll see if he can face the women of America when they take up the fight. That girl must be saved if we have to take her out of prison by force or send a steamer to meet the vessel that carries her away—but that would be piracy, wouldn't it?"

Within an hour messages were flashing to Cuba, England, France, Spain, and to every part of the United States. The petition to the Queen Regent was telegraphed to more than two hundred correspondents in various American cities and towns. Each correspondent was instructed to hire a carriage and employ whatever assistance he needed, get the signatures of prominent women of the place, and telegraph them to New York as quickly as possible. Within twenty-four hours the vast agencies of "yellow journalism" were at work in two hemispheres for the sake of the helpless girl prisoner. Thousands of telegrams poured into the *Journal* office. Mrs. Jefferson Davis, the widow of the Confederate President, wrote this appeal, which the *Journal* promptly cabled to the summer home of the Queen Regent at San Sebastian:—

"To HER MAJESTY, MARIA CRISTINA, *Queen Regent of Spain:*—

"*Dear Madam*: In common with many of my countrywomen I have been much moved by the accounts of the arrest and trial of Señorita Evangelina Cisneros. Of course, at this great distance, I am ignorant of the full particulars of her case. But I do know she is young, defenceless, and in sore straits. However, all the world is familiar with the shining deeds of the first lady of Spain, who has so splendidly illustrated the virtues which exalt wife and mother, and who has added to these the wisdom of a statesman and the patience and fortitude of a saint.

"To you I appeal to extend your powerful protection over this poor captive girl—a child almost in years—to save her from a fate worse than death. I am sure your kind heart does not prompt you to vengeance, even though the provocation has been great. I entreat you to give her to the women of America, to live among us in peace.

"We will become sureties that her life in future will be one long thank-offering for your clemency.

"Do not, dear Madam, refuse this boon to us, and we will always pray for the prosperity of the young King, your son, and for that of his wise and self-abnegating mother.

"Your admiring and respecting petitioner,

"VARINA JEFFERSON DAVIS."

Then Mrs. Julia Ward Howe, author of the "Battle Hymn of the Republic," wrote this appeal to the Pope, which the *Journal* cabled to the Vatican:—

"To HIS HOLINESS, LEO XIII.:

"*Most Holy Father:*—To you, as the head of Catholic Christendom, we appeal for aid in behalf of Evangelina Cisneros, a young lady of Cuba, one of whose near relatives is concerned in the present war, in which she herself has taken no part. She has been arrested, tried by court martial, and is in danger of suffering a sentence more cruel than death—that of twenty years of exile and imprisonment in the Spanish penal colony of Ceuta, in Africa, where no woman has ever been sent, and where, besides enduring every hardship and indignity, she would have for her companions the lowest criminals and outcasts.

"We implore you, Holy Father, to emulate the action of that Providence which interests itself in the fall of a sparrow. A single word from you will surely induce the Spanish government to abstain from this act of military vengeance, which would greatly discredit it in the eyes of the civilized world.

"We devoutly hope that your wisdom will see fit to utter this word, and to make not us alone, but humanity, your debtors.

"JULIA WARD HOWE."

The mother of President McKinley signed a petition to the Queen Regent. The wife of Secretary of State Sherman gave her name to the appeal, and soon the most representative women of the nation joined the movement. Fifteen thousand names were cabled by the *Journal* to the palace of San Sebastian. The country began to ring with the story of Evangelina Cisneros. Hundreds of public meetings were convened. The beautiful young prisoner became the protagonist of the Cuban struggle for liberty. Spain was denounced and the President was urged to lend his influence to the patriot cause of Cuba. The excitement grew day by day. It stirred up forces of sympathy that had lain dormant until then. The wily Spanish minister at Washington was in a trap. He did not dare to attack a movement supported by the wives and daughters of the great leaders of every political party in the United States.

How we worked and watched for poor Cuba in those days! How the tired writers stuck to the fight in those hot, breathless nights! And how the palace officials in Spain and the Captain-general in Cuba cursed us for our pains!

Presently there came a message from Cuba. Karl Decker had carried out his instructions. "Yellow journalism" had broken the bars of the Spanish prison. The beautiful young prisoner was safe on the ocean and would be in New York in a few days.

Not only had the girl been lifted out of the prison window through the shattered iron barriers and carried from rooftop to rooftop in the night over a teetering ladder, but she had been secreted in Havana in spite of the frantic search of the Spanish authorities and, disguised as a boy, had been smuggled on board of a departing steamer under the very noses of the keenest detectives in Havana.

"Now is the time to consolidate public sentiment," said Mr. Hearst, "Organize a great open-air reception in Madison Square. Have the two best military bands. Secure orators, have a procession, arrange for plenty of fireworks and searchlights. Announce that Miss Cisneros and her rescuer will appear side by side and thank the people. Send men to all the political leaders in the city, and ask them to work up the excitement. We must have a hundred thousand people together that night. It must be a whale of a demonstration—something that will make the President and Congress sit up and think."

Who, of all the countless multitude that witnessed that thrilling scene in Madison Square, knew the processes by which "yellow journalism," starting with that little message from Havana, had set in motion mighty forces of sympathy, which increased day by day, until Congress met, and the conscience of the nation found its official voice.

The time has not yet come when all the machinery employed by the American press in behalf of Cuba can be laid bare to the public. Great fortunes were spent in the effort to arouse the country to a realization of the real situation. Things which cannot even be referred to now were attempted.

It was my fortune to interview Canovas del Castillo, the Prime Minister of Spain, a few months before the outbreak of the war. As I had been exiled from Cuba—whither I had gone as a special correspondent for the *New York World*—by Captain-general Weyler, the experience in Madrid was doubly interesting.

"The newspapers in your country seem to be more powerful than the government," said the lion-headed Premier.

"Not more powerful, your Excellency, but more in touch with the real sovereignty of the nation, the people. The government is elected only once in four years, while the newspapers have to appeal to their constituents every day in the year."

If the war against Spain is justified in the eyes of history, then "yellow journalism" deserves its place among the most useful instrumentalities of civilization. It may be guilty of giving the world a lop-sided view of events by exaggerating the importance of a few things and ignoring others, it may offend the eye by typographical violence, it may sometimes proclaim its own deeds too loudly; but it has never deserted the cause of the poor and the downtrodden; it has never taken bribes,—and that is more than can be said of its most conspicuous critics.

One of the accusations against "yellow journalism" is that it steps outside of the legitimate business of gathering news and commenting upon it—that it acts. It is argued that a newspaper which creates events and thus creates news, cannot, in human nature, be a fair witness. There is a grain of truth in this criticism; but it must not be forgotten that the very nature of journalism enables it to act in the very heart of events at critical moments and with knowledge not possessed by the general public; that what is everybody's business and the business of nobody in particular, is the journalist's business.

There are times when public emergencies call for the sudden intervention of some power outside of governmental authority. Then journalism acts. Let me give an instance.

When Admiral Camara was preparing to sail with a powerful Spanish fleet to attack Admiral Dewey in Manila Bay, two American monitors armed with ten-inch rifles were on their way across the Pacific to the Philippines. It was a perilous situation, more perilous than the American people were permitted to know. I have seen Admiral Dewey's letters to Consul General Wildman at Hong Kong, begging for news of the movements of the Spanish fleet and confessing that his squadron was too weak to meet it unless the two monitors should arrive in time. The threatened admiral made no secret of his anxiety. The question of victory or defeat or retreat depended on whether the Spanish fleet could be delayed until the powerful monitors had time to reach Manila.

In that critical hour, when the statesmen at Washington were denouncing "yellow journalism," I received the following message in the London office of the *New York Journal:*—

NEW YORK JOURNAL

W. R. Hearst

Dear Mr. Creelman:

I wish you would at once make preparations so that in case the Spanish fleet actually starts for Manila we can buy some big English steamer at the eastern end of the Mediterranean and take her to some part of the Suez Canal where we can then sink her and obstruct the passage of the Spanish warships. This must be done if the American monitors sent from San Francisco have not reached Dewey and he should be placed in a critical position by the approach of Camara's fleet. I understand that if a British vessel were taken into the canal and sunk under the circumstances outlined above, the British Government would not allow her to be blown up to clear a passage and it might take time enough to raise her to put Dewey in a safe position.

Yours very truly,

W. R. Hearst

Camara's fleet left Spain to attack Dewey and actually entered the Suez Canal; but the sinking of a steamer in the narrow channel was made unnecessary by the sudden abandonment of the expedition and the return of the Spanish admiral to the threatened coast of Spain.

One does not have to be a great lawyer to understand that the obstruction of the Suez Canal could not have been undertaken by any responsible representative of the American government without a grave breach of international law. Nor was there any existing private agency that could so well undertake such a costly and serious patriotic service as a newspaper whose correspondents kept it in almost hourly touch with the changing facts of the situation. I will not attempt to defend this contemplated deed as a matter of law. It needs no defense among Americans. The facts are given as an illustration of the part which the journalism of action is beginning to play in the affairs of nations, and the varying methods employed.

But journalism that acts is no new thing, although it is beginning to act on new lines. The *London Times* defended Queen Caroline against the persecutions of George IV, and was denounced as a vulgar meddler. The same newspaper, after compelling the recall of Lord Raglan from the command of the British forces in the Crimea, forced Lord Aberdeen's ministry to resign. That was "yellow journalism," and John Walter was bitterly assailed for his sensationalism. Again, in 1840, the *Times* went beyond the orthodox frontier of journalism and, at enormous risk and expense, exposed gigantic frauds, saving millions of dollars to the merchants of London. A marble tablet over the entrance of the *Times* office records the gratitude of the people of the British metropolis. The *New York Herald* sent Stanley to find Livingstone in Africa, and equipped the *Jeannette* expedition to search for the North Pole. The *New York Times* smashed the great Tweed Ring, which had plundered and defied the public for years. The *New York World* averted a national disgrace by providing a pedestal for the Statue of Liberty presented by the people of France. The same newspaper defeated the famous bond conspiracy and compelled the Cleveland administration to allow the general public to compete in the $100,000,000 loan, saving millions of dollars for the treasury and demonstrating the financial independence of the United States.

Surely, if it be right for a newspaper to urge others to act in any given direction, it is also right for the newspaper itself to act.

3. Department Stores

With dramatic increases in municipal growth and improvements in rapid transit, American retailing underwent radical transformations in the late nineteenth century. Among the era's characteristic innovations was the great department store, a centralized emporium performing functions served by a variety of specialty stores just a few years earlier. Several American cities dispute the claim of possessing the first true department store, but by the eighteen-eighties the pattern which A. T. Stewart in New York, John Wanamaker in Philadelphia, and Marshall Field in Chicago had set was being widely imitated, and the extensive advertising, huge sales forces, and competitive pricing of the modern department store had become an economic and social given.

Because of their size and function department stores provided increased opportunities for female employment. This in turn aroused the interest of economists, clergymen, social workers, and writers of fiction. The hours of work were long, the pay frequently quite low, and the temptations brought by indiscriminate contact with customers and commodities were numerous. Both the facts and fantasies of the sales clerk proved fascinating.

Annie M. MacLean, who concentrated on the facts, was a Canadian who took a Ph.D. from the University of Chicago and wrote extensively on social problems. An active worker for female suffrage and director of sociological investigation for the recently founded YMCA, she also taught for some years at Adelphi College in New York.

O. Henry, the pen name of William Sidney Porter (1862–1910), had far less formal education than Annie MacLean. Born in New York, he left school at the age of fifteen, went to Texas (where he was accused of embezzling funds from an Austin bank), fled to Central America, and eventually served several years in prison in Columbus, Ohio. O. Henry published his first stories while still in prison, and then achieved great popularity in the first decade of the new century. His sentimental vignettes of life among the urban masses contributed to the creation of a new urban folklore, and illuminated the life-styles of the submerged.

Two Weeks in Department Stores

ANNIE M. MacLEAN

It is so common for those who purchase goods to think nothing at all about the clerk in attendance, or the conditions under which the goods were produced, that it seems timely just now, when the Consumers' League has started upon a crusade of educating the public, to give a true picture of some conditions existing in Chicago.

The necessity for a thorough investigation of the work of women and children in the large department stores in the city was apparent, and the difficulties manifold. With a view to ascertaining some things which could be learned only from the inside, the investigation which is to form the subject-matter of this paper was undertaken. It seemed evident that valuable information could be obtained if someone were willing to endure the hardships of the saleswoman's life, and from personal experience be able to pass judgment upon observed conditions. The urgency of the need, coupled with an enthusiastic interest in the work for which the Consumers' League stands, led me to join the ranks of the retail clerks for two weeks during the rush of the holiday trade. It may be urged that just judgments could not be formed at a time when conditions must be abnormal. It is true that conditions were abnormal, but the importance of knowing to what extent cannot be overestimated. The consumer should know how far his Christmas shopping works hardships for the clerks. Moreover, he should concern himself with the question as to whether the abnormal conditions he has helped to create are in part mitigated by adequate payment for the work exacted. The law in Illinois prohibits the employment of children under fourteen years, and limits the working day of those between the ages of fourteen and sixteen to ten hours in manufacturing and mercantile establishments, and it should be a matter of concern to the purchaser if his persistence in late shopping leads the merchant to break, or at least evade, the law. It is admittedly a menace to the social weal to have children and young girls working late at night, and thus exposed to the dangers of city streets at a time when physical and moral

Annie M. MacLean, "Two Weeks in Department Stores," *American Journal of Sociology*, Vol. IV (May, 1899), pp. 721–741.

safety demand that they be at home. One of the objects of this investigation was to find the amount of overtime exacted, and the compensation, if any, that was given. Employers are always ready to tell the best conditions that exist; it remains to others to find the worst. And the Consumers' League utterly refuses to indorse stores that do not live up to its standard all the time.

And yet some will argue that any effort in behalf of the employees in the great stores is unnecessary. Many objections were urged against factory legislation in the early days of that reform. The champions of the movement in England met with strenuous opposition, but finally their frightful revelations of actual conditions overcame their opponents, and a wave of enthusiastic reform set in. The history in this country is similar. From 1830 to 1874 agitation for the protection of women and children in the factories was kept up, till finally, at the latter date, the Massachusetts Act became a reality. Then other states followed the example set, until, at the present time, almost all the states having large manufacturing interests have very good factory laws. Illinois is a notable exception. Such, in a word, has been the history of the factory laws. We are just on the eve of an agitation for the amelioration of the conditions under which a vast army of saleswomen and cash children work. Thoughtful people all over the country have already recognized the necessity for this; but the whole body of the people must be awakened. And to help, in a small way, the educative movement here my labor was undertaken.

The difficulty of finding employment was not so great as might be supposed. Owing to the holiday rush, and the consequent need of large reinforcements to the original help, the employers were not insistent on experience as a requisite for the successful applicant. However, it was not until several visits had been made that I was promised a position at three dollars a week. Work was to begin the following Monday, which would give me just two weeks of the Christmas trade. Employment being promised, it seemed desirous to engage board in some home for working women; for the environment which such a place would provide gave promise of the best results. I was fortunate in finding a most satisfactory place not far from the heart of the city, and there I went as a working-woman. This home is deserving of more than passing mention. It provides board and lodging, together with the use of pleasant parlors and library, to working-women under thirty years of age for two dollars and a half a week, if they are content to occupy a single bed in a dormitory. These dormitories are thoughtfully planned, and accommodate from ten to fifteen each. A large proportion of the sixty-five residents were saleswomen, and they, in the course of conversation, gave me much useful information. All classes of girls were there, and most of them received very low wages. A few entries in the house register are here inserted to show the nature of the records kept, and the way in which the girls fill in the columns.

Name	Age	Nationality	Occupation	Wages per week
	18	American	Saleslady	$4.00
	27	Virginian	Stenographer	6.00
	24	American	Clerk	4.50
	23	American	Clerk	3.00
	29	German	Cashier	6.50
	23	Irish	Saleswoman	6.00
	28	American	Fur worker	5.00
	20	American	Saleslady	3.00

This, then, was the place from which I started out to work on the appointed Monday morning. The hurried breakfast, the rush out into the street thronged with a lunch-carrying humanity hastening to the downtown district, and the cars packed with pale-faced, sleepy-eyed men and women, made the working world seem very real. Hurrying workers filled the heart of the city; no one else was astir. I reached my destination promptly at eight, the time of opening. Then I had to stand in line at the manager's office awaiting my more definite appointment, which was received in due time. But the manager had changed his mind about wages, and said he would give me two dollars a week plus 5 per cent commission on sales, instead of the regular salary he had mentioned in our former interview. I was then given a number, and by "424" I was known during my stay there. I was sent to the toy department, where I found sixty-seven others who were to be my companions in toil. The place was a dazzling array of all kinds of toys, from a monkey beating a drum to a doll that said "mamma," and a horse whose motor force was to be a small boy. Our business was first to dust and condense* the stock, and then to stand ready for customers. We all served in the double capacity of floorwalkers and clerks, and our business was to see that no one escaped without making a purchase. The confusion can be readily imagined. As soon as the elevators emptied themselves on the floor, there was one mad rush of clerks with a quickly spoken, "What would you like, madam?" or, "Something in toys, sir?" And the responses to these questions were indicative of the characters of the people making them. The majority were rude, some amused, and a few alarmed at the urgency of the clerks. One young boy, on being assailed by half a dozen at once, threw up his hands in horror, and said:

* This meant to pile like things together in as small space as possible.

"For God's sake, let me get out of here!" and fled down the stairs, not even waiting for the elevator. The cause of such watchful activity on the part of so many employees was the 5 per cent commission which was to eke out the two or three dollars a week salary. Those who were experienced received the latter sum. And the extra nickels earned meant so much to many of them. Most of the girls in that department lived at home or with relatives, but in many cases the necessity for money was most urgent.

One of the difficult things at first was keeping track of the prices, for they were frequently changed during the day, and the penalty for selling under price was immediate discharge, while selling above price met with no disapproval.

Every morning there were special sales. Sometimes articles that had sold for one dollar would be reduced to ninety-eight cents, with much blowing of trumpets, while, again, twenty-five cent articles would be offered at a bargain for *forty cents* "today only." But we soon learned what things were to be "leaders" from day to day, and the manager's brief instructions each morning were sufficient to keep us posted on the bargains. The charms of the bargain counter vanish when one has been behind the scenes and learned something of its history. The humor of it seemed to impress the clerks, for often knowing winks would be exchanged when some unwary customer was being victimized.

Oh, the weariness of that first morning! The hours seemed days. "Can I possibly stand up all day?" was the thought uppermost in my mind, for I soon learned from my companions that abusive language was the share of the one who was found sitting down. Later in the week I found this to be true. One of the girls who was well-nigh exhausted sat a moment on a little table that was for sale—there was not a seat of any kind in the rooms, and the only way one could get a moment's rest was to sit on the children's furniture that was for sale on one part of the floor. The manager came along and found the poor girl resting. The only sympathy he manifested was to call out in rough tones: "Get up out of that, you lazy huzzy, I don't pay you to sit around all day!" Under such circumstances it is small wonder that the stolen rests were few. By night the men as well as the women were limping wearily across the floor, and many sales were made under positive physical agony.

How well I remember my first service there! The people were slow in coming that morning; in fact, they were every morning. We scarcely ever had any business worth mentioning till eleven o'clock, and the greatest rush came about six. From half-past twelve to two was a busy time also. People seemed determined to shop when we ought to be getting our meals. My first two customers were of a type that abounds. First an angular woman with a business-like expression came to me and in peremptory tones demanded that I show her building blocks. They were dutifully shown, but proved unsatisfactory. Then dolls' buggies, boys' sleds, laundry sets, and skates were examined in slow succession, and I was catechized in a thoroughly pedagogical manner regarding the prices and merits of the same. When the last skate had been critically examined, she fixed a patronizing gaze upon me and said: "I do not intend to buy today; I merely wished to examine your goods." "Was she a revenue officer?" was the first thought that came to my mind. Oh, no! in the language of the shop, she was only a "rubber-neck." I afterward estimated the distance walked with her, and found it to be about one-twelfth of a mile, and still I had not a sale on my book. She took half an hour of my time.

The next customer who fell to my lot was a man of vinegary mien who wanted a boy's sled at a cost of one dollar and a half. Now, we had none at that particular price, but we had them at one dollar and thirty-five, and one dollar and sixty-five cents, either of which I thought would suit him. But I was mistaken, for he turned upon me a look of utter scorn, and then proceeded to denounce me for advertising things we did not have in stock. I meekly suggested that I was not responsible for the advertisements which appared in the morning papers, but he was not at all mollified, and left in high dudgeon. I felt rather blue, but the comforting voice of a little cash girl said: "Don't yer mind him, he's only a cheap skate." Thus reassured I started out on another venture. This time it was a small boy who wanted to buy, and the bright-faced little fellow did me good. He had eighty cents, he said, and he wanted presents for the baby, and Tom, and Freda, and cousin Jack, and several others. I suggested one thing after another, till finally he had spent his money; so I made out my first check and looked at it with pride. It read thus:

X. Y. Z. HOUSE.			
Sold by			*Am't Rec'd*
424			.80
1	"Dewey" bank		05
2	Sets dishes	15	30
1	Laundry set		15
1	Mother Goose ladder		12
1	Rubber ball		10
2	Bb'ls clothespins	04	08
			.80
Cash No.			*Amount*
127			.80
			.80

The boy was happy, and so was I. I looked admiringly at the eighty cents set down on my index sheet. It meant that I had earned four cents. After that the sales came frequently. They were all small, of course, and amounted to only $14.98 for the day. But this was more than I sold any succeeding day. It has often been noticed that new clerks do better at first than they do later. With me, freshness and interest in the novelty helped to banish weariness and invite sales.

My first day ended at half-past six. Through some oversight, a supper ticket was not given to me, and so I was allowed to go home. I went wearily to the cloak-room and more wearily to my boarding place. When I arrived there, I could only throw myself upon my little white cot in the dormitory and wildly wonder if it would be all right for a working girl to cry. Presently I was dreaming that blows from an iron mallet were falling fast upon me; and in a little while it was morning, and another day was begun. Hundreds of clerks in the city were starting out for work just as weary as I, but with them there was not the knowledge that labor could be ended at will.

It must be understood that "our house" was open every evening till about ten o'clock, and the only compensation given for the extra work was a supper, the market value of which was about fifteen cents. That, like the lunch, had to be eaten in great haste. The maximum time allowed, in either case, was thirty minutes, but our instructions were to "hurry back." That half an hour was wholly inadequate one can readily imagine. It sometimes took ten or fifteen minutes to get a simple order filled in the crowded restaurants near by. The lunch outside meant from ten to fifteen cents a day out of our small earnings, but the breath of even the smoky outdoor air was worth that to us. The air inside was always foul, and the continual noise was fairly maddening. We were obliged to eat our supper in the store, where it was provided. The second day I partook of what the management magnanimously called the "free supper." We were fed in droves and hurried away before the last mouthful was swallowed. The menu consisted of a meat dinner and an oyster stew, the latter of which I always elected with the lingering hope that it had not been made of scraps left from the regular café dinner earlier in the day. The said stew consisted of a bowl of hot milk, in the bottom of which lurked *three* oysters, except on that memorable day when I found *four*.

The days in the store were much the same, with their endless fatigue. At times the rush would be great; then again we would have nothing to do but stand around and talk. Thus we became surprisingly well acquainted in a short time. We talked about our wages and compared index sheets on every possible occasion. Some sold very little and at the end of the week had no more than three dollars.* The mental anguish of some of the girls when they saw at night how small their sales had been is impossible to describe. One may elect to become a worker, and endure the hardships of the toil, and live the life of the laborer, and receive the same starvation wages, but he can never experience the abject wretchedness of not knowing where to turn when the last dollar is gone. Three dollars a week to a girl alone in the city means starvation or shame.

The fourth day of the week was one I remember well. There had been special sales the day before, and everyone was more tired than usual; consequently those in charge were more than usually harsh and discourteous. One girl was ill. She should not have left home, but she feared losing her place if she remained away. She found after an hour or two that she could not work, so she asked permission to go home. The answer given was that she need not return if she left then. The floorwalker, who had a spark of humanity in his breast, told her that she could go to the toilet-room to lie down, if she would come out to her place once in a while to show that she was there. That poor girl spent the day on the rough, dirty floor, with a cash girl's apron for a pillow. At intervals she dragged herself out to her place in the department, only to crawl back more wretched than before. We wondered sometimes why there was no large chair or couch provided for an emergency case of that kind. There were comforts in the customers' waiting-rooms, but discharge was the fate of the employee who dared go in there.

A shop girl might die on the bare, hard floor, while easy chairs and couches in another room were unoccupied. Surely it would not be unreasonable that suitable rest-rooms be provided for the employees. Undue advantage could not well be taken of such a thing, for we could not leave the floor without asking the floorwalker—a man—for a pass, and his injunction always was, "Don't stay long." The unpleasantness of asking for a pass was sometimes overcome by girls slipping away in the crowd without permission. We thought some woman might be commissioned to grant such requests. We had to endure so many unnecessary hardships.

---

* On Saturday night all those whose sales averaged less than five dollars a day were discharged.

The cloak-, toilet-, and lunch-rooms were the gloomiest and filthiest it was ever my misfortune to enter. The cobwebs and dirt-smeared floors looked "spooky" under the flickering glare of insufficient gaslight. The only ventilation came through a foul basement, and there the little girl attendants stayed all day and late into the night. And that was where the girls who brought lunches had to eat them. A few rough board tables and chairs in a more or less advanced state of ruin were provided, and scores of hungry girls sat around and ate lunches from newspaper parcels and drank coffee from tin cans. It was not a healthful atmosphere, either physically or morally, and yet it was typical of the poorer class of stores. The slang of the streets, interspersed with oaths, formed the staple medium of communication. A young and innocent newcomer could not fail to feel shocked at what she heard. But the surroundings were not conducive of elevated thoughts. Refinement of thought and speech would soon disappear in such an environment. I never saw a clean towel in the toilet-room. Several hundred pairs of hands were wiped on the coarse, filthy piece of crash each day, and there was no woman in attendance to see that things were kept in a sanitary condition. Two little girls were in the cloak-room, but they had nothing to do with the adjoining places. The rooms were merely narrow hallways. The wretchedness of all these appointments was forced upon me the day my fellow-worker was so ill. It was so hard to get our wraps at night, for then all the employees were there pushing their way to the front. One night a young girl in the line was rather restless, and one of the store officials charged her with crowding, and jerked her out of line so that she struck against a counter on the right. He then shoved her back with such force that she fell against another on the left. She was badly hurt, and the uproar which followed was mob-like in its intensity. The boys were going to shoot the offender, they said, but he only smiled, secure in the justness of his attack. The case was afterward reported to the managers, but no reparation was ever made. The girl was unable to work the next day on account of the soreness of her back. In addition to the physical discomfort she had to endure, she lost a day's wages. From that warlike atmosphere we went forth into the night, and many of us had to go alone. That night I felt timid; so I asked if anyone was going my way. A little cash girl of only thirteen years spoke up and said: "I'll go wid yez." She had eight blocks to walk after she left me. The only mitigating circumstance was her total lack of fear. She was used to sights and sounds to which I was a stranger. There were always men on the street corners ready to speak to a girl alone, and one hesitating step meant danger.

Almost every morning the girls had some story to tell of encounters with men of that class; and that they were not exaggerating was proved satisfactorily to me by an experience of my own. I stepped from the car one night after midnight, and soon found that I was being followed. The chase continued for two blocks, when I staggered breathless into my doorway, with my pursuer not five feet away. My terror had given me power to outrun him.

I always pitied the cash children. Many of them were too young to be working, but the sin was at their parents' door. They placed on file the required affidavits, and the employer asked no questions. One little girl confessed to me that she was *not quite twelve years old,* but she told me not to tell anyone, because her mother told her to say she was fourteen. This burst of childish confidence came when I was pitying her because she had a toothache. The poor little things always had the toothache. There seems to be something about enforced work that brings on that malady in a child! But their trouble was probably more real than imagined. They often carried some cheap candy in one apron pocket and a little vial of toothache drops in the other, but they thought of no relationship existing between the two. The little girls frequently responded to the cry of, "Cash! Here cash!" with tears streaming down their faces; and the cause was always the one just mentioned, or sore feet. They got tired, of course. They were only children, and the instinct for play was strong. They would kiss the dolls and trundle the carts they were taking to the wrapping-room. A change of any kind was hailed with delight, as for instance the "running" of a C.O.D. check, which occasioned a trip to another floor. The added labor entailed was not considered. There were a great many extra ones employed at that time, and there was a continual war between the regulars and extras. The latter were engaged every morning at thirty-three cents a day, while the former were paid two dollars a week. The "enunciator," or one who had charge of the others, received two dollars and a half a week. In that particular store the little girls looked down on the boys, of whom there were comparatively few. The latter were supposed to clear away rubbish from under the counters, and on one occasion, when no boy was in sight, the floorwalker told a girl to carry away some waste papers, and she replied with a toss of her head: "You bloke you, I ain't no cash boy!" Childlike, they had their favorites among the clerks, and the fortunes of those they watched with much interest. One day the manager of the store appeared on our floor, and in ringing tones called out "424!" As I was starting to answer the summons, my young friend threw her arms around me and said: "Don't you mind Tom Jones, he can't hurt you. Tell him you're a new girl, if he scolds you; and if he's ugly, tell him to go to h—." I did not do any of those things, and I got away unhurt. He had no grievance against me, but he had such a rude way of addressing the clerks that they were all afraid of him.

We had our troubles with the manager and other officials, but they were not all. Some of the customers were so hard to please and so uncivil; and they made us feel like criminals because of our inability to do what apparently could not be done. Then there was the well-meaning buyer who persisted in asking us how much wages we got. Just why saleswomen should be subjected to such rudeness by seemingly intelligent people is difficult to see. One rather independent girl, on being asked this question for the fifth time one day, replied that she got ten dollars a week, and added: "How much do you get?" The questioner was a gentleman of clerical appearance, and he replied: "My dear young woman, I am afraid your surroundings are corrupting your good manners!" Then he passed on, doubtless feeling very righteous over his reproval.

On the whole, the week there passed quickly, and on Saturday night I decided to leave and try my fortune elsewhere. I thought that one week each in two stores would be better than the whole time spent in one. I told the manager that I wanted my pay because I was going to leave. He was rather abusive and said: "What do you want to leave for? You are making good money; you girls want the earth." I left that night with my two dollars in my pocket; my commission could not be obtained till the following week. Wages are always paid weekly there.

I was "out of a job," and trusted to luck to find another.

Sunday in the home was a quiet day. Everybody was tired and discouraged. There had been extra work, but no extra pay, and there were so many Christmas things to be bought. Sunday had to be the general mending day, and that day many were making little gifts for friends at home. Most of the girls were sensible about dress, and they guarded their small earnings carefully. I guided my expenditure by theirs and kept an accurate account of my expenses for the week. The items are here presented:

Board for one week	$2.50
Car fare, 6 days, @ 10 c.	.60*
Lunch, 5 days, @ 15c.	.75
" 1 day, @ 10c.	.10

* Many of the girls walked as far as two miles to save car fare.

For charity dinner .... .13°
Paper, 3 nights .... .06
Postal cards .... .05
Candy .... .10
Stamps .... .10
Oranges .... .09
Present for table girl .... .05
    "   " matron .... .10
Laundry .... .16

    Total expense $4.79

What I earned for the week was as follows:

Wages $2.00
Commission 3.25

                                              $5.25
Less fines .... .30°°

    Total earnings $4.95

Thus I had a balance of sixteen cents after my bills were paid, and that was as much as many had. At that rate it would take a long time to earn enough to buy a pair of boots.

The next week I started out again to look for a place, and I found one where I most wished to work. When I first sought employment I was an unskilled laborer, but the next time I was an experienced saleswoman, and as such I was engaged at a salary of four dollars a week plus 1 per cent commission on sales. This time my work was selling dolls, and there were four of us at the one counter. I realized at once that this was a much better place than the first one. The managers and floorwalkers were gentlemanly and kind, and the work was carried on in a thoroughly business-like way. I breathed freely when I found that no one would swear at me. There it was no crime to sit down, and behind each counter could be found one or two little boxes which the girls used for seats. They were awkward things, though, and very much in the way when we were moving around, waiting on customers. A hinged seat that could be swung under the counter would be such a boon.

    ° The matron asked for contributions from two cents up. Every girl in the home responded.

    °° A fine of ten cents was imposed for each tardiness, unless over half an hour; then twenty-five cents was charged.

The hours were very long. We worked from eight in the morning till eleven at night, with the exception of Christmas eve, when we worked until twelve. Half an hour was the time allowed for each meal. The only extra pay given was thirty cents each night for supper money. There was a very good cheap restaurant in the store, and there we bought our suppers for from twenty to thirty cents. Many of the clerks ate two cold lunches a day in order to save the money, while others were quite reckless and bought what they considered dainties. One day a girl who had a very bad headache went to lunch with me, and this is what she ordered:

Plum pudding with wine sauce $0.10
Swiss cheese sandwiches .... .05
Chocolate ice cream .... .05
Strong coffee .... .05

My astonishment was too great for words.

The work in this store was in many ways not so difficult as in the first. Our work was confined to one counter, and then we could sit down for a moment once in a while; but the customers were just as hard to suit and equally regardless of our feelings. And how long the days were! It seemed to me that my thoughts were always centered on my feet! Our arms got tired, too; we had to reach a good deal for stock. A man made me open and take the dolls from nineteen boxes to see if I could not find him one with black eyes and yellow hair. I told him they were all gone, at the price he desired, but he wanted me to verify my statement. As if it would matter to his two-year-old baby whether the doll had black or green eyes! He was evidently buying one for his own delectation. That is only one instance of the many exacting customers we met.

There the sanitary conditions were good, lunch- and cloak-room accommodation ample, and the treatment kind and courteous; but the wages were woefully insufficient. From four to five dollars a week was the average. The commission given was only temporary, and designed to give an extra impetus to the sale of the holiday goods. One girl who had worked there for seven years told me that she had never received more than five dollars a week; and she had to keep up a respectable appearance. It was an openly acknowledged fact among the girls there that the paths of dishonor were traversed to supplement their small incomes. Some of them did not hesitate to advise newcomers of this lucrative employment. They viewed the matter solely from a commercial standpoint, and justified their conduct by the urgency of the need. The girls themselves said that more than a third of them were leading lives of shame. It was common to hear such expressions as this uttered in agonized seriousness: "If I don't get

more wages I'll have to go bad. But I'd hate to disgrace my family."
Lecherous men were always around ready to offer aid. They came, pro-
fessedly, to buy, but it was not the wares of the store they wanted. The
young and pretty girls yielded most easily. They would weep, sometimes,
and say: "Good people look down on us. But they don't know—they don't
know. *We have to earn our living.*"

Surely any effort which is being made to bring the saleswoman's wages
up to a point where she can live without the wages of sin is worthy of
the most respectful consideration. Whatever is done in this direction is
manifestly a social good. And, moreover, the best interests of society
demand that thinking people should consider this matter seriously. All
the hardships of the shop girl's life fade into insignificance before this
grave danger she has to face. Adequate support is the first necessity.
Improved sanitary conditions and opportunity for rest may well take a
second place. They can be secured by legislation; the other must come
from united action on the part of the buyers, and the organization of the
saleswomen themselves. The trades-union spirit should be fostered, and
the working-women taught the power of united effort.

Many merchants in this city do give living wages, but there are others
who do not. I know from actual experience, and I know from reliable
testimony.

My earnings for the first week have already been presented, and those
of the second are here given:

Salary	$4.00
Commission on sales	1.53
Supper money	1.80
Total	$7.33
Less fines	.40°
Week's wages	$6.93

My expenses for the week were as given below:

Board	$2.50
Car fare, 6 days @ 10.	.60
Lunch, 4 days, @ 15c.	.60
" 2 days, @ 10c.	.20
Supper, 6 days, @ 25c.	1.50
Paper, 3 days, @ 2c.	.06
Stamps	.04

° These were unavoidable owing to the crowds of employees using the elevators, and the shortness of the time allowed for meals.

Toy dog for cook's baby	.11
Bananas	.10
Witch hazel	.10
Chewing gum	.06**
Laundry	.18

$6.05

Thus my balance was eighty-eight cents. One girl at the home had only two cents left when her bills were paid. And she it was who said in answer to someone's expressed wish one night that "tomorrow would be Sunday": "I wish there wouldn't be any tomorrow." So many times they were overcome by the utter hopelessness of the future. They have to grapple with the wages problem in a most practical way.

It is true that the present rate of women's wages has been brought about by forces over which the public has or can have but little control; yet it is equally true that a conscientious investigation of the whole subject in this city could not be valueless. While it is impossible to improve matters at once, or perhaps ever, it is yet certainly worthy of an attempt. That women in other vocations may be in dire straits does not preclude the legitimacy of centering public efforts on one occupation.

In the two weeks I was employed I worked one hundred and seventy-five hours and received eleven dollars and eighty-eight cents, or a little more than six cents an hour. Under normal conditions the hours would be about one hundred and twenty for the same length of time. This, of course, would be exclusive of Sunday work, which is required all the year, at least in some stores. A certain number of clerks are needed for two or more hours during the day. In my first place no remuneration of any kind was given for this; in the second, car fare was always given, and lunch if the duties did not end before noon. The cash children in those two stores earned three and one-third cents an hour. When kept overtime, as they were in the first store in which I worked, they earned not quite two and one-third cents an hour. It must be said, however, that the managers did not insist upon children who worked at night being there promptly at eight in the morning. Sometimes they did not go until nine.

I am going to present just here in tabulated form some information I gathered from my fellow-workers regarding themselves. The statements are made for the month of December, and refer only to employees in the big down-town stores. In some cases I have had a dozen or more names followed by identical information, so I have inserted in the table but one

** This investment was to enable me to respond affirmatively to the oft-repeated question: "Got any chewin's on you?" .

to serve as a type. As a rule the working-women object to telling the wages they receive, particularly if they are low. They like to give the impression that they receive much more than they do, and this, I suppose, is not characteristic of any one particular class in society. Any figures based on a canvass made from the outside are almost sure to be misleading. The cases here (see p. 87) cited have been carefully examined, and from intimate acquaintance with the individuals I believe them to be correct.

The organization that is attempting to mitigate the evils connected with life in the mercantile establishments has most laudable aims and methods. The ameliorative movement on the part of consumers is a rational one. It is representative of the most enlightened forces in society, and rests on a sound basis. So long as the consumer will patronize bad stores, so long will they exist; so long as people will buy clothing produced under inhuman conditions, so long will they continue to be produced under just those conditions. Has the public no duty in the matter? Women and children are in the industrial world, and it is useless to wrangle over the expediency of their filling the places they do. They are there, and as the weaker members of society they need protection. Inhuman and demoralizing conditions must be removed. Some of the evils here could be speedily remedied by legislation and faithful inspection. Those who have not already considered the matter would do well to peruse carefully the Consumers' standard of a fair house, and ask themselves whether or not they can do something to lessen the hardships of the salespeoples' lives.

CONSUMERS' LEAGUE OF ILLINOIS

Consumers' Standard

Children.—A standard house is one in which no child is allowed to work after six o'clock in the evening, and the requirements of the child-labor law are all complied with.

Wages.—A standard house is one in which equal pay is given for work of equal value, irrespective of sex. In the departments where women only are employed the minimum wages are $6 per week for adult workers of six months' experience, and fall in few instances below $8.

In which wages are paid weekly or fortnightly.

In which fines, if imposed, are paid into a fund for the benefit of the employees.

In which the minimum wages of cash girls and boys are $2.25 per week, with the same conditions regarding weekly payments and fines.

Hours.—A standard house is one in which the hours from 8 A.M. to 6 P.M. (with not less than three quarters of an hour for lunch) constitute the working day, and a general half holiday is given on one day of each week during the summer months.

Name	Employment	Hours A.M. P.M.	Overtime	Weekly wage	For extra work	Cost of living per week	Conjugal condition	Health	Remarks
A	saleswoman	8:00–6:00	none	$ 6.00		$2.50	single	fair	
B	"	8:00–6:30	evenings till 10	3.00		2.50	"	"	
C	"	8:00–6:00	none	5.00		3.00	"		same place 3 years
D	inspector	8:00–6:30	till 10 or 11 P.M.	3.50		lived home		bad	
E	wrapper	8:00–6:00	till 7 sometimes	4.00		"		fair	
F	buyer	8:00–6:00	none	10.00				bad	
G	enunciator	8:00–6:30	till 10 or 11	2.50	supper	$4.75	separated	good	
H	saleswoman	8:00–6:30	"	3.50	"	lived home	single	fair	
I	cashier	8:00–6:30	"	6.50		$2.50	married		husband and 4 children
J	saleswoman	8:00–6:30	till 11	3.00	50c per week	3.00	single		one child
K	"	8:00–6:00	till 10	5.00	35c for supper	2.50	married	good	
L	cash girl	9:30–4:30	none	3.25		2.50	widow	"	
M	saleswoman	8:00–6:30	evenings	5% commission	supper	lived home	single	fair	
N	cash girl	8:00–6:30	"	$2.00	"	"	"	"	
O	saleswoman	8:00–6:30	"	$2.00+5% com.	"	"	"	good	
P		8:00–6:30		$3.00	cup of coffee	$2.50	"	"	
Q	sewer	8:30–5:30	none	6.50		2.50	"	"	one child
R	saleswoman	8:00–6:00	evenings	5.00	30c for supper	2.50	widow	fair	same place 7 years
S	cash girl	8:00–6:00	none	2.00		lived home	single	"	
T	inspector	8:00–6:00	evenings	2.50	30c for supper	"	"	fair	mother to help
U	saleswoman	8:00–6:00	"	$4.50+1% com.	"	$1.50 at home	"	"	
V	"	8:00–6:30	"	4.00+1% com.	"	$2.50	"	bad	
W				2.00+5% com.	supper	$2.00 at home	"	fair	
X	shirt-maker	8:00–6:00	none	40⁷⁄₈c per doz.		lived home	married	bad	husband had no work
Y	wrapper-maker	8:00–6:00	"	12½c each			"	fair	ill; 2 children
Z	saleswoman	8:30–5:30	"	$7.00		$3.75	single	good	

In which a vacation of not less than one week is given, with pay, during the summer season to employees of six months' standing.

In which all overtime is compensated for.

Physical conditions.—A standard house is one in which work-, lunch-, and retiring rooms are apart from each other and are in good sanitary condition.

In which seats are provided for saleswomen and the use of seats permitted.

Other conditions.—A standard house is one in which humane and considerate behavior toward employees is the rule.

In which fidelity and length of service meet with the consideration which is their due.

It is a comparatively easy matter to enlist the sympathy of intelligent and educated people, and through them reform must be brought about. The great body of buyers who regularly patronize the cheap stores will take no interest in the matter. Some may feel that they have done their duty when they cease buying at stores where evils exist; but that is a dwarfed conception of social obligation. We should not rest until the bad stores improve or go out of business.

The Trimmed Lamp

O. HENRY

Of course there are two sides to the question. Let us look at the other. We often hear "shop-girls" spoken of. No such persons exist. There are girls who work in shops. They make their living that way. But why turn their occupation into an adjective? Let us be fair. We do not refer to the girls who live on Fifth Avenue as "marriage-girls."

Lou and Nancy were chums. They came to the big city to find work because there was not enough to eat at their homes to go around. Nancy

O. Henry [William Sidney Porter], "The Trimmed Lamp," *The Trimmed Lamp and Other Stories of the Four Million* (New York, 1906, 1915), pp. 3–21.

was nineteen; Lou was twenty. Both were pretty, active, country girls who had ambition to go on the stage.

The little cherub that sits up aloft guided them to a cheap and respectable boarding-house. Both found positions and became wage-earners. It is at the end of six months that I would beg you to step forward and be introduced to them. Meddlesome Reader: My Lady friends, Miss Nancy and Miss Lou. While you are shaking hands please take notice—cautiously—of their attire. Yes, cautiously; for they are as quick to resent a stare as a lady in a box at the horse show is.

Lou is a piece-work ironer in a hand laundry. She is clothed in a badly-fitting purple dress, and her hat plume is four inches too long; but her ermine muff and scarf cost $25, and its fellow beasts will be ticketed in the windows at $7.98 before the season is over. Her cheeks are pink, and her light blue eyes bright. Contentment radiates from her.

Nancy you would call a shop-girl—because you have the habit. There is no type; but a perverse generation is always seeking a type; so this is what the type should be. She has the high-ratted pompadour, and the exaggerated straight-front. Her skirt is shoddy, but has the correct flare. No furs protect her against the bitter spring air, but she wears her short broadcloth jacket as jauntily as though it were Persian lamb! On her face and in her eyes, remorseless type-seeker, is the typical shop-girl expression. It is a look of silent but contemptuous revolt against cheated womanhood; of sad prophecy of the vengeance to come. When she laughs her loudest the look is still there. The same look can be seen in the eyes of Russian peasants; and those of us left will see it some day on Gabriel's face when he comes to blow us up. It is a look that should wither and abash man; but he has been known to smirk at it and offer flowers—with a string tied to them.

Now lift your hat and come away, while you receive Lou's cheery "See you again," and the sardonic, sweet smile of Nancy that seems, somehow, to miss you and go fluttering like a white moth up over the housetops to the stars.

The two waited on the corner for Dan. Dan was Lou's steady company. Faithful? Well, he was on hand when Mary would have had to hire a dozen subpoena servers to find her lamb.

"Ain't you cold, Nancy?" said Lou. "Say, what a chump you are for working in that old store for $8 a week! I made $18.50 last week. Of course ironing ain't as swell work as selling lace behind a counter, but it pays. None of us ironers make less than $10. And I don't know that it's any less respectful work, either."

"You can have it," said Nancy, with uplifted nose. "I'll take my eight a week and hall bedroom. I like to be among nice things and swell people. And look what a chance I've got! Why, one of our glove girls married a Pittsburg—steel maker, or blacksmith or something—the other day worth a million dollars. I'll catch a swell myself some time. I ain't bragging on my looks or anything; but I'll take my chances where there's big prizes offered. What show would a girl have in a laundry?"

"Why, that's where I met Dan," said Lou, triumphantly. "He came in for his Sunday shirt and collars and saw me at the first board, ironing. We all try to get to work at the first board. Ella Maginnis was sick that day, and I had her place. He said he noticed my arms first, how round and white they was. I had my sleeves rolled up. Some nice fellows come into laundries. You can tell 'em by their bringing their clothes in suit cases, and turning in the door sharp and sudden."

"How can you wear a waist like that, Lou?" said Nancy, gazing down at the offending article with sweet scorn in her heavy-lidded eyes. "It shows fierce taste."

"This waist?" cried Lou, with wide-eyed indignation. "Why, I paid $16 for this waist. It's worth twenty-five. A woman left it to be laundered, and never called for it. The boss sold it to me. It's got yards and yards of hand embroidery on it. Better talk about that ugly, plain thing you've got on."

"This ugly, plain thing," said Nancy, calmly, "was copied from one that Mrs. Van Alstyne Fisher was wearing. The girls say her bill in the store last year was $12,000. I made mine, myself. It cost me $1.50. Ten feet away you couldn't tell it from hers."

"Oh, well," said Lou, good-naturedly, "if you want to starve and put on airs, go ahead. But I'll take my job and good wages; and after hours give me something as fancy and attractive to wear as I am able to buy."

But just then Dan came—a serious young man with a ready-made necktie, who had escaped the city's brand of frivolity—an electrician earning $30 per week who looked upon Lou with the sad eyes of Romeo, and thought her embroidered waist a web in which any fly should delight to be caught.

"My friend, Mr. Owens—shake hands with Miss Danforth," said Lou.

"I'm mighty glad to know you, Miss Danforth," said Dan, with out-stretched hand. "I've heard Lou speak of you often."

"Thanks," said Nancy, touching his fingers with the tips of her cool ones, "I've heard her mention you—a few times."

Lou giggled.

"Did you get that handshake from Mrs. Van Alstyne Fisher, Nance?" she asked.

"If I did, you can feel safe in copying it," said Nancy.

"Oh, I couldn't use it at all. It's too stylish for me. It's intended to set off diamond rings, that high shake is. Wait till I get a few and then I'll try it."

"Learn it first," said Nancy wisely, "and you'll be more likely to get the rings."

"Now, to settle this argument," said Dan, with his ready, cheerful smile, "let me make a proposition. As I can't take both of you up to Tiffany's and do the right thing, what do you say to a little vaudeville? I've got the tickets. How about looking at stage diamonds since we can't shake hands with the real sparklers?"

The faithful squire took his place close to the curb; Lou next, a little peacocky in her bright and pretty clothes; Nancy on the inside, slender, and soberly clothed as the sparrow, but with the true Van Alstyne Fisher walk—thus they set out for their evening's moderate diversion.

I do not suppose that many look upon a great department store as an educational institution. But the one in which Nancy worked was something like that to her. She was surrounded by beautiful things that breathed of taste and refinement. If you live in an atmosphere of luxury, luxury is yours whether your money pays for it, or another's.

The people she served were mostly women whose dress, manners, and position in the social world were quoted as criterions. From them Nancy began to take toll—the best from each according to her view.

From one she would copy and practice a gesture, from another an eloquent lifting of an eyebrow, from others, a manner of walking, of carrying a purse, of smiling, of greeting a friend, of addressing "inferiors in station." From her best beloved model, Mrs. Van Alstyne Fisher, she made requisition for that excellent thing, a soft, low voice as clear as silver and as perfect in articulation as the notes of a thrush. Suffused in the aura of this high social refinement and good breeding, it was impossible for her to escape a deeper effect of it. As good habits are said to be better than good principles, so, perhaps, good manners are better than good habits. The teachings of your parents may not keep alive your New England conscience; but if you sit on a straight-back chair and repeat the words "prisms and pilgrims" forty times the devil will flee from you. And when Nancy spoke in the Van Alstyne Fisher tones she felt the thrill of *noblesse oblige* to her very bones.

There was another source of learning in the great departmental school. Whenever you see three or four shop-girls gather in a bunch and jingle their wire bracelets as an accompaniment to apparently frivolous conversation, do not think that they are there for the purpose of criticizing the way Ethel does her back hair. The meeting may lack the dignity of the deliberative bodies of man; but it has all the importance of the occasion on which Eve and her first daughter first put their heads together to make Adam understand his proper place in the household. It is Woman's Conference for Common Defense and Exchange of Strategical Theories of Attack and Repulse upon and against the World, which is a Stage, and Man, its Audience who Persists in Throwing Bouquets Thereupon. Woman, the most helpless of the young of any animal—with the fawn's grace but without its fleetness; with the bird's beauty but without its power of flight; with the honey-bee's burden of sweetness but without its —Oh, let's drop that simile—some of us may have been stung.

During this council of war they pass weapons one to another, and exchange stratagems that each has devised and formulated out of the tactics of life.

"I says to 'im," says Sadie, "ain't you the fresh thing! Who do you suppose I am, to be addressing such a remark to me? And what do you think he says back to me?"

The heads, brown, black, flaxen, red, and yellow bob together; the answer is given; and the parry to the thrust is decided upon, to be used by each thereafter in passages-at-arms with the common enemy, man.

Thus Nancy learned the art of defense; and to women successful defense means victory.

The curriculum of a department store is a wide one. Perhaps no other college could have fitted her as well for her life's ambition—the drawing of a matrimonial prize.

Her station in the store was a favored one. The music room was near enough for her to hear and become familiar with the works of the best composers—at least to acquire the familiarity that passed for appreciation in the social world in which she was vaguely trying to set a tentative and aspiring foot. She absorbed the educating influence of art wares, of costly and dainty fabrics, of adornments that are almost culture to women.

The other girls soon became aware of Nancy's ambition. "Here comes your millionaire, Nancy," they would call to her whenever any man who looked the role approached her counter. It got to be a habit of men, who were hanging about while their women folk were shopping, to stroll over to the handkerchief counter and dawdle over the cambric squares. Nancy's imitation high-bred air and genuine dainty beauty was what attracted. Many men thus came to display their graces before her. Some them may have been millionaires; others were certainly no more than their sedulous apes. Nancy learned to discriminate. There was a window at the end of the handkerchief counter; and she could see the rows of vehicles waiting for the shoppers in the street below. She looked, and perceived that automobiles differ as well as do their owners.

Once a fascinating gentleman bought four dozen handkerchiefs, and wooed her across the counter with a King Cophetua air. When he had gone one of the girls said:

"What's wrong, Nance, that you didn't warm up to that fellow? He looks the swell article, all right, to me."

"Him?" said Nancy, with her coolest, sweetest, most impersonal, Van Alstyne Fisher smile; "not for mine. I saw him drive up outside. A 12 H. P. machine and an Irish chauffeur! And you saw what kind of handkerchiefs he bought—silk! And he's got dactylis on him. Give me the real thing or nothing, if you please."

Two of the most "refined" women in the store—a forelady and a cashier —had a few "swell gentlemen friends" with whom they now and then dined. Once they included Nancy in an invitation. The dinner took place in a spectacular café whose tables are engaged for New Year's eve a year in advance. There were two "gentlemen friends"—one without any hair on his head—high living ungrew it; and we can prove it—the other a young man whose worth and sophistication he impressed upon you in two convincing ways—he swore that all the wine was corked; and he wore diamond cuff buttons. This young man perceived irresistible excellencies in Nancy. His taste ran to shop-girls; and here was one that added the voice and manners of his high social world to the franker charms of her own caste. So, on the following day, he appeared in the store and made her a serious proposal of marriage over a box of hem-stitched, grass-bleached Irish linens. Nancy declined. A brown pompadour ten feet away had been using her eyes and ears. When the rejected suitor had gone she heaped carboys of upbraidings and horror upon Nancy's head.

"What a terrible little fool you are! That fellow's a millionaire—he's a nephew of old Van Skittles himself. And he was talking on the level, too. Have you gone crazy, Nance?"

"Have I?" said Nancy. "I didn't take him, did I? He isn't a millionaire so hard that you could notice it, anyhow. His family only allows him $20,000 a year to spend. The bald-headed fellow was guying him about it the other night at supper."

The brown pompadour came nearer and narrowed her eyes.

"Say, what do you want?" she inquired, in a voice hoarse for lack of chewing-gum. "Ain't that enough for you? Do you want to be a Mormon, and marry Rockefeller and Gladstone Dowie and the King of Spain and the whole bunch? Ain't $20,000 a year good enough for you?"

Nancy flushed a little under the level gaze of the black, shallow eyes.

"It wasn't altogether the money, Carrie," she explained. "His friend caught him in a rank lie the other night at dinner. It was about some girl he said he hadn't been to the theater with. Well, I can't stand a liar. Put everything together—I don't like him; and that settles it. When I sell out it's not going to be on any bargain day. I've got to have something that sits up in a chair like a man, anyhow. Yes, I'm looking out for a catch; but it's got to be able to do something more than make a noise like a toy bank."

"The physiopathic ward for yours!" said the brown pompadour, walking away.

These high ideas, if not ideals—Nancy continued to cultivate on $8 per week. She bivouacked on the trail of the great unknown "catch," eating her dry bread and tightening her belt day by day. On her face was the faint, soldierly, sweet, grim smile of the preordained man-hunter. The store was her forest; and many times she raised her rifle at game that seemed broad-antlered and big; but always some deep unerring instinct—perhaps of the huntress, perhaps of the woman—made her hold her fire and take up the trail again.

Lou flourished in the laundry. Out of her $18.50 per week she paid $6 for her room and board. The rest went mainly for clothes. Her opportunities for bettering her taste and manners were few compared with Nancy's. In the steaming laundry there was nothing but work, work and her thoughts of the evening pleasures to come. Many costly and showy fabrics passed under her iron; and it may be that her growing fondness for dress was thus transmitted to her through the conducting metal.

When the day's work was over Dan awaited her outside, her faithful shadow in whatever light she stood.

Sometimes he cast an honest and troubled glance at Lou's clothes that increased in conspicuity rather than in style; but this was no disloyalty; he deprecated the attention they called to her in the streets.

And Lou was no less faithful to her chum. There was a law that Nancy should go with them on whatsoever outings they might take. Dan bore the extra burden heartily and in good cheer. It might be said that Lou furnished the color, Nancy the tone, and Dan the weight of the distraction-seeking trio. The escort, in his neat but obviously ready-made suit, his ready-made tie and unfailing, genial, ready-made wit never startled or clashed. He was of that good kind that you are likely to forget while they are present, but remember distinctly after they are gone.

To Nancy's superior taste the flavor of these ready-made pleasures was sometimes a little bitter; but she was young; and youth is a gourmand, when it cannot be a gourmet.

"Dan is always wanting me to marry him right away," Lou told her once. "But why should I. I'm independent. I can do as I please with the money I earn; and he never would agree for me to keep on working afterward. And say, Nance, what do you want to stick to that old store for, and half starve and half dress yourself? I could get you a place in the laundry right now if you'd come. It seems to me that you could afford to be a little less stuck-up if you could make a good deal more money."

"I don't think I'm stuck-up, Lou," said Nancy, "but I'd rather live on half rations and stay where I am. I suppose I've got the habit. It's the chance I want. I don't expect to be always behind a counter. I'm learning something new every day. I'm right up against refined and rich people all the time—even if I do only wait on them; and I'm not missing any pointers that I see passing around."

"Caught your millionaire yet?" asked Lou with her teasing laugh.

"I haven't selected one yet," answered Nancy. "I've been looking them over."

"Goodness! The idea of picking over 'em! Don't you ever let one get by you Nance—even if he's a few dollars shy. But of course you're joking—millionaires don't think about working girls like us."

"It might be better for them if they did," said Nancy, with cool wisdom. "Some of us could teach them how to take care of their money."

"If one was to speak to me," laughed Lou, "I know I'd have a duck-fit."

"That's because you don't know any. The only difference between swells and other people is you have to watch 'em closer. Don't you think that red silk lining is just a little bit too bright for that coat, Lou?"

Lou looked at the plain, dull olive jacket of her friend.

"Well, no I don't—but it may seem so beside that faded-looking thing you've got on."

"This jacket," said Nancy, complacently, "has exactly the cut and fit of one that Mrs. Van Alstyne Fisher was wearing the other day. The material cost me $3.98. I suppose hers cost about $100 or more."

"Oh, well," said Lou lightly, "it don't strike me as millionaire bait. Shouldn't wonder if I catch one before you do, anyway."

Truly it would have taken a philosopher to decide upon the values of the theories held by the two friends. Lou, lacking that certain pride and fastidiousness that keeps stores and desks filled with girls working for the barest living, thumped away gaily with her iron in the noisy and stifling laundry. Her wages supported her even beyond the point of comfort; so that her dress profited until sometimes she cast a sidelong glance of impatience at the neat but inelegant apparel of Dan—Dan the constant, the immutable, the undeviating.

As for Nancy, her case was one of tens of thousands. Silks and jewels and laces and ornaments and the perfume and music of the fine world of good-breeding and taste—these were made for woman; they are her equitable portion. Let her keep near them if they are a part of life to her, and if she will. She is no traitor to herself, as Esau was; for she keeps her birthright and the pottage she earns is often very scant.

In this atmosphere Nancy belonged; and she throve in it and ate her frugal meals and schemed over her cheap dresses with a determined and contented mind. She already knew woman; and she was studying man, the animal, both as to his habits and eligibility. Some day she would bring down the game that she wanted; but she promised herself it would be what seemed to her the biggest and the best, and nothing smaller.

Thus she kept her lamp trimmed and burning to receive the bridegroom when he should come.

But, another lesson she learned, perhaps unconsciously. Her standard of values began to shift and change. Sometimes the dollar-mark grew blurred in her mind's eye, and shaped itself into letters that spelled such words as "truth" and "honor" and now and then just "kindness." Let us make a likeness of one who hunts the moose or elk in some mighty wood. He sees a little dell, mossy and embowered, where a rill trickles, babbling to him of rest and comfort. At these times the spear of Nimrod himself grows blunt.

So, Nancy wondered sometimes if Persian lamb was always quoted at its market value by the hearts that it covered.

One Thursday evening Nancy left the store and turned across Sixth Avenue westward to the laundry. She was expected to go with Lou and Dan to a musical comedy.

Dan was just coming out of the laundry when she arrived. There was a queer, strained look on his face.

"I thought I would drop around to see if they had heard from her," he said.

"Heard from who?" asked Nancy. "Isn't Lou there?"

"I thought you knew," said Dan. "She hasn't been here or at the house where she lived since Monday. She moved all her things from there. She told one of the girls in the laundry she might be going to Europe."

"Hasn't anybody seen her anywhere?" asked Nancy.

Dan looked at her with his jaws set grimly, and a steely gleam in his steady gray eyes.

"They told me in the laundry," he said, harshly, "that they saw her pass yesterday—in an automobile. With one of the millionaires, I suppose, that you and Lou were forever busying your brains about."

For the first time Nancy quailed before a man. She laid her hand that trembled slightly on Dan's sleeve.

"You've no right to say such a thing to me, Dan—as if I had anything to do with it!"

"I didn't mean it that way," said Dan, softening. He fumbled in his vest pocket.

"I've got the tickets for the show to-night," he said, with a gallant show of lightness. "If you—"

Nancy admired pluck whenever she saw it.

"I'll go with you, Dan," she said.

Three months went by before Nancy saw Lou again.

At twilight one evening the shop-girl was hurrying home along the border of a little quiet park. She heard her name called, and wheeled about in time to catch Lou rushing into her arms.

After the first embrace they drew their heads back as serpents do, ready to attack or to charm, with a thousand questions trembling on their swift tongues. And then Nancy noticed that prosperity had descended upon Lou, manifesting itself in costly furs, flashing gems, and creations of the tailors' art.

"You little fool!" cried Lou, loudly and affectionately. "I see you are still working in that store, and as shabby as ever. And how about that big catch you were going to make—nothing doing yet, I suppose?"

And then Lou looked, and saw that something better than prosperity had descended upon Nancy—something that shone brighter than gems in her eyes and redder than a rose in her cheeks, and that danced like electricity anxious to be loosed from the tip of her tongue.

"Yes, I'm still in the store," said Nancy, "but I'm going to leave it next week. I've made my catch—the biggest catch in the world. You won't mind now Lou, will you?—I'm going to be married to Dan—to Dan!—he's my Dan now—why, Lou!"

Around the corner of the park strolled one of those new-crop, smooth-faced young policemen that are making the force more endurable—at least to the eye. He saw a woman with an expensive fur coat and diamond-ringed hands crouching down against the iron fence of the park sobbing turbulently, while a slender, plainly-dressed working girl leaned close, trying to console her. But the Gibsonian cop, being of the new order, passed on, pretending not to notice, for he was wise enough to know that these matters are beyond help, so far as the power he represents is concerned, though he rap the pavement with his nightstick till the sound goes up to the furthermost stars.

4. Labor and Management

No problem excited more comment in the last third of the century than the condition of labor. The railroad strikes of 1877 were followed in the next twenty years by other explosions of violence and bitter reprisal. Many Americans saw in the future a bitter class war which would shatter the social fabric and disrupt all existing relationships unless the organization of industry and the conditions of work were dramatically changed.

Some American employers, like George Pullman, sought to avoid labor problems and achieve greater efficiency at the same time, by providing a carefully controlled environment for their employees. While Pullman's example was widely discussed, it was not generally followed. One reason for this lay in the disastrous strike at Pullman in 1893, which seemed to condemn the firm's industrial practices, but other, subtler problems were explored by Richard T. Ely* in an article some years earlier. Ely, born in 1854, was one of a group of young American scholars who received their graduate training in Germany in the seventies and eighties. Ely took a Ph.D. at Heidelberg in 1879, and then taught political economy at Johns Hopkins and the University of Wisconsin. A prominent spokesman for economic reforms, Ely was a founder of the American Economic Association in 1885, and wrote extensively on problems of labor, taxation, and philanthropy.

Walter A. Wyckoff (1863–1908), a Princeton graduate, was less influential than Ely as an academic figure, but pioneered as a writer of documentary sociology. Wyckoff had originally begun to prepare himself for the ministry, but he soon became convinced that his knowledge of social problems was much too abstract. He determined, therefore, to make his way across the country as a common laborer, in a strenuous effort to perceive life from the bottom up. Never fully divesting himself of middle-class values and prejudices, Wyckoff nonetheless persisted in a trip of two years, from 1891 to 1893, and he traveled all the way from Connecticut to San Francisco. His observations were published first as articles in *Scribner's Magazine*, and then in two separate volumes. Wyckoff returned to Princeton where he served as assistant professor of political economy.

* Richard T. Ely, "Pullman: A Social Study," *Harper's New Monthly Magazine*, Vol. LXX (February, 1885), pp. 452–466.

The Workers

WALTER A. WYCKOFF

Chicago, Ill.

A new phase of my experiment is begun. Hitherto I have been in the open country, and have found work with surprising readiness. Now I am in the heart of a congested labor market, and I am learning, by experience, what it is to look for work and fail to find it; to renew the search under the spur of hunger and cold, and of the animal instinct of self-preservation until any employment, no matter how low in the scale of work, that would yield food and shelter, appears to you the very Kingdom of Heaven; and if it could suffer violence, it would seem as though the strength of your desire must take that kingdom by force. But it remains inpregnable to your attack, and baffled and weakened, you are thrust back upon yourself and held down remorselessly to the cold, naked fact that you, who in all the universe are of supremest importance to yourself, are yet of no importance to the universe. You are a superfluous human being. For you there is no part in the play of the world's activity. There remains for you simply this alternative: Have you the physical and moral qualities which fit you to survive, and which will place you at last within the working of the large scheme of things, or, lacking these qualities, does there await you inevitable wreck under the onward rush of the world's great moving life?

That, at all events, is pretty much as it appears to-night to Tom Clark and me. Clark is my "partner," and we are not in good luck nor in high spirits. We each had a ten-cent breakfast this morning, but neither has tasted food since, and to-night, after an exhausting search for work, we must sleep in the station-house.

We are doing our best to pass the time in warmth and comfort until midnight. We know better than to go to the station-house earlier than that hour. Clark is in the corner at my side pretending to read a newspaper, but really trying to disguise the fact that he is asleep.

An official who walks periodically through the reading-room, recalling nodding figures to their senses, has twice caught Clark asleep, and has threatened to put him out.

Walter A. Wyckoff, *The Workers. An Experiment in Reality. The West* (New York, 1899), pp. 1–4, 72–84, 247–256, 258–259, 274–286.

I shall be on the alert, and shall warn Clark of his next approach, for after this place is closed we shall have long enough to wait in the naked street before we can be sure of places in the larger corridor of the station, where the crowding is less close and the air a degree less foul than in the inner passage, where men are tightly packed over every square foot of the paved floor.

We are tired and very hungry, and not a little discouraged; we should be almost desperate but for one redeeming fact. The silver lining of our cloud has appeared to-night in the form of falling snow. From the murky clouds which all day have hung threateningly over the city, a quiet, steady snow-fall has begun, and we shall be singularly unfortunate in the morning if we can find no pavements to clean.

In the growing threat of snow we have encouraged each other with the brightening prospect of a little work, and for quite half an hour after nightfall we stood alternately before the windows of two cheap restaurants in Madison Street, studying the square placards in the windows on which the bills of fare are printed, and telling each other, with nice discriminations between bulk and strengthening power of food, what we shall choose to-morrow.

It is a little strange, when I think of it, the closeness of the intimacy between Clark and me. We never saw each other until last Wednesday evening, and we know little of each other's past. But I feel as though the ties that bound me to him had their roots far back in our histories. Perhaps men come to know one another quickest and best on a plane of life, where in the fellowship of destitution they struggle for the primal needs and feel the keen sympathies which attest the basal kinship of our common humanity. Ours are not intellectual affinities—at least they are not consciously these—but we feel shrewdly the community of hunger and cold and isolation, and we have drawn strangely near to each other in this baffling struggle for a social footing, and have tempered in our comradeship the biting cold of the loneliness that haunts us on the outskirts of a crowded working world.

❀ ❀ ❀

It was hard, but it was not impossible through that Saturday morning to keep one's purpose fairly firm. From the ebb of the city's traffic in the darkness before the dawn I felt it flowing to its full tide. However destitute a man may be he cannot fail to share the quickening to waking life of a great city. The mystery of deepest night enfolds the place, and from out its veiling darkness the vague conformations of streets and buildings gradually emerge to the sharp outlines of the day's reality. An occasional delivery wagon from the market, or a milkman's cart goes rattling down a street, awaking echoes as of a deserted town, or a heavy truck laden with great rolls of white paper for the printing press passes slowly, drawn by gigantic horses whose flat, hairy hoofs patiently pound the cobbles in their plodding pace, while whiffs of white vapor puff from their nostrils with their deep, regular breathing. The driver's oath can be heard a square away.

Standing at the curb along an open space in front of a public building are a few "night hawks." The horses are heavily blanketed and their noses buried in eating-bags. The cabmen have drawn together in social community on the pavement, where, as they gossip in the cold, they alternately stamp the flagging with their feet and clasp themselves in hard, sweeping embraces of the arms to stir the sluggish blood to swifter movement. An empty cable-car goes tearing round a "loop" with noise to awake the dead, and sets off again to some outermost portion of the town with a sleepy policeman on board and a newsboy, his bundle, damp from the press, upon his lap, who is bent on being first with news to that suburban region. The cars fill first with workingmen who are bound for distant factories and workshops and their posts along the lines of railways.

The streets are echoing now to the sounds of increasing traffic and to the steps of the vanguard of workers. These are the wage-earners, men for the most part, but there are women, too, and children. Here is humanity in the raw, hard-handed and roughly wrought for the Atlasian task of sustaining, by sheer physical strength and manual skill, the towering, delicate, intricate structure of progressive civilization.

The first of the salaried workers follow these, and youth swarms upon the streets moving with swift steps to the great co-educational schools of practical business. There are countless "cash" children in the throng, and office boys, and saleswomen and men, and clerks, and secretaries, and fledgling lawyers. There are marks of poverty on the faces and in the garments of the children, but most of the older ones are dressed in all the warmth and comfort of the well-to-do, while the young women who form so large a portion of the crowd step briskly in dainty boots carrying themselves with figures erect and graceful, clothed with the style and *chic* which are theirs as a national trait. Many of the men are, in contrast, markedly careless and unkempt.

All these are at work by eight o'clock, the wage-earners having been at it an hour already. Then come, mingling in the miscellaneous concourse of business streets which have taken on the full day's complexity, the superintendents and managers, and the heads of business houses and of legal firms, and bankers, and brokers, and all the company of rare men, whose native gifts of creative power or organizing capacity or executive ability, joined to great energy and resolution, have placed them in command of their co-workers, and made them responsible, as only the few can be responsible, for the lives and well-being of their fellows.

I recognize an eminent lawyer in the moving crowd, who, in democratic fashion, is walking to his office. He is a nobleman by every gift of nature, and his sensitive, expressive face, responsive to the grace of passing thought, is an unconscious appeal to my flagging courage, and to that, perhaps, of many another man in the pressing throng.

I see in a jolting omnibus a noted merchant, his head bowed over a morning paper as he rides to his business house. He holds a foremost place in business, yet it is fully equalled by his standing as a Christian gentleman and as a wise and most efficient philanthropist.

Almost touching elbows we pass each other on the street, a fellow-alumnus of my college and I, he an inheritor of great wealth and of a vast enterprise far-reaching in its scope to distant portions of the earth. And yet, so unmarred has he remained under the lavish gifts of fortune that his is already the dominant genius in the administration of immense productive power, and his influence is increasingly felt as a helpful and guiding force in great educational institutions of the land.

But this resurgence of the city's life, while it quickens the pulses for the time, is not an inspiration to last one through a day of disappointing search. By noon I had been turned many times away, and a sharp refusal to a polite request to be given a chance to work cuts deeper than men know who have never felt its wound. You try to ignore it at the first, and you bring greater energy to bear upon the hunt, but your wounds are there; and, in each succeeding advance, it is a sterner self-compulsion that forces you to lay bare again the shrinking quick of your quivering sensibilities. How often have I loitered about a door, passing and repassing it again and yet again before I could summon courage for the ordeal of a simple request for work!

Early in my experience I learned never to ask after a possible vacancy. Employers have no vacancies to be filled by such an inquirer. I simply said that I was looking for a job, and should be glad of any work that I could do; and that, if I could be given a chance to work, I would do my best to earn a place.

This request in practically the same terms produced often the most opposite effects. One man would answer with a kindliness so genuine and a regret so evidently sincere that it was with an utmost effort at times that

I could control myself. And but a few minutes later another man might answer, if not with oaths and threats of violence, yet with a cynical sharpness which would leave a sorer rankling.

Despondency had almost conquered hope at last, and well-nigh worn one's courage out, and all but brought your drooping spirits to the brink of that abyss, where men think that they can give the struggle up. It is marvellous how the external aspect of all things changes to you here. The very stones beneath your feet are the hard paving of your prison-house; the threatening winter sky above you is the vaulted ceiling of your dungeon; the buildings towering to nearly twenty stories about you are your prison walls, and, as by a keen refinement of cruelty, they swarm with hiving industry, as if to mock you in your bitter plight.

Suddenly there dawns upon you an undreamed-of significance in the machinery of social restraint. The policeman on the crossing in his slouching uniform bespattered with the oozing slime of the miry streets where he controls the streams of traffic, even as the Fellaheen direct the water of the Nile through the net-work of their irrigation ditches, is the outstretched hand of the law ready to lay hold on you, should you violate in your despair the rules of social order. Behind him you see the patrol wagon and the station-house and the courts of law and the State's prison and enforced labor, the whole elaborate process by means of which society would reassimilate you, an excrement, a non-social being as a transgressor of the law, into the body politic once more, and set you to fulfilling a functional activity as a part of the social organism.

This result, with the means of living which it implies and the link that it gives you to your kind, even if it be the relation of a criminal to society, may become the object of a desire so strong that the shame and punishment involved may lose their deterring force for you.

There are simple means of setting all this process in motion in your behalf. Men break shop-windows in full view of the police, or voluntarily hold out to them hands weighted with the spoils of theft.

Perhaps it is in the moving crowds upon the pavements that one, in such a mood, feels most of all this change in external aspect. The loneliness, the sense of being a thing apart in the presence of your working kind, a thing unvitalized by real contact with the streams of life, is the seat of your worst suffering, and the pain is augmented by what seems an actual antagonism to you as to something beyond the range of human sympathy.

By the middle of that Saturday afternoon I had fairly given up the search for work, and I found myself on State Street, wandering aimlessly in the hope of an odd job. Hunger and utter weariness were playing their part, as well as the loneliness and the sense of imprisonment. One had the feeling that, if he could but sit down somewhere and rest, all other troubles would vanish for the time at least. And there were, I knew, many public rooms to which I could go in unquestioned right or privilege, but once within their warmth, I was well aware that to keep awake would tax all my power of will, and that, as a sleeping lounger, I should soon be turned adrift again.

The street was coated with a murky mire, kneaded by hoofs and wheels to the consistency of paste, and tracked by countless feet upon the pavements, where it lay as thick almost as on the cobbles. The skyline on both sides was a ragged *sierra*, mounting from three to five and seven stories, then leaping suddenly on the right to the appalling height of the Masonic Temple, and grotesque in all its length with rearing signs and flagstaffs that pierced the smoky vapor of the upper air, while the sagging halyards fluttered like fine threads in the icy gusts from off the lake. Whole fronts of flamboyant architecture were almost concealed behind huge bombastic signs, while other advertising devices hung suspended overhead, watches three feet in diameter, and boots and hats of a giant race.

The shop windows were draped with the scalloped fringes of idle awnings, and merely a glance at their displays was enough to disclose a commercial difference separated by only the width of the thoroughfare, a difference like that between Twenty-third Street and the Bowery.

From Polk Street and State I drifted northward to the river. No longer was there any stimulus in contact with the intermingling crowds. All that was hard and sordid in one's lot seemed to have blinded one to all but the hard and sordid in the world about. Beneath its structural veiling you could not see the warm heart of life, tender and strong and true. Multitudes of human faces passed you, deeply marked with the lines of baser care. Human eyes looked out of them full of the unconscious tragic pathos of the blind, blind to all vision but the light of common day; eyes of the money grubbers, sharpened to a needle's point yet incapable of deeper insight than the prospect of gain; eyes of the haunted poor, furtive in the fear of things, and seeing only the incalculable, threatening hand of fateful poverty; eyes of ragged children who were selling papers on the streets, their eyes old with the age of the ages, as though there gazed through them the unnumbered generations of the poor who have endured "long labor unto aged breath;" eyes of the rich, hardened by a subtler misery in the artificial lives they lead in sternest bondage to powers in whom all faith is gone, but whom they serve in utter fear, scourged by convention to the acting of an unmeaning part in life, seeking above all things escape from self in the fantastic *stimuli* of fashion, yet feeling ever, in the dark, the remorseless closing in of the contracting prison-walls of self-indulgence narrowing daily the scope of self, and threatening life with its grimmest tragedy, in the hopeless, faithless, purposeless *ennui* of existence.

And now there passed me in the street two sisters of charity walking side by side. Their sweet, placid faces, framed in white, reflected the limpid purity of unselfish useful living, and their eyes, deep-seeing into human misery and evil, were yet serene in the all-conquering strength of goodness.

It was in some saner thought inspired by this vision that I walked on across the river to the comparative quiet of the North Side. I needed all the sanity that I could summon. The setting sun had broken for a moment through snow-laden clouds, and it shone in blazing shafts of blood-red light through the hazy lengths of westward streets. Its rays fell warmly upon a wide, deep window as I passed, and the rich reflection caught my eye. For some time I stood still, a prey to conflicting feelings. Just within the window with the shades undrawn, sat a friend in lounging ease before an open fire, absorbed in his evening paper. There flashed before me the scene of our last encounter. We stood at parting on a wharf in the balmy warmth of late winter in the far South. Behind my friend was the brilliant carpeting of open lawns and blooming beds of flowers, and beyond lay the deep olive green of forests of live-oak with palmettos growing in dense underbrush, and the white "shell road" gleaming in the varied play of lights and shadows until it lost itself, in its course to the beach, in the deepening gloom of overdrooping boughs weighted with hanging moss in an effect of tropical luxuriance. And from out that vivid mental picture there came again, almost articulate in its reality, the graceful urging of my friend that I should visit him in his Western home.

It was so short a step by which I could emerge from the submerged, and the temptation to take it was so strong and inviting. The want and hardship and hideous squalor were bad enough, but these things could be endured for the sake of the end in view. It was the longing for fellowship that had grown to almost overmastering desire, the sight of a familiar face, the sound of a familiar voice, the healing touch of cultivated speech to feelings all raw under the brutalities of the street vernacular.

And after all, what real purpose was my experiment to serve? I had set out to learn and in the hope of gaining from what I learned something worth the while of a careful investigation. I had discovered much that was new to me, but nothing that was new to science, and the experience of a single individual could never furnish data for a valid generalization, and all that I had learned or could learn was already set forth in tabulated, statistical accuracy in blue books and economics treatises. Moreover it was impossible for me to rightly interpret even the human conditions in which I found myself, for between me and the actual workers was the infinite difference of necessity in relation to any lot in which I was. How could I, who at any moment could change my status if I chose, enter really into the life and feelings of the destitute poor who are bound to their lot by the hardest facts of stern reality? It was all futile and inadequate and absurd. I had learned something, and as for further inquiry of this kind, I would better give it up, and return to a life that was normal to me.

The sense of futility was strong upon me. Never before had the temptation to abandon the attempt assailed me with such force. It was no clean-cut, definite resolution that won in favor of continued effort. Not at all. I think that when I turned away I was more than half-resolved to give over the experiment. But even as a man, who, contemplating suicide, allows himself to be borne upon the aimless stream of common events past the point of many an early resolution to the deed, so I found myself gradually awaking to the thought, "Ah, well, I will try it a little longer."

A ROAD BUILDER ON THE WORLD'S FAIR GROUNDS

Columbian Anniversary Hotel—No. 1.
Chicago, Ill., Wednesday, April 27, 1892.
From the time that I began to work on the Exposition grounds, early in this month, it has grown increasingly difficult to hark back in imagination to the unemployed *régime* of the winter. The change is a revolution of condition. Hundreds of us live all together within this vast enclosure, and have rare occasion to go out except on Sundays, and then only if we choose. We get up in the morning to an eight-hour day of wholesome labor in the open air, and return in the late afternoon with healthy appetites to our temporary "hotel," which is fragrant of clean, raw pine, and stands commandingly on the site of the future "court of honor" near the quiet waters of the lake. About four hundred of us are housed and fed in this one building; men of half a score of nationalities and of as many trades, ranging from expert carpenters and joiners and staff-moulders and steel-workers to the unskilled laborers who work in gangs, under the direction of the landscape-gardeners or, as in my case, on the temporary plank roads which are built for the heavy carting.

Guarded by sentries and high barriers from unsought contact with all beyond, great gangs of us, healthy, robust men, live and labor in a marvellous artificial world. No sight of misery disturbs us, nor of despairing poverty out in vain search for employment. Work is everywhere abundant and well paid and directed with highest skill. And here, amid delicate, web-like frames of steel which are being clothed upon with forms of exquisite beauty, and among broad, dreary wastes of arid dunes and marshy pools which are being transformed by our labor into gardens of flowers and velvet lawns joined by graceful bridges over wide lagoons, we work our eight hours a day in peaceful security and in absolute confidence of our pay.

Complete as this revolution is, it is yet in perfect keeping, in some strange way, with the general change wrought by the coming of the spring. This spring, in its effect upon the labor market in Chicago, was like the heralding of peace and plenty after war.

There was no longer any real difficulty in securing work. The employment-bureaus offered it in abundance in the country, and there was some revival of demand even within the city limits. This by no means solved the problem of the unemployed, however. Many of the men were so weakened by the want and hardship of the winter that they were no longer in condition for effective labor. Some of the bosses who were in need of added hands were obliged to turn men off because of physical incapacity. One instance of this I shall not soon forget. It was when I overheard, early one morning, at a factory-gate, an interview between a would-be laborer and the boss. I knew the applicant for a Russian Jew who had at home an old mother and a wife and two young children to support. He had had intermittent employment throughout the winter in a sweater's den, barely enough to keep them all alive, and, after the hardships of the cold season, he was again in desperate straits for work.

The boss had all but agreed to take him on for some sort of unskilled labor, when, struck evidently by the cadaverous look of the man, he told him to bare his arm. Up went the sleeve of his coat and of his ragged flannel-shirt, exposing a naked arm with the muscles nearly gone, and the blue-white, transparent skin stretched over sinews and the outlines of the bones. Pitiful beyond words was his effort to give a semblance of strength to the biceps which rose faintly to the upward movement of the forearm. But the boss sent him off with an oath and a contemptuous laugh, and I watched the fellow as he turned down the street, facing the fact of his starving family with a despair at his heart which only mortal men can feel and no mortal tongue can speak.

Other men there were in large numbers who during the winter had swelled the ranks of the unemployed, but who now, in the reviving warmth and the growing demand for labor, drifted out upon the open country to their congenial life of vagrancy. There still remained, however, and apparently in full force, the shrewd gentry who stop pedestrians on the street with apologetic explanations of hard luck and with begging appeals for a small sum wherewith to satisfy immediate needs. Clark and I had soon come to know this as a recognized occupation among the men with whom we were thrown. A highly profitable trade it often proved, for a dollar a day is a gleaning not at all uncommon to these men, and the more skilful among them can average a dollar and a half. They are rather the sporting spirits among the professionally idle; gambling is their chief diversion, and their contempt for honest work is as genuine as that of a snob.

But within this chaotic maelstrom of the unemployed, which in every industrial centre seethes with infinite menace to social safety, is always a large element which is not easily classified. It was still to be found on the streets and in the lodging-houses of Chicago when the winter was gone, in seemingly undiminished numbers and in much its accustomed thriftlessness. The class has to be defined in negative terms. The men are not physically incapable of work, nor are they habitual tramps, nor yet the beggars of the pavements, and they lack utterly the grit for crime. If they have a distinctive, positive characteristic as a class, it is that they are victims of the gregarious instinct. By an attraction which is apparently irresistible to them, they are drawn to congested labor markets, and there they cling, preferring instinctively a life of want and squalor in fellowship with their kind to one of comparative plenty in the intolerable loneliness of the country.

There is a semblance of sincerity in their search for work, but they are cursed with the rudiments of imagination which makes cowards of them all, and their incapacity is a weakness of will rather than of brawn. Shrinkingly they walk the narrow ledge which in many planes of life separates from tramphood and crime, while lacking the wit for the latter and the courage for both lives, and looking ever for something to turn up instead of resolutely turning something up. Civilization is hard on such men, and their sufferings are none the less real because chiefly due to their incapacity for the struggle for existence. And not only their own misery must be reckoned with in any fair estimate of the case, but far more the misery of their women and children, for these men are proletarians in the literalist meaning of the word.

Finding now that I could not only get work, but that I could actually be eclectic in the matter, I gladly took advantage of an opportunity of employment among the unskilled laborers on the Exposition grounds.

A sharp-eyed, energetic American, who superintends the gangs of un-skilled laborers, took me on, and at once assigned me to duty under an Irish sub-boss by the name of O'Shea. When I became one of its number, Mr. O'Shea's gang of eight or ten men had torn up a considerable section of the plank road near the Transportation Building, for the purpose of altering the level. Most of us were put in charge of wheel-barrows. These we filled with sand at a neighboring pile and then emptied it in heaps on the roadbed, while the remaining members of the gang spread the sand with shovels to the desired depth before replacing the planks. It was a cloudy morning early in April, with a cold, raw wind blowing in from the lake, and the work, not very fatiguing in itself, kept one comfortably warm until noon. We had a free hour for dinner then, and I simply accompanied the other gang-men to "Hotel No. 1," where my employment ticket, issued by the general superintendent of construction, procured for me without delay a meal-and-lodging ticket on trust.

A large, zinc-lined trough half full of water stood against the wall in an ante-chamber. Here men by the score were washing their hands and faces and drying them near by on roller towels. They then passed singly through the wicket at the dining-room door, where stood a man who punched each boarder's ticket as he entered.

Long wooden tables, heaped with dishes and lined with round-bot-tomed stools, ran the great length of the room. The men took places in the order of their coming, until they had filled one table, when they would begin upon another, and there arose a deafening clatter of knives and forks and dishes and a tumult of mingled speech.

That dinner serves as a good illustration of our fare, both in what it offered and in what it lacked. A bowl of hot soup was at each man's place when he sat down, and, after finishing this, he was given a choice between roast beef and Irish stew. There were potatoes boiled in their jackets, and pork-and-beans, and bread in wide variety and in enormous quantity, and a choice of tea or coffee, and finally a pudding for dessert. Some of this was good, but all of it smacked of wholesale preparation, and appe-tites nicer than those of workingmen would have found difficulties with the dinner. Even ours were not proof against it all. I was struggling with a slice of tough roast-beef out of which the virtue had been cooked, when suddenly I caught an expression of comical dismay stealing over the ruddy, bristling face of the man opposite me. He was eating a piece of meat from a plate of Irish stew, and he spat it out upon the floor with a deep-drawn oath, and a frank assurance to his neighbors that "the meat was rotten," while his facial muscles were contorted with strong disgust. And the pudding was of such uncertain nature as to recall vividly the oft-repeated saying of a classmate at a college eating-club, that "flies in a pudding are quite as good as currants." Still the pork-and-beans were excellent and the bread and potatoes fine, and the coffee, which was served in large cups with the roast, was not impossible; certainly it was a well-fed crowd which sat smoking for a quarter of an hour or more on the rough embankments overlooking the Agricultural Building before going back to work.

Our gang was divided in the afternoon, and Mr. O'Shea left three of us, a German, an Irishman, and me, to open up a way for the teamsters through two long piles of paving-stones, which obstructed the road near the Fisheries Building. His parting word to us was that the stint was an afternoon's job, and we could easily have finished it in the four hours from one o'clock until five, had we worked with moderate swiftness.

The German and the Irishman fell to lifting stones to one side of the desired opening and I to the other. Every condition favored us. We had a definite task and not a difficult one, and no one to watch us at our work, nor drive us in its doing. The clouds had disappeared, and in the soft spring sunshine, with the bushes blossoming about us and the air full of the sounds of multiform labor, there was every stimulus to energetic effort for four hours. Not that the hours seemed short—they never do, I am convinced, even to well-seasoned unskilled workmen—but the difference between four hours of manual labor at a stretch and five is enormous, and to see my *confrères* quite as impatient of their flight, even under these most favoring conditions, and to mark that the sober business of their lives was still an abhorrent drudgery to be shirked if possible, led the way to very sad reflection.

❋ ❋ ❋

That was on a Saturday. On Monday morning Mr. O'Shea singled out us three for as stiff a cursing as a boat's crew often gets, but to little purpose, apparently, in its effect upon the other men. On that very day I was again a member of a gang, a gang of four this time, which was left without an overseer. We were ordered to unload a car of timber and pile the boards near the mammoth framework on the east side of the Manufactures Building.

❋ ❋ ❋

Noon found us with a pitiful showing for the morning's work. In the afternoon I secured the post inside the car, and passed the boards out to the three other men, who piled them near the building. By hastening the work at that end, I hoped to quicken the pace at which the job was being done. To be caught a second time in a delinquent gang I feared would endanger my position, and I was anxious to remain on the grounds, and even more anxious to secure a promotion if I could. It was easy to keep ahead of the men, but it was impossible, apparently, to urge them beyond the languid deliberation with which they shouldered the timber and carried it to the piles.

"Let up on that, John," they were shouting at me presently. "Go easy with that; there ain't no rush, and you'll make nothing by your pains."

It was the view which I had heard again and again in gangs of unskilled laborers. One could understand it in a measure among the older men, who could hope at the best only to eke out an existence free from the poorhouse to the end. But these and many others from whom it came were relatively young men, with every chance, one would suppose, of winning some preferment through effective, energetic work.

❉ ❉ ❉

Among the workmen on the grounds whom I have come to know, none has interested me more as a type than an American carpenter with whom I sometimes spend an evening. The man is lonely and uncomfortable in his new surroundings. The novel conditions which here beset him as a workingman are quite as disturbing to him as the unfamiliar setting of his daily life. He clings tenaciously to his individuality, and the new order of things which confronts him here lightly makes strange havoc of all that.

We had not been talking many minutes on the embankment, where one day after dinner we first met, when the man's case shone clear as day. He is a master-carpenter from a village home in Ohio, and the certainty of steady work for many months at four dollars a day was tempting enough to induce him to leave his family behind and come here. He had arrived a few days before and had found instant employment.

Seeing the man, a tall, fine-looking, self-respecting American mechanic, and hearing him speak, and learning even this little of his history, you had a direct vision of his past. You could almost see a comfortable, wooden cottage, of his own building, with a garden-plot about it and flower-beds in front, standing on a well-shaded street. He owns the cottage and the plot of land, and his children were born there, and he is an officer in the village church, and has been justice of the peace, and more than once has served as "school trustee." Social inequality, as applying to himself, is a new idea, and it gives him a hitherto unexperienced sense of self-consciousness. In his native village his family meet the families of all his neighbors on the same footing, except that they recognize in the minister, and the doctor, and the village lawyer, and the school-master, a distinction which attaches to special education. His children study and play at school with the children of all his neighbors, and mingle freely with them at church and in their other social relations.

But here is something new and strange. He is no longer a man with a name to distinguish him, but has become a "hand," having a number which he wears conspicuous on his jacket. He goes to his work as an integer in an army of ten thousand numerals. Home has changed to a barrack, where he, a number, sleeps in a numbered bunk, and eats, never twice at the same place, as one of half a thousand men. His comfort and convenience are never consulted, and his views have no smallest bearing upon the course of things. The superintendent of the building upon which he works, whose energy and skill he admires hugely, shifts him about with scores of other men, with as little regard to him as an individual as though he were a piece of timber. Once he spoke to his superintendent about some detail of the work and found him a most appreciative listener. Then he ventured, in conversation, upon a subject of general interest, only to find that by some mysterious change he was speaking to a stone wall.

And now there confronts him what he regards as another sacrifice of individuality, which he is urged to make, and which gives him no little concern. He had scarcely known of the existence of Trades Unions, and now he is thronged with appeals to join one.

No discrimination is made by the management as between union and non-union men in employing workers on the Exposition; but many of the union men here are making the most of the present opportunity for the propaganda of their principles, and for bringing the desirable non-union men within their organization. My carpenter friend, whom I shall call Mr. Ford, comes in for a large share of attention, and is, as I have intimated, not a little perplexed by the situation.

Two or three times he has asked me to go with him in the evening to meetings which are held near the Fair Grounds, and which are addressed by delegates from the Central Labor Union. These we have not found very enlightening. There has been a good deal of beer-drinking and much aimless speech, which has grown heated at times in the stress of hostile discussion; and now and then a plain, matter-of-fact workingman has given us an admirable talk on the history of Trades-Unionism and its beneficent results, and the imperative need of organization among workers as the only means of safe-guarding their interests and of meeting, on any approach to equal terms, the peculiar economic relations which exist between labor and organized capital.

Mr. Ford, much bewildered, has listened to all this, and we have talked it over together on the way back to our lodgings, and sometimes late into the night. I have tried to explain to him, as well as I understand it, the idea of organization, and the necessity of organization which has grown out of the great industrial change since the middle of the last century. But Mr. Ford, for all practical purposes, belongs to the pre-revolutionary period; the industrial change has little affected him. He served his apprenticeship, and was then a journeyman and then a master-carpenter in due course. In his experience, work has always had its basis in a personal relation, as, for example, between himself as a contractor and the man whose job he undertook and to whom he looked for payment. A like personal relation has always existed between himself and the men whom he has employed.

This new relation between a workman and an impersonal, soulless corporation which hires him, is one that he does not readily grasp. And, for the sake of meeting the new relation, this "fusing all the skirts of self" and merging individuality into an organization which attempts to regulate the hours of labor, and its wages, and for whom one shall work, and for whom not, is a thing abhorrent to him.

"Why," he said to me, "I give up my independence, and I'm no better than the worst carpenter of the lot. We all get union-wages alike. There's no incentive for a man to do his best. He ain't a man any more, anyway; he's only a part of a machine. Why, such work as some I see done here, I'd be ashamed to do by moonlight, with my eyes shut. But it don't make no difference in the union, you're all on the same level, as near as I can make out."

Finally I proposed to him that we should go together, on some Sunday afternoon, to the meeting of the Central Labor Union, where he could become acquainted with some of the members and learn at first hand the objects and ends of organization and something of its actual working. The members whom I particularly wished him to know were some of the Socialists there, who seemed to me to have a considerable knowledge of Trades-Unionism, and who took, I thought, a judicial view of it.

As an unskilled laborer I was not eligible to membership in any union, but I was admitted freely to the central meetings, to which I sometimes went in company with Socialists who were delegates of their respective orders. Under their tutelage, I was shown the operation of an exceedingly complex system, which, seen without guidance, would have appeared to me hopelessly chaotic. I was seeing it, I realized, from the point of view of the Socialists, and I was interested immediately in learning their attitude.

They are, I found, most ardent supporters of the principle of organization among workingmen. They regard the fact of the organization of wage-earners as among the most significant developments in the evolution of a socialistic state. But they are very impatient of the slow rate of progress in Trades-Unionism. The ignorance of the great mass of workers of how to further their own interests is, to the Socialist, the most discouraging feature in labor-organization. "Why," they ask, "when we working people already have so strong a nucleus of organization for economic ends, do we not direct it at once into the field of politics, and secure immediately, by our overwhelming numbers, the legislation which we need, and so inaugurate a co-operative commonwealth?"

Nowhere have the walking-delegates and the general agitators of their class sincerer foes than among the Socialists who, more than to any other active cause, attribute the comparative ineffectualness of unionism to the influence of these men. Very readily they believe them purchasable, and that often they are little else than the paid agents of the capitalists. Their great influence over workingmen is used, the Socialists seem to believe, chiefly in their own interests and particularly for selfish political ends.

This habit of mind serves to illustrate what eventually appeared to me to be highly characteristic of the general attitude of the Socialists. The key to their mental processes in considering things social, lies, I am quite sure, in the idea of existing conditions as being maintained by a vast capitalistic conspiracy. At all events this clew has cleared up for me the mystery which at first I found in many of their ways of thinking.

However natural may have been the social order in some of its historic phases, they evidently regard it at the present as largely artificial. There is no real vitality, they contend, in the political issues upon which the great national parties are divided. The party cries of "free trade" and "protection" and the like, are manufactured by professional politicians who are in the employ of the capitalists. The purpose is to divert the minds of the working classes by these sham contentions and so keep them about evenly divided politically, and thus prevent their coalescing in overwhelming force in political action for their own interests. Nothing seems to anger a Socialist more than the spectacle of workingmen roused to enthusiasm by the crowds and speeches and processions and brass bands of the usual political campaign. They see in them then only the ridiculous dupes of the capitalists, who have contributed to the campaign funds for the very purpose of thus befooling their employees, and who look with about equal indifference upon the momentary triumph of one party or the other so long as no labor party is in the ascendant.

However free in the past the play of purely natural evolutionary forces

may have been in determining social development, and however free may
be their course again in moulding a future state, their operation is checked
for the present to the Socialists' vision by the active intervention of the
capitalists, who, in some way, have succeeded in effecting a social structure which is highly favorable to themselves, and for whose undisturbed
continuance they unscrupulously employ all the resources of wealth and
craft and dark conspiracy. The idea appeared at its plainest, perhaps, in
their more vindictive speeches, where the strong undercurrent of feeling
was—"There is cruel injustice and wrong in society as it is, and someone
is to blame for it, and unhesitatingly we charge the blame against the
capitalists."

It was with this interpretation in mind that I took Mr. Ford with me
one afternoon to the meeting of the Central Labor Union. I was curious
to see the effect of the gathering upon him. A child of another age in his
experience of certain economic relations, he was an interesting phenomenon in the sudden contact with modern industrialism.

When we reached the building, in the upper floor of which in a large
hall are held the weekly meetings of the Central Labor Union, numbers
of workingmen in their Sunday clothes were passing in and out of the
neighboring saloons or loafing about the doors. The intersecting streets
were strewn with small handbills, which we found covering the wide
staircase leading to the hall and scattered over the seats and floor of the
room itself. They were printed notices instructing the members to boycott
the beer of certain breweries which were accused of employing non-union
men, and also the products of this and that manufacturer, against whom
similar charges were made.

We were a little early, but we chanced upon a Socialistic acquaintance
of mine, who took us in with him and seated us well to the front. As the
members entered I had a chance to point out to Mr. Ford those among
them who had been pointed out to me as the officers of their various
unions. He was deeply interested from the first, and much impressed
apparently by the size of the gathering and the enormous numbers of
organized workers which were represented there.

The stage of "new business" was barely reached that afternoon when
matters were well beyond the control of the president. Motions and
amendments and questions of privilege and points of order were fast
driving him mad, when in despair he called upon a fellow-member to take
charge of the meeting and become its temporary chairman. By this time
there was a good deal of confusion; men in many parts of the hall were
clamoring for the floor, and trying to drown one another's voices. But

there was immediate recognition of a change of generalship. The man who had taken the chair was a member of a union of musicians, a person of excellent address and well-appearing, and, as it proved eventually, a masterly parliamentarian. To reduce to quiet an assembly so excited was beyond his power, but he did unravel the skein of its tangled business, and through all the uproar and confusion he kept his temper perfectly, and secured some actual disposition of the affairs in hand.

The intricacies of intermingling interests there represented were beyond measure bewildering. The Cigarmakers' Union had a grievance, which its representatives insisted upon presenting and having righted at once. But the Waiters' Union claimed an antecedent right to the presentation of a question with reference to admitting certain men to their organization. And the Bricklayers' Union demanded an immediate investigation of the account of expenditure for a certain recent Union picnic, charging directly, meanwhile, a flagrant misappropriation of funds.

Passions were running high. The lie direct was passed repeatedly, and men were all but shaking fists in one another's faces. The shouting rose sometimes to such a pitch that the chairman's voice could not be heard. But the passion was that of strong vitality. The Union, to its members, was an intensely living thing, and its issues, touching them so closely, most naturally roused comparatively untutored men to strong emotion.

I watched Mr. Ford with curious interest. Instead of showing any impatience or disgust at the show of temper and the loud disorder, he sat through the long session deeply, intently absorbed. Every question for debate, and every phase of discussion, and all the progress of the business, and the varying claims of the many organizations, and the widely differing personalities of the members, each won his vital interest, and, with amazing discrimination, he seemed to follow them with intelligent understanding. And when there came a report of progress in a strike among certain workers in shoe factories, and a statement of the causes of the strike and the measures which were being taken to carry it to a successful issue, I could see that he was more than ever roused.

"That's the most interesting meeting I ever was to," he said to me, as we walked down the street together. "I ain't never realized before how mixed up things can be when there's so many working people, and the men that hire them are mostly all organized in big companies. Why, the working people ain't got nothing else they can do but organize too, to get their just rights. They have a pretty hot time in their meetings, if that's a sample, but I guess they'll know what they're about. I guess I'll join."

THE ARCADE AND PUBLIC SQUARE.

PULLMAN: A SOCIAL STUDY.

COMMUNISM, socialism, nihilism, are international words. Understood by people of both hemispheres and of many tongues, and printed daily in ten thousand journals, they are evidence of a momentous social movement. They mean far more than the creeds which under these names find a comparatively limited acceptance. They bear witness to a widespread discontent with things as they are in modern society—a discontent which but rarely goes to the extreme length of what is ordinarily designated by the generic term socialism. The pretty dream of a perfect, natural order of things brought about by the free play of unrestrained social forces has vanished. It has given place on the one hand to pessimism; on the other, and more generally, to a determination not to let things go on of themselves, but to make them go in such manner as may be desired. The conviction has become general that the divine order never contemplated a social and economic world left to itself. Material is furnished out of which man must construct a social fabric according to his lights. This is what modern socialism means, and for this reason it is practical, not romantic, and leaving the dim, artificial light of the study, goes forth into the broad sunlight, seeking immediate realization among the people. This is what co-operation means. It is looked upon as a new social form. For this reason it is preached as a gospel, and its spread in England heralded with joy by men like Thomas Hughes. Finally, for brevity's sake, passing over numerous manifestations of this spirit in our times, this is what is meant by the many attempts of "captains of industry" to step in between those they lead and the unrestrained action of existing economic forces. The variety of methods to which recourse is had is great. Insurance of one kind and another, gratuitous instruction, amusements, reading-rooms, participation in profits, rewards for special merit, occur at once to the mind. Several employers have attempted more far-reaching establishments which should embrace the home life of laborers, and thus include wives and children in their beneficence. Interesting examples are the "Social Palace" of M. Godin at Guise, France, and the town of Saltaire, founded by Sir Titus Salt, on the banks of the Aire, in England, both of which have been described in the pages of this Magazine. Another instance is afforded by the works of the Willimantic Company, at Willimantic, Connecticut. But the most extensive experiment of this character is that now in progress at Pullman, Illinois. It is social experimentation on a vast scale, and this is its significance.

For this reason it challenges attention and discussion at a time when dynamite bombs and revolutionary murmurings terrify monarchs, when an enlarged human sympathy encircles the earth with beneficent institutions, and when an eager interest in social and economic facts more than atones for general indifference to the dogmatic assumptions of classic political economy.

Pullman, a town of eight thousand inhabitants, some ten miles from Chicago, on the Illinois Central Railroad, was founded less than four years ago by the Pullman Palace Car Company, whose president and leading spirit is Mr. George M. Pullman. Its purpose was to provide both a centre of industry and homes for the employés of the company and such additional laborers as might be attracted to the place by other opportunities to labor. Simply as a town, Pullman has not sufficient interest to justify a description of it in a great magazine. Its natural beauties are not remarkable, situated as it is on the low prairie land surrounding Chicago, and its newness makes such romances impossible as one can associate with villages like Lenox, and Stockbridge, and other ancient towns in New England. Like many other Western cities, its growth has been rapid, its population having increased from four souls in January, 1881, to 2084 in February, 1882, and to 8203 in September, 1884. A manufacturing town, it embraces the principal works of the Pullman Palace Car Company, in addition to the Allen Paper Car-wheel Company, the Union Foundry and Pullman Car-wheel Company, the Chicago Steel-works, the Steel-forging Company, and numerous less important enterprises.

Many of the last-mentioned are connected with building operations in the town of Pullman, or furnish commodities to its residents, and in many cases they also supply customers elsewhere, such as the gas-works, the ice-houses, the brick-yards,

A STREET IN PULLMAN.

the carpenter shops, and the large farm which receives the sewage of Pullman. The number of men employed in the place is at present about four thousand, of whom over three thousand are employed by the Palace Car Company. The products of the various establishments are valued at many millions of dollars. As all the Pullman enterprises are conduct-

SUBURBS OF CHICAGO.

THE MARKET-HOUSE.

ed with what seems to the writer a needless air of secrecy, reliable statistics are obtained with difficulty. However, the car-works claim a capacity to turn out $8,000,000 worth of passenger and freight cars per annum, and it is expected that they will be able to manufacture forty of the latter per day hereafter. On August 18, 1884, one hundred freight cars were built in ten hours. The Allen Paper Car-wheel Company claims a capacity of fifteen thousand paper car-wheels a year. The brick-yards are large, and two hundred and twenty thousand bricks is one day's work. Many of the men who work in the brick-yards in summer harvest ice in winter, and it is expected to store about twenty-five thousand tons this winter. The carpenter shops, which do considerable work in Chicago, have employed at times as many as five hundred men. These are some of the principal material facts of interest to the general reader. Much could be said of Pullman as a manufacturing centre, but the purpose of this article is to treat it as an attempt to furnish laborers with the best homes under the most healthful conditions and with the most favorable surroundings in every respect, for Pullman aims to be a forerunner of better things for the laboring classes.

The questions to be answered are these: Is Pullman a success from a social standpoint? Is it worthy of imitation? Is it likely to inaugurate a new era in society? If only a partial success, what are its bright features and what its dark features?

Pullman as an attempt to realize an ideal must be judged by an ideal standard. The measure to be applied is the reasonable ideal of the social reformer. What is this ideal? Is it not that each individual be so situated as to participate, as fully as his nature will allow, in the advantages of the existing civilization? This is a high standard, but not so high as might at first appear. All those who have more than this measure calls for are by no means included in the class of *nouveaux riches*. The writer well remembers a visit to some brass-works in Balti-

SECOND STORY.

PLAN OF COTTAGES AT PULLMAN.

more, where rude, uneducated Welshmen were earning eighteen dollars a week. Society was doing well by these men, and in their case there could be no serious social question as far as wages were concerned. One needed to be with the men but a short time to be convinced that their income enabled them to participate in all the benefits of this nineteenth-century civilization which they were capable of enjoying. Now what the student of society wants to know is the nearness with which Pullman approaches the social ideal.

THE STABLES.

Very gratifying is the impression of the visitor who passes hurriedly through Pullman and observes only the splendid provision for the present material comforts of its residents. What is seen in a walk or drive through the streets is so pleasing to the eye that a woman's first exclamation is certain to be, "Perfectly lovely!" It is indeed a sight as rare as it

INTERIOR OF ARCADE—THE LIBRARY.

is delightful.   What might have been taken for a wealthy suburban town is given up to busy workers, who literally earn their bread in the sweat of their brow.   No favorable sites are set apart for drones living on past accumulations, and if a few short stretches are reserved for residences which can be rented only by those whose earnings are large, this is an exception; and it is not necessary to remain long in the place to notice that clergymen, officers of the company, and mechanics live in adjoining dwellings.

THE SCHOOL-HOUSE.

One of the most striking peculiarities of this place is the all-pervading air of thrift and providence.   The most pleasing impression of general well-being is at once produced.   Contrary to what is seen ordinarily in laborers' quarters, not a dilapidated door-step nor a broken window, stuffed perhaps with old clothing, is to be found in the city.   The streets of Pullman, always kept in perfect condition, are wide and finely macadamized, and young shade trees on each side now ornament the town, and will in a few years afford refreshing protection from the rays of the summer sun.

Unity of design and an unexpected variety charm us as we saunter through the town.   Lawns always of the same width separate the houses from the street, but they are so green and neatly trimmed that one can overlook this regularity of form.   Although the houses are built in groups of two or more, and even in blocks, with

ingenious designs secure variety, of which the most skillful is probably the treatment of the sky line.   Naturally, without an appearance of effort, it assumes an immense diversity.   French roofs, square roofs, dormer-windows, turrets, sharp points, blunt points, triangles, irregular quadrangles, are devices resorted to in the upper stories to avoid the appearance of unbroken uniformity.   A slight knowledge of mathematics shows how infinite the variety of possible combinations of a few elements, and a better appreciation of this fact than that exhibited by the architecture of Pullman it would be difficult to find.   The streets cross each other at right angles, yet here again skill has avoided the frightful monotony of New York, which must sometimes tempt a nervous person to scream for relief.   A public square, arcade, hotel, market, or some large building is often set across a street so ingeniously as to break the regular line, yet without inconvenience to traffic.   Then at the termination of long streets a pleasing view greets and relieves the eye—a bit of water, a stretch of meadow, a clump of trees, or even one of the large but neat workshops.   All this grows upon the visitor day by day.   No other feature of Pullman can receive praise needing so little qualification as its architecture.   Desirable houses have been provided for a large laboring population at so small a cost that they can be rented at rates within their

WORKING-MEN'S COTTAGES.

the exception of a few large buildings of cheap flats, they bear no resemblance to barracks; and one is not likely to make the mistake, so frequent in New York blocks of "brown-stone fronts," of getting into the wrong house by mistake.   Simple but

means and yet yield a handsome return on the capital invested.   Rents are probably about three-fifths what they are in Chicago, and, all things considered, this seems not to be an unfair standard of comparison.   It is a mere matter of course that there are architectural defects even in Pullman. The diversity is not quite all that could be desired. What may be called the public buildings, that is to say, the hotel, school-house, arcade, etc., are detached, but no private house stands by itself, though there are quite a number of detached double houses. Spaces have, however, been reserved for a few detached private residences, which will improve the appearance of the town. With the exception of the church and parsonage, built of green serpentine stone from Philadelphia, all the buildings are of brick. This is monotonous, and rather wearying to the eye, but the slate roofs, and a large use of light stone trimmings, and stripes of black across the houses, help matters somewhat. The general character of the architecture is what has been called advanced secular Gothic. This is skillfully varied, and in the hotel particularly there is a feeling of the Queen Anne style. But there ought to be some bold break in the general design. The newness of things, which time will remedy, is a little distressing, as is also the mechanical regularity of the town, and it is this, perhaps, which suggests the epithet "machine-made." The growth of shade trees will break into the sameness, and the magnificent boulevard which divides the shops on the north from the residences on the south, stretching from east to west across the town, and bordered with double rows of elms, will, twenty years from now, be a vast improvement. Great overarching trees will hide one part of the town from another, and give opportunity for pleasant surprises in nature and art.

The interior of the houses affords scarcely less gratification than their exterior. Even the humblest suite of rooms in the flats is provided with water, gas, and closets, and no requisite of cleanliness is omitted. Most of the cottages are two stories in height, and contain five rooms, besides a cellar, closets, and pantry, as seen in the accompanying plan and illustrations. Quite a large number of houses contain seven rooms, and in these larger dwellings there is also a bath-room.

Outside of the home one finds other noteworthy provisions for the comfort, convenience, and well-being of the residents in Pullman. There is a large Market-house, 100 by 110 feet in size, through which a wide passage extends from east to west. This building contains a basement and two stories, the first divided into six-

teen stalls, the second a public hall. The dealers in meat and vegetables are concentrated in the Market-house. The finest building in Pullman is the Arcade, a structure 256 feet in length, 146 feet in width, and 90 feet in height. It is built of red pressed brick, with stone foundations and light stone trimmings, and a glass roof extends over the entire wide central passage. In the Arcade one finds offices, shops, the bank, theatre, library, etc. As no shops or stores are allowed in the town outside of the Arcade and Market-house, all shopping in Pullman is done under roof—a great convenience in wet weather, and a saving of time and strength.

The theatre, situated in the Arcade as just mentioned, seats eight hundred people, and is elegantly and tastefully furnished. The illustration on page 456 of the Arcade includes a view of the boxes, which are Moorish in design. It was intended to embrace in this theatre many of the best features of the Madison Square Theatre, but the scope of the present article does not admit of a detailed description of them, exquisite and perfectly appointed as they are. Representations are given by various troupes about once in two weeks. There is nothing peculiar in the management. The company rents it to applicants, but attempts to exclude immoral pieces, and admit only such as shall afford innocent amusement and instruction. The prices for tickets are thirty-five, fifty, and seventy-five cents, which have been found to be the most profitable in Pullman, higher prices keeping the people away, and lower ones not attracting enough more to compensate for the diminished return on each ticket.

In the interior of the Arcade a balcony extends around the passage in front of the rooms and offices of the second story, which it thus conveniently connects. It produces a pleasing effect, and affords a favorable position from which to view the busy throng below. The library, which opens on this balcony, contains six thousand volumes, the gift of Mr. Pullman, and numerous periodicals, among which were noticed several likely to be of special importance to mechanics, such as the *Railway Age*, the *Iron Age*, *Scientific American*, and *Popular Science Monthly*. The library rooms are elegantly furnished with Wilton carpets and plush-covered chairs, and the walls are beautifully painted. Objection has been raised to this luxuri-

ousness by those who think it repels the ordinary artisan, unac-
customed in his own home to
such extravagance; but it must
be remembered that it is avowed-
ly part of the design of Pullman
to surround laborers as far as
possible with all the privileges of
large wealth. The annual charge
for the use of the Public Library,
for nothing in Pullman is free,
is three dollars—rather high for
workmen in these days of free libraries. The management of the
librarian is most commendable,
and every aid is given to those
who patronize it to render it as
instructive and elevating as possible. A special effort has been
made to induce the subscribers to
choose a superior class of literature, but the record shows that
seventy-five per centum of the
books drawn are still works of
fiction, which is about the usual
percentage in public libraries.

The educational facilities of
Pullman are those generally afforded in larger American villages by the public-school system.
The school trustees are elected by
the citizens, and rent of the Pullman Company a handsome building, which harmonizes in architecture and situation with the remainder of the town.

There are no barns in the place,
but a large building provides accommodation for livery-stables,
and a fire department sustained
by the Pullman Company. The
hotel, the property of the company, and managed by one of its
officers, is a large structure, surrounded on three sides by beautiful public squares covered with
flowers and shrubbery. It is
luxuriously furnished, admirably
kept, and contains the only bar-
room allowed in Pullman, though
there are thirty on the outskirts
of the place in Kensington. However, the temptation "to drink"
does not constantly stare one in
the face, and this restriction has
not entirely failed to accomplish
its end, the promotion of temperance.

There is nothing so peculiar in

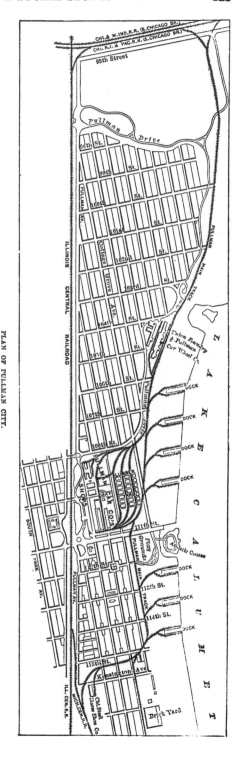

PLAN OF PULLMAN CITY.

these features of Pullman as to require further description. It was necessary to make brief mention of them to help the reader to understand the nature and extent of the experiment called Pullman.

The whole is the work of the Pullman Palace Car Company and the Pullman Land Association, which are both under one management, and, to a considerable extent, the same practically, although two separate legal persons. Colonel James Bowen, who appears to have been one of the interesting characters in the early history of Chicago, had long prophesied that the true. site for a great city was upon the shores of Lake Calumet—an expanse of water some six feet deep, about three miles long, and a mile and a half wide, and connected with Lake Michigan by the Calumet River. Having found a believer in Mr. Pullman, he was commissioned by that gentleman to purchase quietly four thousand acres in the neighborhood, and this has become the site of Pullman. The entire town was built under the direction of a single architect, Mr. S. S. Beman, an ambitious young man whose frequently expressed desire for an opportunity to do a "big thing" was here gratified. This is probably the first time a single architect has ever constructed a whole town systematically upon scientific principles, and the success of the work entitles him to personal mention. The plans were drawn for a large city at the start, and these have been followed without break in the unity of design. Pullman illustrates and proves in many ways both the advantages of enterprises on a vast scale and the benefits of unified and intelligent municipal administration. All articles employed in the construction of the town were purchased at the lowest figures, as orders were given for unusually large quantities, and thus the outlay was far less than it would have been had each building, or even each block, been built by a separate individual. It is manifest, for example, that a man will obtain hinges at the most favorable rates who orders twenty-five thousand pairs at one time. An additional saving was effected by the establishment of the carpenter shops and brick-yards, which enabled the company to avoid the payment of profits on the wood-work and on the bricks. The bricks were manufactured of clay from the bottom of Lake Calumet, and thus the construction of the town helped to deepen its

harbor and prepare it for the large shipping which is one day expected there, for its proprietors prophesy that vessels will yet sail from Pullman to London. Then, as there is no competition at Pullman, and no conflicting municipal boards, gas, water, and sewerage pipes were laid once for all, and the pavement, when completed, not again disturbed. The money saved by this wise, unified, and consequently harmonious action must be reckoned by the hundred thousand.

There are over fifteen hundred buildings at Pullman, and the entire cost of the town, including all the manufacturing establishments, is estimated at eight millions of dollars. The rents of the dwellings vary from $4 50 per month for the cheapest flats of two rooms to $100 a month for the largest private house in the place. The rent usually paid varies from $14 to $25 a month, exclusive of the water charge, which is generally not far from eighty cents. A five-roomed cottage, such as is seen in the illustration, rents for $17 a month, and its cost is estimated at $1700, including a charge of $300 for the lot. But it must be understood that the estimated value of $1700 includes profits on brick and carpenter work and everything furnished by the company, for each industry at Pullman stands on its own feet, and keeps its own separate account. The company's brickyards charge the company a profit on the brick the latter buys, and the other establishments do the same; consequently the estimated cost of the buildings includes profits which flowed after all into the company's coffers.

The Pullman companies retain everything. No private individual owns to-day a square rod of ground or a single structure in the entire town. No organization, not even a church, can occupy any other than rented quarters. With the exception of the management of the public school, every municipal act is here the act of a private corporation. What this means will be perceived when it is remembered that it includes such matters as the location, repairs, and cleaning of streets and sidewalks, the maintenance of the fire department, and the taking of the local census whenever desired. When the writer was in Pullman a census was taken. A superior officer of the company said to an inferior, "I want a census," and told what kind of a census was desired. That was the whole matter. The people of the place had no more to say about it than a resident of Kamtchatka. All this applies only to what is generally known as Pullman, which is in reality no political organization, and is called a town or city simply in a popular sense for the sake of convenience. Pullman is only a part of the large village and town of Hyde Park, but the latter appears to have relinquished the government of this portion of its territory bearing the name of Pullman to private corporations, and the writer was not able to find that a single resident of Pullman, not an officer of the Pullman companies, was either in the board of trustees of Hyde Park or in the staff of officers. The town clerk and treasurer are both officers of the Pullman Palace Car Company, and the directory of Hyde Park reveals the fact that with one exception every member of the board of education of the Pullman school district is an officer of the Palace Car Company or some concern which bears the name of Pullman.

One of Mr. Pullman's fundamental ideas is the *commercial value of beauty*, and this he has endeavored to carry out as faithfully in the town which bears his name as in the Pullman drawing-room and sleeping cars. He is one of the few men who have thought it a paying investment to expend millions for the purpose of surrounding laborers with objects of beauty and comfort. In a hundred ways one sees in Pullman to-day evidences of its founder's sagacious foresight. One of the most interesting is the fact that the company finds it pays them in dollars and cents to keep the streets sprinkled with water and the lawns well trimmed, the saving in paint and kalsomine more than repaying the outlay. Less dust and dirt are carried and blown into houses, and the injury done to walls and wood-work is diminished. For the rest, the neat exterior is a constant example, which is sure sooner or later to exert its proper effect on housewives, stimulating them to exertion in behalf of cleanliness and order.

It should be constantly borne in mind that all investments and outlays in Pullman are intended to yield financial returns satisfactory from a purely business point of view. The minimum return expected is six per centum on expenditure, and the town appears to have yielded a far higher percentage on cost up to the present time. Much of the land was bought at less than $200 per acre, and it is

likely that the average price paid did not exceed that. A large part of this now yields rent on a valuation of $5000 per acre, and certain sections in the heart of Pullman are to-day more valuable, and will continue to increase in value in the future, if the town grows as is expected. The extreme reluctance of the officers of the company to make precise statements of any kind renders it impossible to obtain the accurate information desired. Yet there seems to be no reason to doubt the emphatic assertion that the whole establishment pays handsomely. A large part of Pullman belongs to the Palace Car Company, which claims to have paid nine and one-half per centum on its entire stock for the last three years, and to have averaged about ten per centum since its organization in 1867. As far as the Land Association is concerned, it is sufficient to know that all its houses are rented at a high valuation, and the land put in at twenty-five times its cost.

It pays also in another way. The wholesome, cheerful surroundings enable the men to work more constantly and more efficiently. The healthy condition of the residents is a matter of general comment. The number of deaths has been about seven in a thousand per annum, whereas it has been about fifteen in a thousand in the rest of Hyde Park.

It is maintained that Pullman is truly a philanthropic undertaking, although it is intended that it should be a profitable investment, and this is the argument used: If it can be shown that it does pay to provide beautiful homes for laborers, accompanied with all the conditions requisite for wholesome living both for the body and the mind, the example set by Mr. Pullman will find wide imitation. If what is done for the residents of the town were simply a generous gift, another might argue, "If Mr. Pullman chooses to spend his money this way, very well! I have no objection, but I prefer to keep a stable of blooded horses. Each one according to his taste!" We may feel inclined to shrug our shoulders at the philanthropy which demands a good round sum for everything it offers, but certainly it is a great thing to have demonstrated the commercial value of beauty in a city of laborers.

The wages paid at Pullman are equal to those paid for similar services elsewhere in the vicinity. In a visit of ten days at Pullman no complaint was heard on this score which appeared to be well founded. Unskilled laborers—and they are perhaps one-fourth of the population —receive only $1 30 a day; but there are other corporations about Chicago which pay no more, and Pullman claims to pay only ordinary wages. Many of the mechanics earn $2 50 or $2 75 a day, some $3 and $4, and occasionally even more. Those who receive but $1 30 have a hard struggle to live, after the rent and water tax are paid. On this point there is unanimity of sentiment, and Pullman does comparatively little for them, and the social problem in their case remains unsolved. They are crowded together in the cheap flats, which are put as much out of sight as possible, and present a rather dreary appearance, although vastly better than the poorer class of New York tenements.

The great majority at Pullman are skilled artisans, and nearly all with whom the writer conversed expressed themselves as fairly well satisfied with their earnings, and many of them took pains to point out the advantages of the steady employment and prompt pay they always found there. The authorities even go out of their way to "make work" for one who has proved himself efficient and faithful.

There are many other pleasant and interesting features of Pullman, to which it is possible only to allude here. One is the perfect system of sewerage, similar to that which has been found so successful in Berlin, Germany. The sewerage is all collected in a great tank under the "water tower," and then pumped on to a large garden farm of one hundred and seventy acres, called the "Pullman Farm." This is already profitable, and it is hoped that in time it will pay interest on the cost of the entire sewerage system of the town, which was $300,000. It is worthy the careful study of municipal authorities.

There are a thousand and one little ways in which the residents of Pullman are benefited, and in many cases without cost to the company. Considerable care is taken to find suitable employment for those who in any way become incapacitated for their ordinary work. A watchman with a missing arm was seen, and a position as janitor was found for a man who had become partially paralyzed. These are but examples. Men temporarily injured receive full pay, save in cases

of gross carelessness, when one dollar a day is allowed. Employés are paid with checks on the "Pullman Loan and Savings Bank," to accustom them to its use and encourage them to make deposits.

Encouraging words from superiors are helpful. One warm-hearted official, to whom the welfare of the laboring classes appears to be a matter of momentous concern, wrote a note of thanks to the occupant of a cottage which was particularly well kept and ornamented with growing flowers. In another case he was so well pleased with the appearance of a cottage that he ordered a couple of plants in pots sent from the greenery to the lady of the house, with his compliments. The effect of systematic persistence in little acts of kind thoughtfulness like these is seen in the diffusion of a spirit of mutual helpfulness, and in frequent attempts to give practical, even if imperfect, expression to the truth of the brotherhood of man. Several ladies were especially prominent in this way, and among them may be mentioned the librarian. When the humbler young women see her home, which was designed for an ordinary mechanic, they often ask: "Can this be the same kind of a house we live in? Oh! how did you make all these pretty things? Please tell us." And a ready response is always given to their appeals. At a charming picnic, where a large number of residents were met, the writer had the pleasure of making the acquaintance of a great-hearted motherly German lady, the wife of a manager of the shops, whose life is spent in good works among the employés. The strangers are visited and brought into congenial social circles, and the poor and sick relieved in their distress, by this noble Christian woman. An interesting and successful experiment was tried in connection with wall-paper. Great quantities were bought at wholesale, and a man sent to the poorer houses with a number of varieties, from which the tenant was requested to select one, the company offering the paper at the very low figures at which they purchased it, and agreeing to hang it without charge. The architect assured the writer that this was doubtless the first time many women had been called upon to exercise taste and consider the beautiful in color in any matter pertaining to their dwellings. Great interest was aroused in the selection of wall-paper, and friends and neighbors were called in to aid in the discussion of colors and in the final choice. The small charge made was only beneficial, as it led the people to value what they had acquired.

These are the devices which, together with the constant example set by the company, have awakened a very general desire in the residents to adorn and beautify their dwellings. Everywhere, even in a flat of two rooms in the third story, one sees prints and engravings on the walls, Christmas and other cards, with cheap bric-à-brac on brackets in the corner, or on some inexpensive ornamental table, and growing plants in the windows. It is comparatively a small matter that a highly developed æstheticism could not approve of much that is seen, for it is only the beginning of an education of the higher faculties, and better things will be seen in the children.

In the way of material comforts and beautiful surroundings, Pullman probably offers to the majority of its residents quite as much as they are in a position to enjoy, and in many cases even more. There are those who do not feel it a hardship to live in a dark alley of a great city, and there are men and women at Pullman incapable of appreciating its advantages. But they are learning to do it, and many who go away dissatisfied return, because they can not find elsewhere that to which they have become accustomed there. The pure air and perfect sanitary condition of the houses and of the entire city are more and more valued, especially by mothers, one of whom exclaimed to the writer, in speaking of Chicago: "I just hate the ugly old city." Pullman had taught her better things than she formerly knew, and thus it is becoming a great school, elevating laborers to a higher plane of wholesome living. The Commissioner of Health of Chicago, who holds that "healthy houses whose incumbency does not hint at the acceptance of charity are the best, in fact the only, means of teaching sanitation to the working classes," calls the emigrants from Pullman "sanitary missionaries."

But admirable as are the peculiarities of Pullman which have been described, certain unpleasant features of social life in that place are soon noticed by the careful observer, which moderate the enthusiasm one is at first inclined to feel upon an inspection of the external, plainly visible facts, and the picture must be completed before judgment can be pronounced upon it.

One just cause of complaint is what in government affairs would be called a bad civil service, that is, a bad administration in respect to the employment, retention, and promotion of employés. Change is constant in men and officers, and each new superior appears to have his own friends, whom he appoints to desirable positions. Favoritism and nepotism, out of place as they are in an ideal society, are oft-repeated and apparently well-substantiated charges.

The resulting evil is very naturally dissatisfaction, a painful prevalence of petty jealousies, a discouragement of superior excellence, frequent change in the residents, and an all-pervading feeling of insecurity. Nobody regards Pullman as a real home, and, in fact, it can scarcely be said that there are more than temporary residents at Pullman. One woman told the writer she had been in Pullman two years, and that there were only three families among her acquaintances who were there when she came. Her reply to the question, "It is like living in a great hotel, is it not?" was, "We call it camping out." The nature of the leases aggravates this evil. As already stated, all the property in Pullman is owned by the Pullman associations, and every tenant holds his house on a lease which may be terminated on ten days' notice. A lease which lies on the table before the writer reads: "From —— to ——, unless sooner cancelled in accordance with the conditions of the lease." It is not necessary that any reason be assigned for the notice; "and it is expressly agreed that the fact that rent may have been paid at any time in advance shall not be a waiver of the right to put an end to the term and tenancy under this lease by such notice." Furthermore, three-fourths of the laborers in Pullman are employed by the Palace Car Company, and many of those who do not work for it are employed in establishments in which the company as such or a prominent member of it is interested. The power of Bismarck in Germany is utterly insignificant when compared with the power of the ruling authority of the Pullman Palace Car Company in Pullman. Whether the power be exercised rightfully or wrongfully, it is there all the same, and every man, woman, and child in the town is completely at its mercy, and it can be avoided only by emigration. It is impossible within the realm of Pullman to escape from the overshadowing influence of the company, and every resident feels this, and "monopoly" is a word which constantly falls on the ear of the visitor. Large as the place is, it supports no newspaper, through which complaints might find utterance, and one whose official position in the town qualified him to speak with knowledge declared positively that no publication would be allowed which was not under the direct influence of the Pullman Company. A Baptist clergyman, who had built up quite a congregation, once ventured to espouse the cause of a poor family ejected from their house, and gave rather public expression to his feelings. Shortly after his support began to fall away, one member after another leaving, and it has since never been possible to sustain a Baptist organization in Pullman. It is indeed a sad spectacle. Here is a population of eight thousand souls where not one single resident dare speak out openly his opinion about the town in which he lives. One feels that one is mingling with a dependent, servile people. There is an abundance of grievances, but if there lives in Pullman one man who would give expression to them in print over his own name, diligent inquiry continued for ten days was not sufficient to find him.

One gentleman, whose position ought to have exempted him from it, was "warned" in coming to Pullman to be careful in what he said openly about the town. It required recourse to some ingenuity to ascertain the real opinion of the people about their own city. While the writer does not feel at liberty to narrate his own experience, it can do no harm to mention a strange coincidence. While in the city the buttons on his wife's boots kept tearing off in the most remarkable manner, and it was necessary to try different shoemakers, and no one could avoid free discussion with a man who came on so harmless an errand as to have the buttons sewed on his wife's boots. This was only one of the devices employed. The men believe they are watched by the "company's spotter," and to let one of them know that information was desired about Pullman for publication was to close his lips to the honest expression of opinion. The women were inclined to be more outspoken.

An evil worthy of attention is the neglect of religion. There are scarcely accommodations for one-eighth of the population in the halls where religious exercises are conducted on Sunday. There is but one church building in Pullman, and that, the property of the company, is unoccupied because no denomination can pay the rent. The Presbyterians offered $2000 a year for it, and this was refused. The company, owning all the property of the place, does nothing for the support of religion. The Presbyterians receive $700 a year from the Presbyterian Board, and pay $600 of it over to the company for rent. The Methodists and Episcopalians also support small organizations with difficulty. The men say: "The company care nothing for our souls. They only want to get as much work as possible out of our bodies;" and forthwith they begin to neglect the provision others have made for their spiritual welfare. This may be illogical conduct, but it is human nature.

The town-meeting of New England has ever been regarded by writers of the highest authority on American government as one of the bulwarks of our liberties. The free discussion of local affairs, and the full responsibility for what is done and not done, have ever been held to be an education of the mind, a means to develop the qualities most useful in a citizen of a republic and a training for larger public duties. People of other countries are striving after a nearer approach to this in an improved local self-government, and the renowned German publicist Gneist is perhaps chiefly esteemed for what he has done to promote the movement in Germany. Yet in Pullman all this disappears. The citizen is surrounded by constant restraint and restriction, and everything is done for him, nothing by him.

The desire of the American to acquire a home is justly considered most commendable and hopeful. It promotes thrift and economy, and the habits acquired in the effort to pay for it are often the foundation of a future prosperous career. It is a beginning in the right direction. Again, a large number of house owners is a safeguard against violent movements of social discontent. Heretofore laborers at Pullman have not been allowed to acquire any real property in the place. There is a repression here as elsewhere of any marked individuality. Everything tends to stamp upon residents, as upon the town, the character expressed in "machine-made." Not only are strikes regarded as the chief of social sins, a view too widely disseminated by works like Charles Reade's *Put Yourself in His Place*, but individual initiative, even in affairs which concern the residents alone, is repressed. Once several of the men wanted to form a kind of mutual insurance association to insure themselves against loss of time in case of accident, but it was frowned down by the authorities, and nothing further has been heard of the matter. A lady attempted to found a permanent charitable organization to look after the poor and needy, but this likewise was discouraged, because it was feared that the impression might get abroad that there was pauperism in Pullman.

In looking over all the facts of the case the conclusion is unavoidable that the idea of Pullman is un-American. It is a nearer approach than anything the writer has seen to what appears to be the ideal of the great German Chancellor. It is not the American ideal. It is benevolent, well-wishing feudalism, which desires the happiness of the people, but in such way as shall please the authorities. One can not avoid thinking of the late Czar of Russia, Alexander II., to whom the welfare of his subjects was truly a matter of concern. He wanted them to be happy, but desired their happiness to proceed from him, in whom everything should centre. Serfs were freed, the knout abolished, and no insuperable objection raised to reforms, until his people showed a decided determination to take matters in their own hands, to govern themselves, and to seek their own happiness in their own way. Then he stopped the work of reform, and considered himself deeply aggrieved. The loss of authority and distrust of the people is the fatal weakness of many systems of reform and well-intentioned projects of benevolence.

Pullman ought to be appreciated, and high honor is due Mr. George M. Pullman. He has at least attempted to do something lasting and far-reaching, and the benefits he has actually conferred upon a laboring population of eight thousand souls testify that his heart must be warm toward his poorer brother. Mr. Pullman has partially solved one of the great problems of the immediate present, which is a diffusion of the benefits of concentrated wealth among wealth-creators.

Pullman is still in its infancy, and great things are promised in the future. On an adjoining tract lots are now offered for sale, and workmen will be aided in the purchase of these, and encouraged to build houses thereon. Other manufacturing establishments are expected soon, and a more extended and diversified industry will render the laborers less dependent. Mr. Pullman has also at heart numerous plans, the purpose of which is to give employment to women and young people. It is further proposed to establish a manual training school, and the inevitable Western university is talked about. It is to be hoped that what has been begun at Pullman will be continued in a larger spirit, and that a grander structure will arise on foundations already laid. It is especially to be desired that means should be discovered to awaken in the residents an interest and a pride in Pullman. It is now thought a praiseworthy thing "to beat the company," which phrase in itself points to something radically wrong. It is quite practicable to develop a democracy, or at least what might be called a constitutional monarchy, out of the despotism of Pullman. It is not more than has been done elsewhere, as, for example, by M. Godin, at Guise, France, where the affairs of the "Social Palace" are managed by committees of laborers elected by laborers. Some co-operative features might be added, which would be a move in the right direction, and every great philanthropic enterprise ought as soon as possible to be placed on such a footing as not to be dependent upon the life of any one individual. Not a few have ventured to express the hope that Pullman might be widely imitated, and thus inaugurate a new era in the history of labor. But if this signifies approval of a scheme which would immesh our laborers in a net-work of communities owned and managed by industrial superiors, then let every patriotic American cry, God forbid! What would this mean? The establishment of the most absolute power of capital, and the repression of all freedom. It matters not that they are well-meaning capitalists; all capitalists are not devoted heart and soul to the interests of their employés, and the history of the world has long ago demonstrated that no class of men are fit to be intrusted with unlimited power. In the hour of temptation and pressure it is abused, and the real nature of the abuse may for a time be concealed even from him guilty of it; but it degrades the dependent, corrupts the morals of the superior, and finally that is done unblushingly in the light which was once scarcely allowed in a dark corner. This is the history of a large share of the degeneracy of manners and morals in public and private life.

No; the body is more than raiment, and the soul more than the body. If free American institutions are to be preserved, we want no race of men reared as underlings and with the spirit of menials. John Stuart Mill and others have regarded the relation of master and servant, employer and employed, as unworthy of the highest attainable average type of manhood and womanhood, and have prophesied the abolition of such relationship, and the establishment of some kind or another of co-operation, where men will work for and with one another. Perhaps that may seem Utopian, but it is possible to strive for it as an ideal, and it is the goal toward which the wisest philanthropists are pushing. Shall we turn about and forge new bonds of dependence? Is not a tendency to do this observable as one of the signs of the time? Are we not frequently trying to offer the gilded cage as a substitute for personal liberty? When John Most, in an address to the laborers of Baltimore, sneered at this much-vaunted American liberty, and asked, "Of what value is it? Has any one ever been able to clothe himself with it, to house himself in it, or to satisfy with it the cravings of his stomach?" did he not give a gross expression to a kind of materialism which is becoming too common? It is idle to deny the spread of luxury, and numerous defalcations and embezzlements bear witness to wide-extended extravagance, an overvaluation of material comforts, and an undervaluation of the higher ethical goods. So when we see such splendid provision for the body as at Pullman, we clap our hands and stop not to ask how all this is to effect the formation of character. And the impassioned pleas for liberty which moved Americans mightily one hundred years ago fall to-day on the ear as something strange and ridiculous. Such thing are straws floating on the stream of social life. Have we reason to be pleased with the direction in which the current is setting?

5. Minorities

Urban congestion and the strains of industrial discipline led many Americans to a renewed interest in recreation in the late nineteenth century. The growth of amusement parks, the popularity of professional sports, and the prominence of the new conservation movement testified to this interest. Some portions of the population, however, demanded an atmosphere of privacy in which to spend their leisure time and release their taut nerves. Caspar Whitney (1861–1929), sportsman and author, chronicled this demand. Whitney found the new country clubs which were springing up in the suburbs, evidence of a healthy, outdoors preference by the wealthier classes. He emphasized not their increasing isolation, but the wholesomeness of this new taste. Whitney, a member of several country clubs, editor of *Outing*, explorer and war correspondent, was also active in promoting the popularity of golf.

If life was becoming more varied for one minority group in America, it was growing more desperate for another. Less than a generation out of bondage, American Negroes experienced a steadily increasing legal segregation in this period, so aptly labeled "The Nadir" by Rayford Logan. This segregation was not voluntary, like the withdrawal of the wealthy, but a symbol and cause of an intensified social and political degradation. Among the chief problems American Negroes faced was a rapid increase of mob violence. Careful commentators estimated that several thousand Americans, most of them black, were killed by lynch mobs in the twenty years between 1880 and 1900. Ida B. Wells (1862–1931), a Chicago newspaper editor, published this searing indictment of the atrocities committed on her fellow blacks in the mid nineties, but the revolting facts her pamphlet contained, aroused little action. Newspapers editorialized, ministers sermonized, authors like Mark Twain proclaimed their indignation, but the lynching epidemic grew in strength after 1900, and it took years before even minimal physical protections could be extended to the millions of black citizens of America.

Evolution of the Country Club

CASPAR W. WHITNEY

It used to be said Americans did not know how to live, but that was before we were "discovered" by the journalistic missionaries of Great Britain. It used also to be said we did not know how to enjoy ourselves; but again, that was before the dawn of the country club. If we knew neither how to live nor how to enjoy ourselves until comparatively recent years, it must be acknowledged we have made excellent use of both time and opportunity since our enlightenment. Even yet our efforts to acquire more intimate acquaintance with the leisurely side of life are parodied by those who cannot understand the demands of this great throbbing work-a-day country of ours.

It must be admitted unhesitatingly that we are only just learning how to play; we have not been, nor are we yet, a nation of pleasure-seekers. We are a practical people; we build our living-house before undertaking landscape-gardening. If we have been long in turning our attention to material enjoyments, we have atoned somewhat for early indifference by modernizing the paraphernalia and investing in the pursuit all that earnestness which characterizes the American in whatever field he launches. Indeed, we have entered upon our recreation with such vigor, I often question if even yet we have attained wisdom with the recreative incentive. I confess to a doubt whether full enjoyment for our joys is an American attribute. We steal away for our holidays (likely as not with a portmanteau filled with work to do at odd moments), determined to rest and take life at its easiest; we promise ourselves to foreswear all thoughts of business and the outer world; to loll about under the trees, and seek some of the lessons nature is said to have for us. We hold bravely to our resolutions for a day or so, but the third or fourth is certain to find us bargaining for city newspapers. Perhaps our grandchildren may see the day they can separate themselves from the office as effectually as though it existed in name only, but the present-day American, at least he who fills any active

Caspar W. Whitney, "Evolution of the Country Club," *Harper's New Monthly Magazine*, Vol. XC (December, 1894), pp. 17–32.

part in this great progressive movement, has not yet reached that development in the cultivation of holiday amusement.

In this particular we may indeed learn from the Englishman, who knows to the fullest how to take his recreation; nothing hurries him; little worries him when he goes on his holidays, only collapse of the Bank of England would recall him to the business world. He has gone from town to enjoy himself, and he does so to the utmost of his capability, which is considerable. Truly it is restful to observe the Britisher at play; there is no doubting he is bent on recreation. Every movement bespeaks leisure. But then his disposition is and his training has been totally different from those of the American, to whom the Englishman's comfortable way of conducting his business would of itself be recreation. Even the boys at play reveal the difference in temperament; the American school-boy engages in his games with as much light-hearted enthusiasm as the English lad, but the former shortly exhibits the national characteristic when, as university undergraduate, he gives so serious a turn to his sports, making preparation for contest a matter of considerable expense and elaboration, and giving results the greatest possible importance.

We Americans do nothing by halves—perhaps we should enjoy life more if we did—and the history of the country club, as much as anything else, bears witness to our tendency to superlative development. From having not a single country club in the entire United States of America twenty-five years ago, we have in a quarter of a century, in half that period, evolved the handsomest in the world. But here at least the reaction has been beneficial, for the country club has done appreciable missionary work in bringing us in contact with our fellows, where another than the hard business atmosphere envelops us, and in enticing us for the time being to put aside the daily task.

Apropos of the desire for relaxation that now and again fastens upon us when we have been driving the mind at the expense of the body, I recall a story once told me by an old army officer, who was well on his allotted years, illustrating my point so fittingly as to be worthy of recital here. It was while he was a cadet at West Point, and during the days when recreation as a tonic to study had not been recognized; whatever there was of muscular activity came as a *nolens volens* part of the daily curriculum; no out-door games of any description were tolerated, or at least encouraged. The desire to play became a disease that spread throughout the academy, and grew irrepressible, until one day marbles, surreptitiously taken into the barracks and half-ashamedly exhibited, suddenly filled the pockets of every cadet in the corps, as though by a sportive Santa Claus, and plebs and first classmen played at marbles with all the abandon of ten-year-old schoolboys. The West Point management has grown more sensible and liberal since that time, and marbles are no longer a necessity.

The country club in America is simply one of the results of a final ebullition of animal spirits too long ignored in a work-a-day world; it is nature's appeal for recognition of the body in its co-operation with the mind.

Only a careful study of our country's history and its social traditions will give us a full appreciation of what the country club has done for us. It has, first of all, corrected to a large extent the American defect of not being able or at least not willing to stop work and enjoy ourselves; it has brought together groups of congenial, cultivated people, that often as not might be sweltering in the midsummer sun in town, or at isolated country houses, or in crowded, ill-kept "summer hotels." It has given them a club and country villa combined in one, where, having practically all the comforts and delights of housekeeping, they are called upon to assume none of its cares or responsibilities. For here the steward attends to the early morning market, worries with the servants, and may be held to account for the shortcomings of the *chef*, and at a cost below that on which a separate establishment of equal appointment could be maintained.

It is impossible to overestimate the blessings of the country club in adding comforts to country living that before were utterly unattainable, and in making it possible to enjoy a degree of that rural life which is one of England's greatest attractions. I say degree, for we have not yet attained the full delights of suburban residence as they are enjoyed in England, where a large and wealthy leisure class make wellnigh every great hall virtually a country club. In its present development the country club is really an American institution; there is little occasion for it in England, and nowhere is it so elaborated in the Old World as in the New.

To Boston must be given the credit of first revealing the possibilities and delights of the country club. I never journey to the "Hub" that I do not envy Bostonians the geographical situation of their city, which is superior, from a sportsman's point of view, to that of any other in the United States. What with rural New England within a very few hours' railway travel, and the "North Shore," that ideal summer resting spot, at their very gates, there is out-door entertainment for those of every disposition.

What nature has done for the Bostonian, a visit to the "North Shore," or perusal of Mr. Robert Grant's charmingly realistic pen-picture of its beauties, alone can show. Really it was not very neighborly of Mr. Grant to awaken so abruptly to our rural shortcomings those of us who had pitched our tents on less-favored ground.

A quarter of a century ago the residents of the north shore of Massachusetts Bay—to which no self-respecting Bostonian nowadays ever dreams of alluding otherwise than as the "North Shore"—differed little from those on the remainder of the much-broken New England coastline. If you seek the pioneer in the modern movement you must go to Mr. Grant for information. I shall tell you only how by degrees the busy American began to appreciate that "all work and no play makes Jack a dull boy," and gradually to stop for a breathing-spell. And thus, one at a time, slowly at first, the value of wholesome air and a bit of relaxation made converts. Slowly the underestimated farms passed from rustic to urban ownership, and became at once the most economical and best sanitariums in America, while the erstwhile proprietors withdrew farther into the New England fastnesses. Gradually, too, the entire scene changed from the up-at-sunrise-to-bed-at-sunset monotony of the simple-minded country folk to the brisk atmosphere of refined people; Nature herself seemed to welcome the more congenial surroundings, and the country assumed a brightened aspect. Where the leg-weary family hack, silhouetted against the autumn sky had toiled over the hills to the solitary cross-roads store, the village cart now dashed along, drawn by a good-blooded horse, and driven by a fashionably gowned woman. Man and womankind improved in health, horseflesh in quality, and we began to learn how to use to advantage our opportunities for recreation and health.

Its contiguity to Boston, and the completeness of individual establishments, made a country club in its initial sense along the north shore unnecessary in the very first years of its popularity, and not until it had grown beyond the country abode of a few individuals, and taken on the air of a country retreat of the comparatively many, did the need of a co-operative amusement institution become apparent. Therefore but five years ago the Casino was established near Nahant, and only in the last couple of years the first country club (Essex) of the immediate north shore has been opened at Manchester-by-the-Sea.

On the southern shore of Massachusetts Bay, nature has not been so ·lavish in her setting of the country; beautiful it is, indeed, but wanting in that grandeur of coast-line which is the chief charm of the north. Here there are handsome homes, and many of them, but the settlement of this shore differed from that of the other, insomuch as those who went first to the latter did so as individuals, whereas, on the south, the pioneer fresh-air seekers settled in little bands of chosen ones. Thus the need of a rendezvous was early experienced, and realized in the establishment, in 1882, of the Brookline Country Club, the first of the genus in America, albeit some of the hunting clubs had been and are to this day filling a similar sphere.

Probably the country club has rendered its greatest service in tempting us out of doors, and cultivating a taste for riding and driving that has so largely benefited both sexes. With the evolution of the country club we have been developing into a nation of sportsmen and sportswomen. Indeed, sport of one kind or another and the origin of the country club are so closely connected, it is exceedingly difficult to decide which owes its existence to the other. It may be asserted that country clubs, generally speaking, have been created by the common desire of their incorporators to make a home for amateur sport of one kind or another. Some grew directly out of sport, as, for instance, the Country Club of Westchester County, which was originally planned for a tennis club, the Rockaway, Meadow Brook, and the Buffalo clubs, that were called into existence by the polo and hunting men. Others owe their existence to a desire to establish an objective point for drives and rides, and a rendezvous within easy access of town like the Brookline and Philadelphia Country clubs. Others have been called into being as the centralizing force of a residential colony, as Tuxedo. And yet others have been created by fashion for the coast season, as the Kebo Valley, at Bar Harbor.

If sport had not been the *raison d'être* of every club's establishment, it is at all events, with extremely few exceptions, the chief means of their subsistence. Practically every country club is the centre of several kinds of sport, pursued more or less vigorously as the seasons come and go. A few of them maintain polo teams, and all supply implements and encouragement for as many kinds of games as its members will admit.

After all, the country club is nothing more than a rendezvous for a colony of congenial spirits; at least that, with more or less variation, is its cardinal virtue; but in our restless progressive way we have pursued the revelations of the new life with such tireless energy, I sometimes fear we run the risk of neutralizing the good to be otherwise derived. The ultra-fashionable side of the country club we must always deplore. The effort, happily in only isolated cases, to drag all the pomp and vanity and inane parade of town into the country, where it is in touch with neither the surroundings nor one's inclinations, presents quite as incongruous a situation as that other inanity, where much time and money, and not so much brains, combine to enforce the formalities of full dress at a yachting-cruise dinner upon those who have got into their flannels for a week's relaxation.

The intrusion of "fashion," so called, into some of our choicest summer resting-places has robbed them of all that charm which superb scenic surroundings and relief from society's conventionality formerly gave. One goes into the country in summer to rest and be rid of the set scene of the winter functions. Newport has long been given over to society's star performers, and to simple-minded provincials who journey thither to gape at the social menagerie.

As great an offence, however, is the desecration of the country by attempts to citify it. Citified country is not often a pleasing picture to contemplate, never so when it greets us at the club whither we have flown to escape it. I am inclined to agree with Miss French's sometimes irritable but always philosophical Professor in his lament at finding neither a lily in the ponds nor a solitary mud-puddle anywhere on the roads in the country-club vicinity; who finds, instead, asphaltum walks, and brooklets which you make sure are turned on in the morning and shut off again at night, and where "little bird-cage cottages are all about, with little birds in them, all singing the same song. Big clubhouse, same people, same rocking-chairs, same people rocking in them, same waiters, same floor, same band, same dead monotony, until you feel as if you would like to blow up one half of it to give the other half a new and real sensation." But this is a phase of one or two country clubs only, for not many spoil what they have by attempting what they cannot obtain—natural results with artificial propagation. Where nature has left off, man has stepped in to complete—and not infrequently, too, to mar—the picture. What marvellous displays of taste do we see by those privileged to erect country houses! What a heterogeneous array of architectural nightmares is presented for one's torture—particularly at the sea-side resorts, where the majestic splendors of the coast-line demand the more of the builder! Nowhere does recent architecture harmonize more thoroughly with its surroundings than in California, where many of the country houses and suburban clubs seem almost to have been modelled as a fitting and crowning complement by the same hand that had fashioned the ideal setting.

Really, country-club life has two sides—its domestic, if I may so call it, and its sporting, and not every club has both. Nor do I mean social for domestic. Every club has a social side, and that of the country club is particularly festive in season. But the domestic side is given only to those that have been the magnet in the founding of a colony of residents. Its domesticity may not be of the nursery order, but it goes so far as apportioning a part of its house for the exclusive use of its women members, and in some instances, at the mountain and sea-side resorts, the house is common to members of both sexes. One or two in the West carry the domestic feature so far as to give it somewhat of a family aspect, which, it must be confessed, is a hazardous experiment. One roof is not usually counted upon to cover more than one family harmoniously. The one distinguishing feature of the country club, however, is its recognition of the gentle sex, and I know of none where they are not admittted either on individual membership or on that of *paterfamilias*.

Clubs like the Meadow Brook and the Rockaway, which were organized for hunting and polo pure and simple, have no domestic side and make no especial provision for women, though both entertain, the latter in its pretty little club, the former more often at the home of one of its members.

It is the sporting side of the country club, however, that gives it life and provides entertainment for its members; the club and our sporting history are so closely interwoven as to be inseparable. Polo, hunting, and pony-racing owe to it their lives, and to the members we are largely indebted for the marked improvement in carriage horseflesh during the past five years. They founded the horse show, made coaching an accepted institution, and have so filled the year with games that it is hard to say whether the country-club sporting season begins with the hunting in the autumn or with tennis in the spring, for there is hardly any cessation from the opening to the closing of the calendar year.

Once upon a time the country was considered endurable only in summer, but the clubs have changed even that notion; all of them keep open house in winter, some retain a fairly large percentage of members in residence, and one or two make a feature of winter sports. Tuxedo holds a veritable carnival, with tobogganing, snow-shoeing, and skating on the pond, which in season provides the club table with trout. The Essex Country Club of New Jersey owns probably the best-equipped toboggan-slide in America, and on its regular meeting nights electric illumination and picturesque costumes combine to make it a most attractive scene.

Spring opens with preparation for polo, lawn-tennis, and yachting. Not all country clubs have polo and yachting, but every one has courts, and several hold annual tournaments that are features of the tennis season, and where the leading players are brought together. Of the country clubs proper, only Westchester, Philadelphia, Essex, Brookline, St. Louis, Buffalo, really support polo teams, besides which there are the Meadow Brook and Rockaway, the two strongest in the country, and Myopia hunt clubs. Two only enjoy yachting facilities, the Country Club of Westchester

County and the Larchmont Yacht Club. The latter, although strictly speaking devoted to yachting, is, nevertheless, virtually a country club, with one of the handsomest homes of them all, a fleet second in size only to that of the New York Yacht Club, and a harbor that is one of the safest and most picturesque on the coast. Westchester has no especial fleet aside from the steam and sailing yachts owned by a few individuals of the club; but its harbor is a good one, and its general location very attractive.

All the clubs dabble in live-pigeon trap-shooting, which is regrettable, for it is unsportsmanlike, to say nothing of the cash prizes, professionalizing the participants. It is a miserable form of amusement and unworthy the name of sport; but it is not so popular as formerly, and that, at all events, is something in its favor.

The polo season begins in the latter part of May, and continues more or less intermittently to the middle of September, and sometimes even as late as the first week of October. But usually October sees the end of it, for by that time the interest in hunting is quickening, and active preparations are making for the field. Hunting and polo in the early days constituted the sole sport of the country-club members, but the introduction of other games in the last five years has divided the interest that was once given to them entirely. Neither has retrograded; but they have not expanded as they should. However, that's another story. Whatever may be lacking in its progression, polo is the game that furnishes the country club with its most spirited scenes. The rivalry between the teams is always of the keenest, and the spectators, made up largely of the members of the contesting clubs, are quite as susceptible to its enthusiasm as the players.

Probably the most characteristic country-club scene, however, is created by the pony-race meetings given on the tracks with which several of the clubs are provided. Here there is ample opportunity for the hysterical enthusiasm so dear to the feminine soul, and plenty of time between events for them to chatter away to their hearts' content. Here, too, there is the certainty of seeing one's friends not only in the carts and on top of the coaches that line the course, and on the temporary little grand stand, erected for the near-by residents of the club colony, but frequently riding the ponies. Formerly more gentlemen rode than is the case now, but one day some one, who evidently cared more for the stakes than for the sport, put a professional jockey on his pony, and many others with equally strong pot-hunting tendencies have followed the example. So to-day we go to a meeting expecting, hoping to see our friends, or at least club men, in the saddle, and find instead at least eight out of every ten ponies ridden by second-rate professionals or stable-boys.

Only, therefore, when racing is under strictly club auspices, and partakes of the nature of a hunt meet, with gymkana and other equestrian sports of more or less acrobatic nature, do we have the Simon Pure sport, with "gentlemen up." On such an occasion the social and sporting sides of the club are revealed at their best. Turn your back to the racecourse and you well might fancy yourself at a huge garden party; go to the paddock, and you will find the same scene with a different setting; the same well-groomed men and women that out yonder are drinking tea are here, every last one of them talking horse for dear life, and, what is more to the point, talking it understandingly. Some of the clubs, notably the Genesee Valley Hunt, hold annual meetings, where very skilful tent-pegging, lemon-cutting, and rough-riding creditable to a Cossack, show the practical results of this sporting age. Some, again, on their point-to-point runs give us the only really amateur steeple-chasing of a high class in America. The country club has, indeed, as many sides and many charms as a fascinating woman—merciless in the live-pigeon-shooting, equal to any emergency in the hunting field, and a veritable coquette in the bewitchery of the hunt ball.

There is so much that is entirely delightful in the country club, we wait patiently and in confidence for the correction of the few incongruities that drew forth the "Professor's" pointed criticism. Probably when we have been enjoying ourselves awhile longer we will learn to do so a bit more comfortably to all concerned; just now we make of it a little too much business, and lay out the day's routine for our guest as though it were a "brief" to be completed by the evening, whether or no we have the inclination for the undertaking. The English excel us in this small but important particular of entertaining, by knowing that the secret of pleasing one's guests is in permitting each to follow the bent of his own inclinations. On the other side your host gives you to understand that you can best please him by pleasing yourself. You may join the party that is putting up a luncheon-basket for a day's drive, or go for a round on the golf-links, or have a run with the hounds, or stop at home, as one often feels like doing, for a few quiet hours in the library. The average American host is more solicitous for your day's pleasure—aggressively so, let us say; he is determined you shall enjoy yourself—at least he will keep you on the go. He makes up the parties, and thrusts his guests into them with apparently never a thought of its being quite possible that all may not be of a like turn of mind. He works hard in his endeavor to keep the interest of his guests constantly aroused; he wants no *ennui* under his roof. Our big-hearted, energetic American host means it all for our pleasure, but has not been "at play" long enough to have thoroughly mastered the art.

The club furnishes more independent recreation than most hosts are able to provide, which is one of the reasons why men who do not care to be raced hither and thither in a perspiring search for pleasure prefer the club hearth-stone to that of the individual.

But country-club benefits remain so abundant as not to be easily computed. While being a family physician whose prescriptions are always agreeable, it has at the same time cultivated a love of out-doors for itself, and stood as the rallying-point for every sport in America in which the horse is a factor. Modern organized hunting in America began in 1877 with the Queens County drag hounds (though it must not be forgotten that fox-hunting has existed in the vicinity of Philadelphia for about one hundred and fifty years, and in parts of the South for the same length of time), and immediately found support from the men who afterwards made country clubs possible; so also with polo, introduced in '76; and pony-racing, first centralized under an association in '90. Probably coaching and driving generally, however, have profited most by the country club, in that it has given an objective point in the days' outing where intelligent care for the animals, congenial spirits, and a good dinner were assured. Too much credit cannot be given the Coaching Club, founded in '75 by Messrs. James Gordon Bennett, Frederick Bronson, William P. Douglas, Leonard W. Jerome, William Jay, De Lancy Kane, S. Nicholas Kane, Thomas Newbold, and A. Thorndike Rice, not only for its encouragement of four-in-hand driving, but for the general impetus, and consequent improvement in horseflesh, that has shown such satisfactory results in the past ten years. The club's influence on horsemanship and sportsmanship has been considerable, and with the creation of country clubs long drives became a possible and delightful feature of the year. Nor have the Coaching Club's pleasures and lessons been altogether esoteric; it has from the very beginning given the public an almost annual opportunity of enjoying the exhilaration of coaching, to say nothing of acting as a general educator in coaching ethics.

• • •

This paper would not be complete without a glance at some of the country clubs that have been instrumental in setting in motion and keeping moving this out-door wave that has swept over us in a dozen years.

As the eldest and one of the most picturesquely located, the Country Club of Brookline deserves precedence. It had its origin in J. Murray

Forbes's idea of an objective point for rides and drives, and was organized in 1882. No other club possesses a hundred acres of such beautiful land within such easy access, for it is only five and a half miles from the State House, and can be reached from Boston without going off pavement, and, better still, in its immediate neighborhood none of the rural effects have been marred.

The club-house, originally a rambling old building, is very picturesque, and has been enlarged from time to time to meet requirements. Its piazza overlooks the race-course, in the centre of which is one of the best of polo fields. Before the organization of the club the Myopia Hunt, then in its infancy, held steeple-chase meetings on its property, and in these races, and in those given in the early years of Brookline, "gentlemen up" was the invariable rule. Of late years, however, professionals have been admitted, and with no advantage to the sport. In those days the regular working ponies and hacks of the members were entered: now horses come from New York and Canada, trained to the hour, and in some respects the racing is of a higher order, but the sport is not so enjoyable, and the old-time flavor has departed.

There is a shooting-box, where clay pigeons are used, a toboggan-slide, golf-course, and good tennis-courts, both grass and gravel; and it is not improbable that some day will see cottages for members similar to the plan adopted at Tuxedo.

In the winter, one evening a week has a *table d'hôte* and an informal dance, to which the members and friends from town are sure to come. In fact, nearly all the seats are booked far in advance, and the informality of these occasions lends the essence of ideal country-club life. Indeed, no country club in America so nearly approaches that ideal as Brookline.

The Country Club of Westchester developed from a suggestion to organize a tennis club into a determination to found a club where all country sports could be enjoyed. The newly organized club leased the house and racing-grounds of Dr. George L. Morris, at Pelham, and after some alterations, including a large addition, took possession April 4, 1884, fully equipped with tennis-courts, a race-track, polo field, baseball grounds, traps for pigeon-shooting, a pack of hounds, boats, and bath-houses.

The sale of Dr. Morris's property made it necessary to find other quarters, and in December, 1887, the Country-Club Land Association organized and bought Van Antwerp Farm, of about eighty acres, located on East Chester Bay, between Pelham Bridge and Fort Schuyler, and in the spring of '88 began to lay out the grounds and build the present club-house and stables, into which they moved the following year.

From its inception the club has kept up all the sports of the day: polo and tennis tournaments, baseball, pigeon-shooting, golf, boating (having two launches for the use of the members), and tobogganing and skating in winter. There is also quite a colony of handsome cottages on the grounds, owned by members, and altogether Westchester has probably more than any other encouraged sport of all kinds, both by precept and example.

Although entirely given over to hunting and polo, the Meadow Brook and Rockaway clubs were the pioneers in the country-club movement, and have been the most active workers in encouraging its growth. Both are strictly devoted to the horse, and the Meadow Brook men more particularly have been most prominent in the culture of the American breed.

The Meadow Brook Hunt Club was organized in 1879, though it had hunted two years previously with a pack that was taken over to West-chester. Its club-house is a quaint affair, with absolutely no pretensions to architectural beauty, and made up of two wooden buildings, each two stories high, joined together at their second story by a covered bridge, under which the driveway goes to the stables in the rear.

Rockaway has a modern home and more space for entertaining. Tuxedo has a modern and very handsome club, that was opened in 1886 with a colony of handsome cottages, which, in fact, called it into being. Phila-delphia's country club was organized in 1892, with polo as a *raison d'être*. It has none of the features of Brookline, Westchester, or Tuxedo, but is a charming objective point for an afternoon drive. As a matter of fact, any other sort of club around Philadelphia is uncalled-for. There is no need of country clubs in Philadelphia suburbs, with its handsome homes, and miles of beautiful lawns and orchards and gardens that load the air with rich perfumes, and where fields of daisies grow in such profusion they look like fields of snow which refuse to melt under the rays of the summer sun. Chestnut Hill and Bryn-Mawr and the rest are more English in their method of entertaining than any other suburbs in America.

The Elkridge Fox-hunting Club is Baltimore's country club, and delight-fully situated it is in Multavideo Park, about five miles out on St. Charles Avenue. As its name implies, fox-hunting is its sport, for which purpose it was organized in 1878, the country-club feature being added to gratify the wishes of the non-hunting set in 1887. There is no attempt at lavish display here, but its appointments are in the best of taste and judgment, and its *chef* unexcelled.

I cannot undertake, of course, to touch upon every country club—it would be stupid reading and take too much space—and therefore confine myself to representative ones only, but I must mention the Burlingame Country Club, of California, because, architecturally speaking, it is the most picturesque in America, and altogether a unique member of club-dom, and because it has an interesting history. It is situated in an 800-acre park, with splendid roads and attractive views, surrounded by a colony of cottages, all of the English half-timber style, and shaded by the magnificent wide-spreading oaks which are at once the charm and peculiarity of this beautiful park.

Riding, driving, polo, golf, and tennis are the sporting attractions, and the stables are filled with ponies and horses and traps of all sorts, which are hired out to members—rather a novel departure, but an exceedingly successful one in this case. The club was originally planned by Mr. Burlingame, who will be remembered as minister to China in the early sixties, and author of the treaty which bears his name. He returned to California very wealthy, and interested in the scheme W. C. Ralston, the Napoleon of finance on the Pacific coast in those days; both lost their money before they perfected the plans, and the property passed to the Sharon estate, to which it now belongs. In the past two years this estate has undertaken to carry out the programme devised by Burlingame and fostered by Ralston twenty years ago.

Who shall deny the country club to have been a veritable blessing, what with its sport and pleasure and health-giving properties that have brushed the cobwebs from weary brains, and given us blue sky, green grass, and restful shade in exchange for smoke-laden atmosphere, parboiled pavements, and the never-ceasing glare and racket of the city? And womankind too has partaken of country-club as she should of all blessings, in relaxation from the petty trials of housekeeping, and the parade and deceits of "society," while the hue of health has deepened in her cheeks. It has been a wholesome growth all round. Beginning life as somewhat of a novelty, the country club has become so familiar an institution that we wonder, as about the New York elevated railway, how we ever managed to get on without it.

A Red Record

IDA B. WELLS

THE CASE STATED

The student of American sociology will find the year 1894 marked by a pronounced awakening of the public conscience to a system of anarchy and outlawry which had grown during a series of ten years to be so common, that scenes of unusual brutality failed to have any visible effect upon the humane sentiments of the people of our land.

Beginning with the emancipation of the Negro, the inevitable result of unbridled power exercised for two and a half centuries, by the white man over the Negro, began to show itself in acts of conscienceless outlawry. During the slave regime, the Southern white man owned the Negro body and soul. It was to his interest to dwarf the soul and preserve the body. Vested with unlimited power over his slave, to subject him to any and all kinds of physical punishment, the white man was still restrained from such punishment as tended to injure the slave by abating his physical powers and thereby reducing his financial worth. While slaves were scourged mercilessly, and in countless cases inhumanly treated in other respects, still the white owner rarely permitted his anger to go so far as to take a life, which would entail upon him a loss of several hundred dollars. The slave was rarely killed, he was too valuable; it was easier and quite as effective, for discipline or revenge, to sell him "Down South."

But Emancipation came and the vested interests of the white man in the Negro's body were lost. The white man had no right to scourge the emancipated Negro, still less has he a right to kill him. But the Southern white people had been educated so long in that school of practice, in which might makes right, that they disdained to draw strict lines of action in dealing with the Negro. In slave times the Negro was kept subservient and submissive by the frequency and severity of the scourging, but, with freedom, a new system of intimidation came into vogue; the Negro was not only whipped and scourged; he was killed.

Ida B. Wells, *A Red Record. Tabulated Statistics and Alleged Causes of Lynchings in the United States, 1892–1893–1894* (Chicago, n.d.), pp. 9–15, 20, 43, 45–48.

Not all nor nearly all of the murders done by white men, during the past thirty years in the South, have come to light, but the statistics as gathered and preserved by white men, and which has not been questioned, show that during these years more than ten thousand Negroes have been killed in cold blood, without the formality of judicial trial and legal execution. And yet, as evidence of the absolute impunity with which the white man dares to kill a Negro, the same record shows that during all these years, and for all these murders only three white men have been tried, convicted, and executed. As no white man has been lynched for the murder of colored people, these three executions are the only instances of the death penalty being visited upon white men for murdering Negroes.

Naturally enough the commission of these crimes began to tell upon the public conscience, and the Southern white man, as a tribute to the nineteenth century civilization, was in a manner compelled to give excuses for his barbarism. His excuses have adapted themselves to the emergency, and are aptly outlined by that greatest of all Negroes, Frederick Douglass, in an article of recent date, in which he shows that there have been three distinct areas of Southern barbarism, to account for which three distinct excuses have been made.

The first excuse given to the civilized world for the murder of unoffending Negroes was the necessity of the white man to repress and stamp out alleged "race riots." For years immediately succeeding the war there was an appalling slaughter of colored people, and the wires usually conveyed to northern people and the world the intelligence, first, that an insurrection was being planned by Negroes, which, a few hours later, would prove to have been vigorously resisted by white men, and controlled with a resulting loss of several killed and wounded. It was always a remarkable feature in these insurrections and riots that only Negroes were killed during the rioting, and that all the white men escaped unharmed.

From 1865 to 1872, hundreds of colored men and women were mercilessly murdered and the almost invariable reason assigned was that they met their death by being alleged participants in an insurrection or riot. But this story at last wore itself out. No insurrection ever materialized; no Negro rioter was ever apprehended and proven guilty, and no dynamite ever recorded the black man's protest against oppression and wrong. It was too much to ask thoughtful people to believe this transparent story, and the southern white people at last made up their minds that some other excuse must be had.

Then came the second excuse, which had its birth during the turbulent times of reconstruction. By an amendment to the Constitution the Negro was given the right of franchise, and, theoretically at least, his ballot became his invaluable emblem of citizenship. In a government "of the people, for the people, and by the people," the Negro's vote became an important factor in all matters of state and national politics. But this did not last long. The southern white man would not consider that the Negro had any right which a white man was bound to respect, and the idea of a republican form of government in the southern states grew into general contempt. It was maintained that "This is a white man's government," and regardless of numbers the white man should rule. "No Negro domination" became the new legend on the sanguinary banner of the sunny South, and under it rode the Ku Klux Klan, the Regulators, and the lawless mobs, which for any cause chose to murder one man or a dozen as suited their purpose best. It was a long, gory campaign; the blood chills and the heart almost loses faith in Christianity when one thinks of Yazoo, Hamburg, Edgefield, Copiah, and the countless massacres of defenseless Negroes, whose only crime was the attempt to exercise their right to vote.

But it was bootless strife for colored people. The government which had made the Negro a citizen found itself unable to protect him. It gave him the right to vote, but denied him the protection which should have maintained that right. Scourged from his home; hunted through the swamps; hung by midnight raiders, and openly murdered in the light of day, the Negro clung to his right of franchise with a heroism which would have wrung admiration from the hearts of savages. He believed that in that small white ballot there was a subtle something which stood for manhood as well as citizenship, and thousands of brave black men went to their graves, exemplifying the one by dying for the other.

The white man's victory soon became complete by fraud, violence, intimidation and murder. The franchise vouchsafed to the Negro grew to be a "barren ideality," and regardless of numbers, the colored people found themselves voiceless in the councils of those whose duty it was to rule. With no longer the fear of "Negro Domination" before their eyes, the white man's second excuse became valueless. With the Southern governments all subverted and the Negro actually eliminated from all participation in state and national elections, there could be no longer an excuse for killing Negroes to prevent "Negro Domination."

Brutality still continued; Negroes were whipped, scourged, exiled, shot and hung whenever and wherever it pleased the white man so to treat them, and as the civilized world with increasing persistency held the white people of the South to account for its outlawry, the murderers invented the third excuse—that Negroes had to be killed to avenge their assaults upon women. There could be framed no possible excuse more harmful to the Negro and more unanswerable if true in its sufficiency for the white man.

Humanity abhors the assailant of womanhood, and this charge upon the Negro at once placed him beyond the pale of human sympathy. With such unanimity, earnestness, and apparent candor was this charge made and reiterated that the world has accepted the story that the Negro is a monster which the Southern white man has painted him. And today, the Christian world feels, that while lynching is a crime, and lawlessness and anarchy the certain precursors of a nation's fall, it cannot by word or deed, extend sympathy or help to a race of outlaws, who might mistake their plea for justice and deem it an excuse for their continued wrongs.

The Negro has suffered much and is willing to suffer more. He recognizes that the wrongs of two centuries can not be righted in a day, and he tries to bear his burden with patience for to-day and be hopeful for to-morrow. But there comes a time when the veriest worm will turn, and the Negro feels to-day that after all the work he has done, all the sacrifices he has made, and all the suffering he has endured, if he did not, now, defend his name and manhood from this vile accusation, he would be unworthy even of the contempt of mankind. It is to this charge he now feels he must make answer.

If the Southern people in defense of their lawlessness, would tell the truth and admit that colored men and women are lynched for almost any offense, from murder to a misdemeanor, there would not now be the necessity for this defense. But when they intentionally, maliciously and constantly belie the record and bolster up these falsehoods by the words of legislators, preachers, governors and bishops, then the Negro must give to the world his side of the awful story.

A word as to the charge itself. In considering the third reason assigned by the Southern white people for the butchery of blacks, the question must be asked, what the white man means when he charges the black man with rape. Does he mean the crime which the statutes of the civilized states describe as such? Not by any means. With the Southern white man, any mésalliance existing between a white woman and a black man is a sufficient foundation for the charge of rape. The Southern white man says that it is impossible for a voluntary alliance to exist between a white woman and a colored man, and therefore, the fact of an alliance is a proof of force. In numerous instances where colored men have been lynched on the charge of rape, it was positively known at the time of lynching, and indisputably proven after the victim's death, that the relationship sustained between the man and woman was voluntary and clandestine, and that in no court of law could even the charge of assault have been successfully maintained.

It was for the assertion of this fact, in the defense of her own race, that the writer hereof became an exile; her property destroyed and her return to her home forbidden under penalty of death, for writing the following editorial which was printed in her paper, the Free Speech, in Memphis, Tenn., May 21, 1892:

"Eight Negroes lynched since last issue of the 'Free Speech' one at Little Rock, Ark., last Saturday morning where the citizens broke (?) into the penitentiary and got their man; three near Anniston, Ala., one near New Orleans; and three at Clarksville, Ga., the last three for killing a white man, and five on the same old racket—the new alarm about raping white women. The same programme of hanging, then shooting bullets into the lifeless bodies was carried out to the letter. Nobody in this section of the country believes the old threadbare lie that Negro men rape white women. If Southern white men are not careful, they will over-reach themselves and public sentiment will have a reaction; a conclusion will then be reached which will be very damaging to the moral reputation of their women."

But threats cannot suppress the truth, and while the Negro suffers the soul deformity, resultant from two and a half centuries of slavery, he is no more guilty of this vilest of all vile charges than the white man who would blacken his name.

During all the years of slavery, no such charge was ever made, not even during the dark days of the rebellion, when the white man, following the fortunes of war went to do battle for the maintenance of slavery. While the master was away fighting to forge the fetters upon the slave, he left his wife and children with no protectors save the Negroes themselves. And yet during those years of trust and peril, no Negro proved recreant to his trust and no white man returned to a home that had been dispoiled.

Likewise during the period of alleged "insurrection," and alarming "race riots," it never occurred to the white man, that his wife and children were in danger of assault. Nor in the Reconstruction era, when the hue and cry was against "Negro Domination," was there ever a thought that the domination would ever contaminate a fireside or strike to death the virtue of womanhood. It must appear strange indeed, to every thoughtful and candid man, that more than a quarter of a century elapsed before the Negro began to show signs of such infamous degeneration.

In his remarkable apology for lynching, Bishop Haygood, of Georgia, says: "No race, not the most savage, tolerates the rape of woman, but it may be said without reflection upon any other people that the Southern people are now and always have been most sensitive concerning the honor of their women—their mothers, wives, sisters and daughters." It is not the purpose of this defense to say one word against the white women of the South. Such need not be said, but it is their misfortune that the chivalrous white men of that section, in order to escape the deserved execration of the civilized world, should shield themselves by their cowardly and infamously false excuse, and call into question that very honor about which their distinguished priestly apologist claims they are most sensitive. To justify their own barbarism they assume a chivalry which they do not possess. True chivalry respects all womanhood, and no one who reads the record, as it is written in the faces of the million mulattoes in the South, will for a minute conceive that the southern white man had a very chivalrous regard for the honor due the women of his own race or respect for the womanhood which circumstances placed in his power. That chivalry which is "most sensitive concerning the honor of women" can hope for but little respect from the civilized world, when it confines itself entirely to the women who happen to be white. Virtue knows no color line, and the chivalry which depends upon complexion of skin and texture of hair can command no honest respect.

When emancipation came to the Negroes, there arose in the northern part of the United States an almost divine sentiment among the noblest, purest and best white women of the North, who felt called to a mission to educate and Christianize the millions of southern ex-slaves. From every nook and corner of the North, brave young white women answered that call and left their cultured homes, their happy associations and their lives of ease, and with heroic determination went to the South to carry light and truth to the benighted blacks. It was a heroism no less than that which calls for volunteers for India, Africa, and the Isles of the sea. To educate their unfortunate charges; to teach them the Christian virtues and to inspire in them the moral sentiments manifest in their own lives, these young women braved dangers whose record reads more like fiction than fact. They became social outlaws in the South. The peculiar sensitiveness of the southern white men for women, never shed its protecting influence about them. No friendly word from their own race cheered them in their work; no hospitable doors gave them the companionship like that from which they had come. No chivalrous white man doffed his hat in honor or respect. They were "Nigger teachers"—unpardonable offenders in the social ethics of the South, and were insulted, persecuted and ostracized, not by Negroes, but by the white manhood which boasts of its chivalry toward women.

And yet these northern women worked on, year after year, unselfishly, with a heroism which amounted almost to martyrdom. Threading their way through dense forests, working in schoolhouse, in the cabin and in the church, thrown at all times and in all places among the unfortunate and lowly Negroes, whom they had come to find and to serve, these northern women, thousands and thousands of them, have spent more than a quarter of a century in giving to the colored people their splendid lessons for home and heart and soul. Without protection, save that which innocence gives to every good woman, they went about their work, fearing no assault and suffering none. Their chivalrous protectors were hundreds of miles away in their northern homes, and yet they never feared any "great dark faced mobs," they dared night or day to "go beyond their own roof trees." They never complained of assaults, and no mob was ever called into existence to avenge crimes against them. Before the world adjudges the Negro a moral monster, a vicious assailant of womanhood and a menace to the sacred precincts of home, the colored people ask the consideration of the silent record of gratitude, respect, protection, and devotion of the millions of the race in the South, to the thousands of northern white women who have served as teachers and missionaries since the war.

The Negro may not have known what chivalry was, but he knew enough to preserve inviolate the womanhood of the South which was entrusted to his hands during the war. The finer sensibilities of his soul may have been crushed out by years of slavery, but his heart was full of gratitude to the white women of the North, who blessed his home and inspired his soul in all these years of freedom. Faithful to his trust in both of these instances, he should now have the impartial ear of the civilized world, when he dares to speak for himself as against the infamy wherewith he stands charged.

It is his regret, that, in his own defense, he must disclose to the world that degree of dehumanizing brutality which fixes upon America the blot of a national crime. Whatever faults and failings other nations may have in their dealings with their own subjects or with other people, no other civilized nation stands condemned before the world with a series of crimes so peculiarly national. It becomes a painful duty of the Negro to reproduce a record which shows that a large portion of the American people avow anarchy, condone murder and defy the contempt of civilization.

These pages are written in no spirit of vindictiveness, for all who give the subject consideration must concede that far too serious is the condition of that civilized government in which the spirit of unrestrained outlawry constantly increases in violence, and casts its blight over a continually growing area of territory. We plead not for the colored people alone, but for all victims of the terrible injustice which puts men and women to death without form of law. During the year 1894, there were 132 persons executed in the United States by due form of law, while in the same year, 197 persons were put to death by mobs who gave the victims no opportunity to make a lawful defense. No comment need be made upon a condition of public sentiment responsible for such alarming results.

The purpose of the pages which follow shall be to give the record which has been made, not by colored men, but that which is the result of compilations made by white men, of reports sent over the civilized world by white men in the South. Out of their own mouths shall the murderers be condemned. For a number of years the Chicago Tribune, admittedly one of the leading journals of America, has made a specialty of the compilation of statistics touching upon lynching. The data compiled by that journal and published to the world January 1st, 1894, up to the present time has not been disputed. In order to be safe from the charge of exaggeration, the incidents hereinafter reported have been confined to those vouched for by the Tribune.

RECORD FOR THE YEAR 1892

While it is intended that the record here presented shall include specially the lynchings of 1893, it will not be amiss to give the record for the year preceding. The facts contended for will always appear manifest—that not one-third of the victims lynched were charged with rape, and further that the charges made embraced a range of offenses from murders to misdemeanors.

In 1892 there were 241 persons lynched. The entire number is divided among the following states:

Alabama 22; Arkansas, 25; California, 3; Florida, 11; Georgia, 17; Idaho, 8; Illinois, 1; Kansas, 3; Kentucky, 9; Louisiana, 29; Maryland, 1; Mississippi, 16; Missouri, 6; Montana, 4; New York, 1; North Carolina, 5; North Dakota, 1; Ohio, 3; South Carolina, 5; Tennessee, 28; Texas, 15; Virginia, 7; West Virginia, 5; Wyoming, 9; Arizona Territory, 3; Oklahoma, 2.

Of this number 160 were of Negro descent. Four of them were lynched in New York, Ohio and Kansas; the remainder were murdered in the South. Five of this number were females. The charges for which they were lynched cover a wide range. They are as follows:

Rape, 46; murder, 58; rioting, 3; race prejudice, 6; no cause given, 4; incendiarism, 6; robbery, 6; assault and battery, 1; attempted rape, 11; suspected robbery, 4; larceny, 1; self defense, 1; insulting women, 2; desperadoes, 6; fraud, 1; attempted murder, 2; no offense stated, boy and girl, 2.

In the case of the boy and girl above referred to, their father, named Hastings, was accused of the murder of a white man; his fourteen-year-old daughter and sixteen-year-old son were hanged and their bodies filled with bullets, then the father was also lynched. This was in November, 1892, at Jonesville, Louisiana.

LYNCHED FOR ANYTHING OR NOTHING

In nearly all communities wife beating is punishable with a fine, and in no community is it made a felony. Dave Jackson, of Abita, La., was a colored man who had beaten his wife. He had not killed her, nor seriously wounded her, but as Louisiana lynchers had not filled out their quota of crimes, his case was deemed of sufficient importance to apply the method of that barbarous people. He was in the custody of the officials, but the mob went to the jail and took him out in front of the prison and hanged him by the neck until he was dead. This was in November, 1893.

Details are very meagre of a lynching which occurred near Knox Point, La., on the 24th of October, 1893. Upon one point, however, there was no uncertainty, and that is, that the persons lynched were Negroes. It was claimed that they had been stealing hogs, but even this claim had not been subjected to the investigation of a court. That matter was not considered necessary. A few of the neighbors who had lost hogs suspected these men were responsible for their loss, and made up their minds to furnish an example for others to be warned by. The two men were secured by a mob and hanged.

One of the most notable instances of lynching for the year 1893, occurred about the 20th of September. It was notable for the fact that the mayor of the city exerted every available power to protect the victim of the lynching from the mob. In his splendid endeavor to uphold the law, the mayor called out the troops, and the result was a deadly fight between the militia and mob, nine of the mob being killed.

The trouble occurred at Roanoke, Va. It is frequently claimed that lynchings occur only in sparsely settled districts, and, in fact, it is a favorite plea of governors and reverend apologists to couple two arrant false-hoods, stating that lynchings occur only because of assaults upon white women, and that these assaults occur and the lynchings follow in thinly inhabited districts where the power of the law is entirely inadequate to meet the emergency. This Roanoke case is a double refutation, for it not only disproves the alleged charge that the Negro assaulted a white woman, as was telegraphed all over the country at the time, but it also shows conclusively that even in one of the largest cities of the old state of Virginia, one of the original thirteen colonies, which prides itself of being the mother of presidents, it was possible for a lynching to occur in broad daylight under circumstances of revolting savagery.

When the news first came from Roanoke of the contemplated lynching, it was stated that a big burly Negro had assaulted a white woman, that he had been apprehended and that the citizens were determined to summarily dispose of his case. Mayor Trout was a man who believed in maintaining the majesty of the law, and who at once gave notice that no lynching would be permitted in Roanoke, and that the Negro, whose name was Smith, being in the custody of the law, should be dealt with according to law; but the mob did not pay any attention to the brave words of the mayor. It evidently thought that it was only another case of swagger, such as frequently characterizes lynching episodes. Mayor Trout, finding immense crowds gathering about the city, and fearing an attempt to lynch Smith, called out the militia and stationed them at the jail.

It was known that the woman refused to accuse Smith of assaulting her, and that his offense consisted in quarreling with her about the change of money in a transaction in which he bought something from her market booth. Both parties lost their temper, and the result was a row from which Smith had to make his escape. At once the old cry was sounded that the woman had been assaulted, and in a few hours all the town was wild with people thirsting for the assailant's blood. The further incidents of that day may well be told by a dispatch from Roanoke under the date of the 21st of September and published in the Chicago Record. It says:

"It is claimed by members of the military company that they frequently warned the mob to keep away from the jail, under penalty of being shot. Capt. Bird told them he was under orders to protect the prisoner whose life the mob so eagerly sought, and come what may he would not allow him to be taken by the mob. To this the crowd replied with hoots and derisive jeers. The rioters appeared to become frenzied at the determined stand taken by the men and Captain Bird, and finally a crowd of excited men made a rush for the side door of the jail. The captain directed his men to drive the would-be lynchers back.

"At this moment the mob opened fire on the soldiers. This appeared for a moment to startle the captain and his men. But it was only for a moment. Then he coolly gave the command: 'Ready! aim! fire!' The company obeyed to the instant, and poured a volley of bullets into that part of the mob which was trying to batter down the side door of the jail.

"The rioters fell back before the fire of the militia, leaving one man writhing in the agonies of death at the doorstep. There was a lull for a moment. Then the word was quickly passed through the throng in front of the jail and down the street that a man was killed. Then there was an awful rush toward the little band of soldiers. Excited men were yelling like demons.

"The fight became general, and ere it was ended nine men were dead and more than forty wounded."

This stubborn stand on behalf of law and order disconcerted the crowd and it fell back in disorder. It did not long remain inactive but assembled again for a second assault. Having only a small band of militia, and knowing they would be absolutely at the mercy of the thousands who were gathering to wreak vengeance upon them, the mayor ordered them to disperse and go to their homes, and he himself, having been wounded, was quietly conveyed out of the city.

The next day the mob grew in numbers and its rage increased in its intensity. There was no longer any doubt that Smith, innocent as he was of any crime, would be killed, for with the mayor out of the city and the governor of the state using no effort to control the mob, it was only a question of a few hours when the assault would be repeated and its victim put to death. All this happened as per programme. The description of that morning's carnival appeared in the paper above quoted and reads as follows:

"A squad of twenty men took the Negro Smith from three policemen just before five o'clock this morning and hanged him to a hickory limb on Ninth Avenue, in the residence section of the city. They riddled his body with bullets and put a placard on it saying: 'This is Mayor Trout's friend.' A coroner's jury of Bismel was summoned and viewed the body and rendered a verdict of death at the hands of unknown men. Thousands of persons visited the scene of the lynching between daylight and eight o'clock when the body was cut down. After the jury had completed its work the body was placed in the hands of officers, who were unable to keep back the mob. Three hundred men tried to drag the body through the streets of the town, but the Rev. Dr. Campbell of the First Presbyterian church and Capt. R. B. Moorman, with pleas and by force prevented them.

"Capt. Moorman hired a wagon and the body was put in it. It was then conveyed to the bank of the Roanoke, about two miles from the scene of the lynching. Here the body was dragged from the wagon by ropes for about 200 yards and burned. Piles of dry brushwood were brought, and the body was placed upon it, and more brushwood piled on the body, leaving only the head bare. The whole pile was then saturated with coal oil and a match was applied. The body was consumed within an hour. The cremation was witnessed by several thousand people. At one time the mob threatened to burn the Negro in Mayor Trout's yard."

Thus did the people of Roanoke, Va., add this measure of proof to maintain our contention that it is only necessary to charge a Negro with a crime in order to secure his certain death. It is well known in the city before he was killed that he had not assaulted the woman with whom he had had the trouble, but he dared to have an altercation with a white woman, and he must pay the penalty. For an offense which would not in any civilized community have brought upon him a punishment greater than a fine of a few dollars, this unfortunate Negro was hung, shot and burned.

6. Amusements

If blacks in America were treated with increasing hostility by many Americans in the eighties and nineties, immigrant groups aroused more complex reactions. Sentiment for immigration restriction waxed and waned along with larger social tensions, but a number of sympathetic journalists and litterateurs had begun to sketch the undeniable vitality and exoticism of ghetto life with sensitivity and affection. Jacob Riis, Hutchins Hapgood, and John Corbin were among those exploring the cultural life of these newest Americans. Corbin, who paid particular attention to immigrant theater, was born in Chicago in 1870 and taught English at Harvard before turning to professional criticism. Becoming dramatic critic for *Harper's Weekly* in 1899, Corbin also wrote for several New York newspapers, and took an active role in the management of the New Theatre in New York.

Immigrants also contributed to the ranks of vaudeville actors, but vaudeville audiences, housed in splendid new palaces built for them by magnates like B. F. Keith, were dominated by native Americans. The rapidly stereotyped variety of the vaudeville circuits, which Royle* described in *Scribner's*, served symbolic as well as recreational purposes for these urban audiences. The demand for novelty was continual but, as Royle discovered, the keenest pleasure was taken in formulas and repetitions which avoided the need for sustained analysis. William Glackens, who illustrated Royle's article, would later become famous as a member of the Ash Can School, one of the artists who revolted against the traditionalism of the National Academy of Design, and became a painter of urban, especially theatrical, life.

*Edwin Milton Royle, "The Vaudeville Theatre," *Scribner's Magazine*, Vol. XXVI (October, 1899), pp. 485–495.

How the Other Half Laughs

JOHN CORBIN

The East Side is scarcely the place in which one would look to find much
heed paid to the shows and the gayeties of life. We have heard of the
terrors of the tenements, and of sweat-shops where workman and sweater
alike risk body and soul for a few pieces of silver, whole families sewing
day and night amid squalor and disease; but the reports of organized
charity have neglected to remind us that the people who support the
theatres of the Bowery get as much fun of their sort out of life as most
of us. You may pity the people of the East Side, if you must, ten hours a
day, but when the arc-lights gleam beneath the tracks of the elevated, if
you are honest you will envy them.

To any one who cares for the stage and for the art of the player in
America, the theatres of the lower Bowery are of special interest. Once
the haunt of Mose, the Bowery boy, and Lise, his "steady," they are now
the homes of foreign actors, who will give you a good time in almost any
language. And whereas our plays in English are apt to be either imported
or stupid, and are often both, many of these foreign plays are written in
New York, and—sure sign of a genuine artistic impulse— they treat the
life and the history of the people who swarm to see them. They are crude
and often absurd enough, but when the curtain rings down, a candid
observer will admit that the artistic spirit is more vital and spontaneous
in them than in the plays of the most prosperous uptown theatres.

The Americans who are familiar with the Teatro Italiano might almost
be counted on one's fingers. The theatre is closed now, and the company
is disbanded; but for those who knew it, it has a curious and very intimate
interest that still keeps its memory warm. This was due in the first place,
I think, to the Italians we met. They were bootblacks, and banana-venders,
East-Side barbers, and ex-members of Colonel Waring's Street-cleaning
Brigade. In some theatres the people you sit next are reserved, and conscious of distinctions, but these men were more truly in sympathy with
life. They would speak to you on the slightest pretext, or on none, and

John Corbin, "How the Other Half Laughs," *Harper's New Monthly Magazine*, Vol. LXCVIII (December, 1898), pp. 30–48.

would relate all that was happening on the stage, which was useful of them, for the plays were for the most part in popular dialect. The only visitor I ever knew to be neglected was a lady who carried a bottle of smelling-salts. The reproach of this was scarcely obvious, but it was not as the Romans do. In the end we came to think very well of the Italian plays and actors; and if we thought unduly well of them it must have been because, in some unconscious fashion, our neighbors imparted a measure of the grace and ease with which they succeeded in having a good time.

They were for the most part men. If this fact had any special significance I was never quite sure what it was; yet it is certain that the arts in their more primitive stages have always been masculine, and one can find fair warrant for saying that when women have come in for a share, they have lost primal force. It is also true, no doubt, that in Italian communities women are apt to be mothers at an early age: babies are sad impediments to many kinds of gayeties and shows. Yet there was always a sprinkling of women, and no audience I ever saw was without a baby or two. They were good babies, and never made the least disturbance. While they were awake, they looked at the lights and the brilliant people on the stage with those marvelling eyes we would all give so much to have back again; and when the tired little head toppled over, as it soon did, its mite of an owner was passed from one to another of a party, so that no one was very much put out. If a baby grew peevish, it was sure to be for hunger, and the simplest thing in the world was to nurse it quiet again. There are so many more troublesome things in the world than babies, even when you have the full Italian complement. Or if you don't quite feel so, it is still the part of philosophy to recognize that life could not be without them.

Between the acts trays of penny candies were passed around, the brilliant colors of which were alone worth the price, and highly charged soft drinks, equal in glamour, which even the women drank out of the bottles. They were not half bad—that is, if one was well resolved not to strain at a microbe in swallowing the camel. The orchestra was scarcely less a feature than the players. In the American theatres on the Bowery the concord of sweet sounds is to be explained only on the assumption that the conscientious band plays the fly-specks as well as the notes. Even if they did not do this, they would still be jeered at. But the Italian audiences hung on every bar, whether it was *Faust* or a patriotic air; and when the tunes one has a right to were over, they implored for more. "Let's have another, now! Come on, we'll give you a hand, all right." And they held forth the bribe of a pair of eager palms.

When the curtain was up, they gave way to the full gamut of human emotions. In the American theatres of the East Side the audiences shout and whistle their appreciation; but a handful of Italians can give them cards and spades in the matter of mere noise; and it has, besides, infinite shadings of expression. If one was pleased, he laughed softly; and if the actors stumbled over their lines, or over the crude entrances and exits of the scenery, he laughed softly too, but with what a difference! When it came to really stirring passages, everybody made a row, and then on the instant everybody hissed himself quiet again, even though this took several seconds, while the actors complacently waited.

As the plot developed, the audience discussed it in brief sentences. "The play is *Othello,* the Venice nigger," one man explained to us. For though scholars may differ as to whether Shakespeare meant the Moor for a white or a blackamoor, no doubt was permitted in the Teatro Italiano. Iago was a prime favorite. The horror with which his villainy was resented disturbed my conventional ideas of Italian wickedness. "If that nigger knew what man-a that is, he would-a not trust heem," said one worthy, with a grave shake of the head. His companion replied, "Ain't he a *son-a-gun-a!*" and again, with with increasing horror, "*Ain't* he son-a-gun-a!" I am not saying that this gentleness of instinct always went the full length of our moral code; even in the horror at Iago there was a keen spice of delight. A striking example of Latin morals occurred in a play written by a member of the Mulberry Street colony, *O' Tuocco,* which took its name from the game the Romans call *mora,* that one sees Italian bootblacks playing with their fingers. The husband here quarrels with his wife because she interferes with his gambling and carousing; and when he finds that while he was in prison for his misdeeds she has proved unfaithful, he stabs her in the back. "That's the way," he cries; "when a woman betrays you, stab her. And I've stabbed her." The curtain rang down amid loud and unqualified applause. A flash of this kind now and again is suggestive. The instinctive strength and delicacy of Italian affections may be more nearly allied to the animal than a sympathetic observer suspects.

The scenery was old-fashioned and tattered, and not too varied or appropriate. The drama of *O' Tuocco* began in a backwoods log house, with bear-skins stretched on walls that trembled to shouts of *cinque.* It was doubtless the derelict of some long-forgotten Bowery melodrama of American frontier life, and had trembled in ages past to the shouts of quarrelsome cowboys and to the rifles of whooping Indians. The second act of this play took place before a Grecian portico that might have stood on the Acropolis; and the husband stabbed his wife in an East Side parlor, above which downy clouds floated in blue ether. In *Othello,* while Desdemona and Emilia were awaiting their cues, they could plainly be seen through a hole in the castle wall seated on soap boxes and gossiping companionably. In the bed scene we noticed that Desdemona's gown was inconveniently long in front; but until as she was going up stage to her couch her heels and ankles showed, we did not see that she had got it on wrong side before. When Brabantio was mounting to his window to answer Iago's summons, the whole wall quaked with his misguided struggles; and we quaked too, for we had heard of a Brabantio who missed the shutters and stuck his head out of the chimney.

Our main joy was the prompter's box in the front middle. The bill was changed every day, according to the Continental custom, and there were sometimes two and even three plays in an evening; so that, as happened in similar circumstances on the Elizabethan stage, the prompter was commander-in-chief. His long brown finger could often be seen indicating where the actors were to stand, and whose cue it was to speak; and throughout the evening his tired and raucous voice could be heard, eagerly galloping half a line ahead of the actors. Iago managed his lines with great astuteness. In his long argument with Roderigo, when he wanted the word he would put his palm to his ear, and with one eye devouring his victim and the other on the prompter, he would whisper, "*Ascolto!*"—(I am listening!).

Notwithstanding all this—and one very soon gets used to it and accepts it like any other stage convention—the acting had surprising quality. Its virtue was simplicity and unconsciousness, traits which, in whatever surroundings, are allied to the best in art. In *O' Tuocco* the gamblers in the log-hut café were simply gamblers in a café. Whether they were supers and drank their wine in silence, or took the leading parts and quarrelled vociferously over who should pay for it, the conviction of their acting was so great that one forgot the logs and the bear-skins.

The comedian of the troupe had the genius of his quality: he could not move a foot or a shoulder without getting a laugh, and his occasional speeches were greeted with roars. One of his favorite devices was to spit on the shoes of the people he was talking with, which, as he did not speak a word of our language, could scarcely have been an Americanism.

Of the leading man it is hard to give a just idea. He owed much beyond question to the Italian convention of acting, which is said by those who know to be on the whole the best in Europe. In *Othello*, which is the most successful classic part I saw him in, he doubtless had profited by the example of the elder Salvini. And the very limitations of his stage and his support may have emphasized by contrast his passages of real power. Yet the fact remains that he played throughout with intelligence and dignity. In the scenes in the Venetian council-chamber his presence was fine, and his manner full of repose; his delivery quiet and impressive. His voice is rich and flexible and strong, and he does not squander it. It rose to whatever volume or pitch the lines required. In the scenes where Othello's love and jealousy are struggling for the mastery, the effect was ultimate. One could not fail to feel that a dramatic illusion has no necessary relation to the property-man and the stage-manager—that a touch of vital art transcends most limitations.

The only trace of what would generally be thought overacting was in the death-scene. The first time I saw the play, Othello stabbed himself in the throat many yards from Desdemona's couch, and crawled with grewsome gurglings to throw himself beside her. The second time, some of this horror was abated, but in strangling Desdemona he leaped upon her with both knees. Each of these passages the audience greeted with laughter that seemed to us hysterical. I am inclined to think that this fact has a special significance. In primitive expression there is an almost unfailing tendency to run to grotesque extremes. The sculptures of the cathedrals attest this, as also many a passage of preposterous comedy in our early religious drama. It almost seems that there was a convention of grotesque expression that persisted for centuries, and was used to provoke laughter even by Shakespeare, many of whose most highly organized characters—Caliban, the Witches in *Macbeth*, Shylock, Edgar, even Lear and Hamlet—have traces of the old delight in the grotesque. What we thought worst in the acting of our Bowery Othello may not have been the farthest removed from the Elizabethan spirit. And the audience was an audience to be trusted—they made few mistakes in appreciation. At the tragic climaxes they shouted with delight, and at the end of each act yelled at the top of their lungs. When the stage closed on the sad last scene, it was plain that there were heavy hearts among them, and minds turned upon the soberest realities of life.

The drop was scarcely down, however, when, as was the custom in Elizabethan theatres, and as one might have expected in a theatre where Desdemona's death caused laughter, the comedian—the sometime Duke of Venice—bounded out in a song-and-dance costume, and bellowed forth a Neapolitan ditty. Then, with an equally violent mingling of moods, Cassio came out in black street clothes, somewhat threadbare and shiny, if the truth be told, and sang us a sentimental song while we were putting on our coats. Alas, for our uptown manners! The simple and kindly Italians did not turn from the delights of the stage until the last mournful cadence was ended.

In seeking further acquaintance with the company I was presented to Iago. I own I had a certain timidity as regards so very subtle and wicked a man; but he seemed as much in awe of me as I was of him, a circumstance which I learned later to attribute to the fact that I was introduced as a reporter. Those cunning, evil eyes of his, that could embrace both Roderigo and the prompter, sank from mine, and though he seemed pleased to meet me, he was no less eager to give way modestly to Othello. I could not convince him that his photograph was worthy of being given to the world.

When I left the theatre I was dogged by a swarthy young Italian who carried one hand suspiciously in his breast pocket. As I was new to the Bowery, and had the conventional fear of its ways, I resolved not to be done away with without a struggle. What he drew on me was a tintype of himself as Romeo. He said he could play a very good Romeo, if he was only given a chance, and was going to make a great deal of fame and money. Wouldn't I take his photograph? It was owing to my stupidity, no doubt, that I was surprised to find the same varieties of character, the same degrees of hope and ambition, I had found in the theatres I was used to.

Othello and Desdemona were married. When we went to the little tenement where they lived, Desdemona was on her knees scrubbing the floor in a crimson waist, and swarms of children were romping unheeded about her. One of the youngest of these was lighting scraps of paper in the range and tossing them in the air with delight! The mother merely motioned to an older child to stamp them out, and went on peacefully with what she was doing. The surest way not to be troubled with household cares is not to let them trouble you. And nature has wise ways of bringing up children when cheerfully left to itself. On our last visit Desdemona was in the parlor bathing her younger child (all except two of the children, I found, belonged to the other families in the tenement), and she was as unconscious and charming as when playing Desdemona. It was all very different from what we might have wished, and it would have been easy to make ourselves unhappy over it; but she seemed so pleased and contented that pity could only have been an impertinence. Her life on the stage was in sad contrast, to be sure, to this life at home, for the real Desdemona—poor lady—never lived to have a parlor, to say nothing of a baby to bathe in it.

Othello was twenty-eight years old—much older than his wife. At the age of nineteen, I found, he was already playing leading parts in Naples and Rome. When the time came for him to serve his four years in the Italian Army, he had either to leave Italy or abandon all he had achieved in his art. He went to Paris, where he acted two years. "It was a mistake," he says, "and now I repent myself that I did it." Seven years ago he came to America. A year or two ago he had an engagement to play with Duse in Paris and in Germany, but before he crossed the ocean she changed her plans and returned to Italy, whither he could not follow her. His repertory is large, and includes both melodrama and tragedy. His best play he considers to be Giacometti's *Morte Civile*. He has played Othello only a dozen to a score of times. He has lately given his first performance of *Hamlet*.

I expected soon to see a second performance, which was announced; but happening one day to pass the Italian theatre, a glare of pink fleshings smote my eyes. It was from an array of billboards announcing that an athletic and vaudeville troupe were holding forth inside. The theatre was no longer the Teatro Italiano; it was the Columbia Opera-House, and like any other cheap American show-place, only possibly worse. I looked up the manager. The Italian theatre, he said, was no good. He was going to run an American theatre. That was the beginning of the end. For some weeks the theatre changed regularly from Italian to American; but its luck did not change. Toward the end of the season somebody set it on fire, after which the Italians acted at rare intervals and in various places.

An obvious reason for the failure of the Italian theatre lies in the fact that the Italians in America are largely from rural districts, and even if they were educated to the theatre are too parsimonious for its pleasures. They are here to work and to save; and when they have a hundred dollars or two, they go home to Italy and buy a little piece of farmland that stands in their eyes for all prosperity and content. A letter I received from one of the actors of the company is a document in point:

> As all the Colonies, even the Chinese, have their National Theatre, I hoped that ours could also start up with one through my sacrifices but I was soon disillused.
> All my countrymen who live here are such a kind of people who can not judge anything above them. They are almost ignorant and positively different from all the good Italian peoples living in our country. They come here from their mountains without any knowledge of art or bello as we use to say. They land here only in order to accumulate a little money, even through privations and starving, to go then back to their farms and pose as proprietors. I am perfectly convinced now that it is of no use to work for the Italian people of America.

Yet this is not the whole truth; thousands of Italians regard America as home, and by nature they are one of the most pleasure-loving of all our foreign colonies. The trouble is with their assimilative natures. In a few years even the older immigrants are apt to pick up our language, and one by one to abandon their native customs and ways of thought. Even in the theatre they spoke to each other mainly in English. In seeking amusement they fall prey to the flash and glare of our variety bill-posters. The new generation, who lack the traditions of the home country, and sometimes the knowledge of Italy to appreciate its drama, are almost certain to become Americanized in their tastes. An Italian theatre could appeal only to new arrivals and to those of the past generation who have not forgotten their old life and the joy of true acting. The company struggled bravely. The leading man went to Boston, Philadelphia, and other of our cities where the Italians are numerically strong; but the conditions were the same. As a last resort they planned to go to South America, where the Italians are as numerous, and are less influenced by indigenous customs and tastes. While this plan was pending the *Maine* was destroyed, and one afternoon I learned that the playwright who got up most of their new pieces had just begun one on *La Catastrofe della Maine*. A few days later it was given. Though it was said not to be a first-rate play, the theatre, for the only time in my experience, was filled. The display of patriotism was superb. The next night the theatre was empty as ever.

The fate of the Italians is a repetition of what happened a generation ago to the French theatre. For a time it had its own stock company, and a good one, I am told; but little by little it lost ground, and finally disbanded. The assimilative French people now have no plays but American plays, except during the rare visits of Bernhardt, Coquelin, or Mounet-Sully, when they invade the gallery.

The ill fortunes of the Italians seemed so sad to a philanthropist of our party that, though he had grave doubts as to how well they would apply his charity, he made up his mind to help them. He seemed to fear that they would try to keep the wolf from the door with a song and a bunch of flowers. I thought they might too, and secretly hoped they would; but it was not the wolf that was nearest their door. The next time we saw our friend we learned that his eldest child was dead. Diphtheria, the ancient scourge of the tenements, had done its work in two days. "We had five doctors," he said; "three Americans and two Eyetalians." He spoke of a few other details that would not add to anybody's cheerfulness. "I loved that child too much," he concluded. The philanthropist's conscience was satisfied.

A few days later we were stopped in the Bowery by a funeral procession such as we had never seen before. There were six carriages, with six or eight women folk in each. At this kind of show, it seems, the men are apt to be few. The mothers had bare heads and shawls, as peasant women in Italy have; but the children wore hats with flowers on them. One could see at a glance how an Italian becomes an American. The few men relatives walked in front with little switches with which they waved the street children away from their games of pussy-cat. The hearse and casket were white, and a white angel with gold crown and gold feathers in his wings knelt on the roof of it, with hands folded in prayer. There were four horses, before which marched a band of twelve instruments playing an Italian death-march, so gentle and complaining that the philanthropist caught his breath. As they passed, the women on the curb-stone looked after with set faces—the mothers in the Italian colony know such things too well.

The procession went through Roosevelt Street and beneath the elevated trestle in Park Row to Baxter Street. It was blocked by electric cars, and now and then it was joined by trucks loaded with rolls of paper for the war extras of Newspaper Row, or with whatever merchandise. We asked a postman who was dead. "Nobody at all but a little Eyetalian kid," he explained. "The parents all does that if they can scrape up the means." Half an hour later we saw the procession return, playing the same gentle and complaining march. Its tour through the crowded city had been a journey of state—a tribute out of a narrow and sordid life to the hope and the beauty of death. The musicians disbanded at the ferry to Greenwood, and one more East Side show was ended.

If the philanthropist was shocked that death as well as life should be decked out to cheat it of its poverty, he did not say so, though some days later he remarked that for himself he preferred fresh air and open plumbing. Of course, he was right; and we Americans have beaten the world in making life comfortable and in prolonging it. Yet we have no contrivance to make life simple and cheerful, and not even open plumbing can make the death that we all owe beautiful.

The atmosphere of the Yiddish—which is to say the Judisch or Jewish—theatres is in sharp contrast to that of the Italians. A down-trodden people, used through generations to hopeless persecutions, is leaping into individuality and power through the new liberty they have found. Their very bill-boards, compared to the modest placards of the Italians, speak of prosperity; but when I went to photograph their announcement of *Trilby*, I found that they were far from satisfied to have it represent them in the eye of the broader public. "You will misrepresent us," the cashier of the theatre explained. "We have borrowed the poster of the burlesque *Thrilby*, and have written the notice of our play above it. You cannot read it. You will turn us into ridicule." I had to confess that I could not read it, though, like the Irishman, I felt that if I had my fiddle, begorra! I could play it.

The question of ridicule was not so easily set aside. "A reporter came here the other day," the cashier explained, "and wrote this about me. I pay no attention to it." He handed me a carefully folded newspaper and pointed to a passage which told, among other things, how the cashier staid in the box-office all day and wrote stories of life in the Bowery. "He turns us into ridicule," he repeated.

I pointed out that it is a reporter's business to speak of the amusing things he finds, and added that I was interested to know what he had to say about the life of the foreign people in America. "Ah!" he exclaimed, with quick intuition, "I see you will turn me into ridicule! I don't care. By-and-by I will write about you." I accept the challenge; and if I am unable to disguise the fact that I was provincial enough to find keen delight in the strange people and strange sights I met, I stand in danger of swift retribution. If we laugh first, it behooves us to laugh as heartily as we can, for these Yiddish people are hot on our trail in the arts as well as in commerce.

The racial instincts of the audience are as plain as the nose on your face—or on theirs. If you leave your seat between acts, the probability is that you will find a standee in it when you come back. No array of checks will save you. The usher will plead and argue in your behalf, but the standee sits it out in defiance. If you persist until the curtain rises, you speedily realize that you have become a public nuisance. The people will shout "Sit down!" "Get out!" "Put him out!" There is scarcely a murmur of sympathy. If the usurper says a word, it is, "I paid to get in!" or, "Didn't I give my fifty cents?" I seldom went to a Jewish theatre that some such row did not take place. At the afternoon performances the disturbance is continual. The babies who cannot be left at home to sleep are amply in evidence. They are not like the polite Italian babies, who are nursed quiet in an instant. They whine, and squall, and kick. The neighbors say " 'S-s-s-h!" The people in the balcony cry "Shut up!" And from the gallery there are shouts of "Put him out!" until finally, the mother gets up and walks her offspring quiet in the foyer. When she comes back she gets her seat, perhaps. At one matinée the noise was so loud and continual that, though I stood in the flies, I could not hear what the actors were saying, and finally they stopped talking and waited, with the utmost *gemüthlich-keit* for the baby to be put out.

The revelation of Yiddish traits in the plays has the frankness and intimacy of spontaneous artistic expression. The prevailing theme is perhaps the immemorial strife against the golden idols of the Gentiles. In two very popular operas I saw, *Rabbi Shabshi's Daughter* and *Zirele the Rabbi's, or the Beauty of Krakow*, a Yiddish maiden becomes alienated from her people and tastes all the splendor and the power of Christendom. Rabbi Shabshi's daughter is torn from her people during a religious persecution, and becomes an adoptive princess in Bohemia. Zirele is betrayed by a Christian student, afterward a Russian priest, and is sent on the scarlet way of the Babylonian. I own that I was delighted to find that for the Yiddish maiden the primrose way to the everlasting bonfire had so many primroses. It seems as if there is no end of bouquets to be thrown at almost any young Yid who goes out from among her people. But the foretaste of the bonfire was proportionately bitter. Fate haled the wanderers back, humbled and suppliant, to the people and the religion of their childhood, with its sweet and sacred rites, its homeliness and severity. *"Ein Yid bleibt ewig ein Yid!"* exclaims Rabbi Shabshi's daughter at the last, and the sentiment rouses boundless enthusiasm. The fundamental tragedy of this historic race lies here: the mainspring of their life is in a faith that was old when history began, and is still one of the purest and noblest of religions, rich in the mystery of the East; yet the very Oriental luxuriance of their temperament makes them respond to the glamour of the Gentile world about them. Like Mr. Zangwill's child of the Venetian Ghetto, born and bred in the awful simplicity of the synagogue, they awake some day to find themselves in the gayety of the Piazza of Venice and in the splendor of the Cathedral of St. Mark. The Yiddish playwright had a right, perhaps, to make his villain a Christian priest. And the audience was right to hiss him and hoot him. At the end of each act he came out to receive his ovation of groans and jeers, and the audience was not to be placated until he gave a very un-Christian shrug of deprecation, and—or so at least it seemed to me—thrust forward his nose in evidence.

There is no end of plays and operas drawn from Josephus and the Old Testament, plays which bear the same relation to Jewish national life that the Chronicle histories of the Elizabethan stage bore to the life of England. Such plays are often produced on appropriate feast-days, celebrations of which are to be witnessed in this odd corner of New York in precisely the form in vogue since hundreds of years before the Christian era. One of the most popular themes is afforded by the persecutions of the Yiddish peoples in their homes across the sea. There are struggles between labor and capital, with strikes and riots enough; and there are Nihilists who are dynamiters, and suffer for it. But with all this there is a strong infusion of the life of the Bowery. The first time I made inquiries at the theatre I found that the historical opera of *Bar Kochba* was to be given, and that on the following night there was to be "a play by one of the managers' wives, called *Annie the Finisher*." It was "about a girl here in New York what finishes." A *finisher* is the technical name for the sweat-shop woman who "finishes" or puts the last touches on the garments they call "pants," which they make and finish at four or five dollars a week. Annie, I found, was an operative with whom the son of her employer fell in love. There is much in the play about poor Yids and rich Yids, about love and plutocracy. After the usual course of true love the young people are happily married. The play is very popular.

In a melodrama called *The Aristocracy of a Province*, a humble servingman in Bessarabia is bequeathed a fortune of two million dollars by a relative who had become rich in America. His landlord—the provincial aristocrat—finds this out, steals the vital documents, comes to America, impersonates his old servant, and enjoys his stolen millions. The action takes place in New York, where the thief is marrying his son to the daughter of a Broadway merchant, while the true heir lives in poverty as an East Side coal-man. On the one hand is shown the life of the struggling Yiddish people—tenement life, street life, the brutality of the New York police; while on the other is shown the life of a prosperous resident of Fifth Avenue. The leading juvenile is the son of the merchant, and a student in Columbia University. When he makes his first entrance, the friends of the family—that is to say, the chorus girls—welcome him with a vociferous Columbian yell. The usurping villain is utilized also as a comic character. His favorite gesture is to stroke the forks of a long black beard, displaying beneath his chin a diamond solitaire somewhat smaller than an egg. No gesture could have been funnier than the Yiddish audience thought this. His pet vanity was that he could "speken Engleesch." I jotted down some of the flowers of his speech on my programme. "Ich danke dir, dear, dear Mr. Blumenfeld. Tankaiou [thank you]." "Oh, du, my swittest. Oh du, meine lufly goil,"—and other like phrases. When his foolish son makes love to a poor tenement girl instead of to the Fifth Avenue heiress, he storms at him: "Was ist de matter mit you?" "Gunnisht [*gar nicht*]," answers the son, defiantly. "Shut up!" the villanous father retorts; "I break your nuis [nose]." Once, when hungry, he exclaims, rubbing his waistcoat, "Kom on, und let's have a little lunch-room!" On another occasion he says, urbanely: "Ah, there! Was willst du, Mister High-tone Sport?" At all of these essays the audience howl with laughter, for they talk the English of the Bowery fluently, and, in addition to their Yiddish newspapers, read the yellow journals.

An interesting example of the influence of the life about them is in the play of *Trilby*. The plot is from the American play, and many passages are almost identical. The local color and character, however, have suffered as complete a translation into Yiddish terms as the language. Trilby's name easily becomes Tilly. Taffy is Herr Gottlieb, and Little Billee is Herr Werner. Svengali is Herr Hartmann, and the racial distinction of which Du Maurier made so much is perforce ignored. The characters seem all to belong to one family, and Svengali is Little Billee's uncle. Yet the permanence of stage tradition crops out in his nose. Not content with what nature has lavished on him, he built it a story or two higher on the bridge.

I hoped to see all the best Yiddish plays, and asked my friend the cashier to book me and let me know whenever Herr Adler, the leading man at the Windsor Theatre, was to appear, for I was helpless before the Yiddish announcements. He failed me; and when I spoke of my regret, he said he had been so interested in the stories he had been writing that the matter had quite slipped his mind. The explanation was more than adequate, and I make no apologies for the fact that I can speak of some of Herr Adler's best plays only by name. *Kabale und Liebe, Der Schwartze Yid,* and *Die Raüber* are all, I believe, adaptations of classical German plays. *Der Odessa Bettler* is an adaptation of the *Rag-Picker of Paris. Solomon Caus,* or *Cardinal Richelieu,* turns on the theft of Caus's invention of the mechanical use of steam. *The Russian Jew in America* explains itself. I was especially sorry to miss it, because it is said to be full of local color, many of the scenes being presented in English. There is also a Yiddish adaptation of *King Lear,* which, from all I could find out, is most interesting. It is a tragedy in four acts, and, as in *Trilby,* not only the language, but the scenes and characters have been translated into terms of modern Yiddish life. King Lear wears a long Yiddish beard and gown. Herr Adler considers Lear his best part. In the first act, he explains, Lear is a king; in the second, he has given away his throne; in the third, he is an outcast; in the fourth, he dies a beggar and blind. "Every act is worse than the other," he says. "When I give it, there is sobbing and weeping all through the house. It is better than Shakespeare."

Uriel Acosta is founded on the life of Gabriel da Costa, a Portuguese philosopher, whose romantic love-story Mr. Zangwill has told in *Dreamers of the Ghetto.* The heart of the situation is in the strife between the philosopher's loyalty to freedom of thought and action, and the lover's necessity of bowing to rabbinical power. The play is taken from a German classic; the lines are largely classical German; as Herr Adler renders them, they are full of the fire and dignity of intellect; his interpretation is broad and simple, and every effort springs directly from the heart of the dramatic situation. I found that the play had been several times acted during the winter, and always to audiences rapt in enthusiasm. I know of no American theatre where so nobly intellectual a theme would meet with so keen an appreciation.

A play called *Der Wilde Mensch* (The Madman) was as intellectual a bit of drama, and in many ways was more suggestive of the æsthetic medium of the Yiddish theatres. The theme bears a resemblance to the theme of *Hamlet*, which is all the more curious because quite unconscious. The father of a family marries a young woman who deceives him in the face of his children. A daughter is driven into the streets by her bad influence; and a son, a student, remains with the utmost abhorrence. There is a third child, an idiot son, who, despised because of his infirmity, witnesses the step-mother's full guilt. In spite of the incoherence of his reason he has a certain fulness of nature and flashes of intuition that make him instinctively rebel against his step-mother and her accomplices, and strive to bring them to justice. Like Hamlet, fate has given him a task too great for his powers. His mind is incapable of grasping the offence, and when he tries to report it to his elder brother he is tortured by his inability to speak coherently. In its outlines the tragedy has a simplicity and breadth that is Elizabethan; and though it differs widely from *Hamlet* in the circumstances of the sin, as also in the fact that the hero is actually mad, the similarities in the situation are striking. The madman's reverence for his dead mother is as strong as that of Hamlet for buried Denmark. He holds deep and agonized discourse with his student brother, questioning him as to life and death, the past of the soul and its future. Most striking of all, the hero's madness, like Hamlet's, is made the theme for grotesquely comic relief, which the audience gave ample evidence of relishing, and which Mr. Hitchcock and I found it impossible not to laugh at. This treatment of madness is more nearly related to the lost *Hamlet*, presumably by Thomas Kyd, than to Shakespeare's play; but there are passages in the text as it stands to-day—for instance, Hamlet's incoherrent passages with the ghost ("truepenny," "old mole") and with Ophelia ("to a nunnery")—which cannot be rightly read without remembering that such incoherences could not fail to strike an Elizabethan audience as grotesquely amusing. Altogether *De Wilde Mensch*, like the Italian *Othello*, is more nearly related æsthetically to the crude strong youth of the English drama than to modern English or American plays.

Adler's conception of the leading part was at times illuminating. He told me that when studying it he haunted mad-houses and mimicked the inmates; and when he produced it, he had in the physicians and medical students of the Yiddish community to criticise him. As first acted, I was interested to find, he conceived the part as wholly tragic. He found, however, that the audience was disposed to laugh at the madness, and that when they did so they were more appreciative of the tragic scenes. Little by little he has developed passages of genuine comedy.

In our efforts to see more of the people behind the scenes we were aided by an American scene-shifter with whom we scraped acquaintance. He was a son of the ancient Bowery, and though he had lived so long among the Yiddish actors that he had learned their language, he was only the more American. His account of the company was loud, and so broadly satirical that I feared he might give offence. He laughed at my fears, and let me see how he got on with the Yids. Alone and unabetted he assailed the entire chorus with Rabelaisian opprobrium, to all of which they had only the old reply that he could not be of their people if he wanted to. In the end he routed them, every mother's girl of them. It was not nice, but it was very funny, and it gratified my Saxon pride to feel that this derelict of our people had through all these years maintained his racial pride in the face of the immigrating people. It is almost compensation for our lack of the sympathies and the assimilative powers that make up an artistic people.

There were other respects in which these chorus girls were under American influences. They mostly spoke English; and those who have grown up in the country had been to our public schools. They are to be seen at Coney Island in swarms as great as the swarms of their richer kinswomen who resort to the roof gardens of Fifth Avenue hotels. One of them evinced such a mingling of the traits of her native and adopted country-people while Mr. Hitchcock was sketching her that I jotted down a word or two of what she said. She had taken a position square in front, and Mr. Hitchcock moved about so as to get the eyelids, nose, and lips more in profile. "What's the matter with taking all of my face?" she objected with primeval vanity, and was quieted with difficulty. When the sketch was finished she tossed her shoulder in a way worthy of Lise of old, and said, "Come again to-morrow and take the other side." For the life of me I could not say whether her tone held more of the ancient irony of the Bowery or its modern instinct for getting all there is in a transaction.

The leading actors and singers were all from the old country, and some of them had not yet learned English. The story of their lives is, in a general way, the story I heard of Adler's wanderings. His first theatre, in Odessa, was closed by reason of the Russian hatred of the Jews. He opened it again as a German theatre, was discovered, and again put down. As a last resort he engaged a Russian to manage him and secure him against persecution. The shift succeeded, but the Russian laid hands on so large a proportion of the proceeds that the company rebelled, and left the country. After wandering through the Continent, he brought up in the London Ghetto, where he made his longest stand. Six years ago he came to America, and travelled through the West as far as Denver and San Francisco, playing chiefly in Chicago. In New York he began at the modest theatre lately occupied by the Italians, prospered, and took the Windsor. Every year in the early summer he travels about among his people in the cities of the Atlantic States, and even in those of the middle West, so that his reputation is virtually national. It was not unnatural that Adler is recognized as the leading Yiddish actor in America, but, though he may be, I could not make certain that this is the case. There are Yiddish theatres also in Philadelphia, Chicago, and spasmodically in San Francisco, in any one of which, I suppose, much of the same kind of plays and acting are to be found. It is Adler's ambition to come out in an uptown theatre before American audiences. I cannot imagine a more amusing experiment; and it would be interesting to discover whether it would teach us more of Yiddish art or of the limitations of an American audience.

The manager of the Thalia, which is the rival theatre of the Windsor, has written some fourteen plays and operas, among them *The Aristocracy of a Province*. He has translated the leading tragedies of Shakespeare, and gives them at intervals every season. The new plays are written by Gordin, who wrote *Der Wilde Mensch,* by Latainer, and by Horwitz. Much of the music for the operas is adapted from operas well known in New York by the conductors and some of the actors. Both of these Yiddish theatres are in effect stock companies. At the Windsor, where the talent is on the whole greater and more varied, there are, besides Herr Adler, nearly a dozen actors of distinct artistic power; and at least one of the singers, Mrs. Kalisch, has a voice not unworthy of the Metropolitan stage.

The importance of the theatres of the Yiddish colony are best seen in their auditoriums. The Windsor is the equal of most of the theatres of Broadway. The Thalia, which is directly opposite in the Bowery, is one of the very best in the city; the prices of the seats range from a quarter of a dollar to a dollar, and the rental is eighteen thousand dollars a year. To hundreds of thousands of Americans who travel in the East-Side elevated trains perhaps no sight is more familiar than the four cream-colored Roman columns that uphold the entablature on which is written in letters of gold "Thalia Theatre"; but only a score or two of them, I suppose, are aware that the building is the most interesting theatrical monument in America. The first theatre on this site was opened in 1826, when, according to the records of Ireland, "the vast improvements made in the eastern section of the city, . . . and its great increase of population, including many wealthy and fashionable citizens," led to the building of a theatre, in comparison with which, it was hoped, all other theatres "would sink subordinate." The opening of the theatre was revolutionary enough. "The brilliant experiment of lighting the stage with gas, then first attempted, was hailed with the greatest satisfaction." The early history of the theatre is curiously prophetic. The opening address proclaimed the high ambition of the managers.

> At last, as Hope, bright, sandalled Hope, went by,
> She calls on Shakespeare, and her throne is won!
> And *ours* is Shakespeare.

In the following year, however, the dominance of our classic drama was gravely threatened. "After a performance of *Much Ado about Nothing*, a grand *pas seul*—'La Bergère Coquette'—was executed by Madame Francisquy Hutin, her first appearance in America, and the first introduction of the modern French school of dancing on the American stage. The house was crowded, and an anxious look of curiosity and expectation dwelt in every face; but when the graceful *danseuse* came bounding like a startled fawn upon the stage, her light and scanty drapery floating in air, and her symmetrical proportions liberally displayed by the force of a bewildering *pirouette*, the cheeks of the greater portion of the audience were crimsoned with shame, and every lady in the lower tier of boxes immediately left the house. But time works wondrous changes, and though for a while Turkish trowsers were adopted by the lady, they were finally discarded, and the common ballet dresses, indecent though they be, were gradually endured." To-day the Americans who care for the classic English plays and can judge of them are a handful; the disciples of Madame Hutin number hundreds of thousands; but, by a curious trick of fate, the Old Bowery has remained true for the most part to its traditions.

The Germans, who first took the place of the elder American managers, and called the theatre The Thalia, prospered in presenting their national plays, light and serious; and when the elevated road and the gradual shifting of the German population made its situation less desirable, they moved up town to the Irving Place Theatre. Here they continue the traditions of the Thalia, and to-day present a range and variety of interesting performances as great perhaps as those of any theatre in America.

During the holidays the theatre is given over to dramatic fairy-tales, and to operas by Humperdinck and others, founded on the lore of the nursery; for the rest of the season the mainstays of the Irving Place Theatre are the German classic drama, Ibsen, and Sudermann. The actors are frequently the leaders on the Germany stage. In 1897–8, Frau Sorma held the theatre for months.

The Yiddish troup that took the Thalia from the Germans are working along the same general lines. Every spring, after the Passover, which the Yiddish people refer to as "our Easter," light plays are brought out, filled with characteristic songs and dances. For the rest of the year serious drama holds the boards.

Their performances are not yet up to those of the Germans, but for all who are interested in bringing American influence to bear upon our foreign populations, I can imagine no better field of study, nor one more likely to alter some of their fundamental preconceptions with regard to sweat-shop existence. "Life itself," says Mr. Jacob A. Riis, in his epoch-making book, *How the Other Half Lives,* is here "of little value compared with even the meanest bank account. . . . Over and over again I have met with instances of these Polish and Russian Jews deliberately starving themselves to the point of physical exhaustion while working from daylight until eleven at night to save a little money. . . . In no other spot does life wear so bald and materialistic an aspect." Night after night I have seen the two Yiddish theatres swarmed with men, women, and children largely from the sweat-shops. I referred the question to my friend the cashier. "That is how you all misrepresent us!" he exclaimed. "There are many poor Jewish families that spend sometimes three, four, five dollars a week here at this theatre." A brief calculation will show that, compared with their earnings, this represents a patronage of art infinitely beyond that of the families uptown who parade their liberality in supporting the Metropolitan Opera House. In the Yiddish version of *Trilby,* Svengali shows his hardness of heart by scoffing at art and artists, insolently crying: *"Die Kunst ist für Narren. Ich will Geld haben—Millionen Millionen."* It is the simple and sufficient evidence of villainy, as the lack of music in one's soul was to Shakespeare.

The artistic life of the Ghetto is not confined to playwrights and actors, composers, musicians, and singers. There are five Yiddish newspapers, which Yiddish newsboys cry daily through the streets. One paper, *The Dramatic World,* is devoted to the Yiddish theatres. There are novelists whose tales are hawked from tenement to tenement, and sell in great numbers. Of the most popular of the novelists, Schorner, it is related, that in order to meet the demand he has to keep three or four tales under way at once; and to keep all his printers supplied, he goes almost daily from shop to shop, writing only long enough in each to meet the present demand for copy. There are poets, too, one of whom, Morris Rosenfeld by name, is said by those capable of judging to have the native gift for song. In all the artistic output of the Ghetto there is the same correspondence between the life and history of the people and their art that is evident in the theatres; and, by means of it, Russians and Galicians are, as in the theatres, made known to Poles, Austrians, and Prussians. The arts of the Ghetto, as is usually the case when arts spring from the masses, are imbuing their patrons with a sense of the community of their life and interests. In the truest sense of the word, they are national arts.

If you are a philanthropist, you will of course be distressed to find people whose fortunes are so wretched so light of heart. A truly charitable person, I suppose, would advise them to buy soap instead of theatre tickets. But if you are a lover of your kind—which has somehow come to be very different from a philanthropist, and not at all so respectable— you will perhaps wonder whether we have not a thing or two to learn from these pitied foreigners. It is worth questioning, for instance, whether there is not a pretty definite tie between the primitive, the elemental, in life and the beautiful in art. The people that built the cathedrals lived in no grander state than these peoples of the East Side; and the age of Shakespeare had gone some two hundred years and more before Englishmen found out that life is not worth living without the daily bath. Even in the court theatre of the time, it would seem, cleanliness and ventilation were not always to be looked for. "Some sweet odors suddenly coming forth, without any drops falling," says Bacon, in the essay on "Masques and Triumphs," "are in such company, as there is steam and heat, things of great pleasure and refreshment." The "company" were, of course, Elizabeth and her court. The "steam and heat" would doubtless find their modern parallel in a sweat-shop. If one had his choice between carving an angel in the stone of a cathedral portal, or tuning an Elizabethan song, and his morning tub,—but life has solved the problem for us; and, after all, much as this Yiddish community resembles in outward conditions the great artistic generations of our past, it may not be relevant.

It is a fair question, though, whether the artists of the Ghetto, if allowed to develop spontaneously, would produce any really great works of art. Unfortunately it is one that can never be answered. On all sides American life is pressing in on them; in every corner children are coming under the spell of its outward glamour. It is Morris Rosenfeld's badge of fame among his people that he was discovered by a Harvard professor, and has read his poems before the leading literary men of New York. Even the language he uses is affected by the out-lying idiom. Mr. W. D. Howells, who speaks very highly of the poems, tells me that many of the words were plain English. A resident of the Ghetto, Abraham Cahan, has written stories of Yiddish life in New York for American magazines, and has published two successful books. In describing the influence of American life, he told me of a mother who said: "I don't speak English, but I shall soon learn. There" (pointing to her son), "that is my teacher." The children mostly go to the public schools, and, except in their homes, have discarded the Yiddish language. "I like to talk about the old country," a Yiddish mother said to me one evening at the Windsor, "and some day I think I go back; but my children make fun of me and call me 'Dutchman.'" Here the father chirped in: "Yes, they say, 'What hell good the old country? This here is United States.'" He confessed to me that he preferred Proctor's to the Windsor. This was during the Spanish war, and the Windsor was draped with American flags and banners, and some of them wrought in silk. The orchestra began with Sousa's "Stars and Stripes." I found that the Yiddish people were proud of the fact that they had sent a larger proportion of soldiers to the front than any of the other colonies. For all the minglings of outlandish jargons, the bits of quaint life and character on the stage, the insistence of Jewish customs and religious usages, those Yiddish sons were right—that was United States. In a generation or two the native color of Yiddish life will fade, and the theatres with them.

It would be pleasant to think that in change for the cleanliness and comfort we teach we may receive a part of the love of pleasure, the sympathy with merely amusing things, the aspiration for an ampler life, that have cheered these downtrodden people. Something of their spirit we may of course imbibe, but not all, for nature is apt to work things out on a different plan. In a democratic community the genius for artistic creation is most likely to be manifested when the community falls heir to aspirations above its worldly condition—as occurred when these Yiddish people reached our shores. If in the course of years our souls should cease to fulfil their largest hopes in out-of-door sports and porcelain baths, is it more than reasonable to suppose that the longing for ampler life can be satisfied only by something very beautiful?

THE VAUDEVILLE THEATRE

By Edwin Milton Royle

ILLUSTRATED BY W. GLACKENS

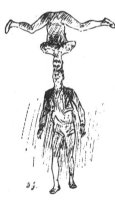

THE Vaudeville Theatre is an American invention. There is nothing like it anywhere else in the world. It is neither the Café Chantant, the English music-hall, nor the German garden. What has been called by a variety of names, but has remained always and everywhere pretty much the same—reeky with smoke, damp with libations, gay with the informalities of the half-world — is now doing business with us under the patronage of the royal American family.

Having expurgated and rehabilitated the tawdry thing, the American invites in the family and neighbors, hands over to them beautiful theatres, lavishly decorated and appointed, nails up everywhere church and army regulations, and in the exuberance of his gayety passes around ice-water. He hasn't painted out the French name, but that is because he has been, as usual, in a hurry. Fourteen years ago this may have been a dream in

a Yankee's brain ; now it is a part of us. The strictly professional world has been looking for the balloon to come down, for the fad to die out, for the impossible thing to stop, but year by year these theatres increase and multiply, till now they flourish the country over.

Sometimes the vaudeville theatre is an individual and independent enterprise ; more often it belongs to a circuit. The patronage, expenses, and receipts are enormous. One circuit will speak for all. It has a theatre in New York, one in Philadelphia, one in Boston, and one in Providence, and they give no Sunday performances ; and yet these four theatres entertain over 5,000,000 people every year, give employment to 350 attachés and to 3,500 actors. Four thousand people pass in and out of each one of these theatres daily. Ten thousand dollars are distributed each week in salaries to the actors and $3,500 to the attachés. Take one theatre for example, the house in Boston. It is open the year round and it costs $7,000 a week to keep it open, while its patrons will average 25,000 every week. On a holiday it will play to from ten to twelve thousand people. How is it possible ?

Persons who secrete campaign rations about them, and camp there from 9.30 A.M. to 10.30 P.M.—Page 486.

A holiday to an American is a serious affair, so the doors of the theatre are open and the performance begins when most people are eating breakfast ; 9.30 A.M. is not too soon for the man who pursues pleasure with the same intensity he puts into business. There are no reserved seats, so one must come first to be first served. One may go in at 9.30 A.M. and stay until 10.30 at night. If he leaves his seat, though, the nearest standing Socialist drops into it and he must wait for a vacancy in order to sit down again.

Not over two per cent. of an audience remains longer than to see the performance through once, but there are persons who secrete campaign rations about them, and camp there from 9.30 A.M. to 10.30 P.M., thereby surviving all of the acts twice and most of them four or five times. The management calculate to sell out the house two and a half times on ordinary days and four times on holidays, and it is this system that makes such enormous receipts possible. Of course I have taken the circuit which is representative of the vaudeville idea at its best, but it is not alone in its standards or success, and what I have said about the houses in New York, Boston, and Philadelphia applies more or less to all the principal cities of the country, and in a less degree of course to the houses in the smaller cities.

Some of these theatres are never closed the year round. Some are content with three matinees a week in addition to their night performances. Others open their doors about noon and close them at 10.30 at night. These are called "continuous" houses. It is manifest, I think, that the vaudeville theatre is playing an important part in the amusement world and in our national life. Perhaps we should be grateful. At present it would seem that the moral tone of a theatre is in the inverse ratio of the price of admission. The higher the price, the lower the tone. It is certain that plays are tolerated and even acclaimed on the New York stage to-day which would have been removed with tongs half a dozen years ago.

On the eighteenth day of last April the member of Parliament for Flintshire made a formal query in the House of Commons in relation to the drama, asking "if the Government will, in view of the depraving nature of several plays now on the stage, consider the advisability of controlling theatres by licenses." The honorable member appeared to think one censorship in the person of the Lord Chamberlain not enough for the growing necessities of London. As we are no longer manufacturers but importers of plays, and largely by way of London, it is not strange that there should be some talk here of a legal censorship for our playhouses.

Begged me " to soften the asperities."—Page 488.

So far as the vaudeville theatres are concerned, one might as well ask for a censorship of a "family magazine." It would be a work of supererogation. The local manager of every vaudeville house is its censor, and he lives up to his position laboriously and, I may say, religiously. The bill changes usually from week to week. It is the solemn duty of this austere personage to sit through the first performance of every week and to let no guilty word or look escape. But this is precautionary only.

"You are to distinctly understand," say the first words of the contracts of a certain circuit, "that the management conducts this house upon a high plane of respectability and moral cleanliness," etc.

A Ballad Singer.

But long before the performer has entered the dressing-rooms, he has been made acquainted with the following legend which everywhere adorns the walls:

NOTICE TO PERFORMERS.

You are hereby warned that your act must be free from all vulgarity and suggestiveness in words, action, and costume, while playing in any of Mr. ——'s houses, and all vulgar, double-meaning and profane words and songs must be cut out of your act before the first performance If you are in doubt as to what is right or wrong, submit it to the resident manager at rehearsal.

Such words as Liar, Slob, Son-of-a-Gun, D e v i l, S u c k e r, Damn, and a l l o t h e r words unfit for the ears of ladies and children, also any reference to questionable streets, resorts, localities, and bar-rooms, are prohibited under fine of i n s t a n t discharge.

———— ——,
General Manager.

And this is not merely a literary effort on the part of the management; it is obligatory and final. When we have about accepted as conclusive the time-honored theory that "You must give the public what it wants," and that it *wants* bilge-water in champagne glasses, we are confronted with the vaudeville theatre, no longer an experiment, but a comprehensive fact.

The funniest farce ever written could not be done at these houses if it had any of the ear-marks of the thing in vogue at many of our first-class theatres. Said a lady to me: "They (the vaudeville theatres) are the only theatres in New York where I should feel absolutely safe in taking a young girl without making preliminary inquiries. Though they may offend the taste, they never offend one's sense of decency." The vaudeville theatres may be said to have established the commercial value of decency. This is their corner-stone. They were conceived with the object of catering to ladies and children, and, strange to say, a large, if not the larger, part of their audiences is always men.

What I have said does not describe all theatres which may have "fashionable vaudeville" over their doors. Godliness has proved so profitable that there be here, as elsewhere, wolves masquerading in woollens, but the houses I have described are well known. Nor have the stringent regulations of these theatres exiled the "song-and-dance man," who was wont to rely on risqué songs and suggestive jokes —they have only forced him to happier and saner efforts, and the result is not Calvinistic; on the contrary, nowhere are audiences jollier, quicker, and more intelligent, and the world of fashion even is not absent from these theatres primarily designed for the wholesome middle classes.

I never for a moment suspected that these admirable regulations c o u l d b e meant for me, or that indeed I was in need of rules and regulations, but my self-righteousness, as was meet, met with discipline. I had a line in my little farce to this effect: "I'll have the devil's own time explaining," etc. I had become so familiar with the devil that I was not even aware of his presence, but the management unmasked me and I received a polite request (which was a command) to cast out the devil. I finally got used to substituting the word "dickens." Later on, the local manager, a big,

She ruled, she reigned, she triumphed.—Page 492.

handsome man, faultlessly attired, in person begged me "to soften the asperities." Need I add that this occurred in Boston? When I travel again I shall leave my asperities at home.

A friend of mine was leaving a spacious vaudeville theatre, along with the audience, and was passing through the beautiful corridor, when one of the multitude of uniformed attachés handed him this printed notice :

Gentlemen will kindly avoid carrying cigars or cigarettes in their mouths while in the building, and greatly oblige
The Management.

My friend was guilty of carrying in his hand an unlighted cigar.

How careful of the conduct of their patrons the management is may be seen from the following printed *requests* with which the employees are armed :

Gentlemen will kindly avoid the stamping of feet and pounding of canes on the floor, and greatly oblige the Management. All applause is best shown by clapping of hands.

Please don't talk during acts, as it annoys those about you, and prevents a perfect hearing of the entertainment.
The Management.

When we were playing in Philadelphia a young woman was singing with what is known as the "song-sheet," at the same theatre with us. Her costume consisted of silk stockings, knee-breeches, and a velvet coat—the regulation page's dress, decorous enough to the unsanctified eye; but one day the proprietor himself happened in unexpectedly (as is his wont) and the order quick and stern went forth that the young woman was not to appear again except in skirts— her street-clothes, if she had nothing else, and street-clothes it came about.

These are the chronicles of what is known among the vaudeville fraternity as "The Sunday-school Circuit," and the proprietor of "The Sunday-school Circuit" is the inventor of vaudeville as we know it. This which makes for righteousness, as is usual, makes also for great and abiding cleanliness—physical as well as moral. I almost lost things in my Philadelphia dressing-room — it was cleaned so constantly. Paternal, austere perhaps, but clean, gloriously clean!

The character of the entertainment is always the same. There is a sameness even about its infinite variety. No act or "turn" consumes much over thirty minutes. Everyone's taste is consulted, and if one objects to the perilous feats of the acrobats or jugglers he can read his programme or shut his eyes for a few moments and he will be compensated by some sweet bell-ringing or a sentimental or comic song, graceful or grotesque dancing, a one-act farce, trained animals, legerdemain, impersonations, clay modelling, the biograph pictures, or the stories of the comic monologuist. The most serious thing about the programme is that seriousness is barred, with some melancholy results. From the artist who balances a set of parlor furniture on his nose to the academic baboon, there is one concentrated, strenuous struggle for a laugh. No artist can afford to do without it. It hangs like a solemn and awful obligation over everything. Once in a

while an artist who juggles tubs on his feet is a comedian, but not always. It would seem as if a serious person would be a relief now and then. But so far the effort to introduce a serious note, even by dramatic artists, has been discouraged. I suspect the serious sketches have not been of superlative merit. Though this premium is put upon a laugh, everyone is aware of the difference between the man who rings a bell at forty paces with a rifle, and the man who smashes it with a club, and the loudest laugh is sometimes yoked with a timid salary. The man who said: "Let me get out of here or I'll lose my self-respect—I actually laughed," goes to the vaudeville theatres, too, and must be reckoned with.

So far as the character of the entertainment goes, vaudeville has the "open door." Whatever or whoever can interest an audience for thirty minutes or less, and has passed quarantine, is welcome. The conditions in the regular theatres are not encouraging to progress. To produce a play or launch a star requires capital of from $10,000 upward. There is no welcome and no encouragement. The door is shut and locked. And even with capital, the conditions are all unfavorable to

The orchestra's place is filled by pianists.—Page 493.

Singing Soubrettes.

proof. But if you can sing or dance or amuse people in any way ; if you think you can write a one-act play, the vaudeville theatre will give you a chance to prove it. One day of every week is devoted to these trials. If at this trial you interest a man who is looking for good material, he will put you in the bill for one performance, and give you a chance at an audience, which is much better. The result of this open-door attitude is a very interesting innovation in vaudeville which is more or less recent, but seems destined to last—the incursion of the dramatic artist into vaudeville.

The managers of the vaudeville theatres are not emotional persons, and there were some strictly business reasons back of the actor's entrance into vaudeville. We do not live by bread alone, but by the saving graces of the art of advertising. It was quite impossible to accentuate sixteen or eighteen features of a bill. Some one name was needed to give it character and meaning at a glance. A name that had already become familiar was preferred. The actor's name served to head the bill and expand the type and catch the eye, and hence arose the vaudeville term— "HEAD-LINER."

This word is not used in contracts, but it is established and understood, and car-

ries with it well-recognized rights and privileges, such as being featured in the advertisements, use of the star dressing-room, and the favorite place on the bill; for it is not conducive to one's happiness or success to appear during the hours favored by the public for coming in or going out. The manager was not the loser, for many people who had never been inside a vaudeville theatre were attracted thither by the name of some well-known and favorite actor, and became permanent patrons of these houses.

At first the actor, who is sentimental rather than practical, was inclined to the belief that it was beneath his dignity to appear on the stage with "a lot of freaks," but he was tempted by salaries no one else could afford to pay (sometimes as high as $500 to $1,000 per week) and by the amount of attention afforded to the innovation by the newspapers. He was told that if he stepped from the sacred precincts of art, the door of the temple would be forever barred against him. The dignity of an artist is a serious thing, but the dignity of the dollar is also a serious thing. None of the dire suppositions happened. The door of the temple proved to be a swinging door, opening easily both ways, and the actor goes back and forth as there is demand for him and as the dollar dictates. Indeed, the advertising secured by association with "a lot of freaks" oiled the door for the actor's return to the legitimate drama at an *increased salary*.

Manifestly, it has been a boon to the "legitimate" artist. To the actor who has starred ; who has had the care of a large company, with its certain expenses and its uncertain receipts ; who has, in addition, responsibility for his own performance and for the work of the individual members of his company and for the work of the company as a whole, vaudeville offers inducements not altogether measured in dollars and cents. He is rid not only of financial obligation, but of a thousand cares and details that twist and strain a nervous temperament. He hands over to the amiable manager the death of the widely mourned Mr. Smith, and prevalent social functions, Lent and the circus, private and public calamities, floods and railroad accidents, the blizzard of winter and the heat of summer, desolating drought and murderous rains, the crops, strikes and panics, wars and pestilences and opera. It is quite a bunch of thorns that he hands over !

Time and terms are usually arranged by agents, who get five per cent. of the actor's salary for their services. Time and terms arranged, the rest is easy. The actor provides himself and assistants and his play or vehicle. His income and outcome are fixed, and he knows at the start whether he is to be a capitalist at the end

of the year; for he runs almost no risk of not getting his salary in the well-known circuits.

The Monologuist.

It is then incumbent on him to forward property and scene-plots, photographs and cast to the theatre two weeks before he opens, and on arrival, he plays twenty or thirty minutes in the afternoon and the same at night. There his responsibility ends. It involves the trifling annoyance of dressing and making up twice a day. In and about New York the actor pays the railroad fares of himself and company, but when he goes West or South, the railroad fares (not including sleepers) are provided by the management.

The great circuit which covers the territory west of Chicago keeps an agent in New York and one in Chicago to facilitate the handling of their big interests. These gentlemen purchase tickets, arrange for sleepers, take care of baggage, and lubricate the wheels of progress from New York to San Francisco and back again.

A couple of stage hands ran in and shut you out with two flats upon which were painted in huge letters —"N. G."—Page 494.

The Human Lizard and the Human Frog.—Page 494.

The actor's only duty is to live up to the schedule made and provided.

The main disadvantage of the Western trip is the loss of a week going and one coming, as there is no vaudeville theatre between Omaha and San Francisco. To avoid the loss of a week on my return I contracted for two nights at the Salt Lake Theatre. My company consisted of four people all told, and my ammunition, suited to that calibre, was three one-act plays. To give the entire evening's entertainment at a first-class theatre, at the usual prices, with four people was a novel undertaking.

I finally determined to add to my mammoth aggregation a distinctly vaudeville feature, and while in San Francisco I engaged a young woman who was to fill in the intermissions with her song-and-dance specialty. Scorning painful effort to escape the conventional, I billed her as "The Queen of Vaudeville," whatever that may mean. We were caught in a tunnel fire at Summit and delayed thirty-six hours. I threatened the railroad officials with various and awful consequences, but the best I could do was to get them to drag my theatre-trunks around the tunnel by hand over a mile and a half of mountain trail, newly made, and get me into Salt Lake just in time to miss my opening night, with a big advance sale and the heart-rendings incident to money refunded. We were in time to play the second night, but my Queen, starting from 'Frisco on a later train, had shown no signs of appearing when the curtain rose. I made the usual apologies. The evening's entertainment was half over when a carriage came tearing up to the theatre and my Queen burst into the theatre without music, trunks, costumes, make-up, supper.

She borrowed a gown from my ingenue, which was much too small for her ; a pair of slippers from my wife, which were much too big for her ; make-up from both ladies, and went on. She leaned over, whispered the key to the leader of the orchestra and began to sing. The orchestra evolved a chord now and then, jiggled and wiggled, stalled, flew the track, crawled apologetically back, did its amiable best individually, but its amiable worst collectively. No mere man could have lived through it. But the young woman justified my billing. She ruled, she reigned, she triumphed. Pluck and good humor always win, and so did the Queen of Vaudeville.

When high-class musical artists and dramatic sketches were first introduced into vaudeville, I understand policemen had to be stationed in the galleries to compel respectful attention, but now these acts are the principal features of every bill, and if they have real merit the gallerygods are the first to appreciate it. So it would seem that vaudeville has torpedoed the ancient superstition that the manager is always forced to give the public just what it wants. At first his efforts were not taken seriously either by the actor himself or the public, and many well-known artists failed to "make good," as the expression is, largely because they used " canned " or embalmed plays ; that is, hastily and crudely condensed versions of well-known plays; but many succeeded, and the result has been a large increase in the number of good one-act farces and comedies, and a distinct elevation in the performance and the patronage of the vaudeville theatres. This has been a gain to everybody concerned.

It cannot be denied that the vaude-

ville "turn" is an experience for the actor. The intense activity everywhere, orderly and systematic though it is, is confusing. The proximity to the "educated donkey," and some not so educated; the variegated and motley samples of all strange things in man and beast; the fact that the curtain never falls, and the huge machine never stops to take breath until 10.30 at night; the being associated after the style of criminals with a number, having your name or number shot into a slot in the proscenium arch to introduce you to your audience; the shortness of your reign, and the consequent necessity of capturing your audience on sight—all this, and some other things, make the first plunge unique in the actor's experience.

One comedian walks on and says, "Hello, audience!" and no further introduction is needed; for the audience is trained to the quick and sharp exigencies of the occasion, and neither slumbers nor sleeps.

Irish Comedians.

One of the first things to surprise the actor in the "continuous" house is the absence of an orchestra. The orchestra's place is filled by pianists who labor industriously five hours a day each. As they practically live at the piano, their knowledge of current music and their adaptability and skill are often surprising, but they are the most universally abused men I ever met. Everyone who comes off the stage Monday afternoon says of the pianist that he ruins their songs; he spoils their acts; he has sinister designs on their popularity, and he wishes to wreck their future. The pianist, on the other hand, says he doesn't mind his work—the five thumping, tyrannous hours—it is the excruciating agony of being compelled to sit through the efforts of the imbecile beings on the stage. It is the point of view!

The Monday-afternoon bill is a tentative one, but thereafter one's position on the bill and the time of one's performance are fixed and mathematical for the remainder of the week. The principal artists appear only twice a day, once in the afternoon and once in the evening, but there is an undivided middle, composed of artists not so independent as some others, which "does three turns" a day (more on holidays), and forms what is picturesquely known as the "supper bill." The "supper bill" explains itself. It lasts from five o'clock, say, till eight or eight-thirty. Who the singular people are who do not eat, or who would rather see the undivided middle than eat, will always be a mystery to me. But if they were not in esse, and in the audience, the management would certainly never retain the "supper bill."

The man who arranges the programme has to have some of the qualities of a general. To fix eighteen or nineteen different acts into the exact time allotted, and so to arrange them that the performance shall never lapse or flag; to see that the "turns" which require only a front scene can be utilized to set the stage for the "turns" which require a full stage, requires judgment and training; but there is very little confusion even at the first performance, and none thereafter.

Many of our best comedians, men and women, have come from the variety stage, and it is rather remarkable that some of our best actors have of late turned their attention to it. This interchange of courtesies has brought out some amusing contrasts. A clever comedian of a comic-opera organization was explaining to me his early experience in the "old days," when he was a song-and-dance man. "The tough manager," he said, "used to

German Dialect Comedians.

stand in the wings with a whistle, and if he didn't like your act he blew it and a couple of stage hands ran in and shut you out from your audience with two flats upon which were painted in huge letters 'N. G.,' and that was the end of your engagement." Then he proceeded to tell with honest pride of his struggles, and his rise in the world of art. "And now," said he to me, "I can say '*cawn't*' as well as you can."

Our first day in vaudeville was rich in experience for us, and particularly for one of the members of my little company. He was already busy at the dressing-table making up, when the two other occupants of his room entered—middle-aged, bald-

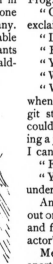

headed, bandy-legged little men, who quickly divested themselves of their street-clothes, and then mysteriously disappeared from sight. Suddenly a deep-drawn sigh welled up from the floor, and turning to see what had become of his companions, the actor saw a good-humored face peering up out of a green-striped bundle of assorted legs and arms. He was face to face with the Human Lizard, and his partner in the Batrachian business, the Human Frog.

"Good Lord! what are you doing?" exclaimed Mr. Roberts.

"Loosenin' up!"—laconically.

"But do you always do that?"

"Yes. *Now!*"

"Why *now?*"

"Well, I'm a little older than I was when I began this business, and yer legs git stiff, ye know. I remember when I could tie a knot in either leg without cracking a joint, but now I am four-flushing until I can get enough to retire."

"Four-flushing?"

"Yes, doin' my turn one card shy. You understand."

And the striped bundle folded in and out on itself and tied itself in bows, ascots, and four-in-hands until every joint in the actor's body was cracking in sympathy.

Meanwhile his partner was standing apart with one foot touching the low ceiling, and his hands clutching two of the clothes-hooks, striving for the fifth card to redeem *his* four-flush.

"Number fourteen!" shouts the call-boy through the door.

"That's us!"

And the four-flushers unwound and, gathering their heads and tails under their arms, glided away for the stage.

Presently they were back panting and perspiring, with the information that there was a man in one of the boxes who never turned his head to look at their act; that there was a pretty girl in another box fascinated by it ; that the audience had relatives in the ice business and were incapable of a proper appreciation of the double split and the great brother double tie and slide— whatever that may be ; and the two athletes passed the alcohol bottle, and slipped gracefully back into their clothes- and private life.

This unique and original world has its conventions, too, quite as hard and fast as elsewhere. The vaudeville dude always bears an enormous cane with a spike in the end of it even though the style in canes may be a bamboo switch. The comedian will black his face, though he never makes the lightest pretence to negro characterization, under the delusion that the black face and kinky hair and short trousers are necessary badges of the funny man. The vaudeville "artist" and his partner will "slang" each other and indulge in brutal personalities under the theory that they are guilty of repartee ; and with a few brilliant exceptions, they all steal from each other jokes and gags and songs and " business," absolutely without conscience.

So that if a comedian has originated a funny story that makes a hit in New York by the time he reaches Philadelphia he finds that another comedian has filched it and told it in Philadelphia, and the originator finds himself a dealer in second-hand goods.

It is manifest, I think, that vaudeville is very American. It touches us and our lives at many places. It appeals to the business man, tired and worn, who drops in for half an hour on his way home ; to the person who has an hour or two before a train goes, or before a business appointment; to the woman who is wearied of shopping ; to the children who love animals and acrobats ; to the man with his sweetheart or sister; to the individual who wants to be diverted but doesn't want to think or feel; to the American of all grades and kinds who wants a great deal for his money. The vaudeville theatre belongs to the era of the department store and the short story. It may be a kind of lunch-counter art, but then art is so vague and lunch is so real.

And I think I may add that if anyone has anything exceptional in the way of art, the vaudeville door is not shut to that.

Rag-time Dance.

7. Women

The status of women in America had posed a dilemma since the days of the American Revolution, when Abigail Adams tauntingly asked her husband John whether females would be granted the same rights as male revolutionaries. Despite many legal and social inequalities, which the Revolution failed to end, American women continued to struggle for more freedom through the nineteenth century. The aggressiveness of their protests caused some alarm, particularly among those who feared that extension of the suffrage and job competition with men would erode the softness of the gentler sex.

Anna Bowman Dodd was one such conservative. A novelist and travel writer who was born in Brooklyn, Mrs. Dodd wrote her dystopia one year before Edward Bellamy published *Looking Backward*. Anticipating changes as revolutionary as those Bellamy described, Mrs. Dodd was far more pessimistic about their ultimate value. Machinery, socialism, and women's rights seemed to her an unholy and inextricably linked trinity, which would stunt the nation's progress.

The most infamous woman of the period, however, had little to do with radicals or social reform. Lizzie Andrew Borden (1860–1927), was a quiet, respectable spinster living in Fall River, Massachusetts in the summer of 1892, active in the Women's Christian Temperance Union and the Christian Endeavor. But in July of that year, when her wealthy father and stepmother were found butchered in their home, Lizzie achieved national celebrity, for circumstances seemed to point to her guilt. Despite a jury verdict of innocent the following summer, Lizzie was convicted by public opinion and a series of subsequent commentators. Immortalized in doggerel, Lizzie was one of the period's fascinations, and a difficult subject for the prosecuting attorney to handle, as his trial summation indicates.

The Republic of the Future

ANNA BOWMAN DODD

NEW YORK SOCIALISTIC CITY

December 1st, 2050 A.D.

Dear Hannevig:

At last, as you see, my journey is safely accomplished, and I am fairly landed in the midst of this strange socialistic society. To say that I was landed, is to make use of so obsolete an expression that it must entirely fail to convey to you a true idea of the processes of the journey. Had I written—I was safely *shot* into the country—this would much more graphically describe to you the method of my arrival.

You may remember, perhaps, that before starting I found myself in very grave doubt as to which route to take—whether to come by balloon or by tunnel. As the latter route would enable me to enjoy an entirely novel spectacle, that of viewing sub-marine scenery, I chose, and wisely I now know, to come by the Pneumatic Tube Electric Company. The comforts and luxuries of this sub-marine route are beyond belief. The perfection of the contrivances for supplying hot and cold air, for instance, during the journey, are such that the passengers are enabled to have almost any temperature at command. The cars are indeed marked 70° Fahr., 80° and 100°. One buys one's seat according to his taste for climate. Many of the travellers, I noticed, booked themselves for the bath department, remaining the entire journey in the Turkish, Russian, vapor or plunge department—as the various baths attached to this line surpass a Roman voluptuary's dream of such luxuries. I, however, never having been through the great tunnel before, was naturally more interested in what was passing so swiftly before my eyes. The speed at which we were shot was terrific—five miles to the minute—making the journey of three thousand miles just ten hours long. In spite of the swiftness of our transit, we were enabled by the aid of the instantaneous photographic process, as applied to opera-glasses and telescopes, to feel that we lost nothing by the rapidity of our meteor-like passage. I was totally unprepared for the

Anna Bowman Dodd, *The Republic of the Future; or, Socialism a Reality* (New York, 1887).

beauties and the novelties which met my eye at every turn. The sight-seers' car is admirably arranged. Fancy being able to take in all the wonders of ocean-land through large glass port-holes in the concave sides of circular cars. The tube itself, which is of iron, enormously thick, has glass sides, also of huge thickness, running parallel with the windows of the car so that the view is unobstructed. The sensations awakened, there-fore, both by the novelty of the situation and by the wonders we passed in review, combined to make the journey thrillingly exciting. We were swept, for instance, past armies of fishes, beautiful to behold in such masses, shimmering in their opalescent armor as they rose above, or sank out of sight into the depths below. The sudden depressions and abrupt elevations of the sea-level made the scenery full of diversity. There was a great abundance of color, with the vivid crimson of the coralline plants and the delicate pinks and yellows of the many varieties of the sub-marine flora. It seemed at times as if we were caught in a liquid cloud of amber, or were to be enmeshed in a grove of giant sea-weeds.

Beyond all else, however, in point of interest, was the spectacle of the wholesale cannibalism going on among the finny tribes, a cannibalism which still exists, in spite of the persistent and unwearying exertions of the numerous Societies for the Prevention of Cruelty among Cetacea and Crustacea. We passed any number of small boats darting in and out among the porpoises, dolphins and smaller fish, delivering supplies (of proper Christian food) and punishing offenders. A sub-marine missionary, who chanced to sit next to me, told me that of all vertebrate or inverte-brate animals, the fish is the least amenable to reformatory discipline; fishes appear to have been born, he went on to say, without the most rudimentary form of the moral instinct, and, curiously enough, only flourish in proportion as they are allowed to act out their original degen-erate nature. He also confessed privately to me, that after some twenty-five years active work among them, the results of his labors were most discouraging. Since, however, the Buddhistic doctrine of metempsychosis has come to be so universally accepted, and as each one of these poor creatures is in reality a soul in embryo, it behoves mankind to do all that lies in its power to elevate all tribes and species.

As you may well imagine, my dear Hannevig, with such spectacles and speculations to enliven the journey, I found it all too short. Its shortness was, in truth, the only drawback to my complete enjoyment. The wonders of the journey, I found, were, however, only a fitting prelude to the surprises that awaited me on my arrival. I leave an account of both these surprises and of my first impressions of the great city until my next letter, as this one, I find, has already grown to the proportions of an ancient epistle.

I am, my dear Hannevig,

Your life-long friend and comrade,
Wolfgang.

Dear Hannevig:

The three days' time which has elapsed since my last letter to you, has been so crowded with a confusion of bewildered impressions produced by this astonishing city and its still more astonishing inhabitants, that I am in doubt whether I shall be able to convey to you any clearer pictures than those which fill the disordered canvas of my own mind. I will, however, strive to reproduce my experiences in the order in which they came to me, and allow you to draw your own conclusions.

The first amazing thing that happened to me was the way in which I reached my hotel. Fancy being blown up on the shore, for the pneumatic tube being many hundreds of feet below the shore level, we were literally blown up on the beach; there we found air-balloon omnibuses, into which we and our luggage were transported by means of little electric cars, running on an inclined plane. The balloon rose about a thousand feet into the air, affording a fine view of the city. Great is not a large enough word to describe so vast a city as this city of the Socialists—it has the immensity of an unending plain, and the flatness of one also. In former times, I believe, the original city was an island, on either side of which flowed a river, but as more and more land became necessary new channels for these rivers were dug, and the river-bed filled in, so that now, as far as the eye can reach, there is a limitless expanse of roof-tops.

As seen from an aerial elevation, there was nothing to attract the eye from the picturesque standpoint—there were few large buildings of noticeable size or beauty. The city was chiefly remarkable because of its immensity. When landed at my hotel I found these first impressions confirmed by a nearer view.

First let me tell you, however, that after entering the vestibule of the hotel, I felt as if I had stepped into some dwelling of gnomes or sprites. Not a human being presented himself. No one appeared to take my luggage, nor was a clerk or hall boy visible anywhere. The great hall of the hotel was as deserted and silent as an empty tomb; at first I could not even discover a bell. Presently, however, I saw a huge iron hand pointing to an adjacent table. On the table lay a big book with a placard on which was printed, *"Please write name, country, length of stay and number of rooms desired."* All of which I did. The book then miraculously closed itself and disappeared! The next instant a tray made its appearance where the book had been, on the tray was a key, and on the key a tag with a number and the words, *"Take elevator at your left to third flight."* The elevator as I stepped into it, stopped as if by magic at the third story, when another iron hand shot out of the wall, pointing me to the left. Soon I found the room assigned me, opened it, and entered to discover the apartment in complete order, and the faucets in the bath-chamber actually turned on!

My dear Hannevig, can you believe me when I tell you that I have been in this hotel four mortal days, have eaten three substantial meals a day, have been fairly comfortable, and yet have not seen a human creature, from a landlord to a servant? The whole establishment apparently is run by machinery. There is a complicated bell apparatus which you ring for every conceivable want or need. Meals are served in one's own room, by a system of ingenious sliding shelves, which open and shut, and disappear into the wall in the most wizard-like manner. Of course the reason of all these contrivances is obvious enough. In a society where labor of a degrading order is forbidden by law, machinery must be used as its substitute. It is all well enough, I presume, from the laborer's point of view. But for a traveller, bent on a pleasure trip, machinery as a substitute for a garrulous landlord, and a score of servants, however bad, is found to be a poor and somewhat monotonous companion. I amuse myself, however, with perpetually testing all the bells and the electrical apparatus, calling for a hundred things I don't want, to see whether they will come through the ceiling or up the floor.

Most of my time, however, is spent in the streets. My earlier impressions of the city I find remain unchanged. It is as flat as your hand and as monotonous as a twice-told tale. Never was there such monotony or such dulness. Each house is precisely like its neighbor; each house has so many rooms, so many windows, so many square feet of garden, which latter no one cultivates, as flowers and grass entail a certain amount of manual labor, which, it appears, is thought to be degrading by these socialists. Imagine, therefore, miles upon miles of a city composed of little two-story houses as like one unto another as two brown nuts. There are parks and theatres and museums, and libraries, the Peoples' Clubs, and innumerable state buildings; but these are all architecturally tasteless, as utility has been the only feature considered in their construction. Every thing here, from the laying out of the city to the last detail concerning the affairs of commerce or trade is arranged according to the socialistic principle—by the people for the People. The city itself was rebuilt a hundred years ago, in order that the houses and the public buildings might be in more fitting harmony with the new order and principles of Socialism. What the older City of New York may have been, it is difficult to determine, although it is supposed to have been ugly enough. But this modern city is the very acme of dreariness. It is the monotony I think, which chiefly depresses me. It is not that the houses do not seem comfortable, clean and orderly, for all these virtues they possess. But fancy seeing miles upon miles of little two-story houses! The total lack of contrast which is the result of the plan on which this socialistic city has been built, comes, of course, from the principle which has decreed that no man can have any finer house or better interior, or finer clothes than his neighbor. The abolition of poverty, and the raising of all classes to a common level of comfort and security, has resulted in the most deadening uniformity. Take for example, the aspect of the shop windows. All shops are run by the government on government capital; there is, consequently, neither rivalry nor competition. The shop keepers, who are in reality only clerks and salesmen under government jurisdiction, take naturally, no personal or vital interest either in the amount of goods sold, or in the way in which these latter are placed before the public. The shop-windows, therefore, are as uninviting as are the goods displayed; only useful, necessary objects and articles are to be seen. The eye seeks in vain throughout the length and breadth of the city for any thing really beautiful, for the lovely, or the rare. Objects of art and of beauty find, it seems, no market here. Occasionally the Government makes a purchase of some foreign work of art, or seizes on some of those recently excavated from the ruins of some 19th century merchant's palace. The picture or vase is then placed in the museums, where the people are supposed to enjoy its possession.

To connect the word enjoyment with the aspect of these serious socialists is almost laughable. A more sober collection of people I never beheld. They are as solemn as the oldest and wisest of owls. They have the look of people who have come to the end of things and who have failed to find it amusing. The entire population appear to be eternally in the streets, wandering up and down, with their hands in their pockets, on the lookout for something that never happens. What indeed, is there to happen? Have they not come to the consummation of everything, of their dreams and their hopes and desires? A man can't have his dream and dream it too. Realization has been found before now, to be exceedingly dull play.

As it is, I am free to confess, that the dulness and apathy of these ideally-perfect socialists weighs on me. My views of their condition may change when I come to know them better.

It is late and I must close.

Ever yours, W.

Dear Friend:

Curiously enough, my dear fellow, the very next day after dispatching my last, I found myself involved in a long and most interesting conversation with the daughter of one of the city residents. I had brought letters of introduction to a certain gentleman, and after a search of some hours through the eternal labyrinth of these unending streets, found the house to which I had been directed. The gentleman, or rather citizen, as all men are called here, was not at home. I was, however, received by his daughter, a plain but seemingly agreeable, intelligent young woman. The women dress so exactly like the men in this country that it is somewhat difficult to tell the sexes apart. Women, however, usually betray themselves as soon as they speak, by their voices.

This young lady had an unusually pleasant voice and manner, and we were soon deep in the agreeable intricacies of a lengthy conversation. I had any number of questions to ask, and she appeared to be most willing to answer them.

My first question, I remember, was an eminently practical one. It was on the subject of chimneys and cooking. I had noticed almost immediately on my arrival that, throughout the entire city, not a chimney was to be seen. It was this fact more than any other that gave the city the appearance of a plain, and made the houses seem curiously deformed. It naturally followed that, there being no chimneys, there was also no smoke, which therefore made this already sufficiently clear atmosphere as pure as the air on a mountain-top. All very beautiful, I said to myself, but how do the people get along without cooking? I, in my quality of stranger and foreigner, had made the interesting discovery that my own meals were prepared to my taste by specially appointed State cooks—a law only recently passed to facilitate international relations. The latter, it appears, had become somewhat strained, when travelers had found themselves forced to abide by the rules and regulations governing the socialists' diet. But what was this diet? This was the mystery which had been puzzling me ever since my arrival. When therefore I found myself face to face with my young lady, I promptly implored her to solve my dilemma. "Oh," she replied, "cooking has gone out long ago. To do any cooking is considered dreadfully old-fashioned."

"Has eating also gone out of fashion in this wonderful country?" I asked in amazement.

She laughed as she replied, "Eating hasn't, but we do it in a more refined way. Instead of kitchens we now have conduits, culinary conduits."

"Culinary conduits?" I asked, still in a daze of wonderment.

"Oh, I see you don't understand," she answered; "you haven't been here long enough to know how such things are arranged. Let me explain. The State scientists now regulate all such matters. Once a month our Officer of Hygiene comes and examines each member of the household. He then prescribes the kind of food he thinks you require for the next few weeks, whether it shall be more or less phosphates, or cereals, or carnivorous preparations. He leaves a paper with you. You then touch this spring—see?" and here she put her pretty white finger on a button in the wall. "You whistle through the aperture to the Culinary Board, put in the paper, and it is sent to the main office. You then receive supplies for the ensuing month."

"And where is this wonderful board?"

"It is in Chicago, where all the great granaries are. You know Chicago supplies the food for the entire United Community."

"But Chicago is a thousand miles off. Isn't all the food stale by the time it reaches you?"

Here she laughed, although I could see she tried very hard not to do so. But my ignorance was evidently too amazingly funny. When she had regained composure she answered: "The food is sent to us by electricity through the culinary conduits. Everything is blown to us in a few minutes' time, if it be necessary, if the food is to be eaten hot. If the food be cereals or condensed meats, it is sent by pneumatic express, done up in bottles or in pellets. All such food is carried about in one's pocket. We take our food as we drink water, wherever we may happen to be, when it's handy and when we need it. Although," she added with a sigh, "I sometimes do wish I had lived in the good old times, in the nineteenth century, for instance, when such dear old-fashioned customs were in vogue as having four-hour dinners and the ladies were taken into dinner by the gentlemen and every one wore full dress—the dress of the period, and they used to flirt—wasn't that the old word? over their wine and dessert. How changed every thing is now! However," she quickly added, "if kitchens and cooking and long dinners hadn't been abolished, the final emancipation of women could never have been accomplished. The perfecting of the woman movement was retarded for hundreds of years, as you know, doubtless, by the slavish desire of women to please their husbands by dressing and cooking to suit them. When the last pie was made into the first pellet, woman's true freedom began. She could then cast off her subordination both to her husband and to her servants. Women were only free, indeed, when the State prohibited the hiring of servants. Of course, the hiring of servants at all was as degrading to the oppressed class as it was a clog to the progress of their mistresses' freedom. The only way to raise the race was to put every one on the same level, to make even degrees of servitude impossible."

"But how, may I be permitted to ask, is the rest of the housework accomplished, if no servants exist to take charge of so pretty a house as this one?" (The house, my dear Hannevig, was in reality hideous, as bare and as plain as are all the houses here. Each is furnished by state law, exactly alike).

"Oh, every thing is done by machinery, as at your hotel. Every thing, the sweeping, bed making, window scrubbing and washing. Each separate department has its various appliances and apparatus. The women of every household are taught the use and management of the various machines, you know, at the expense of the state, during their youth; when they take the management of a house they can run it single-handed. Most of the machinery goes by electricity. A house can be kept in perfect order by two hours' work daily. The only hard work which we still have to do is dusting. No invention has yet been effected which dusts satisfactorily without breakage to ornaments, which accounts for the fact, also, that the fashion of having odds and ends about a home has gone out. It was voted years ago by the largest womans' vote ever polled, that since men could not invent self-adjusting, non-destructive dusters, their homes must suffer. Women were not to be degraded to hand machines for the sake of ministering to men's æsthetic tastes. So you see we have only the necessary chairs and tables. If men want to see pictures they can go to the museums."

Perhaps it is this latter fact which accounts for my never being able to find the good citizen A—— at home. He is gone to the public club or to the bath, or to the Communal Theater, I am told, when I appear again and again. This wonderful community has done much, of that I am convinced, in the development of ideal freedom; but there appears to be a fatal blight somewhere in its principles, a blight which seems to have destroyed all delight in domestic life. In my next I will tell you more and at length, of the peculiar development which the race has attained under these now well-established emancipation doctrines, and of their results on the two sexes.

I hope you are not wearying of my somewhat lengthy descriptions, but you yourself are to blame, as you bound me to such rigid promises of detail and accuracy.

Farewell, dear companion, would you were here to use your wiser philosopher's eyes.

I am yours, Wolfgang.

Dear Friend:

No one thing, I think, strikes the foreigner's eye, on his arrival in this extraordinary land so strongly as does the lack of variety and of taste displayed in the dress of either the men or the women. Both sexes dress, to begin with, as I said in my last, precisely alike. As it is one of the unwritten social laws of the people to dress as simply, economically and sensibly as possible, it results that there is neither brightness nor color nor beauty of line in any of the garments worn. In passing Government Clothing Distribution Bureaus, nothing so forcibly suggests the ideal equality existing between the sexes, as does the sight of the big and the little trowsers, hanging side by side, quite unabashed, the straight and the baggy legs being the only discernible difference. Baggy trowsers and a somewhat long, full cloak for the women—straight-legged trowsers and a shorter coat for the men, this is the dress of the entire population. Some of the women are still pretty, in spite of their hideous clothes. But they all tell me, they wouldn't be if they could help it, as they hold that the beauty of their sex was the chief cause of their long-continued former slavery; they consider comeliness now as a brand and mark of which to be ashamed. From what I have been able to observe, however, I should say that the prettiness which has descended to some of the women fails to awaken any old-time sentiment or gallantry on the part of the men. There has, I learn, been a gradual decay of the erotic sentiment, which doubtless accounts for the indifference among the men; a decay which is due to the peculiar relations brought about by the emancipation of woman.

It is now nearly two hundred years since women have enjoyed the same freedom and rights as men. It is interesting and curious to note the changes, both upon the character and nature of the two sexes, which has been the result of this development. One's first impression, in coming here, is that women are the sole inhabitants of the country. One sees them everywhere in all the public offices, as heads of departments, as government clerks, as officials, as engineers, machinists, aeronauts, tax collectors, firemen, filling, in fact, every office and vocation in civil, political and social life. The few men—by comparison, whom I saw seemed to me to be allowed to exist as specimen examples of a fallen race. Of course, this view is more or less exaggeration. But the women here do appear to possess by far the most energy, vigor, vitality and ambition. Their predominance in office just now is owing to their over-powering number, the women's vote polled being ten to one over that of the men. This strong sex influence has been fruitful in greatly changing and modifying the domestic, social and political laws of the community.

Women, for instance, having satisfactorily emancipated themselves from the bondage of domestic drudgery and the dominion of servants, by means of the improvement in machinery and the invention of the famous culinary conduits, found one obstacle still in their path to complete and co-equal man-freedom. There still remained the children to be taken care of and brought up. As motherhood came in course of time to be considered in its true light, as perhaps the chief cause of the degradation of women, it was finally abolished by act of legislature. Women were still to continue to bear children, or else the socialistic society itself would cease to be. A law was passed providing that children almost immediately after birth, should be brought up, educated and trained under state direction to be returned to their parents when fully grown, and ready for their duties as men and women citizens. In this way women stand at last on as absolutely equal a physical plane with men as it is possible to make them.

It has followed, of course, that with the jurisdiction of the state over the children of the community, all family life has died out. Men and women live together as man and wife, but the relation between them has become more nominal than real. It is significant of the changes that have been brought about between the sexes, that the word "home" has entirely dropped out of the language. A man's house has in truth ceased to be his home. There are no children there to greet him, his wife, who is his comrade, a man, a citizen like himself, is as rarely at home as he. Their food can be eaten anywhere—there is no common board; there is not even a servant to welcome the master with a smile. The word *wife* has also lost all its original significance. It stands for nothing. Husband and wife are in reality two men having equal rights, with the same range of occupation, the same duties as citizens to perform, the same haunts and the same dreary leisure.

Is it therefore, my dear Hannevig, to be wondered at, that all ideas of love, and that all strong mutual attraction and affections should have died out between the sexes? Man loves, longs for passionately and protects with tender solicitude only that which is difficult to conquer. The imagination must at least be inflamed. But where there is no struggle, no opposition, no conditions which breed longing, desire, or the poetry of a little healthy despair, how is love or any sentiment at all to be awakened or kindled? Here there is no parental authority to make a wall between lovers, nor is there inequality of fortunes, nor any marked difference between the two sexes, even in their daily duties or in their lives. I am more and more impressed with the conviction, as I look into this question— this question of what we should consider the growth of an abnormal indifference between the sexes—that the latter cause is perhaps the one which has been chiefly instrumental in the bringing about so complete a change over the face of the passions. Woman has placed herself by the side of man, as his co-equal in labor and vocation, only to make the real distance between them the greater. She has gained her independence at the expense of her strongest appeal to man, her power as mistress, wife and mother. How can a man get up any very vivid or profound sentiment or affection for these men-women—who are neither mothers nor housekeepers, who differ in no smallest degree from themselves in their pursuits and occupation? Constant and perpetual companionship, from earliest infancy to manhood and old age has resulted in blunting all sense of any real difference between the sexes. Whatever slight inequalities may still exist between men and women in the matter of muscular energy or physical strength is more than counterbalanced by the enormous disproportion between them, numerically, as voters.

Some very curious and important political changes have been effected by the preponderance of the woman's vote.

Wars, for instance, have been within the last fifty years declared illegal. Woman found that whereas she was eminently fitted for all men's avocations in time of peace, when it came to war she made a very poor figure of a soldier. Wars, therefore, were soon voted down; foreign difficulties were adjusted by arbitration. As women, as a rule, were sent on these foreign diplomatic missions, I have heard it wickedly whispered that the chief cause of the usually speedy conclusion of any trouble with a foreign court was because of the babel of tongues which ensued: a foreign court being willing to concede any thing rather than to continue negotiations with women-diplomatists. But this of course, is to be put down to pure maliciousness. Women since time immemorial, have had the best of man whenever it came to contests of the tongue, and this appears to be the one insignia of their former prestige which the sex insists on claiming.

The Fall River Tragedy

EDWIN H. PORTER

DISTRICT ATTORNEY KNOWLTON'S PLEA

Hosea M. Knowlton, attorney for the State, spoke as follows: May it please your honors, Mr. Foreman and you, gentlemen of the jury—Upon one common ground in this case all human men can stand together. However we may differ about many of the issues in this trial, there can be no doubt, and I do not disguise my full appreciation of the fact, that it is a most heartrending case. Whether we consider the tragedy that we are trying and the circumstances that surround it, the charge that followed it, the necessary course of the trial that has been had before you, the difficult and painful duty of the counsel upon both sides of the case, or the duty that shall finally be committed to your charge, there is that in it all which lacerates the heart strings of humanity. It was an incredible crime, incredible but for the cold and merciful facts which confront and defeat that incredulity.

There is that in the tidings of a murder that thrills the human heart to its depths. When the word passes from lip to lip and from mouth to mouth that a human life has been taken by an assassin, the stoutest hearts stop beating, lips pale and cheeks blanch, strong men grow pale with the terror of the unknown and mysterious, and if that be so with what I may, perhaps, by comparison call an ordinary assassination, what were the feelings that overpowered the community when the news of this tragedy was spread by the lightning to the ends of the world? Nay, gentlemen, I need not ask you to imagine it. You were a part of the community. It came to you in your daily avocations, it sent a thrill through your beings and you felt that life was not secure. Every man turned detective. Every act and fact and thought that occurred to the thousand, to the million men all over the United States, was spread abroad and furnished and given for the identification of the criminal, and still it remained an impenetrable mystery. My distinguished friend says, Who could have done it? The

Edwin H. Porter, *The Fall River Tragedy* (Fall River, 1893), pp. 270–275, 280–284, 291–292, 296–297, 300–303.

answer would have been, nobody could have done it. If you had read the account of these cold and heartless facts in any tale of fiction before this thing happened, would you not have said, Mr. Foreman—you would have said, That will do for a story, but such things never happen.

In the midst of the largest city of this county, in the midst of his household, surrounded by people and houses and teams and civilization, in the midst of the day, right in that household, while they were attending to their household duties in the midst of their families, an aged man and an aged woman are suddenly and brutally assassinated. It was a terrible crime. It was an impossible crime. But it was committed. And very much, very much, Mr. Foreman, of the difficulty of solving this awful tragedy starts from the very impossibility of the thing itself. Set any human being you can think of, put any degraded man or woman you ever heard of at the bar, and say to them, "You did this thing," and it would seem incredible. And yet it was done; it was done. And I am bound to say, Mr. Foreman, and I say it out of a full heart, that it is scarcely more credible to believe the charge that followed the crime. I would not for one moment lose sight of the incredibility of that charge, nor ask you to believe it, unless you find it supported by facts that you cannot explain or deny. The prisoner at the bar is a woman, and a christian woman, as the expression is used. It is no ordinary criminal that we are trying to-day. It is one of the rank of lady, the equal of your wife and mine, of your friends and mine, of whom such things have never been suspected or dreamed before. I hope I may never forget nor in anything that I say here to-day lose sight of the terrible significance of that fact. We are trying a crime that would have been deemed impossible but for the fact that it was, and are charging with the commission of it a woman whom we would have believed incapable of doing it but for the evidence that it is my duty, my painful duty, to call to your attention. But I beg you to observe, Mr. Foreman and gentlemen, that you cannot dispose of the case upon that consideration. Alas, that it is so! But no station in life is a pledge or a security against the commission of crime, and we all know it. Those who are intrusted with the most precious savings of the widow and the orphan, who stand in the community as towers of strength and fidelity, suddenly fall, and their wreck involves the ruin of many happy homes. They were christian men, they were devout men, they were members of some christian church, they had every inducement around them to preserve the lives that they were supposed to be living, and yet, when the crash came, it was found that they were rotten to the core. Nay, Mr. Foreman, those who are installed with the sacred robes of the church are not exempt from the lot of humanity. Time and again have we been grieved to learn, pained to find, that those who are set up to teach us the way of correct life have been found themselves to be foul as hell inside. Is youth a protection against crime? It is a matter of the history of the commonwealth that a boy of tender years was the most brutal, the most unrelenting, the most cruel, the most fiendish murderer that the commonwealth ever knew. Is sex a protection to crime? Is it not a matter of common knowledge that within the remembrance of every man I am talking to, a woman has been found who murdered a whole cart load of relatives for the sake of obtaining a miserable pittance of a fortune. Ah, gentlemen, I do not underestimate, I do not speak lightly of the strength of a christian character. Far be it from me to join in the sneers which are sometimes thoughtlessly indulged in that a man who is a good Christian is not therefore a good man. Most of them are. Many times all of them are. But they are all sons of Adam and Eve. They fall because they are human. They fall all at once because they have never been shown to the light, and their fall is all the greater because their outward lives have been pure before. I do not forget what a bulwark it is to you and me, Mr. Foreman, that we have heretofore borne a reputation that is above the suspicion of crimes and felonies. It is sometimes the only refuge of a man put in straits. But nobody is beyond the rank of men. Else would it not have been said even by the disciples themselves, "Lead not thy servant into presumptuous sins." It was not ordained by the Saviour that the weak and the trembling and the wicked and the easily turned only should utter the prayer, lead us not into temptation. We are none of us secure. Have you led, sir, an honorable, an upright life? Thank your Heavenly Father that the temptations have not been too strong for you. Have you, sir, never been guilty of heinous crime? Is it your strength of character or is it your fortune that you have been able to resist what has been brought against you? Mr. Foreman, let me not be misunderstood. Not for one moment would I urge that because a man or a woman has led an upright and devout life that therefore there should be any reason for suspecting him or her of a crime. On the contrary, it is a buttress to the foundation, to the presumption of innocence with which start to try anybody. I am obliged to tread now upon a more delicate ground. The prisoner is a woman, one of that sex that all high-minded men revere, that all generous men love, that all wise men acknowledge their indebtedness to. It is hard, it is hard, Mr. Foreman and gentlemen, to conceive that woman can be guilty of crime. It is not a pleasant thing to reflect upon. But I am obliged to say what strikes the justice of every man to whom I am talking, that while we revere the sex, while we show our courtesies to them, they are human like unto us. They are no better than we; they are no worse than we. If they lack in strength and coarseness and vigor, they make up for it in cunning, in dispatch, in celerity, in ferocity. If their loves are stronger and more enduring than those of men, am I saying too much that, on the other hand, their hates are more undying, more unyielding, more persistent? We must face this case as men, not as gallants. You will be slow to believe it is within the capacity of a man to have done it. But it was done. You will be slower to believe that it was within the capacity of a woman to have done it, and I should not count you men if you did not, but it was done. It was done for a purpose. It was done by hatred. But who did it? You have been educated to believe, you are proud to recognize your loyalty, your fealty to the sex. Gentlemen, that consideration has no place under the oath you have taken. We are to find the facts. I am said to be impervious to criticism, but those who have said one thing of me may have the consolation of knowing that the shaft has struck home. When it has been said of me that in the trial of this cause, in the prosecution of this case, there entered into it anything but the spirit of duty, anything like a spirit of revenge, any unworthy motives like ambition or personal glory, if they had known how I shrank from this horrible duty, those slanderous tongues would never have uttered those words. Gentlemen, it is the saddest duty of my life—it is the saddest duty of my life. Gladly would I have shrunk from it if I could have done so and been a man. Gladly would I have yielded the office with which I have been intrusted by the votes of this district if I could have done so honorably. And if now any word I say, any evidence I state, any inference I draw, shall be done with any purpose or intent to do that woman an injustice, may my right hand wither and my tongue cleave to the roof of my mouth. With that spirit, gentlemen, let me ask you to enter upon this case. It was a crime that may well challenge your most sober and sacred attention. That aged man, that aged woman, had gone by the noonday of their lives. They had borne the burden and heat of the day. They had accumulated a competency which they felt would carry them through the waning years of their lives, and hand in hand they expected to go down to the sunset of their days in quiet and happiness.

But for that crime they would be enjoying the air of this day. But for that assassin many years of their life, like yours, I hope, sir, would have been before them, when the cares of life were past, when the anxieties of their daily avocation had ceased to trouble them, and together they would have gone down the hill of life serene in an old age that was happy because the happiness had been earned by a life of fidelity and toil. Over those bodies we stand, Mr. Foreman. We sometimes forget the past. Over those bodies we stand, and we say to ourselves, is it possible that this crime cannot be discovered. You are standing, as has been suggested, in the presence of death itself. It is only what comes hereafter, but it is the double death that comes before. There is a place—it is the chamber of death—where all these personal animosities, passions and prejudices have no room, where all matters of sentiment are one side, where nothing but the truth, the naked truth, finds room and lodgment. In that spirit I adjure you to enter upon the trial of this case. It is the most solemn duty of your lives. We have brought before you as fully and frankly as we could, every witness whom we thought had any knowledge of any surrounding of this transaction, I do not know of one that has been kept back.

• • •

We must now go into this establishment and see what manner of family this was. It is said that there is a skeleton in the household of every man, but the Borden skeleton—if there was one—was fairly well locked up from view. They were a close-mouthed family. They did not parade their difficulties. Last of all would you expect they would tell the domestic in the kitchen, which is the whole tower of strength of the defense, and yet, Mr. Foreman, there was a skeleton in the closet of that house which was not adequate to this matter—O, no, not adequate to this thing. There is not anything in human nature that is adequate to this thing—remember that. But there was a skeleton of which we have seen the grinning eyeballs and the dangling limbs. It is useless to tell you that there was peace and harmony in that family. We know better. We know better. The remark that was made to Mrs. Gifford, the cloakmaker, was not a petulant outburst, such as might come and go. That correction of Mr. Fleet, at the very moment the poor woman who had reared that girl lay dead within ten feet of her voice, was not merely accidental. It went down deep into the springs of human nature. Lizzie Borden had never known her mother. She was not three years old when that woman passed away, and her youthful lips had scarcely learned to pronounce the tender word, mamma, and no picture of her lay in the girl's mind. And yet she had a mother—she had a mother. Before she was old enough to go to school, before she arrived at the age of five years, this woman, the choice of her father, the companion of her father, who had lost and mourned and loved again, had come in and had done her duty by that girl and had reared her, had stood in all the attitudes which characterize the tenderest of all human relations. Through all her childhood's sicknesses that woman had cared for her. When she came in weary with her sports, feeble and tired, it was on her breast that girl had sunk as have our children on the breast of their mothers. She had been her mother, faithful persevering, and had brought her up to be at least an honorable and worthy woman in appearance and manner.

This girl owed everything to her. Mrs. Borden was the only mother she had ever known, and she had given to this girl her mother's love and had given her this love when a child when it was not her own and she had not gone through the pains of childbirth, because it was her husband's daughter. And then a quarrel; what a quarrel. What a quarrel, Mr. Foreman. A man worth more than a quarter of a million of dollars, wants to give his wife, his faithful wife who has served him thirty years for her board and clothes, who has done his work, who has kept his house, who has reared his children, wants to buy and get with her the interest in a little homestead where her sister lives.

How wicked to have found fault with it. How petty to have found fault with it. Nay, if it was a man sitting in that dock instead of a woman, I would characterize it in more opprobrious terms than those. I trust that in none of the discussion that I engage in to-day shall I forget the courtesy due from a man to a woman; and although it is my horrible and painful duty to point to the fact of this woman being a murderess, I trust I shall not forget that she is a woman, and I hope I never have. And she repudiated the title that that woman should have had from her. Did you ever hear of such a case as that? It was a living insult to that woman, a living expression of contempt, and that woman repeated it day in and day out, saying to her, as Emma has said, you are not interested in us. You have worked round our father and have got a little miserable pittance of $1,500 out of him, and you shall be my mother no more. Am I exaggerating this thing? She kept her own counsel. Bridget did not know anything about it. She was in the kitchen. This woman never betrayed her feelings except when some one else tried to make her call her mother, and then her temper broke forth. Living or dead, no person should use that word mother to that poor woman unchallenged by Lizzie Borden. She had left it off herself; all through her childhood days, all through her young life Mrs. Borden had been a mother to her as is the mother of every other child to its offspring, and the time comes when they still live in the same house and this child will no longer call her by that name. Mr. Foreman, it means much. It means much. Why does it mean much? They did not eat together.

• • •

When Mrs. Gifford spoke to her, talking about her mother, she said, "Don't say mother to me,"—that mother who had reared her and was her father's companion under the roof with whom she was then living, whose household she shared, to whom every debt of gratitude was due and whom she had repudiated as her mother, she could not find the heart to say to this cloakmaker was her mother, for I believe that you believe this story is true—"she is a mean, good for nothing old thing." Nay, this is not all—"We do not have much to do with her. I stay in my room most of the time."

• • •

I don't know how deep this cancer had eaten in. It makes but little show on the surface. A woman can preserve her appearance of health and strength even when the roots of this foul disease have gone and wound clear around her heart and vital organs. This was a cancer. It was an interruption of what should have been the natural agreeable relations between mother and daughter, a quarrel about property, not her property, but her father's, and property that he alone had the right to dispose of. A man does not surrender his rights to his own until he is dead, and not even then if he chooses to make a will. She could not brook that that woman should have influence enough over her father to let him procure the little remnant of her own property that had fallen to her from her own folks. She had repudiated the title of mother. She had lived with her in hatred. She had gone on increasing in that hatred until we do not know, we can only guess, how far that sore had festered, how far the blood in that family had been poisoned by the misfortune of these unfortunate relations between them. I come back to that poor woman lying prone, as has been described, in the parlor. It is wicked to say it, it is wicked to have to say it, but, gentlemen, there is no escape from the truth. Had she an enemy in all the world? She had one. Was anybody in the world to be benefitted by her taking away? There was one. There was one. It is hard to believe that mere property would have influenced this belief. We are not obliged to, although it appears that property was that which made or broke the relations of that family, and a small amount of property, too. But there was one woman in the world who believed that that dead woman stood between her and her father, and was the enemy of her and the friend of her father, and between whom there had grown up that feeling that prevented her from giving her the title that the ordinary instincts of decency would have entitled her to. Let us examine the wounds upon that woman. So we look at the skull and we look at these wounds, and what do we read there? We know afterwards, by another examination downstairs, that no thief did this thing; there was no object of plunder. We are spared the suspicion that any base animal purposes had to do with this crime. No, Mr. Foreman, there was nothing in these blows but hatred, but hatred, and a desire to kill. What sort of blows were they? Some struck here at an angle, badly aimed; some struck here in the neck, badly directed; some pattered on top of the head and didn't go through; some, where the skull was weaker, went through. A great strong man would have taken a blow of that hatchet and made an end of it. The hand that held the weapon was not the hand of masculine strength. It was the hand of a person strong only in hate and desire to kill.

• • •

There may be that in his case which saves us from the idea that Lizzie Borden planned to kill her father. I hope she did not. But Lizzie Andrew Borden, the daughter of Andrew Jackson Borden, never came down those stairs. It was not Lizzie Andrew Borden, the daughter of Andrew Jackson Borden, that came down those stairs, but a murderess, transformed from all the thirty-three years of an honest life, transformed from the daughter, transformed from the ties of affections to the most consummate criminal we have read of in all our history or works of fiction. She came down to meet that stern old man. His picture shows that, if nothing more, even in death. That just old man, of the stern puritan stock, that most of you are from, gentlemen, that man who loved his daughters, but who also loved his wife, as the Bible commanded him to. And, above all, the one man in all this universe who would know who killed his wife. She had not thought of that. She had gone on. There is cunning in crime, but there is blindness in crime, too. She had gone on with stealth and cunning, but she had forgotten the hereafter. They always do. And when the deed was done she was coming downstairs to face Nemesis. There wouldn't be any question of what he would know of the reason why that woman lay in death. He knew who disliked her. He knew who could not tolerate her presence under the roof. He knew the discussion which had led up to the pitch of frenzy which resulted in her death, and she didn't dare to let him live, father though he was, and bound to her by every tie of affection. It is the melancholy, the inevitable attribute of crime that it is the necessary and fruitful parent of crime. He moved slowly. He went to the back door, as was his custom, but nobody was there to open it, and so he went around to the front door, as very likely he often did, supposing, of course, that he could gain entrance, as any man does into his own house in the day time, by the use of a spring lock. We have heard something about the noise and confusion of that street, but Bridget's ears, which are no quicker than Lizzie's, heard him as he put the key into the lock, and came to the door and let him in. He came in and passed into the dining room, because she was, I presume, working in the sitting room, took off his coat and replaced it with a cardigan jacket and down came Lizzie from the very place where Mrs. Borden lay dead and told him what we cannot believe to be true about where his wife was. I am told, gentlemen, that circumstances are to be regarded with suspicion. Mr. Foreman, a falsehood that goes right to the very vitals of crime is not a circumstance; it is proof. Where was that mother? She knew. She told what never was true. That would pass off for awhile; that would keep the old man quiet for a time, but it would not last.

. . .

I would not lift the weight of my finger to urge that this woman remarkable though she is, nervy as she is, brave as she is, cool as she is, should be condemned because grief, it may have been, but for other things in the case, drove back the tears to their source and forbade her to show the emotions that belong to the sex. But there are some things that are pregnant. My distinguished friend tells of the frequency of presentiments. They are frequent in the storybooks, Mr. Foreman. If they occur in real life they are usually thought of afterward. Did you ever hear one expressed beforehand? Tell me that this woman was physically incapable of that deed? My distinguished friend has not read female character enough to know that when a woman dares she dares, and when she will she will, and that given a woman that has that absolute command of herself . . . a woman whose courage surpassed that of any man I am talking to, I very humbly believe —tell me that she is physically incapable of this act? But those are trifles, Mr. Foreman. Those are trifles. Those are little chips that do not perhaps directly indicate which way the current flows. But there is more in the case than that. Of course the question arises to one's lips. How could she have avoided the spattering of her dress with blood if she was the author of these crimes? As to the first crime, it is scarcely necessary to attempt to answer the question. In the solitude of that house, with ample fire in the stove, with ample wit of woman nobody has suggested that as to the first crime there was not ample opportunity, ample means and that nothing could be suggested as a reason why all the evidence of that crime could not have been amply and successfully concealed. But as to the second murder the question is one of more difficulty. I cannot answer it. You cannot answer it. You are neither murderers nor women. You have neither the craft of the assassin nor the cunning and deftness of the sex.

. . .

I had intended, Mr. Foreman and gentlemen, at this point, to attempt to recapitulate these things to you. I do not think I will do it. If I have not made them plain they cannot be made plainer.

. . .

We find a woman murdered by blows which were struck with a weak and indecisive hand. We find that that woman had no enemies in all the world excepting the daughter that had repudiated her. We find that that woman was killed at half past nine, when it passes the bounds of human credulity to believe that it could have been done without her knowledge, her presence, her sight, her hearing. We find a house guarded by night and by day so that no assassin could find lodgment in it for a moment. We find that after that body had been murdered a falsehood of the very essence of this whole case is told by that girl to explain the story to the father, who would revenge it and delay him from looking for her. We find her then set in her purpose turned into a mania, so far as responsibility is concerned, considering the question of what to do with this witness who could tell everything of that skeleton if he saw fit. He had not always told all he knew. He had forbidden telling of that burglary of Mrs. Borden's things for reasons that I do not know anything about, but which I presume were satisfactory to him, but he would not have so suppressed or concealed this tragedy, and so the devil came to her as God grant it may never come to you or me, but it may. When the old man lay sleeping she was prompted to cover her person in some imperfect way and remove him from life and conceal the evidences, so far as she could in the hurried time that was left her. She did not call Maggie until she got ready. She had fifteen minutes, which is a long time, and then called her down, and without helping the officers in one single thing, but remonstrating with them for going into her room and asking her questions—those servants of the law who were trying to favor her, never opening her mouth except to tell the story of the barn, and then a story of the note, which is all she ever told in the world. We find that woman in a house where is found in the cellar a hatchet which answers every requirement of this case, where no outside assassin could have concealed it, and where she alone could have put it. We find in that house a dress which was concealed from the officers until it was found that the search was to be resumed and safety was not longer assured. The dress was hidden from public gaze by the most extraordinary act of burning that you ever heard of in all your lives by an innocent person.

We say these things float on the great current of our thought and tell just where the stream leads to. We get down now to the elements of ordinary crime. We get hatred, we get malice, we get falsehood about the position and disposition of the body. We get absurd and impossible alibis. We get contradictory stories that are not attempted to be verified. We get fraud upon the officers by the substitution of an afternoon silk dress as the one that she was wearing that morning ironing, and capping the climax by the production of evidence that is beyond all question, that there was a guilty destruction of the dress that she feared the eye of the microscope might find the blood upon. What is the defense, Mr. Foreman? What is the answer to this array of impregnable facts? Nothing, nothing. I stop and think, and I say again, nothing. Some dust thrown upon the story of Mrs. Reagan which is not of the essence of the case, some question about time put upon the acts of Mr. Medley which is not of the essence of the case; some absurd and trifling stories about drunken men the night before and dogs in the yard the night before. Of men standing quietly on the street the same day of the tragedy, exposing their bloody persons for the inspection of passersby, of a pale, irresolute man walking up the street in broad daylight. Nothing, nothing. The distinguished counsel, with all his eloquence, which I can't hope to match or approach, has attempted nothing but to say, "Not proven." But it is proven; it is proven. We cannot measure facts, Mr. Foreman. We cannot put a yardstick to them. We cannot determine the length and breadth and the thickness of them. There is only one test of facts. Do they lead us to firm belief? If they do they have done the only duty they are capable of. You cannot measure the light that shines about you; you cannot weigh it, but we know when it is light because it shines into our hearts and eyes. That is all there is to this question of reasonable doubt. Give the prisoner every vestige of benefit of it. The last question to be answered is taken from these facts together. Are you satisfied that it was done by her?

• • •

I have no other suggestion to make to you than that you shall deal with them with that courage that befits sons of Massachusetts. I do not put it on so low a ground as to ask you to avenge these horrid deaths. O, no, I do not put it even on the ground of asking you to do credit to the good old commonwealth of Massachusetts. I lift you higher than that, gentlemen. I advance you to the altitude of the conscience that must be the final master of us all. You are merciful men. The wells of mercy, I hope, are not dried up in any of us. But this is not the time nor the place for the exercise of it. That mighty prerogative of mercy is not absent from the jurisprudence of this glorious old commonwealth. It is vested in magistrates, one of the most conspicuous of whom was the honored gentleman who has addressed you before me, and to whom no appeal for mercy ever fell upon harsh or unwilling ears. Let mercy be taken care of by those to whom you have intrusted the quality of mercy. It is not strained in the commonwealth of Massachusetts. It is not for us to discuss that. It is for us to answer questions, the responsibility of which is not with you nor with me. We neither made these laws, nor do we execute them. We are responsible only for the justice, the courage, the ability with which we meet to find an answer to the truth. Rise, gentlemen, rise to the altitude of your duty. Act as you would act when you stand before the great white throne at the last day. What shall be your reward? The ineffable conciousness of duty done. There is no strait so hard, there is no affliction so bitter, that it is not made light and easy by the consciousness that in times of trial you have done your duty and your whole duty. There is no applause of the world, there is no station of height, there is no seduction of fame that can compensate for the gnawings of an outraged conscience. Only he who hears the voice of his inner consciousness, it is the voice of God himself saying to him "Well done, good and faithful servant," can enter into the reward and lay hold of eternal life.

8. Social Forms

One response of a generation beset by novel occasions for social conflict, was to codify the ceremonies of daily life. Many of these formulas were outlined in the etiquette books, so essential to the social climber. Because class lines had been blurred for so long in America, these books had been popular for generations. Like so many other things in the late nineteenth century, however, treatises on behavior multiplied rapidly, spurred by demands for information. Eliza Lavin's volume on manners was part of a larger set entitled "Metropolitan Culture"; the title reveals the prominence some gave to courtesy. Cities placed special demands on rural newcomers confronted with many novel experiences. The apparent formlessness of urban life was actually undercoated with elaborate rituals, which newcomers ignored at their peril if they hoped for social success.

Education as an instrument of social control was also far from new in American history, but the era of Calvin Woodward, John Dewey, and William Torrey Harris studied the possibilities for shaping the habits of future generations more vigorously than ever before. Many Americans sought to create in the school a surrogate not only for the workshop but for the home as well. Julia Dewey focused on providing children with an ideal of public behavior, an ideal which, in an earlier period, they might have absorbed more effortlessly from their parents.

Good Manners

ELIZA M. LAVIN

RAISING THE HAT—THE WELL-BRED SMILE—HAND SHAKING

In the days of chivalry did the question "When shall a gentleman lift his hat" ever rise? We think not, and our belief that chivalry is not dead, but existing under another name and practised according to a more modern and practical standard, makes us surprised that the question should be so often asked nowadays. Perhaps it is proof of that earnest desire to acquire the grace which will lend to the sterner qualities of American chivalry the polish that cannot fail to set it far above the standard of any past age.

A gentleman lifts his hat to a lady acquaintance whom he meets on the street and also to any lady whom an acquaintance walking with him happens to salute. He does not look at the lady if she be not an acquaintance of his, neither does he seem to avoid meeting her gaze, which it is safe to say in the brief flash of recognition permitted by a street bow is directed wholly toward his friend. If he is driving and his right hand be unencumbered, he lifts his hat; even if he is carrying the whip he may free his hand so as to lift his hat, though some claim the privilege of saluting by touching the hat brim.

In the country, where in cold and windy weather the *chapeau* is not always as easily transferable as a silk hat or derby, a salute with the free hand or whip is in order, and this pleasing custom is practised to a gratifying degree by the rural population in most country places. This form of salutation is generally considered sufficient between gentlemen who are driving rapidly or enjoying a brisk canter in the saddle, but the man who desires to both possess and express the art of perfect horsemanship takes pride in being able to lift his hat while holding the reins.

In passing a lady in a hotel corridor, in handing her fare for her in a street car, in performing any of the little courtesies which good breeding calls for, a gentleman lifts his hat; and if there be any circumstances connected with the offering of the service which tends to develop awkward-

Eliza Lavin, *Good Manners*, 2nd ed. (New York, 1889), pp. 39–44.

ness or delay on the part of the lady, he remains with uncovered head until the adjustment of the difficulty.

A gentleman expresses the same deference in his mode of saluting his own family that he shows to others. He lifts his hat to wife, mother, or sister when he meets her, and he recognizes a chance meeting with either of them as politely as he would with an acquaintance.

The question, should a gentleman remove his hat when he enters the lobby of a theatre, hall, etc., or not until he is about to pass through the passage-way to the auditorium, is often asked. A general answer to this would involve considerable research into the architectural provisions of such buildings. Some of the more modern theatres have luxurious lobbies and foyers containing interesting objects of art; these places are as clearly divided from the outer entrance as they are from the auditorium, and if he lingers there he should certainly remove his hat whether he be accompanied by ladies or not; but good sense should teach us that to stand with uncovered head in a draughty passage-way simply because it is in a building, is not rational, and, as a matter of course, not demanded by etiquette. Etiquette, however, voices all the censure which good breeding feels when a man walks down the aisle of a theatre, remains in the reception room of a hotel or advances into a restaurant, with his hat on his head.

When a gentleman meets a lady on the street for the first time after he has been introduced to or entertained by her, he may, if he perceives she is in doubt as to his identity, help her memory by quickly going through his part of the recognition and lifting his hat. A lady who has any defect of vision or who entertains largely is apt to pass by strangers, even though she may have greeted them under her own roof, without recognizing them; and while the privilege of speaking first is always the lady's, still it is the spirit and not the letter of the law which should be considered. Very young men sometimes take a melancholy pleasure in resenting the offence they imagine has been conveyed by this most simple and natural error on the part of ladies who have entertained them, and their conduct is often amusing.

A gentleman should remove his hat when he enters a private business office, when he makes use of an elevator in an establishment devoted mainly to the use of ladies, and always when he makes inquiries which involve the bestowal of information for purely courteous reasons. Even from a merely practical stand-point, young men cannot afford to overlook the advantage of attention to such details, and the practice of youth becomes the habit of maturity.

It is a safe and comprehensive rule to follow, that the hat should be removed from the time a gentleman reaches the door leading to the auditorium of a place of amusement. On entering a private house it should be taken off the moment the door is opened, and is not resumed until it closes upon him, even though he takes leave of his host or hostess three rooms removed from it.

From gladness to gloom is but a short step in this busy world, and he who steps aside for a funeral procession in the street of some country village, or pauses to permit the transmission of the casket to the hearse in his passage along the walk of some city street, exalts his manliness when he bows his uncovered head.

A smile or a frown may express a great deal, but, while a frown seems all darkness, a smile is capable of many shadings. It is not beyond the province of etiquette to insist that its influence in street salutations, and, indeed, at any place, shall not be too broad nor too marked. It is upon the promenade that it is apt to depart from the severe elegance of well-bred composure. No doubt this is partly attributable to the exhilaration of oxygen and the sympathy with nature which we all feel, but it is not desirable to place our gladness too conspicuously *en evidence.* Into the greeting which a lady gives a friend on the street the warmth of a slight smile infuses a graciousness that is the refinement of cordiality, but the happy girls, who descry afar off their partners in a divine waltz or the vanquished heroes of yesterday's tennis game, should beware of allowing their countenances to expand too markedly with the memory of the pleasure. "Thank you," or even a slight inclination of the head is very expressive when the light of a smile illuminates it, and a refusal to accede to another's desires is softened without being weakened by a pleasant manner. A certain decorum of countenance is as desirable for the promenade as for a good photograph.

Hand-shaking is a brief ceremonial, meaningless or eloquent, according to the manner of its performance. It may be made the exponent of hearty good-will or the most formal acknowledgment of one's presence. It is needless to say that it should not go to extremes. A gentle pressure is usually sufficient to express one's feelings, and it is all that etiquette demands. If that much cannot be conceded, do not attempt it at all, for it is quite as unpleasant to have one's hand taken in a limp and lifeless fashion as to have it subjected to the pressure which some seem to think due to a cordial manner.

Upon introduction, gentlemen usually shake hands with gentlemen, and so do ladies with ladies, when a pleasant impression is of more consequence than severely elegant formality. But a gentleman should not offer to shake hands with a lady, unless she indicates a desire to do so. If there is any question of who should indicate whether such a salutation is agreeable, the hint should be given in the ready manner of the elder, the one who is at home or the one most distinguished. If there is a preliminary indecision, due to youth or shyness, such as the extending and withdrawal of the hand, do not make it more conspicuous by offering to shake hands after the first opportunity has passed; but, when the next occurs, remember the failing and try to dispel awkwardness by prompt action.

If a lady has offered to shake hands with a gentleman when he enters her presence, he may offer his hand when he bids her adieu, not otherwise. Avoid hand-shaking in the street, unless you are sure of the ready response of a friend.

How To Teach Manners
in the School-Room

JULIA M. DEWEY

1. In teaching manners to young children there is no better example to be followed than that of a careful mother, who takes advantage of incidents of every-day life to impress a truth upon the mind of her child. By such means the ideal standard is kept in close relation to the child's conduct until it is taken up and assimilated into his nature. For this reason it is better to begin the definite teaching of manners with reference to the school, and as far as possible to allow actual occurrences to suggest or illustrate the point to be considered. The lesson that will fit the needs of the occasion is the most effective. Just here it may be remarked that, within bounds, a teacher is justified in taking advantage of these oppor-

Julia M. Dewey, *How To Teach Manners in the School-Room* (New York, 1888), pp. 13–24, 26–28.

tunities, even if it somewhat disturbs the formality of a rigid programme of school-work.

2. The mother's method may be followed still farther in making the definite lesson as informal as possible. Questions should be asked to awaken thought, and the lesson should partake more of the nature of a familiar conversation than of a school exercise. Pupils should be allowed to tell what they know on certain points, and new truths should be "developed" as in other subjects.

3. The instruction to older pupils may be given in a similar manner, but less simply; or the item may be read with or without comment. This lesson serves to instruct those ignorant of prevailing forms, and to keep the matter before the minds of others who are better informed. When pupils are old enough, if not provided with a text-book on manners, it is well for them to make a note of the directions given.

4. The time given to this subject must be regulated by the other work in the school. A few minutes daily will amount to a great deal in the course of years.

5. A plan that has been successfully pursued is to allow ten minutes for the opening exercises of school, and to make a brief lesson in manners a part of these exercises. It is not the aim of the author that the illustrative lessons shall be arbitrarily followed. That would be to aim at an impossibility. If success is expected, it is even more necessary in this branch than in others that the work be stamped with the individuality of the teacher. There must also be a certain compass of expression and force and earnestness of manner in giving these lessons which cannot be imparted to the printed page.

6. Brevity is essential, as the effect sought would be lost if the lesson became tiresome. Moreover, it is not intended to add to the already overburdened curriculum of most schools. Teachers should exercise care in selecting items adapted to the age and capacity of their pupils. It is needless to add that as far as there is opportunity teachers should see that precept and practice go hand-in-hand.

SPECIAL DIRECTIONS TO TEACHERS

1. The manners of pupils are usually similar to those of the teacher. It is therefore of the utmost importance that he should himself exemplify true courtesy, because he will be imitated. His whole bearing and manner in the presence of pupils should be above criticism. If not conversant with the details of a code of manners, it is obligatory upon him to become so, and to conform his manners to it.

2. A high and loud tone of voice should not have place in a school-room.

There is perhaps no more unrefining influence unconsciously exerted by a teacher than that of a loud voice. Emerson says, "Loudness is rude, quietness always genteel," and in nothing is the truth more apparent than in the voice. As children are close imitators, if teachers speak in a loud and dictatorial manner, so will their pupils.

A teacher's voice should be as melodious as nature permits, and its effect should be heightened by all the modulations and intonations used in polite conversation. Suitable language *voiced* in this manner not only has a most refining influence on the character and manners of pupils, but is often the only instrumentality needed in the formal "government" of the school.

3. A teacher should assume no attitude in a school-room which is not proper for the pupils. Here again the natural propensity of children to imitate should be remembered. Teachers have been known to censure children for carelessness in posture when they themselves were guilty of the same. There is no instruction of this kind so impressive as that of example, and if teachers wish their pupils to be patterns of propriety in attitude, motions, actions, they themselves must furnish the model.

4. Teachers should not be careless in personal habits. Besides formal instruction relative to habits of cleanliness and tidiness, the teacher should show the importance of these habits by strict adherence to them. Teachers should dress neatly and in good taste. This does not necessarily involve expense. There should be no gaudiness of dress, but due attention should be paid to harmony of color and suitableness of fabric, and garments should be made in prevailing styles. Attention to these details will help to refine the tastes of pupils.

5. Teachers should watch their tones and words with great care. It is not enough that expressions should be grammatical, but they should be devoid of anything inelegant. All proprieties of speech should be observed, even (or especially) with the youngest children. *Severe* expressions, arising from lack of self-control on the part of the teacher, are productive of demoralization in the school, and have a most unrefining effect on the pupils.

Let teachers observe the direction which they give to their pupils,—

> "Guard well while you are young
> Ear and eye and *Tongue*,—"

and it will be much more effectual than the memorizing of the couplet. A polite request is at any time more refining and effective than a stern command. Instead of saying "Do this" or "Do that," if teachers make a practice of asking "Will you kindly do this?" or "Please do that," they will find their wishes more cheerfully complied with, and less selfishness displayed in the requests made by pupils.

6. Teachers should not only guard their words, but the expression of their countenances. The expression should be pleasant and indicative of kindness and common sense. A stolid expression or constant smiling are both exceedingly objectionable in a school-room, as elsewhere.

Children are very susceptible either to smiles or frowns, and both should be used with discretion. Approving smiles, like approving words, may be given as rewards, but a too liberal use detracts from their value. It may seem to be setting up an ideal standard to say that when in the schoolroom an angry or a petulant look should never come upon a teacher's face. It is sometimes necessary to express regret, sorrow, or severity in this manner, but anger and irritability never, as that shows lack of self-control; and one of the serious results of such a lack is impoliteness.

7. Teachers should not indulge in modes of discipline that are unrefining in their tendencies. Happily the old barbaric modes of punishment are passing away. If complete abolition of corporal punishment does not seem feasible, any teacher ought to be possessed of sufficient delicacy and refinement to avoid making such punishment public. It should *never* be inflicted in the presence of the school.

PRACTICAL TRAINING IN MANNERS

1. Ask the children daily to tell what opportunity they have improved of being kind and polite.

2. The teacher should remark on any improvement shown by the pupils, and lead pupils to talk of it. It is well to allow them to talk without restraint so as to obtain their real opinions. Tact will be needed to ward off a feeling of self-gratulation or conceit, which may otherwise be brought out when pupils tell of their own polite acts.

3. Impress pupils with the idea that good manners is one of the subjects pursued in the schools, and that it will help them in life, and that practice shows progress in this particular branch.

4. Without seeming to demand it, teachers should lead children to offer them any service that is *not menial*. Such attentions as disposing of wraps, umbrellas, etc., fetching them when needed, picking up things accidentally dropped, handling crayon, eraser, etc., lifting or moving things, offering a chair, helping to put things in their places at the close of school, should be rendered to teachers by pupils. If, at first, in order to make

children see what offices are proper, the teacher must ask for them, it should be as one would ask an equal, and not a servant; and any service rendered should be most politely acknowledged.

5. The older children should be made to understand the propriety of assuming some responsibility over the younger. This is almost universally practiced in schools where "busy work" is done, when the older pupils help to distribute materials for such work, and to assist in its execution. They should also assist those who need aid in putting on or taking off wraps, overshoes, etc. Children should understand that girls need not necessarily assist girls, and boys boys, but that help should be offered and accepted, as is convenient.

6. Children should be encouraged to try to settle disputes or to quell disorder in any form. This does not imply a system of monitorship. As young children are pleased to do these things, it needs tact and watchfulness on the teacher's part to keep down an overbearing or officious spirit. This may be accomplished by appointing certain pupils for a definite length of time, and by removing them from "office" when they exceed their authority. These advisers are not to be encouraged in tale-bearing. It should be considered just cause for removal, unless the tale is told in order to get the teacher's advice as to the best mode of settling a difficulty.

7. Pupils should be trained to receive and entertain those who come to visit the schools. They should entertain as politely in a school-room as in a parlor. When visitors come, a pupil should answer the bell, politely invite the company to enter, find them comfortable seats, take their wraps if they wish to dispose of them, and offer any other attention the occasion may seem to demand. To do this properly at the time implies previous training—pupils acting as visitors. In this as in other things, officiousness on the part of pupils should be guarded against. Give opportunities to all pupils in turn to show these attentions.

8. Whenever it is possible, every direction in manners should be exemplified in the school-room. When the school-room does not furnish illustrations, directions should be made as real as possible to the youngest pupils, as, for instance, they should actually be shown how to hold the fork, how to drink from a tumbler, how to enter a room, etc.

9. The polite phrases of society should be used by the teacher to the pupil, and vice versa.

In the discipline of the school, when children have had training in good manners, the question "Is this polite?" will oftentimes prove more effectual than a severe reprimand. This has been demonstrated by actual experience, even in schools difficult of control.

LESSONS ON MANNERS

LESSON I. For the Youngest Pupils.

Purpose.—To awaken an interest in manners in general.

Method.—A common incident in real life briefly described, followed by questions and answers.

The Lesson.

As I was sitting on the piazza the other evening, watching the sunset and listening to the chirp of the birds, a boy passed along the sidewalk, and as he looked up and saw me, he touched his hat and smiled and said, "Good evening, Miss B." I smiled back and answered him, and as he passed on I thought about him. Why did I think about him?

"Because he was so pleasant to you."

Can you tell what I thought?

"You thought he was good."

"You thought he was a nice boy."

Why did I think so?

"Because he touched his hat."

"Because he smiled."

"Because he said, 'Good evening, Miss B.'"

Yes, because he was polite to me. Can you tell why we should be polite?

"It makes people think of us."

"It makes people like us."

What must we learn, then, if we wish people to like us?

"To be polite."

LESSON II.

Purpose.—To suggest kindness as an element of politeness.

Method.—A supposed incident is used, and questions given.

The Lesson.

Suppose a new little girl should come into our room. Perhaps she would come from a country far away from this place. Her dress might be queer, and she might not look like any other little girl in the room. What do you think these boys and girls would do?

"Look at her."

Oh, I hope not, for how would she feel?

"I guess she wouldn't like it."

"I think she would be scared."

"Perhaps she would cry."

If she should speak in her own way, not like ours, what would happen then?

"Like enough we should laugh."

Oh, no, I hope not.

"I should feel sorry for her."

What would you *do* for her, May?

"I would go and stand by her and speak to her."

What would you say?

"Please come and sit with me."

What would you say of May, children, if she should do and say what she thinks she would?

"That she is a good girl."

"She is a kind girl."

"And a polite girl."

What would you say of those children who stared and laughed at her?

"They were not kind."

"They were not polite."

What do you mean by politeness?

"It is to speak kind words."

"And to do kind acts."

Yes. I will tell you what it is, in a pretty verse:

"Politeness is to do and say
The kindest thing in the kindest way"

Note.—This couplet is to be memorized.

LESSON III.

Purpose.—To suggest seeking the happiness of others as an element of good manners.

Method.—A story told founded on an incident liable to happen at any time, and a conversation deduced.

The Lesson.

One day I looked out on the play-ground, where there were many children playing and seeming to have the best kind of a time. On the other side of the ground was one little girl looking as sad and lonely as you can think. I was about to go and see if I could cheer her up, when another little girl whose name was Jennie, and who had been playing with all her might, happened to see her. She left her place and went to the stranger, and said in a sweet way, "Wouldn't you like to come and play too? Come and take my place." And away they went hand-in-hand, looking as happy as two butterflies.

Now, what do you think of Jennie?

"She was good."

"She was kind."

"She asked the new girl to go and play."

Was that all?

"She gave up her place in the game that the little girl might play."

Was that very kind?

"Yes, Miss B."

How did it make the little stranger feel?

"Happy."

What do you say of such acts?

"They are polite."

How, then, shall we be polite to others?

"By trying to make them happy."

Note.—Although all the underlying principles of politeness can be taught unconsciously to the youngest pupils, it is better to teach but two formally, without unfamiliar terms. The end sought in the first year of instruction in this subject is to rouse thought and interest, and to lead the pupil to make simple judgments. In the next higher grade of lessons, other principles may be formally taught, and new terms brought out. In the highest grade all principles should be taught.

LESSONS ON MANNERS

SECOND TWO YEARS

LESSON V.

Purpose.—To suggest as a reason for cultivating good manners that we thus make our manners like those of the best people.

Method.—Questions and answers.

The Lesson.

Of what did we talk in our last lesson?

"Of kindness."

"And trying to make others happy."

What is it to think of the happiness of others before our own?

"Unselfishness."

And if we practice unselfishness, what can be said of us?

"That we have good manners."

But do all kind and unselfish people have good manners?

(Some are in doubt.) Let us see. I do not think a truly kind heart will allow any one to be rude, but how is it in this case? It is not thought polite to eat with the knife. Have you ever known kind people to do it?

"Yes, Miss B."

Why do you think they do it?

"Because they know no better."

Can they learn better?

"Yes, Miss B."

How?

"From other people."

How from other people?

"They can watch, and do what they see nice people do."

And how do these nice people know?

"Perhaps they have watched some other nice people."

If one who has used his knife in eating learns better, what ought he to do?

"To stop using it."

And if he continues to use it, what will be thought of him?

"That he is odd or queer."

Should you like to be thought odd or queer?

"No ma'am."

Then what must you do?

"We must watch people who know what good manners are, and try to make our manners like theirs."

What kind of people are polite?

"The best people."

If we learn to do as the best people do, how shall we be considered?

"To be *best* people."

Now tell me one reason why our manners should be good.

"Because the best people have good manners."

And another?

"Because we wish to be considered *best*."

LESSON VI.

Purpose.—To suggest gaining the esteem of others as a reason why good manners should be cultivated.

Method.—A story.

The Lesson.

A boy once wished to find a place to work. He went to a shop in town where he had heard help was needed. Many were there before him, and he thought he stood no chance at all of getting the work, but much to his surprise he was employed. He said, "Why, sir, I did not expect it when so many were ahead of me." "Do you wish to know why I hired you?" said the gentleman. "You came in quietly, you took off your hat, you gave your chair to an old man, you stood patiently until your turn came, and then you spoke pleasantly and in a manly tone of voice; in fact, I saw you were a well-bred boy, and that is the reason I hired you."

If this boy had been rude, what would have happened?

"He would not have been employed."

How did the gentleman feel toward him?

"He liked him."

What was his one reason for liking him? He had never seen him before.

"His manners were good."

If your manners are good, how will people feel toward you?

"They will like us."

Tell me, then, a reason why you should be polite.

"We should be polite because people like us better for it."

9. Town and Country

In the eighties and nineties the vast majority of Americans still lived on farms or in small country towns, their environment not physically very different from the surroundings of their ancestors. Urban values and ideas, however, now penetrated even the rural hinterlands, and the discrepancy between agrarian ideals and economic constraints was emphasized by the glamour of the rising urban centers, in the West as well as on the eastern seaboard.

John Herbert Quick (1861–1925) grew up in the Iowa of the late nineteenth century. In later life he recalled the texture of rural life as it must have appeared to many of his contemporaries. Teacher, lawyer, political leader, and in time a national spokesman for farmers, Quick remained attached to rural living even while many of his neighbors found the attractions of the city too much to withstand.

Among those spreading information about urban life, and sometimes indignation about its abuses, were a group of American photographers and cartoonists. Joseph and Percy Byron, a father and son team, along with Jacob Riis,* were among the most influential photographers working in the country during this period. Riis used his pictures to dramatize his battle against New York's slums, while the Byrons were more exclusively professional photographers, shooting yacht races, fancy dress balls, hotel life, restaurants, department stores, theaters, and street scenes in thousands of pictures published by magazines and newspapers. Siegmund Krausz,** a Chicago photographer, did not, like the Byrons, attempt spontaneity in his pictures, preferring to pose his subjects in conformity with already existing stereotypes about city life. His pictures and text, however, form a valuable record of how some Americans rationalized the contrasts of metropolitan living. And Michelangelo Woolf,*** like the Byrons an English emigrant, caught the sentimentalized tone of contemporary attitudes toward children. His bittersweet comments focused on city waifs, deprived of the pleasures of a secure childhood, but finding pleasure in the diversions of sidewalk life.

* Pictures by Riis and the Byrons are reproduced from the collections of, and through the permission of the Museum of the City of New York.
** Sigmund Krausz, *Street Types of Great American Cities* (Chicago, 1896), pp. 10–11, 18–19, 54–55, 150–151, 174–175.
*** M. A. Woolf, *Sketches of Lowly Life in a Great City*, ed. Joseph Henius, (New York and London, 1899), pp. 65, 87, 149.

The Tragedy of the Wheat

HERBERT QUICK

Who of my readers remembers Frank Norris, who died in the midst of writing his trilogy on wheat, after finishing *The Octopus* and *The Pit?* I should like to read those novels again. Norris died in 1902 at the early age of thirty-two. If he had lived, he would, I feel sure, have escaped from the influence of Zola and given us even greater fiction than the books I have named, and they were powerful. But if he had lived my life, he could have written a story of wheat which would have outdone anything he had planned on the grain which keeps us alive. It might have been called *The Tragedy of Wheat.*

We grew wonderful wheat at first; the only problem was to get it to market and to live on the proceeds when it was sold. My father hauled his wheat from the Iowa River to Waterloo, and even to Iowa City, when it was the railhead for our part of the country; hauled it slowly over mere trails across the prairie. It took him three days to market a load of wheat in Waterloo. I remember his telling us one morning of a dream he had had. His dream was that after hauling a load to Waterloo, he was offered only thirty cents a bushel for it.

"I'll be goshblasted," he thought he replied, "if I'll take thirty cents! I'll haul it back home first and give it to the poor."

My mother gave him a long look and burst into a gale of laughter. Father looked dazed for a moment; and then the huge joke came to him also of the Quick family giving anything to the poor. It was a jolly breakfast. The poor! Good heavens and earth, where could any one be found poorer than we? We were impoverished by wheat growing.

But the worst, however, was yet to come. A harvest came when we found that something was wrong with the wheat. No longer did the stalks stand clean and green as of old until they went golden in the sun. The broad green blades were spotted red and black with rust. Still it grew tall and rank; but as it matured it showed signs of disease. The heads did

Herbert Quick, *One Man's Life* (Indianapolis, 1923), pp. 207–210, 212–217, 340–347, 354–357, 398–408. Reprinted by permission of the Bobbs-Merrill Company.

not fill well. Some blight was at work on it. However, we thought next year all would be well again. And when it grew worse year by year, it became a blight not only on the life of the grain but on human life as well. Wheat was almost our sole cash crop. If it failed, what should we do? And it was failing!

We were incurring, of course, the penalty for a one-crop system. We ought to have known that it was inevitable. Yet even the agricultural experts did not know what was the trouble until a quarter of a century afterward; when it was worked out, I believe, by the scientists of the North Dakota College of Agriculture. Preying on the wheat were fungi, bacteria, and molds. We sowed wheat after wheat until every field became a culture bed for every antagonistic organism; but instead of finding a remedy, we were only amazed and driven to despair by the calamity.

Some of our people thought that one crop of wheat after another had robbed the soil of some necessary property; but my father pointed out the fact that not even on newly broken sod could good wheat now be grown. It must be something else. Maybe the climate had changed. If it had, why it would change back next year. So we went on, as farmers nearly always do, sticking to the system which had become established. The new breaking, we now know, had become infected with the wheat diseases from the surrounding fields or the infections were blown to it by the winds.

This era gave me my first contact with the phenomenon which puzzles so many city people. If the farmers are losing money on a certain crop, why in the world don't they change to something else? It is not so easy to change as the city man may think. . . . The manufacturer can shut down when the market is bad, or specialize for a few weeks or months on a thing which pays. The business man may slow up on purchases and narrow his operations, pursuing one policy one month and making a change the next, always trying things out in a small way and feeling his projects out. But the farmer's experiment always takes a year and involves so great a loss in case of bad judgment or misfortune that he perforce becomes very conservative. We were so in our devotion to wheat. It was tragic, but natural.

• • •

The fields of grain had always been a delight to me. Nothing can be more beautiful than a gently rolling landscape covered with growing wheat. The shadows of the clouds swept over it majestically. The waves of shadow as the grain bent to the breeze, straightened and then bent again, used to bring tears to my eyes—tears of sheer delight—it was so marvelously lovely. But now all the poetry went out of it. There was no joy for the soul of the boy who was steeped in such poetry as he could stumble upon, in these grain-fields threatened by grasshoppers, eaten by chinchbugs, blackened with molds and rusts, their blades specked as with the shed blood of the husbandman, their gold dulled by disease, their straw crinkling down in dead brittleness instead of rising and falling and swaying with the beautiful resiliency of health and abundance.

• • •

We looked about in vain for aid, and none came. Some, of course, looked to the government for aid. Other people had help, they said, why not the farmers? The government gave the manufacturers a tariff, didn't it, so they could have the whole market to themselves? Then why couldn't it do something for us? This was about the time that specie payments were resumed, and "resumption" was a word much bandied about.

The silver question had not yet reached us, to puzzle and divide. We were on a paper-money basis. We looked to Congress to make times better by the issuance of greenbacks. Tom Brown, one of our neighbors, stopped in the front yard one morning, and, of course, the hard times became the subject of conversation. He brought the news that Congress had just passed a law calling for the issuance of some thirty million dollars of new greenbacks. This ought to help us some, he thought. I doubt if he or any of us had any idea of the way in which such an issue affected trade and prices through inflation; the argument merely was that it would make money plentier. My mother looked out over the wheat-fields and refused to show enthusiasm.

"Thirty millions is a lot of money," she admitted—though it seems ridiculous now—"but by the time it gets spread out as far as Iowa, it won't make much difference. It's like pourin' a pail of water in the river."

I can't help thinking that her summing up of the case was a good one.

All this time, while we were playing the role of the tortured victims in the tragedy of the wheat, we were feeling our way toward some way out. We knew that our fields would grow great crops of maize—it was a good corn country. But if there was more than one person who grew and fed cattle for the market there, I did not know of it. The average small farmer grew into the combination of hogs and corn. Gradually we changed over from wheat farming to big corn-fields and populous hog lots. And then the price of both corn and pork went down, down, down, until corn sold for less than ten cents a bushel in our depreciated money and hogs for even less than three cents a pound. We had not found out about the balanced ration and the hog's need of pasture; and after a few generations of a diet of corn, the swine lost vitality and the crop of young pigs failed, save where there was milk for them. The villain of misfortune still pursued us.

Our fuel was now soft coal, and the cold winters of Iowa called for much fuel. A time came when a load of corn drawn to market would just about pay for a load of coal to haul home; so to save the long-drawn dragging of the two loads over the fourteen miles to the railway and back, we began using the corn itself for fuel. To the older people who had been reared in an atmosphere of the cheap fuel of the forests and the scarcity of cereals for food, there was something sinful in this. My Grandmother Coleman had a language of her own which consisted of groans, and this she used whenever she saw the great ears of corn going into the stove.

"When I think," she would say, "of the folks in this world that are hungry, it seems a sin to burn up victuals like this."

"Well," my father would reply, "I don't see as it's my duty to put in my time and freeze myself to death haulin' corn to town to trade it for coal, an' maybe pay some boot for the sake of gettin' it."

Gradually we worked out a better *modus vivendi*—worked it out in a welter of debt and a depression which has characterized the rural mind to this day. Corn and hogs came to pay us as little as had wheat; yet for a while they were our only recourse, for the soil refused to grow wheat. For a long time there was plenty of open prairie on which cattle could be grazed freely. My first economic usefulness was that of a herd boy. I was a very bad rider and was in the habit of falling off when my horse turned quickly, owing to my feebleness of spine; and I was never able to leap upon my horse's back from the ground, or even climb up. So I developed the scheme of getting on his neck when he put his head down to graze and sliding to place when he lifted it. Yet I herded the cattle summer after summer. Then the expanding acres of wheat land cut us off from any extended range of free grass. We had no fencing until barbed wire came in. So our cows were picketed on the prairie, led to water and cared for much as the Danes handle their cows now.

In spite of these difficulties, however, it gradually dawned upon us that by the sale of butter we were getting a little money from time to time. And though eggs were sometimes as low as eight cents a dozen, they brought in some funds. The skim milk restored our hogs to health. Without conscious planning, we were entering the business of mixed farming. My mother's butter was famed in all the near-by villages. In view of all the pains she took with it, it should have been; for she met the hot weather of our Iowa summers by hanging both cream and butter down the well where it was cool. Finally a creamery was started in Holland, a small town near us; and by this time we had a nice little herd of cows. A tank was made where water could be pumped through it and in this we set our cans of milk; and the cream hauler of the creamery came, skimmed off the cream, gave us tickets for it and hauled it away, thus giving us the cash when we went to town and saving the women the work of making the butter. It was the first contact of the factory system with the Iowa farm.

All this made life easier both as to labor and money. But it was not our only amelioration. We began to have a better food supply. Our apple trees never did anything, for the varieties which thrive in Iowa were not known when our orchard was set out. But our strawberries, raspberries, grapes, gooseberries, currents, and cherries yielded abundantly. I had a patch of raspberries which I pruned and tended on a system of my own which gave us all we could consume and furnished dividends for our friends. In place of the old regimen of dried fruits and just dry groceries, we were surfeited on jams, jellies, preserves and other delicious viands; and with our supply of milk and cream, found the pioneer epoch definitely past so far as the larder was concerned.

The prairie had been tamed. Iowa had been civilized. Our eighty-acre farm was furnishing us a real living for the first time. The era of extensive farming and the consolidation of farms into larger holdings had scarcely begun. The curse of high land values had not yet come upon us. Though our incomes were very low and we were still oppressed by debts, I am inclined to believe that the years which definitely marked the end of the tragedy of the wheat were the best years Iowa agriculture has seen.

The farmer is often accused by the city dweller of being a confirmed calamity howler. He is. He is such because almost every calamity which comes on the land hits him sooner or later. Whenever any other industry shifts from under an economic change it shifts it in part upon the farmer, and the farmer is unable to shift it in his turn; while most other shiftees can, by adding to prices or wages, get from under the load. The farmer is so placed that there is nothing beyond him but the wall. He is crushed against it. There is nothing under him but the earth. He is pressed into it. He is the end of the line in the economic game of crack the whip, and he is cracked off. He has been cracked off into city life by the million.

The utterances of some great men to the effect that this is not a bad thing leave out of account the pregnant truth that, after all, the basis of civilization is agriculture; that our farming class, not being composed of fools, will not stay on the soil with better city opportunities open to them; that once divorced from the soil a people never have returned to it; and that what we are observing is in danger of becoming the progressive ruin of our cities and our civilization. I have been describing the history of one family and one generation of farmers so that my readers may understand, if they try, why farmers are likely to be calamity howlers. The howl comes from the contact place of the calamity.

SOME NEGLECT OF THE JEALOUS MISTRESS

One of our novelists of condemnation could revel in the crude materialism of Mason City at that time—or now; or of New York or Philadelphia, either. We had no institution of learning higher than our public school. There was in the city no club devoted to the study of literature, history, or science. We had no Y.M.C.A. to arrange lectures for us, nor any other organization with the same functions. Parker's Opera House took the attractions which came along, and many of these I saw; because my friend Klinefelter, through his newspaper, very often had press tickets for me. These shows in a town of three or four thousand people were not often of a very high order; but occasionally the Andrews Opera Company, a family organization with headquarters somewhere in southern Minnesota, gave us excellent presentations of light opera; and such actors as Thomas W. Keene presented Shakespearean plays once in a while. Such cultural activities as we had grew mainly out of church activities.

Our family has always had a flair for music; at least since my father in his young manhood was chorister in his little church at Danby or Candor, in Tompkins County, New York. I had no musical training, but somehow —I forget how—I found myself a member of the choir of the First Methodist Church, under the leadership of a man who was one of those intellectual Robinson Crusoes, a person wrapped up in art in an undeveloped and materialistic society, L. L. Huntly. He was a good organist and had an excellent tenor voice. He confided to me one day that he was a cousin of the American Hemans, Lydia Huntly Sigourney, most of whose poems are now forgotten along with those of the British versifier with whom she was so often compared.

Mrs. Sigourney's poems still commanded some rather unmerited attention in the 'eighties. It rather startled me to hear Professor Huntly refer to her as Lyd. Huntly agreed that if I would sing for him in the church, he would do what he could with my voice. This was not very much, and yet it enabled me to earn a little money afterward at a time when I needed it, and it brought me into close relations with some musicians, many singers, and a few churches. It gave me an intimate familiarity with the palms of the hands of many ministers, as they stood with their hands behind their backs and preached. All these things are worthy of study.

Huntly had the artist's temperament and loved to talk with me about his music. When musicians of real aquirements came to us, Huntly used to revel in meetings with them. Blind Boone, the pianist, came occasionally; and he and Huntly used to amuse themselves with a sort of a musical puzzle system. Each would play a selection, picking out passages supposed to be unfamiliar to the other, and ask the name of the composer. Once Huntly played a slow, stately largo movement with dainty little embellishments.

"That's Beethoven," said Blind Boone; "but what's it from?"

Huntly accelerated the movement, and it became *Yankee Doodle*, greatly to Boone's astonishment.

I have heard Huntly play this *Yankee Doodle* adaptation as a voluntary in church. I have heard him sing a Kyrie eleison in a perfectly angelic way, to his own accompaniment, as the people walked out of church. I feel sure they would have been shocked at this music had they known what it was. Among the things which were thought by Mr. Cliggitt to have interfered with my slavish devotion to that jealous mistress, the law, were the choir meetings I attended and the musical events in which I soon came to take part. They did cut into my evenings a bit.

This was the era of Gilbert and Sullivan. Mrs. James E. Moore, one of our musicians, undertook the presentation of *The Pirates of Penzance* with local talent. The role of Mabel went to Mrs. Moore, since she was a good soprano—and why else get the thing up? She found a tenor in C. B. Higgins, who did the Frederick part very well; and she managed to pick up people for the other solo parts. It was taken for granted that our best baritone, W. E. Ensign, would be The Pirate King; but Will began, rehearsed a few times and backed out. Everyone thought it was because he was jealous of the prominence of Mabel and Frederick; but he took me aside and assured me that his real reason was that he couldn't mingle music with the comic. Give him an oratorio part, he said, and he was at home; but he was too stately for any pirate king.

"The fact is, Quick," he said, dropping his voice, "folks think I'm stuck on myself, and stuck up; but I'm not. I act just the same way when I'm mowing the lawn or washing the buggy. I simply can't take this part."

So Mrs. Moore asked me to be the pirate king; and willing to try anything once, I consented. The thing went off—not my part, but the opera—with great success. We sang it and repeated it. And a year or so afterward it was staged again, and I went back from Sioux City to take my old part in it. We also sang *The Chimes of Normandy*. I have proof that my part was excellently well done, for Klinefelter so stated in his write-up of the event in the *Express-Republican*. He was still strong for his discovery, and any sort of a noise made by me would have gained recognition as great stuff in his paper.

We thought we did the *Pirates* mighty well; but I have sometimes been harassed by doubts. I remember a dress rehearsal just before we gave our first show. Back in the wings were two strangers who, I discovered, belonged to the theatrical profession. The sopranos and the policemen who did the bass parts were rehearsing their part of the full chorus which closes the first act. The pirates were for the moment off watch; and in my kingly robes I was leaning against one of the flies, listening to the remarks which our two professional visitors were making. They were impressed, I could see that; but there was something in the tempo which disturbed them. I now know that we sang it twice too slow. General Stanley's daughters were not "climbing over rocky mountains" half fast enough. And when the policemen "slapped their chests" and sang "Ta-ran-ta-ra," they failed to put their clubs to their mouths as trumpets. The two members of the profesh looked at each other and grinned.

"Do you think we ought to tell her about it," asked one.

"No, for the love of heaven!" replied the other. "It would ruin 'em. They couldn't make the change at this late day—and, you know, some of it ain't so rotten!"

Rather considerate of them when one comes to think of it. I was somewhat disillusioned by this comment on our work. One experiences that feeling once one gets back of the scenes. When the flies were all run back on the stage of Parker's Opera House, the audience saw painted on the back wall of the stage a marine view, rather well done. It was a scene of green islands, waving palms and rocky shores. I had often admired what I took to be a sailboat represented as skimming across the bay, its sail dipping to the freshening breeze. But when, in my royal capacity, I went back to that wall, I was astonished to find that my white-winged yacht was nothing but a spot of plaster which had been knocked off by the awkwardness of some stage mechanic. The last touch of romance proved to be a bit of disrepair. That represents the difference between the view of the poor illuded occupant of a seat in the audience and the sophisticated one behind the scenes.

I have been away back behind the scenes in our national life since then; and I have noted many things in the highly exalted which to the public appeared as the finishing touches to a beautiful picture, but were to the one back on the stage merely marred spots in the scenery. The generous heartiness of a great man turned out to be not much more than a rather good-hearted stupidity and carelessness. The intense devotion to the welfare of the people and to even-handed justice of another was on close inspection just a hole through the plaster of devotion to special interests. The inflexible rectitude of a third was largely obstinacy and self-esteem. The devotion to a great moral movement of another was a pose as far from the truth as the mark of the plank on the wall from the picture of a yacht. The deep knowledge of the law and the Spartan patriotism of another—as seen from the front—was intellectual denseness, lethargy, and laziness. The public viewing the bad spots in the wall through the haze of distance and the mirage created by press, platform, and pulpit, beholds every defect turned by our conventions in such cases to a perfection, every vice to a virtue. And the man who calls the hole in the wall by its true name soon finds how much more comfortable he would be if he cried, "Beautiful! Perfect!" with the rest.

Our opera company was largely recruited from the church choirs, and many of our beauties were members of the churches. Hence not a few of the best people were greatly scandalized. I think my friend Klinefelter was responsible for a part of this high tide of reproach. Kline said—not in his paper, but where it circulated just as far—that in his judgment, the Episcopalian ladies were the best dancers but the Methodists had the prettiest legs. Great heavens! To mention a portion of the human underpinning in this manner, and to have had the ocular basis for the remark, was something not to be endured—not in the eighteen-eighties. It is different now, very different indeed.

So great the departure from the norm of churchly behavior was this deed of enrolling in an opera company, rehearsing, actually dancing, and making possible such shocking comparisons among them as this of their dancing and one thing and another; and finally of presenting on the stage a profane piece like *The Pirates of Penzance,* so wrought upon the mind of the pastor of the Methodist church in which I was a humble choir member, that he prepared and preached a terrible sermon in which he condemned yieldings to worldly tendencies in scathing terms. He did not refer directly to the Pirates—he just scorched things so close to piracy that it hurt. I remember his text—and it was the text that most deeply harrowed up tender feelings; for while no one could say that it referred to anything of recent date, it had a swinging lash to it which hit everything and which was all the more cutting because of its apparent generality. It was Revelations 19:2: "For true and righteous are his judgments;

for he hath judged the great whore which did corrupt the earth with her fornications, and hath avenged the blood of his servants at her hand."

How could one discuss such a text as that? Clearly it was, as the diplomats say, outside the field of discussion. Professor Huntly, who had not had a role in the opera, because he said he was too old to make love, looked quizzically at the ladies of the choir who had given Kline the chance to make his ill-timed and his really improper jest. They blushed, more with indignation than anything else, and swept with stately dignity from the church in which they felt that they had received an insult which they could not resent. One offended young matron left before the services were over. It was not what the text actually meant; nobody stopped to analyze the text; it was those awful words in it. I never heard any deliverance which could not be strictly construed to mean anything definite, or to be addressed to any one in particular, which made so distinct an impression. Several of our nicest members felt as if they had been called dreadful names. And this, I believe, is exactly the result which the minister wished to attain. How long ago this was!

As for me, I had no chips in the game. The pastor was not talking to me. I had already made for myself a position as a sort of free-lance, who did as he mighty well pleased, and laughed at criticism. I was on the whole rather titivated by the part I had taken. I had felt myself rising in the community out of my former obscurity. It is not every day that a principal of a ward school late from the country can become a pirate king, and have friends of the press to shield him from the criticism which no doubt he deserved.

In the summer of 1887 I had my first glimpse of a great city—Chicago. The National Teachers' Association held its annual convention there, and the sleeping car on the Chicago, Milwaukee and St. Paul train was pretty well filled with people taking advantage of the excursion rates to make a visit to the great metropolis of the West. I was one of the party, and in it were Klinefelter, Tom Miller, Art Sale, Judge Cummings, and many more, both teachers and members of the laity. The sleeping car was a new thing to me. I remember that the extravagance of paying the porter a tip of a whole quarter impressed me as uncalled for, though I yielded to custom. Tom Miller invented several remarks attributed to me, the point of which was my verdancy.

"Did you hear what Quick said when he came into the city?" he asked so that all could hear. "He said, 'There's a house bigger than John West's. Why, Chicago's built up on both sides of the track!'"

This was an exaggeration; but the city was a great sight for me. The

Iowa headquarters were in a hotel across the street north of the Palmer House. The street between was paved with Belgian-block pavement. All that first day I was dazed by the throngs; and Tom said they found me once standing in a doorway as if waiting for something. When they asked me what I was waiting for, he said I remarked that I had stopped to give the crowd a chance to get by! This also was a statement colored somewhat by the mentality of its author.

I went to bed late that first night and slept heavily after the wakefulness of the night before and the weariness of a day of excitement. As I slept I dreamed I was out in Iowa, and that a fearful storm had risen. I heard its roar in my ears, deafening me. Surely this was a tornado. I was terrified, I leaped out of bed. The sun was shining in the window; but the roar went on. It was the thunder of traffic on the pavement outside. I crawled back into bed, but I slept no more; and I did not tell Tom or Cummings about my dream. They would have based a tradition on it.

Two inventions have mitigated the tornado which beat upon the sensorium of city dwellers then—the soft-tired motor-car and asphalt and concrete pavements; but still my dream proves what a revolution has taken place in the environment of a nation of country people, accustomed for ages to the stillness of the country-side, who have become city dwellers. The sounds of the city are only one element in this new world in which humanity has learned to live; but the noises alone mark a change from peace to a tornado. No wonder the neurologists have a busy life.

I never found out where the meetings of the National Teachers' Association took place. I began my career as a visitor to such gatherings, as I have in the main continued it, by ignoring the ostensible objects of them. I took my dip into the night life of the city. I rode in street-cars drawn swiftly along by horses and carrying one to the end of the line for a nickel. I stood on the shore of Lake Michigan and for the first time gazed out across water so broad as to form the horizon. And all the time I was filled with such a crowd of new impressions that they grew dim even as I looked and listened.

There was a landing for steamers then at the foot of Madison Street, at a place which is now nearly half a mile inshore from the lake. One evening an excursion for the Iowa delegation was planned. I started for the landing, alone, I think, when I saw one fire engine after another dash off southward, their horses running madly, their gongs clanging. I forgot all about the excursion and followed the crowd to the fire. It was miles away, but its flares beckoned to us. It was in fact away down in the railway yards; but it was worth seeing. The great soap works of N. K.

Fairbank & Co. were burning. It would be a great spectacle for me even now. The next day a member of the Chicago Fire Department told me that so large a proportion of the department had not been called out to any conflagration since the Great Fire.

To see the rushing streams of water turned to steam as they entered the flames, to see the great oil tanks heated one after another until they sent off huge clouds of black smoke, and then to see them burst into soaring beacons of flame, rising away above the surrounding buildings, laughing at the puny efforts of the firemen to control them—it was a marvelous sight. I feasted my rural eyes on it until it had begun to burn low and its spread was under control, and then went back to the hotel. I had seen something that none of the rest of the party had witnessed—an immense crowd at a Chicago fire, and one of the most spectacular conflagrations of the time.

I SEE A GREAT LIGHT

There be those called teachers who say to us that the villages, towns, and when the full truth is told, the cities, are almost without witnesses as to the great things of the spirit and the intellect. As for the rural regions, they instruct us, they are lost, as a matter of course. Does not "pagan" mean "paganus" which being interpreted meaneth a countryman? Brethren, it's a sad tale, this description of this world. Now Mason City is one of these lost towns in which the aspiring soul expires merely, or runs away to Lower Manhattan and spends its time running around, a merely spiral soul with more of its kind. But here is what happened to me in Mason City, Iowa, which I take it is another name for Gopher Prairie.

It was before I was admitted to the bar, I know; but just how long before I have no way of telling. Reverdy Miller, a young man reared in the town and educated in the colleges of the state, was one day when I came upon him, reading a thick paper-bound book.

"I was looking for some one to give this to," said he, handing it to me. "Take it and read it."

I looked at it with contempt; for it was a book greatly reprobated in the crowd with which I had been training; a book never read by those who condemned it; a book already known in most civilized lands, and often answered. It had been published for some years. I ranked its author with the two awful examples of destroying heterodoxy of those days, Herr Johann Most, and O'Donovan Rossa. Who of my readers remember those two disturbers? Few, of course, but they loomed large as agents of coming cataclysm then. This book handed me by Reverdy Miller, and the man who wrote it, were in my opinion as bad as Most, Rossa and their writings. Yet I took it and read it.

From childhood I had read everything I could find dealing with the structure of society. Analysis of institutions was familiar to me. I was not widely read on these subjects, and much of my reading had been rather inferior stuff, like the greenback propaganda of my teens, and the partisan outgivings of the days when I took as correct what the Republican orators and writers sent out. The best of my readings had been the compositions of the fervent minds of the abolition era—Wendell Phillips, Lowell, Whittier, Emerson and their contemporaries. These were strong morally and weak economically. These were not economists—we had no "sociologists" then—but reformers. All of them but Phillips had accepted the Republican Party as the Lord's Anointed, and in so far as they continued to think on social matters, had become conservatives and reactionaries. They thought the crusade for national righteousness ended when the slaves were freed. Phillips knew better; but even James Russell Lowell settled down in the belief that his eyes had seen the glory of the coming of the Lord, and there was nothing more to do. When Miller handed me that paper-bound book, my mind was in agreement with those of the poets and apostles of the pre-Civil-War period who were still living. I had no desire to read the works of a mischief-maker and disturber; but I took pride in having an open mind, and possessed a curiosity as to what the fellow had to say.

The preface, dated November, 1880, while its sweeping generalizations rather took away my breath, was so calm, so quiet, so free from that blatancy which marks the howl of the demagogue that I went on to the Introduction, entitled "The Problem" with half my hostility removed. This man appealed to thought rather than to passion. But in the introduction, I began to feel the swell of a suppressed fervor, and I sensed the confidence of the writer in the fact that he had attained to truth. He spoke calmly of the failure of political economy as then taught to explain, to say nothing of proposing a remedy for, the social evils which every one could see. This failure he urged came not from the inability of the human mind to solve the problem, but from false steps in various more or less accepted explanations. "And," he concluded, "as such mistakes are generally concealed by the respect paid to authority, I propose in this inquiry to take nothing for granted, but to bring even accepted theories to the test of first principles, and should they not stand the test, freshly to interrogate facts in the endeavor to discover their law. I propose to beg no question, to shrink from no conclusion, but to follow truth wherever it may lead. Upon us is the responsibility of seeking the law, for in the very heart of our civilization to-day women faint and little children moan. But what that law may prove to be is not our affair. If the conclusions that we reach run counter to our prejudices, let us not flinch; if they challenge institutions that have long been deemed wise and natural, let us not turn back."

What could be fairer, nobler, or bolder than this; and fairness, boldness and nobility thrilled me. I plunged into the book and read until I had finished it. The writer was Henry George, and the book was *Progress and Poverty*.

I have often wondered whether many men have passed through such an experience as mine in the reading of this book. I found the very foundations of my philosophy in the process of dissolution. Like the foundations of the Cathedral of St. Paul's, they turned out to be nothing but sand and rubble, and the structure of conviction and theory so dear to me was tottering to its fall; but the book did not destroy alone. It poured into the rotten base the concrete of a new and perfectly correlated doctrine, which has stood firm and unshaken ever since. But these foundations of belief which were moving, dissolving and undergoing reconstruction, were those of my very life. The dome which was trembling was that of the convictions which I had publicly proclaimed before my little world. Consistency is a very precious jewel, especially to him who even in a modest way has been a speaker and a writer; and I saw that if these were veritable truths which I was drinking in, I should be forced to repudiate my doctrines which I had held, and which constituted the bond between me and many dear friends. I was facing a crucial test of character, or I was being misled.

I struggled hard against conversion. Surely, I said to myself, there must be some error in this man's logic, some sophistry which I could not detect. I saw the power of his presentation, and felt the charm of his style. I knew that my mind was at close grips with an intellect of the first order, moved by an apostolic fervor. I said to myself in effect, that if this were really truth, I should be a lost soul if I rejected it; for it was not only a call to the discipleship of truth, but the most completely redemptive truth ever set before the world. It was true that all history was strewn with the wrecks of civilizations. It was true that progress had always been associated with growing poverty. It was true that all civilizations which had possessed the power of protecting themselves against destruction from dangers from the outside, had eventually rotted from within. It was true that the increase of wealth had been accompanied by the increase of poverty in America.

And here was an analysis of the factors which were not only at work in our own society, but must inevitably have been at work all through history, which not only had produced the disease in the past everywhere, but must generate it in us as surely as decade should follow decade. Here was at last a perfectly plain and irrefutable exposition of the way in which wealth is distributed as it is produced. As every one has agreed, it fell into the divisions of interest, wages and rent; but George, for the first time, defined these three so that each included no portion of either of the others. He gave perfect definitions of interest, wages and rent. Then he showed that as rent increased with the increase of population, and the progress of the arts and sciences, it is always subtracted, and must in the nature of things be subtracted, from the portions of wealth produced going into wages and interest.

He demonstrated that with land reduced to private possession, the economists before him had been correct in asserting that rent is measured by the superior productive capacity of any land in question, in site value in cities, and in farming value or the like in the country, over the least desirable land in use. In other words, rent depends upon the margin of cultivation, as Ricardo, Mill and others had said. But George showed that interest also depends on the margin of cultivation, as it must take its share of what is left after rent is satisfied; and that wages also depend upon it for the same reason. Thus the land question became the fundamental fact in economics as well as in sociology.

I was surprised to find here a reformer saying a good word for interest; but George proved not only the necessity, but the righteousness of interest. He showed that rent is at the expense of interest, and thus takes from capital a part of a larger share which it should have. But the crux of his demonstration lay in the proof that it is rent which crushes labor down to the returns from the poorest land in cultivation, and that this really means down to the smallest wage on which labor can live and reproduce. He was not content with the really mathematical demonstration of this. He proved it inductively, and deductively. He scanned history for evidence. He stated all the objections which have ever been made against his system in a stronger form than they have ever been stated by his opponents; and answered them beforehand. And he proposed a remedy for the social disease of increasing poverty with the development of a civilization which was simple and just.

He showed that rent arises in the nature of things. No one is to blame for it. As land in a new society is occupied the superior land must bear rent. But rent comes, not from the labor of the owner, so far as the mere land is concerned; but from the progress of society. Hence, morally, it belongs to society. There this "unearned increment" of land values, in city and country, should be collected yearly by the government as belonging to the whole people. All public expenditures should be paid for with it. No one under such circumstances would hold land for any purpose except use, and he would pay only what the use was worth. All wealth produced by human activities would be untaxed. Nothing would be taxed save that which was created by the taxing power. Really the single tax would not be a tax at all, in the ordinary sense, since it would be merely a payment to the whole people for a benefit enjoyed. All titles would remain as now. There would be no disturbance of any occupation. Things would gradually readjust themselves. Wages and interest would rise to their proper level. The problem of poverty and want would be cured, and that without revolution. People freed from the trammels of a rigid land system could readjust themselves to any system of public order they might choose. Even the benefits claimed by socialism could be realized in so far as they might be realizable through voluntary cooperation, without the tryanny of state socialism. This is in a very sketchy form the vision which dawned on me as I read *Progress and Poverty.*

A perfectible society, and the obvious means of perfecting it. The ancient riddle of ruin solved at last. The abolition of involuntary poverty in view. Eternal racial life attainable for us of the end of the century, under terms of freedom, and with no need for revolution. I moved for days in a plane of exaltation such as I have never experienced before or since. I was uplifted to the skies. Again I suffered. It was the breaking up of the fountains of the great deep, and the opening of the windows of my spiritual heaven. I can not wish any young reader a better thing than some such experience. I have never for a moment since lost that something like a transformation which came to me then.

Of course no such book ought to have been given me by a young man born and brought up in Gopher Prairie; and no young man from a still more sordid plane of our lost and damned American life ought to have read it—not if we are to believe what recent pictures of such life depict. Yet Reverdy Miller gave and commended it to me, and I read it. And when I went back to him with a new light in my face, I suspect obscured by some clouds of doubt, and asked him if he believed what George had written, he said he did.

"Nobody can refute it," said he. "It's the real stuff!"

But I was not ready to take what he said as any strong buttress of a thing which must stand against every attack. He was a Democrat, for one thing, and I had a feeling that he had a weakness for the new and untried. So I went to Richard Montague, who had been our prize student in the

Mason City High School, and had come back from the state university trailing clouds of academic glory and a lawyer's sheepskin. He had a mind, the reaction of which it was worth while to get.

"Have you read *Progress and Poverty*?" I asked him.

"Yes," said he.

"What do you think of it?"

"It's the political economy of the future," he replied. "It is a discovery in the realm of thought. It's truth."

Then, even in Mason City, I had another mind to which I could appeal. I could ask Duncan Rule what he thought of it.

"I've been reading *Progress and Poverty*," said I. "Have you read it, Dunc?"

"Yes," said he, "I've given it a pretty close study."

"What do you think of it?" I asked.

"Well," said Duncan, who unlike Miller and Montague had an official position to maintain, "it makes the other political economists look like infants. If you grant George's premises, you can't avoid his conclusions."

I sat a while in thought, weighing what he had said. These were men who did their own thinking, to whom I had appealed. They had seen nothing wrong with the book. I realized that in Rule's mind the doubtful point was not in the system itself, but in getting it applied.

"Well," said I at last, "I think I'm as good a judge of his premises as any one. It was his logical processes I was inquiring about. Anything wrong with them?"

"Not a thing!" said Duncan.

I don't believe I could have found more intelligent men anywhere with whom to confer on this matter of "weighing a philosopher and gauging a philosophy," than these three natives and lifelong residents of this little burg on the Iowa prairie. I have always found such men wherever I have gone. The writers who condemn our society for its lack of people of brain and vision merely describe what they have wished to find. The masses of our people are rich in every desirable human trait. All they need is a state of things calculated to bring these virtues to the surface, rather than to stunt and dwarf them. In this fact lies the hope of all our future.

As for the philosophy with which I became acquainted, a search of forty years for truth has never shaken my faith in its correctness, nor in the belief that it must be accepted, not only in America but all over the world if civilization is not to rot down into ruin as have those of the past. I have tried to find the answer to it; but there is none. I do not mean that I agree with Henry George in everything, but in every vital point in his system,

I believe more strongly than ever. My experience as a man of affairs, and a student of world history as well as of sociology, has confirmed this faith. I have long since ceased to expect any progress of any consequence toward it in my time. At first I could not see how it could fail to win a great victory soon; but I made no allowance for the inevitable "drag" between the discovery of truth and its acceptance and adoption in human affairs.

And it may never be accepted. If not, our civilization will not last, and the world, it seems to me, will be worse off than in past ages when dominant cultures have broken down through the conflict between the House of Want and the House of Have; for we can now see no fresh barbarians to come in and take our places. It may be that the last Great Experiment is now going on. It may be that in Henry George we have in America produced the mind which will make it a success. If there is any such thing as overruling guidance of our affairs, this must be so.

1. *Siegel Cooper Company's Bargain Counter, 1897.*

2. *Daughters of the American Revolution Meeting, 1898.*

3. *The Lower East Side, 1898.*

4. Fifth Avenue North from 65th Street, Showing the J. J. Astor House in the Foreground, 1898.

5. *T. E. Fitzgerald's Bar.*

6. Vantine's Tea Room.

7. *Hotel Marie Antoinette, Foyer, 1896.*

8. *Dishwashers at Astor Hotel.*

9. *Park Avenue Hotel, The Court.*

10. Lodging House.

11. Home of Mr. Ed Lauterbach, 2 East 78th Street, Hall, 1899.

12. *Black and Tan Dive on Broome Street.*

260

13. Home of Mr. Blakeley Hall, 11 West 45th Street, Parlor, 1896.

14. Coming Home from Fresh Air Vacation.

15. *Home of Mr. Ed Lauterbach, Dining Room.*

16. Child's Restaurant, 1899.

TERRIBLE.

"Yes, it 's just too awful to think I 've got to grow so old that gents won't make room for me in the cars!"

17. City Waifs.

HER SMALL WISH.

"See w'ot I found in the ash-barril. What a pity it ain't got no stummick!"
"I envies it. If I didn't have no stummick I would n't want no grub!"

TEN CENTS' WORTH.

Consuelo (reading): "The viz-count entered the apartment with a languid h'air, and puffed his cigaroot with wiolence. 'Air you alone?' he inkwired in a nongshallnot manner of the countiss. She rose from the turkeys otterman with a diluted nostril, her eyes flashed with a fire which almost consoomed their lids, and shakin' her jewilled left hand in the viz-count's face, she gave a majestic sweep with her right foot an' lef' the room."

Omnes: "My!"

WHEN THE THERMOMETER IS MELTING
IN THE SHADE.

"Oh! But this is bully; it's more coolin' than ice-cream, an' makes me feel better 'n pink leminade does!"

18. Contrasts.

ONE OF THE FINEST.

The moral status of the policeman is the moral status of the city he serves. Complain as you will of the scandalous conduct of this or that member. Mourn at the seeming general depravity of the men who wear the blue. They are yet a reflex of the people who employ them. When Cromwell ruled, officers were praying men. When Louis was king, they intrigued for mistresses. In America they travel on the average lines of intelligence, honesty and fidelity followed by the mass.

Policemen are men. They—unlike poets—are made, not born. What a man was in former life he is as a policeman. Putting on blue, thatching his poll with a helmet, filling his hand with a club or a revolver does not make him braver, or abler, or more honest than he was at the beginning. Also, it cannot make him worse. Remember in your sweeping condemnation the officers who stand indifferent to weather; who brave danger every time they help a child across the street; who invite mutilation every time they make an arrest; who are knit of the fibre of rectitude and strength, and who stand for the best that is in their employer. Remember, as there are heights of holiness, there are sinks of iniquity. Laving in these polluted waters are human brutes whose venomous hate is leveled at no one with such deadly purpose as at the officer. They delight in "slugging" him. They are the tigers of a city's jungle. They rend without reason—only because they hate that typified Right. They would peril their life to injure it. They would give their life to obliterate it.

Between the Bad, who hate him upon one side, and the Good, who distrust him on the other, the life of "One of the Finest" is far from serene.

COMPETITORS.

This conflict is not only irrepressible; it is hopelessly unending. Oil and water are not more diverse than are the black man and the white. Good humor may bridge the gulf. Hilarity may gloss the scar. But when the laughter and dance are ended, there lies an ocean of difference, of antagonism, of scorn on the one side and spite on the other—for the Caucasian and the Ethiopian are at war. The land which gave the latter birth was pushed in creation far away, below and apart from the land of light. It was divided by seas, and bulwarked by deserts. It was all but cut off, and kept its tiny tendon of connection at the most forbidding point—where the simoom of the South was wasted and lost in the measureless sands of the East. Yet Fate, "whose stepping-stones are ages," pierced through all barriers, to leaven with the African the lighter life of Europe and the West. But dominance is not shifted. By a Suez isthmus the darker lad still clings to human recognition. By the preponderance of mighty seas the white denies it.

" I am a master; you, my slave ! ''

'' Prove it—for I am a man ! ''

The street boys, with all humanity in common, with enjoyments akin, with efforts alike, with accomplishments equal, revert to the primal struggle—and force alone can determine. For force is the one language in common, down deep below acquired courtesy. Has Sambo trespassed on the claim of Jim ? Then Sambo must move on. Has Jim, in arrogance of fairer skin, pushed his frontiers beyond Sambo's reserves ? Then he shall maintain them there. The black may struggle. He will struggle, because he is upright, because he can laugh; but in the end he shall fail. Land of Goshen shall be taken from him.

Two gamins typify the feud of the races, and the circling sun can find but one solution.

SCISSORS.

One of the types that haunt the residence parts of the city in preference to the business district is the scissors-grinder. He is generally an Italian, though other nationalities also contribute to this "sharp" profession. The scissors-grinder is a man who is always welcome to the cook, who, if she happens to be a daughter of Erin, will for the moment forget her innate prejudice against the "Eyetalian" and intrust her dull knives to his care. Whether he carries his apparatus on his back or pushes it before him on wheels, his mind reverting to his sunny home or to his native maccaroni pots, his brown hand does not tire of swinging the bell with which he reminds our housewives of a dull carving-knife or a rusty pair of scissors. The boys also welcome him and are interested spectators during the process of putting an edge on the pocket-knives which Santa Claus had brought them last Christmas. What a pleasure it is for the children to stand around that spark-emitting grindstone! They don't disturb the taciturn Italian, who grinds away with the stoical equanimity of a Marc Aurelius until he tests the edge with his horny thumb and demands his ten or "fifteen centi."

The scissors-grinder likes America, but not always enough to be willing to die here. His ambition is to save a few hundred dollars—if possible more—with which to return to his sunny country. There, on the beautiful plains of the Lombardy or in the picturesque mountains of Calabria he will enjoy the eve of his life with plenty of polcuta and maccaroni. Mayhaps he will look compassionately at the poor Lazzaroni in Naples, compared to whom, he imagines himself a Crœsus.

RAG PICKERS.

Born in streets that "echoed to the tread of either Brutus," under the wall-shadows that have fallen on a Cæsar's triumphal march, beneath a sun that could not find a foe for Romans—born so, but in a later day when alien blood has sunk a race of warriors—this last residuum in Time's great goblet that once brimmed over with the best of earth, these ancient crones have wandered from the Old world to glean a living from the refuse of the New. The dames of ancient Rome—the garbage barrels of an American city! There is the satire of the centuries. The stylus that painfully engrossed the learning of that day has swept across the page of Time with swiftly growing speed, till lightning presses end the cycle of improvement. And these old crones, dark fishing in the dawn, dig up the crumpled leaves: "Decline and Fall!" Shall any matron, proud of present empire, live in lines to be digged out of dust-bins in that brighter age when our descendants, sunk to slaves, shall crouch and shiver in the noisome ways? Is there a city somewhere hid in Earth and Time through whose dim alleys Columbia's final son shall grope inferior for food? Why not? Did the Tigris promise less? Do our streams promise more? Where stood the fate that crushed the kings of earth? What fate for us lies crouching in the twilight—centuries away?

BICYCLE GIRL.

Though a " fin de siècle" product she is not necessarily a new woman. If not always a picture of feminine grace on the wheel, she represents, as a rule, vigor and health off the wheel. The world has arrived at a point where it does not look askance at a maiden devoted to healthful, invigorating sport.

The bicycle girl does not necessarily loose any of the sweet feminine graces that the sturdier sex so much admires, for indulging in an outdoor exercise which can only be beneficial to her constitution. If "*mens sana in corpere sano*" applies to man why not to woman? If the lord of creation needs a sturdy constitution to fulfill his part during his short sojourn in the universe why not woman? Long enough has she been kept from the pleasures and benefits of athletic exercises by the conventionalities of society. She can only be congratulated for breaking loose from long established prejudices. The world will be all the better off for it, as the result can be no other than happier matrimony and strong and vigorous motherhood.

The question has been raised as to the moral influence of bicycle exercise upon our girls. Some have condemned the whole sport on account of a few exceptional cases that have come under their observation, where a dire result might perhaps be traced indirectly to the innocent bicycle. To condemn a healthful exercise on such trivial grounds is like throwing a beautiful apple away on account of a small speck of dirt on its skin. Looking at our bicycle girl in the illustration one cannot but receive the impression that the American girl can, under all circumstances, well take care of herself. Give her, therefore, more elbow-room. She is all right !

10. The Power of Art

The expansion of information Americans experienced in the last third of the century did not please everyone. Journalists, sociologists, novelists were, after all, now writing about subjects which had either been ignored by respectable publishers and magazines, or translated by them into a language which disguised personal intensity and smothered realistic detail. When the old boundary lines were crossed by writers of fiction and social analysts, when genteel standards no longer governed subject material, warnings appeared. Unofficial censors like Anthony Comstock armed themselves for battle.

The censors were backed up, in many cases, by a group of Protestant clergymen, some of them revivalists, already aroused by immigration, social discord, and urban growth. The present seemed to them filled with perils and dangers requiring not more information, but more self-control. Thomas De Witt Talmage (1832–1902), was one of those angered by the breakdown of older divisions. One of the most celebrated preachers in an age of orators, Talmage was called to the pulpit of the Central Presbyterian Church of Brooklyn, while still a young man, and there he drew some of the largest audiences ever gathered by an American minister. An enormous Tabernacle was built for him (and rebuilt after it burned down), and thousands of newspapers published his sermons weekly. His flamboyance, violent language, and melodramatic gestures landed him in continual controversy, but the popularity of his sermons and books revealed the anxieties of middle-class Protestants, who found in his pulpit respectable entertainment and reassuring advice.

If Talmadge anxiously fought the expansion of the artist's empire, Clarence Darrow (1857–1938) eagerly welcomed it. Already a famous lawyer by the eigtheen-nineties, a friend of reformers like Governor Altgeld of Illinois and Eugene V. Debs, Darrow was also interested in literature and even managed to author a novel. In fiction as in law his tolerances were broad, and he saw in the new material the realists were presenting to the public, a basis for social change. His position may have been oversimplified but it mirrored even while it exaggerated an important body of literary opinion. His article appeared, appropriately, in *The Arena*, a hospitable organ for radical criticism in the nineties.

Immoral Literature

THOMAS DE WITT TALMAGE

Paul stirred up Ephesus with some lively sermons about the sins of that place. Among the most important results was the fact that the citizens brought out their bad books and in a public place made a bonfire of them. I see the people coming out with their arms full of Ephesian literature, and tossing it into the flames. I hear an economist standing by and saying: "Stop this waste. Here are seven thousand and five hundred dollars worth of books—do you propose to burn them all up? If you don't want to read them yourself, sell them and let somebody else read them." "No," said the people, "if these books are not good for us, they are not good for anybody else and we shall stand and watch until the last leaf has turned to ashes. They have done us a world of harm, and they shall never do others harm." One of the wants of the cities of this country is a great bonfire of bad books and newspapers. We have enough fuel to make a blaze two hundred feet high. Many of the publishing houses would do well to throw into the blaze their entire stock of goods. Bring forth the insufferable trash and put it into the fire, and let it be known in the presence of God, and angels and men, that you are going to rid your homes of the overtopping and underlying curse of profligate literature.

The printing press is the mightiest agency on earth for good and for evil. The minister of the Gospel, standing in a pulpit has a responsible position; but I do not think it is as responsible as the position of an editor or a publisher. At what distant point of time, at what far out cycle of eternity, will cease the influence of a Henry J. Raymond, or a Horace Greeley, or a James Gordon Bennett, or a Watson Webb, or an Eratus Brooks, or a Thomas Kinsella? Take the simple statistic that the New York dailies now have a circulation of about eight hundred and fifty thousand per day, and add to it the fact that three of the weekly periodicals have an aggregate circulation of about one million, and then cipher, if you can, how far up, and how far down, and how far out, reach the influences of the American printing-press. What is to be the issue of all this? I believe the Lord

Thomas De Witt Talmage, *Social Dynamite; or, The Wickedness of Modern Society* (Chicago, 1889), pp. 171–181.

intends the printing-press to be the chief means for the world's rescue and evangelization, and I think that the great last battle of the world will not be fought with swords and guns, but with types and presses—a purified and gospel literature triumphing over, trampling down and crushing out forever that which is depraved. The only way to overcome unclean literature is by scattering abroad that which is healthful. May God speed the cylinders of an honest, intelligent, aggressive, Christian printing-press. The greatest blessing that ever came to this nation is that of an elevated literature, and the greatest scourge has been that of unclean literature. This last has its victims in all occupations and departments. It has helped to fill insane asylums and penitentiaries and almshouses and dens of shame. The bodies of this infection lie in the hospitals and in the graves, while their souls are being tossed over into a lost eternity, an avalanche of horror and despair. The London plague was nothing to it. That counted its victims by thousands, but this modern pest has already shoveled its millions into the charnel-house of the morally dead. The longest rail train that ever ran over the Erie or Hudson tracks was not long enough nor large enough to carry the beastliness and the putrefaction which have been gathered up in bad books and newspapers of this land in the last twenty years.

Now, it is amid such circumstances that I put a question of overmastering importance to you and your families. What books and newspapers shall we read? You see a group of them together. A newspaper is only a book in a swifter and more portable shape, and the same rules which will apply to book reading will apply to newspaper reading. What shall we read? Shall our minds be the receptacle of everything that an author has a mind to write? Shall there be no distinction between the tree of a life and the tree of death? Shall we stoop down and drink out of the trough which the wickedness of men has filled with pollution and shame? Shall we mire in impurity and chase fantastic will-o'-the-wisps across the swamps, when we might walk in the blooming gardens of God? O no! For the sake of our present and everlasting welfare we must make an intelligent and Christian choice. Standing, as we do, chin deep in fictitious literature, the first question that many of the young people are asking me is: "Shall we read novels?" I reply: There are novels that are pure, good, Christian, elevating to the heart and ennobling to the life. But I have still further to say that I believe that ninety-nine out of the hundred novels in this day are baleful and destructive to the last degree. A pure work of fiction is history and poetry combined. It is a history of things around us, with the licenses and the assumed names of poetry. The world can never pay the debt which it owes to such fictitious writers as Hawthorne and McKenzie, and Lander and Hunt, and Arthur and Marion Harland, and others whose names are familiar to all. The follies of high life were never better exposed than by Miss Edgeworth. The memories of the past were never more faithfully embalmed than in the writings of Walter Scott. Cooper's novels are healthfully redolent with the breath of the sea-weed, and the air of the American forest. Charles Kingsley has smitten the morbidity of the world, and led a great many to appreciate the poetry of sound health, strong muscles, and fresh air. Thackeray did a grand work in caricaturing the pretenders to gentility and high blood. Dickens has built his own monument in his books, which are an everlasting plea for the poor, and the anathema of injustice.

Now, I say, books like these, read at right times, and read in right proportion with other books, can not help but be ennobling and purifying; but alas for the impure literature that has come upon this country in the shape of novels, like a freshet overflowing all the banks of decency and common sense! They are coming from some of the most celebrated publishing houses of the country. They are coming with recommendation of some of our religious newspapers. They lie in your center table to curse your children, and blast with their infernal fires generations unborn. You find these books in the desk of the school miss, in the trunk of the young man, in the steamboat cabin, on the table of the hotel reception room. You see a light in your child's room late at night. You suddenly go in and say: "What are you doing?" "I am reading." "What are you reading?" "A book." You look at the book; it is a bad book. "Where did you get it?" "I borrowed it." Alas, there are always those abroad who would like to loan your son or daughter a bad book. Everywhere, everywhere an unclean literature. I charge upon it the destruction of ten thousand immortal souls, and I bid you wake up to the magnitude of the theme. I shall take all the world's literature—good novels and bad, travels true or false, histories faithful and incorrect, legends beautiful and monstrous, all tracts, all chronicles, all epilogues, all family, city, state and national libraries—and pile them up in a pyramid of literature, and then I shall bring to bear upon it some grand, glorious, infallible, unmistakable Christian principles. God help me to write with reference to my last account. I charge you, in the first place, to stand aloof from all books that give false pictures of human life. Life is neither a tragedy nor a farce. Men are not all either knaves nor heroes. Women are neither angels nor furies. And yet, if you depended upon much of the literature of the day, you would get the idea that life, instead of being something earnest, something practical, is a fitful and fantastic and extravagant thing. How poorly prepared are that young man and woman for the duties of to-day who spent last night wading through brilliant passages descriptive of magnificent knavery and wickedness! The man will be looking all day long for his heroine, in the tin-shop, by the forge, in the factory, in the counting-room, and he will not find her, and he will be dissatisfied. A man who gives himself up to the indiscriminate reading of novels will be nerveless, inane, and a nuisance. He will be fit neither for the store, nor the shop, nor the field. A woman who gives herself up to the indiscriminate reading of novels will be unfitted for the duties of wife, mother, sister, daughter. There she is, hair disheveled, countenance vacant, cheeks pale, hands trembling, bursting into tears at midnight over the fate of some unfortunate lover; in the day time, when she ought to be busy, staring by the half hour at nothing; biting her finger nails into the quick. The carpet that was plain before will be plainer after having wandered through a romance all night long in tesselated halls of castles. And your industrious companion will be more unattractive than ever now that you have walked in the romance through parks with plumed princesses, or lounged in the arbor with the polished desperado. O, these confirmed novel readers! They are unfitted for this life, which is a tremendous discipline. They know not how to go through the furnaces of trial through which they must pass, and they are unfitted for a world where everything we gain we achieve by hard, long-continuing and exhaustive work.

Again, abstain from all those books which, while they have some good things about them, have also an admixture of evil. You have read books that had two elements in them—the good and the bad. Which stuck to you? The bad! The heart of most people is like a sieve, which lets the small particles of gold fall through, but keeps the great cinders. Once in awhile there is a mind like a loadstone, which, plunged amid steel and brass filings, gathers up the steel and repels the brass. But it is generally just the opposite. If you attempt to plunge through a fence of burrs to get one blackberry, you will get more burrs than blackberries. You can not afford to read a bad book, however good you are. You say: "The influence is insignificant." I tell you that the scratch of a pin has sometimes produced the lock-jaw. Alas, if through curiosity, as many do, you pry into an evil book, your curiosity is as dangerous as that of the man who would take a torch into a gunpowder mill merely to see whether it would really blow up or not.

In a menagerie, a man put his arm through the bars of a black leopard's cage. The animal's hide looked so sleek, and bright, and beautiful. He just stroked it once. The monster seized him, and he drew forth a hand torn, and mangled, and bleeding. O, touch not evil even with the faintest stroke! Though it may be glossy and beautiful, touch it not, lest you pull forth your soul torn and bleeding under the clutch of the black leopard. "But," you say, "how can I find out whether a book is good or bad without reading it?" There is always something suspicious about a bad book. I never knew an exception—something suspicious in the index or style of illustration. This venomous reptile almost always carries a warning rattle. I charge you to stand off from all those books which corrupt the imagination and inflame the passions. I do not refer now to that kind of a book which the villain has under his coat waiting for the school to get out, and then, looking both ways to see that there is no policeman around the block, offers the book to your son on his way home. I do not speak of that kind of literature, but that which evades the law and comes out in polished style, and with acute plot sounds the tocsin that rouses up all the baser passions of the soul. To-day, under the nostrils of this land, there is a fetid, reeking unwashed literature, enough to poison all the fountains of public virtue, and smite your sons and daughters as with the wing of a destroying angel, and it is time that the ministers of the gospel blew the trumpet and rallied the forces of righteousness, all armed to the teeth, in this great battle against a depraved literature. Again, abstain from those books which are apologetic of crime. It is a sad thing that some of the best and most beautiful book-binderies, and some of the finest rhetoric, have been brought to make sin attractive. Vice is a horrible thing, anyhow. It is born in shame, and dies howling in the darkness. In this world it is scourged with a whip of scorpions, but afterwards the thunders of God's wrath pursue it across a boundless desert, beating it with ruin and woe. When you come to paint carnality, do not paint it as looking from behind embroidered curtains, or through lattice of royal seraglio, but as writhing in the agonies of a city hospital.

Cursed be the books that try to make impurity decent, and crime attractive, and hypocrisy noble! Cursed be the books that swarm with libertines and desperadoes, who make the brains of the young people whirl with villainy. Ye authors who write them, ye publishers who print them, ye booksellers who distribute them, shall be cut to pieces, if not by an aroused community, then, at last, by the hail of divine vengeance, which shall sweep to the lowest pit of perdition all ye murderers of souls. I tell you, though you may escape in this world, you will be ground at last under the hoof of eternal calamities, and you will be chained to the rack, and you will have the vultures of despair clawing at your soul, and those whom you have destroyed will come around to torment you, and to pour hotter coals of fury upon your head, and rejoice eternally in the outcry of your pain and the howl of your damnation.

The clock strikes midnight. A fair form bends over a romance. The eyes flash fire. The breath is quick and irregular. Occasionally the color dashes to the cheeks, and then dies out. The hands tremble as though a guardian spirit were trying to shake the deadly book out of the grasp. Hot tears fall. She laughs with a shrill voice that drops dead at its own sound. The sweat on her brow is the spray dashed up from the river of death. The clock strikes four, and the rosy dawn soon after begins to look through the lattice upon the pale form that looks like a detained specter of the night. Soon in a mad-house she will mistake her ringlets for curling serpents, and thrust her white hand through the bars of the prison, and smite her head, rubbing it back as though to push the scalp from the skull, shrieking: "My brain! My brain!" Oh, stand off from that! Why will you go sounding your way amid the reefs and warning buoys, when there is such a vast ocean in which you may voyage, all sail set?

I consider the lascivious pictorial literature of the day as most tremendous for ruin. There is no one who can like good pictures better than I do. The quickest and most condensed way of impressing the public mind is by pictures. What the painter does by his brush for a few favorites the engraver does by his knife for the million. What the author accomplishes by fifty pages the artist does by a flash. The best part of a painting that costs ten thousand dollars you may buy for ten cents. Fine paintings belong to the aristocracy of art. Engravings belong to the democracy of art. You do well to gather good pictures in your homes. Spread them before your children after the tea hour is past and the evening circle is gathered. Throw them on the invalid's couch. Strew them through the rail train to cheer the traveler on his journey. Tack them on the wall of the nursery. Gather them in albums and portfolios. God speed the good pictures on their way with ministries of knowledge and mercy. But what shall I say of the prostitution of this art to purposes of iniquity? These death-warrants of the soul are at every street corner. They smite the vision of the young man with pollution. Many a young man buying a copy has bought his eternal discomfiture. There may be enough poison in one bad picture to poison one soul, and that soul may poison ten, and ten fifty, and the fifty hundreds, and the hundreds thousands, until nothing but the measuring line of eternity can tell the height, and depth, and ghastliness, and horror of the great undoing. The work of death that the wicked author does in a whole book the bad engraver may do on a half side of a pictorial.

Under the guise of pure mirth the young man buys one of these sheets. He unrolls it before his comrades amid roars of laughter, but long after the paper is gone the result may perhaps be seen in the blasted imagination of those who saw it. The queen of death holds a banquet every night, and these periodicals are the printed invitations to her guests. Alas, that the fair brow of American art should be blotched with the plague spot, and that philanthropists, bothering themselves about smaller evils, should lift up no united and vehement voice against this great calamity. Young man, buy not this moral strychnine for your soul. Pick not up this nest of coiled adders for your pocket. Patronize no news-stand that keeps them. Have your room bright with good engravings, but for these outrageous pictorials have not one wall, not one bureau, not one pocket. A man is no better than the pictures he loves to look at. If your eyes are not pure your heart can not be. At a news-stand one can guess the character of a man by the kind of pictorial he purchases. When the devil fails to get a man to read a bad book, he sometimes succeeds in getting him to look at a bad picture. When Satan goes afishing he does not care whether it is a long line or a short line, if he only draws his victim in. Beware of lascivious pictorials, young man, in the name of Almighty God I charge you.

If I have successfully laid down any principles by which you may judge in regard to books and newspapers, then I have done something of which I shall not be ashamed on the day which shall try every man's work, of what sort it is.

Cherish good books and newspapers. Beware of the bad ones. One column may save your soul; one paragraph may ruin it. Benjamin Franklin said that the reading of Cotton Mather's essay on "Doing Good" molded his entire life. The assassin of Lord Russell declared that he was led into crime by reading one vivid romance. The consecrated John Angell James, than whom England never produced a better man, declared in his old days that he had never yet got over the evil effects of having for fifteen minutes once read a bad book. But I need not go so far off. I could come near home and tell you of something that occurred in my college days. I could tell you of a comrade that was great-hearted, noble and generous. He was studying for an honorable profession, but he had an infidel book in his trunk, and he said to me one day: "De Witt, would you like to read it?" I said: "Yes, I would." I took the book and read it only for a few minutes. I was really startled with what I saw there, and I handed the book back to him and said: "You had better destroy that book." No, he kept it. He read it, He re-read it. After awhile he gave up religion as a myth. He gave up God as a nonentity. He gave up the Bible as a fable. He gave up the Church of Christ as a useless institution. He gave up good morals as being unnecessarily stringent. I have heard of him but twice in many years. The time before the last I heard of him he was a confirmed inebriate. The last I heard of him he was coming out of an insane asylum— in body, mind and soul an awful wreck. I believe that one infidel book killed him for two worlds.

Look through your library, and then, having looked through your library, look on the stand where you keep your pictorials and newspapers, and apply the Christian principles I have laid down. If there is anything in your home that can not stand the test, do not give it away, for it might spoil an immortal soul; do not sell it, for the money you get would be the price of blood; but rather kindle a fire on your kitchen hearth, or in your back yard, and then drop the poison in it, and keep stirring the blaze until from preface to appendix there shall not be a single paragraph left, and the bonfire in your city shall be as consuming as that one in the streets of Ephesus.

Realism in Literature and Art
CLARENCE S. DARROW

Man is nature's last and most perfect work; but however high his development or great his achievements, he is yet a child of the earth and the forces that have formed all the life that exists thereon. He cannot separate himself from the environment in which he grew, and a thousand ties of nature bind him back to the long-forgotten past, and prove his kinship to all the lower forms of life that have sprung from that great common mother, earth.

As there is a universal law of being which controls all forms of life, from the aimless movement of the mollusk in the sea to the most perfect conduct of the best developed man, so all the varied activities of human life, from the movements of the savage digging roots to the work of the greatest artist with his brush, are controlled by universal laws, and are

Clarence S. Darrow, "Realism in Literature and Art," *The Arena*, Vol. IX (December, 1893), pp. 98–109, 111–113.

good or bad, perfect or imperfect, as they conform to the highest condition nature has imposed.

The early savage dwelt in caves and cliffs, and spent his life in seeking food and providing some rude shelter from the cold. He looked at the earth, the sun, the sea, the sky, the mountain peak, the forest, and the plain, at the vegetable and animal life around, and all he saw and heard formed an impression on his brain, and aided in his growth.

Like a child he marvelled at the storm and flood; he stood in awe as he looked upon disease and death; and to explain the things he could not understand, he peopled earth and air and sea with gods and demons and a thousand weird creations of his brain.

All these mysterious creatures were made in the image of the natural objects that came within his view. The gods were men grown large, and endowed with marvellous powers, while tree and bird and beast were used alike as models for a being greater far than any nature ever formed.

It was an angry god that made the rivers overrun their banks and leave destruction in their path. An offended god it was who hurled his thunderbolts upon a wicked world or sent disease and famine to the sinning children of the earth; and to coax these rulers to be merciful to man, the weak and trembling people of the ancient world turned their thoughts to sacrifice and prayer.

The first clouded thoughts of these rude men were transcribed on monument and stone, or carved in wood, or painted with the colors borrowed from the sun and earth and sky; in short, the first rude art was born to sing the praise, and tell the fame, and paint the greatness of the gods. But all of this was natural for the time and place; and the graven images, the chiselled hieroglyphics, and all this rude beginning of literature and art were formed upon what men saw and heard and felt, enlarged and magnified to fit the stature of the gods.

As the world grew older, art was used to celebrate the greatness and achievements of kings and rulers as well as gods, and their tombs were ornamented with such decorations as these early ages could create; but yet all literature and art was only for the gods and the rulers of the world. Then, even more than now, wealth and power brought intellect to do their will, and all its force was spent to sing the praises of the rulers of the earth and air.

The basis of all this art of pen and brush was the reality of the world; but this was so magnified and distorted for the base use of kings and priests, that realism in the true sense could not exist.

It would not do to paint a picture of a king resembling a man of flesh and blood, and of course a god must be far greater than a king. It would not do to write a tale in which kings and princes, lords and ladies, should act like men and women—else what difference between the ruler and the ruled? The marvelous powers which romance and myth had given to gods and angels were transferred to those of royal blood. The wonderful achievements of these knights and princes could be equalled only by the gods; and the poor dependents of the world, who lived for the glory of the great, were fed with legends and with tales that sang the praises of the great.

Literature, sculpture and painting, music and archetecture, indeed, all forms of art, were the exclusive property of the great and strong; and the artist, then, like most of those to-day, was retained to serve the great and maintain the status of the weak.

No one dreamed that there was any beauty in a common human life or any romance in a fact. The greatest of the earth had not yet learned to know that every life is a mystery and every death a tragedy; that the spark of the infinite, which alone transforms clay to life, animates alike the breast of the peasant and the soul of the prince. The world had not learned that the ant hill was as great as Mont Blanc and the blade of grass as mysterious as the oak. It is only now that the world is growing so delicate and refined that it can see the beauty of a fact; that it is developing a taste so rare as to distinguish between the false and true; that it can be moved by the gentle breeze as well as by the winter's gale; that it can see a greater beauty in a statement true to life than in the inflated tales which children read.

Most of the literature and art the world has known has been untrue. The pictures of the past have been painted from the distorted minds of visionists and the pliant brains of tools. They have represented impossible gods and unthinkable saints, angels and cherubs and demons—everything but men and women. Saints may be all right in their place, but a saint with a halo around his head was born of myth and not of art. Angels may be well enough, but all rational men prefer an angel with arms to an angel with wings. When these artists were not busy painting saints and Madonnas, they were spending their time painting kings and royal knaves, and the pictures of the rulers were as unlike the men and women whom they were said to represent as the servile spirit of the painter was unlike the true artist of to-day. Of course an artist would not paint the poor. They had no clothes that would adorn a work of art, and no money nor favors that could pay him for his toil. An ancient artist could no more afford to serve the poor than a modern lawyer to defend the weak.

After literature had so far advanced as to concern other beings than gods and kings, the authors of these ancient days endowed their characters with marvellous powers: knights with giant strength and magic swords; princes with wondrous palaces and heaps of gold; travellers who met marvellous beasts and slew them in extraordinary ways; giants with forms like mountains and strength like oxen, and who could vanquish all but little dwarfs. Railroads were not invented in those early days, but travel was facilitated by the use of seven-league boots. Balloons and telescopes were not yet known, but this did not keep favored heroes from peering at the stars or looking down from on high upon the earth. They had but to plant a magic bean before they went to bed at night, and in the morning it had grown so tall that it reached up to the sky; and the hero, although not skilled in climbing, needed simply to grasp the stalk and say, "Hitchety, hatchety, up I go. Hitchety, hatchety, up I go," and by this means soon vanished in the clouds.

Tales of this sort used once to delight the world, and the readers half believed them true. We give them to children now, and even the least of these view them with a half contempt.

The modern man who still reads Walter Scott does not enjoy these ancient myths. He relishes a lie, but it must not be too big; it must be so small that, although he knows in his inmost soul that it is not true, he can yet make himself believe it is not false. Most of us have cherished a pleasant waking dream, and fondly clung to the sweet delusion while we really knew it was not life. The modern literary stomach is becoming so healthy that it wants a story at least half true; should the falsehood be too strong, it acts as an emetic instead of food.

These old fairy tales have lost their power to charm, as the tales of the gods and kings went down before. They have lost their charm; for as we read them now, they awake no answering chord born of the experiences that make up what we know of human life.

When the beauty of realism shall be truly known, we shall read the book, or look upon the work of art, and, in the light of all we know of life, shall ask our beings whether the image that the author or the painter creates for us is like the one that is born of the consciousness which moves our souls, and the experiences that life has made us know.

Realism worships at the shrine of nature. It does not say that there may not be a sphere in which beings higher than man can live, or that some time an eye may not rest upon a fairer sunset than was ever born behind the clouds and sea; but it knows that through countless ages nature has slowly fitted the brain and eye of man to the earth on which we live and the objects that we see, and the perfect earthly eye must harmonize with the perfect earthly scene. To say that realism is coarse and vulgar, is to declare against nature and her works, and to assert that the man she made may dream of things higher and grander than nature could unfold.

• • •

There are realists who look at all the beauty and loveliness of the world, and all its maladjustments, too, and who do not seek to answer the old, old question, whether back of this is any all-controlling and designing power. They do not answer, for they cannot know; but they strive to touch the subtle chord which makes their individual lives vibrate in harmony with the great heart of that nature which they love, and they cannot think but what all parts of life are good, and that, while men may differ, nature must know best.

Other realists there are who believe they see in nature the work of a divine Maker, who created man in His own image as the last and highest triumph of His skill; that not the minutest portion of the universe exists except because He wished it thus. To the realist who accepts this all-controlling power, any imputation against a portion of his Master's work must reach back to the author who designed it all.

• • •

One day the world will learn to know that all things are good or bad according to the service they perform. A great brain which is used by its owner for his selfish ends, regardless of all the purposes that are sacrificed to attain the goal, is as base and bad as the mind can well conceive; while a great brain dedicated to the right and just, and freely given to the service of the world, is high and grand. One day it ought to learn that the power to create immortality, through infinite succeeding links of human life, is the finest and most terrible that nature ever gave to man; and to ignore this power or call it bad, to fail to realize the great responsibility of this tremendous fact, is to cry out against the power that gave us life, and commit the greatest human sin, for it may be one that never dies.

The growth of letters has been like that of art, from the marvellous and mythical to the natural and true. The tales and legends of the ancient past were not of common men and common scenes. These could not impress the undeveloped intellects of long ago. A man of letters could not deify a serf or tell the simple story of the poor. He must write to maintain the status of the world, and please the prince who gave him food. So he told of kings and queens, of knights and ladies, of strife and conquest, and the coloring he used was human blood.

The world has grown accustomed to those ancient tales—to scenes of blood and war, and novels that would thrill the soul and cause the hair to stand on end. It has read them so long that the true seems commonplace and not fit to fill the pages of a book. But all the time we forget the fact that the story could not charm unless we half believed it true. The men and women in the tale we learn to love and hate; we take an interest in their lives; we hope they may succeed or fail; we must not be told at every page that the people of the book are men of straw, that no such beings ever lived upon the earth. We could take no interest in men and women who were myths conjured up to play their parts, reminding us in every word they spoke that, regardless of the happiness or anguish the author made them feel, they were but puppets, and could know neither joy nor pain. It may be that the realistic story is commonplace, but so is life, and the realistic tale is true. Among the countless millions of the earth it is only here and there, and now and then, that some soul is born from out the mighty depths that does not soon return to the great sea, and leave no ripple on the waves.

In the play of life each actor seems important to himself; the world he knows revolves around him as the central figure of the scene; his friends rejoice in all the fortune he attains, and weep with him in all his griefs. To him the world is bounded by the faces that he knows and the scenes in which he lives; he forgets the great surging world outside, and cannot think how small a space he fills in that infinity which bounds his life. He dies; a few sorrowing friends mourn him for a day, and the world does not know he ever lived or ever died. In the ordinary life almost all events are commonplace, but a few important days are thinly sprinkled in among all of those that intervene between the cradle and the grave. We eat and drink, we work and sleep, and here and there a great joy or sorrow creeps in upon our lives, and leaves a day that stands out in the monotony of all the rest, like the pyramids upon the level plains. But these are very, very few, and are important only to ourselves; . . .

The old novel, which we used to read and to which the world so fondly clings, had no idea of relation or perspective. It had a hero and a heroine, and sometimes more than one. The revolutions of the planets were less important than their love. War, shipwreck, and conflagration all conspired to produce the climax of the scene, and the whole world stood still until their hearts and hands were joined. Wide oceans, burning deserts, Arctic seas, impassable jungles, irate fathers, and even designing mothers were helpless against the decree that fate had made; and when all the barriers were passed, and love had triumphed over impossibilities, the tale was done. Through the rest of life nothing of interest could transpire. Sometimes in the progress of the story, if the complications were too great, a thunderbolt or an earthquake was introduced to destroy the villain and help out the match. Earthquakes sometimes happen, and the realistic novelists might write a tale of a scene like this; but then the love affair would be an incident of the earthquake, and not the earthquake an incident of the love affair.

In real life the affections have played an important part, and sometimes great things have been done in the name of love; but most of the affairs of the human heart have been as natural as the other events of life.

• • •

It may be that there are few great incidents in the realistic tale; but each event appeals to life, and cannot fail to wake our memories and make us live the past again. The great authors of the natural school, Tolstoi, Daudet, Howells, Ibsen, Keilland, Flaubert, Zola, Hardy, and the rest, have made us think and live. Their words have burnished up our thoughts and revealed a thousand pictures that hung upon the walls of memory, covered with the dust of years and hidden from our sight. Sometimes, of course, we cry with pain at the picture that is thrown before our view; but life consists of emotions, and we cannot truly live unless the depths are stirred.

These great masters, it is true, may sometimes shock the over-sensitive with the stories they tell of life; but if the tale is true, why hide it from our sight? Nothing is more common than the protest against the wicked books of the realistic school, filled with delineations of passion and of sin; but he who denies passion ignores all the life that exists upon the earth, and cries out against the mother that gave him birth; and he who ignores this truth passes with contempt the greatest fact that nature has impressed upon the world.

Those who condemn as sensual the tales of Tolstoi and Daudet still defend the love stories of which our literature is full—those weak and silly tales that make women fit only to be the playthings of the world, and deny to them a single thought or right except to serve their master, man. These objectors do not contend that stories dealing with the feelings and affecions shall not be told—they approve these, but they simply insist that they shall be false, instead of true.

The old novel filled the mind of the school girl with a thousand thoughts that had no place in life—with ten thousand pictures she could never see. It taught that some time she would meet a prince in disguise, to whom she should freely give her hand and heart. So she went out upon the road to find this prince; and the more disguised he was, the more certain did she feel that he was the prince for whom she sought.

• • •

In these days of creeds and theories, of preachers in the pulpit and out, we are told that all novels should have a moral and be written to serve some end. So we have novels on religion, war, marriage, divorce, socialism, theosophy, woman's rights, and other topics without end. It is not enough that the preachers and lecturers shall tell us how to think and act; the novelist must try his hand at preaching, too. He starts out with a theory, and every scene and incident must be bent to make it plain that the author believes certain things. The doings of the men and women in the book are secondary to the views the author holds. The theories may be very true, but the poor characters who must adjust their lives to these ideal states are sadly warped and twisted out of shape.

The realist would teach a lesson, too, but he would not violate a single fact for all the theories in the world, for a theory could not be true if it did violence to life. He paints his picture so true and perfect that all men who look upon it know that it is a likeness of the world that they have seen; they know that these are men and women and little children whom they meet upon the streets, and they see the conditions of their lives, and the moral of the picture sinks deeply into their minds.

• • •

The world has grown tired of preachers and sermons; to-day it asks for facts. It has grown tired of fairies and angels, and asks for flesh and blood. It looks on life as it exists to-day—both its beauty and its horror, its joy and its sorrow. It wishes to see all; not only the prince and the millionaire, but the laborer and the beggar, the master and the slave. We see the beautiful and the ugly, and know what the world is and what it ought to be, and the true picture which the author saw and painted stirs the heart to holier feelings and to grander thoughts.

• • •

The greatest artists of the world to-day are telling facts and painting scenes that cause humanity to stop and think, and ask why one shall be a master and another a serf—why a portion of the world should toil and spin, should wear away their strength and lives, and the rest may live in idleness and ease.

The old-time artists thought they served humanity by painting saints and Madonnas and angels from the myths they conjured in their brains. They painted war with long lines of soldiers dressed in new uniforms, and looking plump and gay, and a battle scene was always drawn from the side of the victorious camp, with the ensign proudly planting his bright colors on the rampart of the foe. One or two were dying, but always in their comrades' arm and listening to shouts of victory that filled the air, and thinking of the righteous cause for which they fought and died. In the last moments they dreamed of pleasant burial-yards at home, and of a grave kept green by loving, grateful friends, and a smile of joy lit up their fading faces, so sweet that it seemed a hardship not to die in war. They painted peace as a white-winged dove settling down upon a cold and "farewell" earth. Between the two it was plain which choice a boy would make, and thus art served the state and king.

But Verestchagin painted war so true to life that as we look upon the scene we long for peace. He painted war as war has ever been and will ever be—a horrible and ghastly scene, where men, drunk with blind frenzy,—which rulers say is patriotic pride,—and made mad by drums and fifes and smoke and shot and shell and flowing blood, seek to maim and wound and kill, because a ruler gives the word. He paints a battle-field a field of life and death, a field of carnage and of blood. And who are these who fight like fiends and devils driven to despair? And what cause is this that makes these men forget that they are men, and vie with beasts to show their cruel thirst for blood? They shout of home and native land; but they have no homes, and owners of their native land exist upon their toil and blood. The nobles and princes, for whom this fight is waged, are sitting far away upon a hill, beyond the reach of shot and shell; and from this spot they watch their slaves pour out their blood to satisfy their rulers' pride and lust of power. And what is the enemy they fight? Men, like themselves, who blindly go to death at another king's command; slaves who have no land, who freely give their toil or blood— whichever one their rulers may demand. These fighting soldiers have no cause for strife, but their rulers live by kindling in their hearts a love of native land—a love which makes them hate their brother laborers of other lands, and dumbly march to death, to satisfy a king's caprice.

But let us look once more, after the battle has been fought. Here we see the wreck and ruin of the strife. The field is silent now, given to the dead, the beast of prey, and night. A young soldier lies upon the ground. The snow is falling fast around his form. The lonely mountain peaks rise up on every side. The wreck of war is all about. His uniform is soiled and stained. A spot of red is seen upon his breast. It is not the color that his country wove upon his coat to catch his eye and bait him to his death; it is hard and jagged and cold; it is his life's blood that leaked out through a hole that followed the point of a sabre to his heart. His form is stiff and cold, for he is dead. The cruel wound and the icy air have done their work. The government which took his life taught this poor boy to love his native land. As a child he dreamed of scenes of glory and of power, and the great, wide world just waiting to fall captive to his magic strength. He dreamed of war and strife, and of victory and fame. If he should die, kind hands would smooth his brow, and loving friends would keep his grave and memory green, because he died in war. But no human eye was there at last, as the mist of night and the mist of death shut out the lonely mountains from his sight. The snow is all around, and the air above is gray with falling flakes. These would soon hide him from the world; and when the summer time should come again, no one could tell his bleaching bones from all the rest. The only life upon the scene is the buzzard, slowly circling in the air above his head, waiting to make sure that death has come. The bird looks down upon the boy, upon the eyes which first looked out upon the great, wide world, and which his mother fondly kissed. Upon these eyes the buzzard will begin his meal.

Not all the world is beautiful, and not all of life is good. The true artist has no right to choose only the lovely spots, and make us think that this is life. He must bring the world before our eyes, and make us read and think. As he loves the true and noble, he must show the false and bad. As he yearns for true equality, he must paint the master and the slave. He must tell the truth; must tell it all; must tell it o'er and o'er again, till the deafest ear will listen and the dullest mind will think. He must not swerve to please the world by painting only pleasant sights and telling only lovely tales. He must paint and write and work and think until the world shall learn so much, and grow so good, that the true will be all beautiful, and all the real be ideal.

PART THREE

UNITIES

11. The Official Ideal

Well aware of the contrasts and disunities marring their society, many artists, architects, and their wealthy patrons sought to develop physical symbols of unity in the late nineteenth century and objectify standards of virtue, loyalty, and community identity. Despite the fears of men like Talmage and the hopes of critics like Darrow, art's idealizing mission continued to dominate artistic practice. As a result, alongside the photographs, cartoons, and realistic depictions of social problems, there emerged a homogenized if technically impressive art and architecture which consciously recalled the glories of Renaissance Italy and Periclean Greece. Enormous murals, mosaics, and statues filled the country's new libraries, and court houses, designed to inspire their viewers with patriotism and civic pride. Whether the complicated allegories they contained communicated very much to the public was another question, but on at least one occasion, the Columbian Exposition, they scored an undeniable triumph. The dreamland constructed on the shores of Lake Michigan excited rhapsodic praises, and the photographs which survive, as well as their hyperbolic captions, capture this generation's commitment to spiritual visions of spectacular scope.

Photographs of the Exposition, from *The Dream City, A Portfolio of Photographic Views of the World's Columbian Exposition* (St. Louis, 1893); and *Photographs of the World's Fair* (Chicago, 1894).

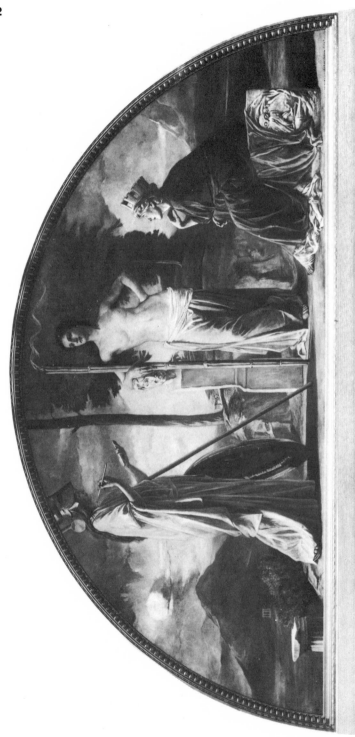

1. "Athens" by John La Farge.

2. *"Venice" by Kenyon Cox.*

3. *"The Mantle of the Law" by Frederick Diehlman.*

4. *"The Arts" by Kenyon Cox.*

5. *"The Sciences" by Kenyon Cox.*

6. *"Corrupt Legislation" by Elihu Vedder.*

7. *"Good Administration" by Elihu Vedder.*

296

THE ADMINISTRATION BUILDING.—This structure nobly sustained the expectations of the public, and held a sovereign position among all the wonders of the Fair. It was designed by Richard M. Hunt, of New York, and, besides serving as headquarters for the chief officers of the Exposition, its spacious rotunda offered a favorite meeting place for friends, and was thronged early and late by admirers of the beautiful and impressive in architecture. Four square edifices (called pavilions) of the general height of the principal facades of the Exposition, were placed at the corners of a quadrangular square of two hundred and fifty feet, and from the inner corners of these edifices rose the beautiful French octagonal dome, which, in addition to its gilding, bore a conspicuous outer ornamentation in relief. Between each pavilion was a space about ninety feet square, making the entrances to the rotunda—that is, the main entrances—about that far from the outer lines of the building. The whole design was in three stages: the first was the four pavilions, and carried the height sixty-five feet, to a level with the facades of the Court of Honor; the next stage was a central one, forty feet high; the third stage was the dome itself. The first stage was Doric, the second Ionic, with a colonnade of great dignity, as viewed from its loggia; the third was the ribbed dome, with its sculptural panels, and reached a height of two hundred and sixty feet from the floor below. The rotunda was ornamented with panels that bore the names of nations and celebrated men, with didactic inscriptions; and in the upper part of the vault were Dodge's allegorical paintings. At night the dome was lighted with incandescent bulbs so as to define its panels, and a corona shone on its crest, making a memorable illumination—the chief beauty of the Fair. The total cost was $650,000.

THE TOWER OF ORANGES.—The engraving shows the attractive exhibit of the people of Los Angeles County, California, in the northern end of the southwestern curtain of Horticultural Hall—that is, near and southwest of the great dome. This tower stood directly before the door as the visitor entered, after having left the rotunda. The base was fourteen feet square, and the tower, beginning with a diameter of five feet, rose to a height of thirty-two feet and tapered gradually to a diameter of less than four feet at the apex. The oranges were selected with reference to their position in the tower, and were the pick of Los Angeles County. The wire fastenings could not be detected until the fruit had shrunken with months of exhibition; one set of oranges lasted through the Fair, though looking much the worse for exposure. A handsome satin gonfalon hung at the base, giving the name of the exhibitor. Near by were spread the finest specimens of Malta Bloods, Mediterranean Sweets, Wilson Seedlings, Joppas, St. Michaels, Konahs, and Australian and Washington Navels. The same county displayed Lisbon, Sicily, Villa Franca, Bonnie Brae and Eureka lemons, shaddocks, pomelos, grape fruit, China lemons, citrons, Mexican limes and apples, with jars containing enormous specimens of fruit.

THE COLUMBIAN FOUNTAIN.—Frederick MacMonnies was entrusted with the design and construction of the central fountain at the Fair, and $50,000 were placed at its disposal for the purpose. Of this amount, it is said that the ardent lover of sculpture actually expended fully $48,000 in bringing his great conception to successful completion. The fountain shows Columbia sitting aloft on the Barge of State, heralded by Fame at the prow, oared by the Arts and Industries, guided by Time at the helm, and drawn by the sea-horses of Commerce. The prow of the barge is ornamented with an eagle's beak; its sides are bordered with dolphins in relief; and horns of plenty pour their abundance over the gunwales. The pedestal on which Columbia sits, bears a national shield in front, and the throne is supported by four kneeling children, who also bear heavy garlands. A torch at rest is in Columbia's hand. The rowers on the right are Music, Architecture, Sculpture and Painting; on the left, Agriculture, Science, Industry and Commerce. Time has improvised a helm by using his scythe. This barge stands in the center of a circular basin, one hundred and fifty feet in diameter, which at its eastern periphery flows in circular cascade in many falls to the surface of the Grand Basin of the Exposition, twelve feet below. In the basin of the fountain, four pair of sea-horses, mounted by riders who represent modern intelligence, draw the barge. Near the semi-circular balustrade which guards the rear of the fountain, dolphins send streams upward, and mermaids and tritons at various places add to the fleecy display of high-thrown water. The general effect of the MacMonnies fountain was marvelously beautiful, and thousands of visitors gained their chief enjoyment in sitting near by and enjoying this principal scene. It was said to be the largest fountain in the world,

A GLIMPSE OF THE COURT OF HONOR.—In the view here presented art may assuredly claim a glory almost unshared by her sister, nature. The prospect is one entirely resulting from man's artistic genius along with his consummate handicraft. Behold the placid waters of the North Canal, bridged by that graceful structure whereon millions have stood enraptured at the scene before them. Glance upon the stately corner of the Manufactures and Liberal Arts Building, which is but the counterpart of three others that indicate well by their massiveness the vast proportions of the structure. To the right, what a magnificent vista is open to the entranced beholder. There are seen the smooth waters of the Grand Basin, shimmering in the light of the sun. In the foreground stands up one of the numerous monoliths that adorn the grounds, permitting just a peep at the noble statue "Republic" looming above the basin. In the extreme background is the Peristyle, a most marvelous conception, with its forty-eight pillars representing all the States and Territories of the Union, while above its great Columbian Arch is faintly outlined the Quadriga group, in illustration of Christopher Columbus' triumphal return after his voyage of discovery. At the extreme right is the beautiful Casino, among the most attractive architectural features of the White City, where bands of music discourse sweet harmony for the visitors who come to repose here from the bewilderment of their surroundings.

300

THE MANUFACTURERS AND LIBERAL ARTS BUILDING.—How dare one attempt a description of this mammoth edifice in 100 words? Three times larger than St. Peter's Church at Rome, four times the size of the Colosseum, having in its construction 17,000,000 feet of lumber, 13,000,000 pounds of iron, 2,000,000 pounds of steel, 1,700,000, it stands as the most gigantic architectural endeavor of human hands. It is by far the largest building in the world, 1,687 x 787 feet in area and in its central hall alone can seat 75,000 people. This hall, unbroken by a single balcony or a projecting column can be seen at a glance though its stupendous size can scarcely be comprehended. It is 1,280 feet long and 380 wide, having a nave surrounding it 107 feet in width. Above the nave and encircling the entire building, is a gallery 50 feet wide. The south end of this building overlooks the Grand Basin and its eastern flank extends northward not far from the shore of Lake Michigan. The building has four grand entrances, one at each end and one at each side. They are eighty feet high and forty feet wide and are adorned as is the whole building inside and out, with magnificent groups of statuary. Extending through the whole length of the central hall is a veritable street, Columbia Avenue, lined on either side with handsome lamp-posts. Thronged with people, this grand avenue could well be likened to a great thoroughfare in some large metropolis; it might well be termed "A Road Through the World."

THE VIRGIN WEST.—It cannot be anything less than an intense satisfaction to the women of this country, nay, of the whole world, to know and realize the high plane upon which the sex now stands as regards many of the fields wherein man has heretofore been the recognized master. The World's Columbian Exposition has been an event of much importance to the gentle sex. In no other line so much as art has its capabilities been shown. The construction of the Woman's Building from beginning to end, so far as design, plans and decorations are concerned, is its work wholly and alone. No masculine hand has here interfered; no idea or suggestion has emanated from the masculine mind. The glory of the structure, entire and undivided, belongs to woman. And the result is one of which any man, no matter how high he stands in his profession, might well be proud. The critics have paid it the homage due to its merits. The interior is considered woman's natural domain, and it might seem a matter of course that the arrangement there should be almost perfection. In the interior, accordingly, are some works of art, paintings and statuary, which demand attention. In the main room stands a female figure representing "The West," exquisite in form and faultless in proportion. The artist chose a happy theme, and has wrought it out with a marked degree of genius.

A VISION OF FAIRYLAND.—Happy must be the birds that fly over the White City of the Columbian Exposition. They can certainly rejoice in such views as are not given to mortals. Even this partial glimpse of the artist at once beggars description. A correspondent of an English magazine despairingly writes of it: "Considered as a coup d' oeil, regardless of the material used in the construction of the buildings, it is, I veritably believe, the grandest sight the human eye has ever encountered. At first you will not believe in its actuality. Your imagination has played you a trick. • • Yet it is still before you, growing more distinct, increasing in grandeur as you gaze. Let me try to describe it to you more in detail. On your left a triumphal arch and lofty colonnades, through which the blue waters of the inland sea laugh and sparkle in the sunlight. Before you a grand canal that would make Venice blush, lined with the finest specimens of the plastic art. Back of these are gilded domes, awnings and colossal statues, and away on your right, at the head of the grand canal, a fountain with basin piled upon basin and presided over by a majestic group, all except the gilded statues, the domes and the awnings white as the driven snow. • • Much as has been said about these buildings enough never can be said. They are the realization of a dream—the dream that childhood sees before it as in the picture of the 'Progress of Life;' the only realization of a complete and perfect beauty I ever expect to behold."

VESTIBULE OF THE WHITE CITY.—If a study of the figures were made it would undoubtedly be discerned that the admissions to the Exposition through the western entrance to the Midway Plaisance exceed those of any other avenue to the Fair. The great popularity of this interesting place is a strong inducement to many visitors to make their first approach by it. To merely walk through the Midway without lingering at any of the attractions affords no end of amusement. Here there is such variety of life, such bustle and animation! Here are all the nations of the earth represented. In one and the same minute the visitor meets the fair-haired Laplander or Scandinavian from the north and the black-eyed and swarthy-faced descendant of Latin stock or native of South Africa. The Arabs of the desert here mingle with the cultured and refined denizens of the Paris salon and Mongolian jostles Caucasian in the hurly-burly throng. Above is a noonday scene at the west end of Midway. Nothing like the great crowd which pours through this channel in the morning, it is still an animated scene that greets the view. In the distance the Ferris Wheel looms up against the sky, revolving in gentle motion and seeming to give welcome to the incoming tide. Ranged along on either side are the various places of entertainment, the Chinese Joss house on the left, "Old Vienna" at the right, and the others stretching away into the beckoning distance.

12. A National Pantheon

In 1900 the construction of a new campus by New York University was suddenly invested with national interest and publicity. Chancellor MacCracken's decision to construct a Hall of Fame on the picturesque site of the campus attracted enormous newspaper attention. Editors praised the proposal as a stimulus to the study of American history, and a possible revelation of national unity. The plan also promised an exciting popularity contest, whose results would cast a great deal of light upon the American taste in heroes.

The decisions of the judges, who included—along with famous historians and college presidents like J. Franklin Jameson, Edward Channing, C. M. Andrews, and Charles W. Eliot—one ex-President of the United States, Grover Cleveland, and two future presidents, Theodore Roosevelt and Woodrow Wilson, generally gave satisfaction. New Englanders exulted that Massachusetts was represented by fourteen of the first twenty-nine selections; Southerners were pleased by the inclusion of Robert E. Lee (although this choice caused a tremendous controversy in the North); Westerners looked to future ballots, which have more than tripled the number of immortals in the past sixty years. No woman was selected, but a number had been nominated. In retrospect the actual inclusions may seem less significant than the desire to construct a national pantheon itself, to define a cordon of great men. Like so many of the period's achievements the Hall of Fame left an indelible mark, as visitors to Cooperstown and other sports shrines can testify.

The Hall of Fame

LOUIS A. BANKS

Chancellor MacCracken, of the New York University, in his account of the inception of the Hall of Fame, says that like many another product of civilization, it was due in considerable part to hard facts of physical geography. In order to secure a large interior campus, it was necessary that the three buildings which composed the west side of the college quadrangle should be placed close by the avenue above the Harlem River. But since the grade of the quadrangle was one hundred and seventy feet above the river, and from forty to sixty feet above the avenue, this arrangement would leave the exterior basement walls of these buildings exposed and unsightly. To conceal these walls, and to present an ornamental effect toward the avenue, a broad terrace was suggested, to be supported upon granite walls and crowned by a colonnade. The colonnade was to stand upon the outer curve of the terrace and extend full five hundred feet in length.

While the argument for this structure, upon the ground of beauty, was most convincing, the trustees of the University did not feel justified in spending so large a sum of money simply upon ornamental work. Chancellor MacCracken felt that he must discover some educational use for such an edifice, and it was in that search that there came to him the idea of "The Hall of Fame for Great Americans." The educational value of such a structure promised to grow with the years and endure for many generations.

It was curious that no plans of an American Pantheon had before this time been presented to the nation.

In Rome still stand the remains of the Pantheon, built by Agrippa (to-day the most perfect of the existing classical buildings in the city), dedicated to all the gods, and goddesses, and deities of Roman mythology.

The Pantheon in Paris, now the Church of St. Geneviève, was consecrated by the Convention to illustrious men.

Munich possesses a Temple of Fame, built by the King of Bavaria,

Louis Albert Banks, *The Story of the Hall of Fame* (New York, 1902), pp. 13–19, 369–372.

while in England, Westminster Abbey serves to commemorate under one roof the names of many of the most famous children of the empire.

• • •

In the Hall of Fame were to be provided one hundred and fifty panels, to be inscribed to the memory of great Americans—not more than fifty to be raised at the present time, and fifty more at the close of every succeeding period of five years.

It was decided that in the first fifty names should be included one or more representatives of the following fifteen classes of citizens: Authors and Editors, Business Men, Educators, Inventors, Missionaries and Explorers, Philanthropists and Reformers, Preachers and Theologians, Scientists, Engineers and Architects, Lawyers and Judges, Musicians, Painters and Sculptors, Physicians and Surgeons, Rulers and Statesmen, Soldiers and Sailors, and distinguished men and women outside the above classes.

No name was to be inscribed except of a person born in what is now the territory of the United States, and who had been deceased for at least ten years.

Nominations were invited from the public, and it was planned that any name that was seconded by a member of the University Senate should be submitted to one hundred judges chosen among these classes of citizens—University or College Presidents and Educators; Professors of History and Scientists; Publicists, Editors, and Authors; and Judges of the Supreme Court, State or National.

There was no lack of nominations. Literary and educational bodies, as well as patriotic, military, and philanthropic societies, scientific associations, and many other organizations, hastened to send in the names of those in which they were interested through the peculiar character of their societies.

Some leading newspapers also added great interest to the occasion by offering prizes to contestants who should approach most nearly to the roll of names finally selected by the judges and University Senate. A very interesting incident occurred in connection with one of these contests. The highest prize of $100 offered by a newspaper went to a schoolgirl, whose list of fifty names contained twenty-seven of the twenty-nine finally elected by the hundred judges.

The University Senate soon had nearly a thousand names presented for its consideration. They selected one hundred names which stood first in popular favor in newspaper contests. Each member of the Senate had the right to make a further nomination from the thousand names sent in by the public; one hundred additional nominations were thus made. The judges also were asked to nominate, and they added something over thirty names.

The list of nominations was sent out from the University Senate to the one hundred judges, June 15, 1900, and they had until October of that year to make up their minds and cast their ballot. Ninety-seven judges acted within the required time.

Only twenty-nine names were chosen, as it had been decided that no name could be selected which had not received a majority, not of the votes cast, but of the one hundred judges, thus requiring fifty-one votes to elect. The following are the twenty-nine names chosen, with the votes cast for each:

George Washington	97
Abraham Lincoln	96
Daniel Webster	96
Benjamin Franklin	94
Ulysses Simpson Grant	93
John Marshall	91
Thomas Jefferson	91
Ralph Waldo Emerson	87
Robert Fulton	86
Henry Wadsworth Longfellow	85
Washington Irving	83
Jonathan Edwards	82
Samuel Finley Breese Morse	82
David Glascoe Farragut	79
Henry Clay	74
George Peabody	74
Nathaniel Hawthorne	73
Peter Cooper	69
Eli Whitney	69
Robert E. Lee	68
Horace Mann	67
John James Audubon	67
James Kent	65
Henry Ward Beecher	64
Joseph Story	64
John Adams	62
Willam Ellery Channing	58
Gilbert Charles Stuart	52
Asa Gray	51

• • •

The names of nine women were submitted to the judges, but in no case did they come near the majority of votes required. On the board of electors were three women, all of whom voted for Mary Lyon, the famous educator, while not more than one voted for any of the other women who were nominated—Helen Hunt Jackson (author), Emma Willard (educator), Lucretia Mott (reformer), Dorothea Dix (reformer), Maria Mitchell (astronomer), Charlotte S. Cushman (tragedienne), Martha Washington (wife of the first President), and Elizabeth A. Seton (philanthropist).

✿ ✿ ✿

Of the hundred judges chosen, ninety-seven acted within the time required. The following table shows the result of their ballot in detail.

CANDIDATES and CLASSES	University Presidents.	Professors of Science and History.	Publicists, Editors, and Authors.	Chief Justices.	Totals.

CANDIDATES and CLASSES	University Presidents.	Professors of Science and History.	Publicists, Editors, and Authors.	Chief Justices.	Totals.

CANDIDATES and CLASSES	University Presidents.	Professors of Science and History.	Publicists, Editors, and Authors.	Chief Justices.	Totals.

CANDIDATES and CLASSES	University Presidents.	Professors of Science and History.	Publicists, Editors, and Authors.	Chief Justices.	Totals.

CANDIDATES and CLASSES	University Presidents.	Professors of Science and History.	Publicists, Editors, and Authors.	Chief Justices.	Totals.

CANDIDATES and CLASSES	University Presidents.	Professors of Science and History.	Publicists, Editors, and Authors.	Chief Justices.	Totals.
(A) AUTHORS AND EDITORS:					
William Cullen Bryant	11	8	19	11	49
James Fenimore Cooper	11	7	7	5	30
Ralph Waldo Emerson	24	26	21	16	87
William Lloyd Garrison	6	5	6	2	19
Horace Greeley	12	10	9	14	45
Nathaniel Hawthorne	21	24	20	8	73
Washington Irving	24	20	23	6	83
Henry Wadsw'th Longfellow	24	21	23	17	85
John Lothrop Motley	8	15	11	7	41
Wendell Phillips	7	2	6	4	19
William Hickling Prescott	8	9	6	10	33
Edgar Allan Poe	9	7	12	10	38
Noah Webster	8	8	10	10	36
(B) BUSINESS MEN:					
James Harper	3	3	4	5	15
Amos Lawrence	5	6	10	1	22
Cornelius Vanderbilt	8	7	6	9	30

(C) EDUCATORS:

Thomas Hopkins Gallaudet .	4	3	4	3	14
Mark Hopkins	17	14	12	5	48
Mary Lyon	12	4	2	2	20
Horace Mann	22	22	12	11	67
Francis Wayland	9	3	5	7	24
Theodore Dwight Woolsey .	3	6	9	3	21

(D) INVENTORS:

Alvin Clark	7	3	2	. .	12
Robert Fulton	21	24	20	21	86
Charles Goodyear	1	6	2	4	13
Richard Marsh Hoe	3	9	4	3	19
Elias Howe	14	12	10	11	47
Cyrus Hall McCormick	3	9	4	9	25
Samuel Finley Breese Morse	23	23	17	19	82
Eli Whitney	18	20	18	13	69
Horace Wells	3	4	6	1	14

(E) MISSIONARIES AND EXPLORERS:

Daniel Boone	6	10	7	12	35
John Charles Fremont	3	4	3	7	17
Samuel Houston	2	6	3	5	16
Adoniram Judson	13	7	10	6	36
Elisha Kent Kane	5	4	6	7	22
Meriwether Lewis	2	6	4	2	14
Marcus Whitman	10	3	. .	6	19
George Rogers Clark	1	9	7	2	19

(F) PHILANTHROPISTS:

John Brown	5	5	4	3	17
Peter Cooper	18	17	19	15	69
Dorothea Lynde Dix	4	1	6	1	12
George Peabody	19	25	12	18	74

(G) PREACHERS AND THEOLOGIANS:

Henry Ward Beecher	17	20	14	13	64
Horace Bushnell ...:.....	12	7	10	3	32
William Ellery Channing ..	18	19	16	5	58
Jonathan Edwards	23	22	22	15	82
Cotton Mather	4	5	5	4	18
Theodore Parker	3	10	5	3	21

(H) SCIENTISTS:

John James Audubon	19	18	14	16	67
Asa Gray	18	16	13	4	51
Joseph Henry	12	13	13	6	44
Matthew Fontaine Maury ..	5	5	2	8	20
Benjamin Peirce	4	4	5	1	14
Benjamin Silliman	7	3	6	1	17
Benjamin Thompson	6	9	4	. .	19

(I)   ENGINEERS AND ARCHITECTS:

George Henry Corliss	5	1	3	3	12
James Buchanan Eads	7	11	6	17	41
Henry Hobson Richardson .	12	13	6	1	32

(J)   JUDGES AND LAWYERS:

Rufus Choate	14	10	11	12	47
James Kent	13	18	13	21	65
John Marshall	22	25	23	21	91
Joseph Story	15	17	13	19	64
Roger Brooke Taney	2	3	3	9	17
Henry Wheaton	5	5	2	1	13

(K)   MUSICIANS, PAINTERS, AND SCULPTORS:

John Singleton Copley	9	10	9	5	33
Hiram Powers	7	10	7	12	36
Gilbert Charles Stuart	11	18	15	8	52
William Morris Hunt	3	4	5	1	13

(L)   PHYSICIANS AND SURGEONS:

Valentine Mott	3	6	5	4	18
Benjamin Rush	12	10	10	10	42
James Marion Sims	11	8	4	5	28

(M)   RULERS AND STATESMEN:

John Quincy Adams	13	14	13	8	48
John Adams	15	19	14	14	62
Samuel Adams	11	8	11	3	33
Thomas Hart Benton	4	2	1	9	16
John C. Calhoun	13	14	10	12	49
Salmon Portland Chase	2	1	5	5	13
Henry Clay	18	21	16	19	74
Benjamin Franklin	24	26	22	22	94
John Hancock	3	2	3	4	12
Patrick Henry	11	9	10	9	39
Andrew Jackson	11	14	10	13	48
John Jay	7	6	5	7	25
Thomas Jefferson	24	25	21	21	91
Abraham Lincoln	25	26	23	22	96
James Madison	11	14	10	14	49
James Monroe	3	4		12	19
William Henry Seward	5	6	6	8	25
Charles Sumner	9	6	4	7	26
George Washington	25	26	23	23	97
Daniel Webster	25	26	23	22	96

(N)   SOLDIERS AND SAILORS:

Stephen Decatur	4	8	5	6	23
David Glascoe Farragut ...	22	23	19	15	79
Ulysses Simpson Grant	25	26	21	21	93

Nathaniel Greene	8	11	7	4	30
Thomas Jonathan Jackson ..	5	6	6	6	23
Robert Edward Lee	16	19	17	16	68
Oliver Hazzard Perry	9	5	5	7	26
Winfield Scott	5	5	..	6	16
Philip Henry Sheridan	4	6	6	7	23
George Henry Thomas	5	6	10	3	24
Albert Sidney Johnston	1	2	3	6	12

(O) DISTINGUISHED MEN AND WOMEN OUTSIDE THE ABOVE CLASSES:

Charlotte S. Cushman	6	1	5	1	13
Martha Washington	2	..	1	11	14

In this list it will be noted that none who received less than twelve votes are included. All receiving a less number of votes were counted "Scattering." The scattering votes were distributed as follows:

AUTHORS

Edward Everett, 9; Richard Hildreth, 1; Francis Scott Key, 2; John Gorham Palfrey, 1; Ray Palmer, 1; John Howard Payne, 4; Jared Sparks, 3; Henry David Thoreau, 3; Helen Hunt Jackson, 3.

BUSINESS MEN

Daniel Appleton, 7; Jonas Chickering, 2; Erastus Fairbanks, 2.

EDUCATORS

Samuel G. Howe, 9; Taylor Lewis, 2; Elias Loomis, 2; William H. McGuffey, 5; Lindley Murray, 7; Eliphalet Nott, 9; Henry Tappen, 7; Emma Willard, 4; Samuel Harvey Taylor, 1.

INVENTORS

Thomas Blanchard, 2; Samuel Colt, 1; Oliver Evans, 3; Charles T. Jackson, 1; William Thomas Green Morton, 6; John Stevens, 2; Alfred Vail, 6.

MISSIONARIES AND EXPLORERS

David Brainerd, 9; John Carroll, 1; Titus Coan, 3; David Crockett, 8; Manasseh Cutler, 9; Gordon Hall, 1; Samuel Kirkland, 1; Charles Wilkes, 2.

PHILANTHROPISTS

Johns Hopkins, 11; Lucretia Mott, 11; Gerrit Smith, 1; James Lick, 1.

PREACHERS AND THEOLOGIANS

Archibald Alexander, 3; J. Addison Alexander, 1; Albert Barnes, 3; Lyman Beecher, 4; Orestes A. Brownson, 2; Peter Cartwright, 8; Timothy Dwight, 11; Charles G. Finney, 4; Charles Hodge, 5; Thomas Starr King, 7; Stephen Olin, 4; Matthew Simpson, 11; Martin John Spaulding, 1; John McClintock, 1.

SCIENTISTS

Spencer F. Baird, 8; Alexander D. Bache, 9; Nathaniel Bowditch, 10; William Chauvenet, 1; Henry Draper, 8; Robert Hare, 2; Edward Hitchcock, 4; Maria Mitchell, 7; David Rittenhouse, 6; John Torrey, 1.

MUSICIANS, PAINTERS, AND SCULPTORS
Thomas Crawford, 9; Lowell Mason, 10.

PHYSICIANS AND SURGEONS
Ephraim McDowell, 5; John Collins Warren, 3.

SOLDIERS AND SAILORS
Nathan Hale, 5; George G. Meade, 6; David Porter, 6; Israel Putnam, 10; Philip Schuyler, 4; Zachary Taylor, 9; George Brinton McClellan, 6.

RULERS AND STATESMEN
Charles Francis Adams, 4; DeWitt Clinton, 8; Stephen Arnold Douglas, 3; James Abram Garfield, 7; Richard Henry Lee, 3; Robert E. Livingston, 3; Gouverneur Morris, 7; James Otis, 4; Charles C. Pinckney, 4; Roger Sherman, 5; Edwin McMaster Stanton, 6; Alexander H. Stephens, 7; Martin Van Buren, 1; Charles Carroll, 2; John J. Crittenden, 1; Samuel T. Tilden, 6.

ENGINEERS AND ARCHITECTS
Horatio Allen, 1; Charles Bulfinch, 7; Ellis S. Chesbrough, 1; Zerah Colburn, 1; James Geddes, 2; Alexander L. Holley, 8; John Bloomfield Jervis, 1; Benjamin H. Latrobe, 4; William Barton Rogers, 5; Benjamin Wright, 1; Henry R. Worthington, 4.

JUDGES AND LAWYERS
Oliver Ellsworth, 10; Charles O'Conor, 8; William Wirt, 6; Lemuel Shaw, 11.

OUTSIDE THE ABOVE CLASSES
Edwin Forrest, 6.

13. The Glories of Consumption

To interest American consumers in the bewildering and expanding series of available products, manufacturers and advertising agencies expanded their promotional activities in the eighties and nineties. The great middle-class magazines like *The Cosmopolitan, McClure's, Scribner's* and the *Ladies Home Journal,* spread before their prosperous readers the marvels of novel inventions like the typewriter, the phonograph, and the safety bicycle, the tastiness of cereals, sauces, canned meats, and soups, the purity of soaps and detergents, the healing power of miraculous medicines. Copywriters turned to puns, jingles, riddles, human-interest stories, and slogans to make their point, while they employed a variety of illustrative techniques. The older promotional expressions of the postwar era, the small crowded ads with their terse descriptions and cluttered typefaces, existed side-by-side in these decades with the newer, more refined, and more psychologically effective appeals to basic social values, allusions to patriotism and mythology, and extravagant promises of well being and content. The economic value of advertising now seemed obvious, and the industry girded for the coming explosion in the next century.

The consumer's ears were assaulted along with his eyes. These were the years when music began to serve a commercial purpose as well, the decades when "The Health Rocking Chair Gavotte," "The New York Produce Exchange Waltzes," and the Southern Pacific's "Down Where the Oil Burners Run Two-Step" were published as melodic offerings. Market orientation, however, was already established independently in the polite arts. Music publishers and song writers, for example, discovered the fortunes to be made in sales of sheet music, and they eagerly turned out thousands of ditties, hoping to gauge the public's mood and strike success. Often they exploited current tragedies like the Johnstown Flood or the Garfield assassination, writing their numbers with the headlines still fresh; at other times they relied on standard favorites—sentimental ballads, tinged with sadness about death, bereavement, and the unnamed terrors of city life, or humorous numbers playing on some of the new inventions or the peculiar speech of immigrants. Introduced by famous entertainers, plugged in advertising campaigns, performed by the popular pianolas, words and music alike catered to the aspirations and anxieties of an enormous new audience.

Advertisements taken from issues of *McClure's* and *Scribner's* published between 1895 and 1900.

The ones we work for and LOVE are ofttimes Hurt by our ignorance ✋ ✋ ✋

"And papa please don't forget we need some more POSTUM CEREAL FOOD COFFEE

You know Doctor says you should never give Mamma and I coffee, and we like POSTUM just as well or better for breakfast and lunch. Mamma says her eyes are so much better, and she is so free from her nervous troubles, since leaving off coffee and using POSTUM, that she never wants to be without; so don't forget, Papa, please; good-bye! Come home early. Can you hear me send you a kiss? Good-bye!"

POSTUM CEREAL FOOD COFFEE cannot be told in color from the finest thick Mocha. Use good cream and it changes to a rich golden brown, while its taste is that of the milder and more expensive grades of Java. It is an absolutely pure and simple product of the cereals intended by nature for man's subsistence, and selected by the highest scientific knowledge of the food elements needed for the human body.

About 70 per cent. is from the gluten, albumens and phosphates of wheat, which go directly to make the gray matter in the nerve cells. (Well-fed nerve centres means health, strength, and success in life.) About 20 per cent. is the starchy particles of grain, which go to make the fat globules of the body, and about 10 per cent. is saccharine matter (sugar) prepared from cereals. That is why "It makes Red blood" when common coffee does exactly the *other* thing. Sold by Fancy Grocers, or will be sent, express prepaid, from factory. Samples free on application.

POSTUM CEREAL CO., Limited, Battle Creek, Mich.

McCLURE'S MAGAZINE.

$200.⁰⁰ FOR CORRECT ANSWERS

Most Unique Contest of the Age — $200.00 Paid for Correct Lists made by Supplying Missing Letters In Places of Stars — No Lottery — Popular Plan of Education — Read All the Particulars.

In the United States four times as much money is expended for education as for the military. Brain is better than brawn. By our educational facilities we have become a great nation. We, the publishers of **Woman's World and Jenness Miller Monthly**, have done much toward the cause of education in many ways, but now we offer you an opportunity to display your knowledge and receive **most generous payment for a little study.** The object of this contest is to give an impetus to many dormant minds to awaken and think; also we expect by this competition of brains to extend the circulation of **Woman's World and Jenness Miller Monthly** to such a size that we shall be able to charge double the present rate for advertising in our columns. By this plan of increasing the number of subscriptions and receiving more money from advertisers of soaps, pianos, medicines, books, baking powders, jewelry, etc., we shall add **$50,000** a year to our income, and with this mathematical deduction before us we have decided to operate this most remarkable "missing letters" contest.

HERE'S WHAT YOU ARE TO DO.

There are **thirty words** in this schedule, from each of which letters have been omitted and their places have been **supplied by stars.** To fill in the blank spaces and get the names properly you must have some knowledge of geography and history. **We want you to spell** out as many words as you can, then send to us with 25 cents to pay for a three months' subscription to WOMAN'S WORLD. For correct lists **we shall give $200.00** in cash. If more than one person sends a full, correct list, the money will be awarded to the fifty best lists in appearance. Also, if your list contains twenty or more correct words, we shall send you a beautiful **Egeria Diamond Scarf Pin** (for lady or gentleman), the regular price of which is **$2.25.** Therefore, by sending your list, you are positively certain of the $2.25 prize, and by being careful to send a correct list you have an opportunity of the **$200.00 cash award.** The distance that you may live from New York makes no difference. All have equal opportunity for winning.

PRIZES WILL BE SENT PROMPTLY.

Prizes will be honestly awarded and promptly sent. We publish the list of words to be studied out. In making your list of answers, be sure to give the number of each word:

1. * R A * I * A country of South America.
2. * A * I * I * Name of the largest body of water.
3. M * D * * E * * A * E * * A sea.
4. * M * * O * A large river.
5. T * A * * S Well known river of Europe.
6. S * * A N * A * A city in one of the Southern States.
7. H * * * * * X A city of Canada.
8. N * A * A * A Noted for display of water.
9. * E * * E * * E * One of the United States.
10. * A * R I * A city of Spain.
11. H * V * * A A city on a well known island.
12. S * M * E * A well known old fort of the United States.
13. G * * R * L * A * Greatest fortification in the world.
14. S * A * L E * A great explorer.
15. C * L * F * * * I * One of the United States.
16. B * S M * * K A noted ruler.
17. * * C T O * I * Another noted ruler.
18. P * R * U * A * Country of Europe.
19. A * S T * A * I * A big island.
20. M * * I N * E * Name of the most prominent American.
21. T * * A * One of the United States.
22. J * F * * R * * N Once President of the United States.
23. * U * * N A large lake.
24. E * E * S * N A noted poet.
25. C * R * A A foreign country, same size as Kansas.
26. B * R * * O A large island.
27. W * M * * S W * R * D Popular family magazine.
28. B * H * I * G A sea.
29. A * L * N * I * An ocean.
30. M * D * G * S * A * An island near Africa.

In sending your list of words, mention whether you want prize money sent by bank draft, money order or registered mail; we will send any way that winners require. The **Egeria Diamond** is a perfect imitation of a **Real Diamond** of large size. We defy experts to distinguish it from real except by microscopic test. In every respect it serves the purpose of **Genuine Diamond of Purest Quality.** It is artistically mounted in a fine gold-plated pin, warranted to wear forever. This piece of jewelry will make a most desirable gift to a friend if you do not need it yourself. At present our supply of these gifts is limited, and if they are all gone when your set of answers comes in, we shall send you $2.25 in money instead of the **Scarf** or **Shawl Pin,** so you shall either receive the piece of jewelry or the equivalent in cash, in addition to your participative interest in the **$200.00 cash prize. This entire offer is an honest one,** made by a responsible publishing house. We refer to **mercantile agencies** and any bank in New York. We will promptly refund money to you if you are dissatisfied. What more can we do? We study, and exchange slight brain work for cash. With your list of answers send **25 cents** to pay for three months' subscription to our great family magazine, **Woman's World.** If you have already subscribed, mention that fact in your letter, and we will extend your subscription from the time the present one expires. To avoid loss in sending silver, wrap money very carefully in paper before inclosing in your letter. Address:

JAMES H. PLUMMER Publisher,

22 & 24 North William Street, - - - - - - New York City, N. Y.

Please mention McClure's when you write to advertisers.

DERMATOLOGICAL INSTITUTE

HOW CUPID RECEIVED AID

By NAM DERIH SYRUBDOOW

This is a story of how two fond hearts were united after years of uncertainty.

Right here I will say that this article is an advertisement, but it is more interesting than fiction because the statements are facts and also because the story is interesting and instructive to all who wish to be better looking.

Alice Gray Smith, three years ago, lived at No. 155 West 98th Street, New York City, which, as almost everyone knows, is an aristocratic section of New York. Her father was wealthy, having five years ago retired from the woolen business with a competency.

Alice, who was his only daughter, was educated at Vassar and afterward studied music, painting and languages in Paris. Her form was superb and her disposition lovable, but her face, unlike that of the dairymaid's, was not her fortune.

Her nose was of a pronounced Roman type, and her face was liberally adorned with pimples and a few moles.

While Alice was at Vassar she met George Holden at a football game in which Yale and Princeton were the contestants.

George, who was a Yale graduate, was infatuated with Alice, and although they saw each other only for a few hours during a jolly supper party, a friendship sprang up which almost immediately ripened into mutual love.

Six months later George sailed for Germany and entered a medical college in Heidelberg, and when he left New York he and Alice had become so much attached to each other that a regular correspondence had been agreed upon.

Before the young medical student sailed he had often remarked to himself that Alice's beauty would be complete were it not for her "humped" nose. At that time she had no other facial blemishes. The moles came soon afterward, and a little later the pimples appeared, which were caused by lack of proper exercise and too generous eating.

The letters between the two young people passed more and more frequently until after two years George returned to New York.

The morning of the day he landed he thought he saw Alice on Fifth Avenue, but after he had seen her face he gazed at her and thought he was mistaken.

Alice had anticipated the return of her sweetheart with both joy and fear. She would be delighted to see him again, but feared her unattractive face might cause his affection to cool.

She had passed hours daily before the mirror, hoping that the brush, crimping iron and other aids would make her more attractive, but her pronounced nose, pimples and moles remained and no embellishment would tend to decrease their effect.

The afternoon of the day George returned to New York he called upon Alice. He was surprised to find that it really was Alice whom

"SHE PASSED HOURS DAILY BEFORE THE MIRROR."

he had seen that morning, and he could hardly realize it was the same girl he had bidden good-by two years before.

When George was being driven to his club he had a feeling that he really did not love Alice as much as he had thought; and his feelings had been anticipated by the unfortunate girl.

No doubt the reader will think George a very flippant lover; if you do, put yourself in his place.

That evening Alice had a long talk with a certain matron who was not only her close friend but a society woman thoroughly up-to-date.

As a result of this interview Alice left home

Please mention McClure's when you write to advertisers.

the next day, and it was announced that she had gone abroad with her aunt Harriet, who lived in Marlboro' Street, Boston.

Four months later she returned looking prettier and more attractive than ever before.

As a matter of fact Alice had not been out of New York.

Acting upon the advice of her friend, she visited a specialist who for twenty-six years has given his life work to the art of making people better looking.

Alice visited the specialist with much doubt, but after the consultation she was satisfied of the probability of her facial beauty being restored.

The first thing done was to change her pronounced Roman nose to an aquiline.

Although the task seemed almost impossible, the transformation occupied only a half hour, and it was rendered entirely painless by anæsthetics.

"HE GAZED AT HER AND THOUGHT HE WAS MISTAKEN."

A skilled surgeon laid the skin back along the bridge of the nose, and then deftly removed enough cartilage to make the line of the nose straight. Then the skin was laid back in its former position, the edges neatly joined, and then small pieces of fine adhesive plaster were applied.

During the operation Alice was conversing with her friend as gaily as if she was having her hair dressed.

Inside of a week the plaster was removed, and no scar was visible.

The pimples on the face of the otherwise fair patient were soon removed by necessary careful living and the use of medicines which destroyed the cause of the pimples, and an external application which removed the pimples themselves.

This course of treatment resulted in restoring Alice's fine complexion in less than two months. The only facial blemishes left were the moles. These were all removed before

the last pimple had disappeared and without the use of a surgical instrument.

The specialist applied a preparation which caused the moles to dry up and drop off without the skin even being broken.

"HE HAD CALLED WITH A BOUQUET."

When Alice returned from her alleged European trip she was more prominent in society than before and more sought after.

George Holden realized that his life could not be happy without Alice for a wife, and one day, after he had called with a bouquet, he proposed and was accepted.

"And so they were married."

The place where Alice was made beautiful was at the John H. Woodbury Dermatological Institute, 127 West 42d Street, New York. Associated with Dermatologist Woodbury are twenty-three skilled surgeons and physicians, each of whom is a specialist in one or more branches of dermatology.

The institute has offices and a corps of surgeons and physicians at 11 Winter Street, Boston; 1218 Walnut Street, Philadelphia; and 155 State Street, Chicago.

There is no blemish in, on or under the skin that Dermatologist Woodbury cannot remove painlessly and permanently. Consultation is free, either personally or by letter, and fees are moderate.

Among the many preparations of the Woodbury Institute is Woodbury's Facial Soap. It beautifies and softens the skin. Woodbury's Facial Cream is the best cream made. Send ten cents to the New York Office for a 132-page illustrated Beauty Book and either a sample cake of Facial Soap or a trial tube of Facial Cream.

McCLURE'S MAGAZINE.

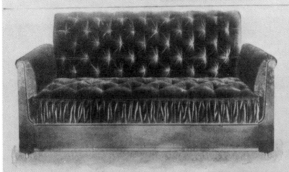

The...
Leonard
Sofa Bed

A luxurious Sofa, Couch length, instantly convertible into a large, soft, hair mattress bed, with large drawer for bedding or dresses. 20 pounds of pure hair and 100 finely tempered steel springs in every one. Ten styles, $28.00 to $65.00. Equally luxurious and serviceable. Freight prepaid. Returnable if unsatisfactory. Catalogues Free. Patented, manufactured and sold only by

THE LEONARD SOFA BED CO.,
403 Erie Street, Cleveland, Ohio.

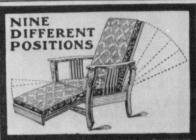

NINE DIFFERENT POSITIONS

SIMILAR to the Morris Chair when closed and combining all the comforts of the $50 Reversible Chairs when open. Made of quartered oak with Golden or Flemish finish, or in imitation mahogany. Reversible cushions of best quality velour and leatherine. State color preference and we will make careful selection.

Delivered east of Mississippi and north of Carolinas on receipt of

$14.25

and can be returned at our expense if not satisfactory. Our booklet gives details and tells how to order. Send for it.

THE AMERICAN CHAIR MFG. CO.
Hallstead, Pa.

Queen Kitchen Cabinets
$7.55 and Upwards. The modern
Household Labor Saving Device.

Queen Cabinets are necessary to the proper equipment of the kitchen. Has a place for everything and gives a neat, tidy appearance to the kitchen.

Roll Top, Sliding Bread Board,

easy running drawers for table linens, are special features

Makes Cooking Easy; Saves Labor–Waste

Made of hard wood, antique finish. Six styles, $4.90 to $11.40. For country and city home or cozy flat, it cannot be excelled. The ideal wedding or birthday gift. Used and recommended by Mrs. S. T. Rorer and other famous American cooks. Everything we sell is guaranteed. Money back if not satisfactory. Write to-day.

Descriptive catalogue "G" including useful household articles, all at factory prices, sent FREE.

QUEEN CABINET COMPANY, Security Bldg., Chicago

WE FURNISH A DINING-ROOM COMPLETE

$19.75 Buys this dainty combination buffet and china closet direct from factory, freight prepaid, sent "On Approval," to be returned at our expense if not positively the best value at so low a price.

The design of this china buffet gives a combination of the practical and pleasing features of both the china closet and buffet. It is made of finely figured quarter sawed oak, golden finish, highly polished, has easy-running casters and cast brass trimmings. It has a 10 x 32 inch French bevel plate mirror, and from a buffet will cost you from $25.00 to $35.00.

We prepay freight to all points east of the Mississippi and north of South Carolina; points beyond on an equal basis.

THE CHARLES F. POWERS COMPANY
87 Pearl Street   Grand Rapids, Mich.
Makers of Dining-Room Furniture.

We can furnish Dining Tables, Dining Chairs, Buffets, Sideboards, China Buffets, China Closets, Hanging Wall Cabinets, Plate Racks, Five O'Clock Tea Tables. Send for our Complete Catalogue A1

AT FACTORY PRICES.

Among Life's Pleasures

All sit steady! The long whip lash flies out, the guard sounds his horn and we are off. High above the dust and traffic of busy streets, past verdant fields, up and down the country roads and lanes! The exhilaration of swift motion, the beautiful scenes, joyous companionships, the pure delight of coaching through a pleasant land. And at the end of the trip a dainty, sufficient, appetizing luncheon of

Cream of Wheat!

Composed of only the part of the grain useful as a food-it is palatable nutritious and digestible. A series of gravures which we issue will interest you. They are really fine, and you get one with two packages of Cream of Wheat. Your grocer has them.

CREAM OF WHEAT CO. MINNEAPOLIS, MINN.

McCLURE'S MAGAZINE.

Wellington No. 2

The Simplest High-Grade Machine Made.

It contains less than one-third the number of parts of the best known machines; has all their advantages together with some peculiarly its own.

Price 60 Dollars

It is the mechanical and practical superior of any machine now on the market and the equal of the very best in its construction and finish, and to convince yourself that all we say about it is true, try it for 10 days free. One profit between maker and user explains the price. Illustrated catalog free.

THE WILLIAMS MFG. CO. Ltd.
Box 40. Plattsburg, N. Y.

Wellington No. 2

The superiority of the

Columbia Bar-Lock Typewriter

is as visible as the writing.

The new No. 10 Model has ball-bearing carriage.

It combines strength of construction and ease of operation.

Send for catalogue and full particulars to

Columbia Typewriter Mfg. Co.
1 West 116th Street, New York City.

Our Business is to make Folks Comfortable

THIS IS ONE OF OUR LATEST ..... It is one of 60 styles illustrated and described in our catalogue "B." for 1900.

The case of invalidism does not exist for which we cannot furnish a suitable chair

ROLLING AND CARRYING CHAIRS

We also make the best types as well as the largest variety to be found of

RECLINING CHAIRS and ADJUSTABLE COUCHES for SICK FOLKS, WELL FOLKS, and LAZY FOLKS

all of which are illustrated and described in our catalogue "C."

In writing for information, particularize.

GEO. F. SARGENT COMPANY
289 c Fourth Ave., next 23d St. New York

"BUSINESS SYSTEM"

is the title of our 64-page book *illustrating and explaining* model business methods used by our largest and most successful business houses—it is free upon request.

It GATHERS ARRANGES CLASSIFIES INDEXES every character of business records and lists—it

Increases Profits and **Reduces Expenses**

YOUR CHOICE of *three* distinct card-locking devices. Our "Macey" **SIDE-LOCKED CARDS** require no *unsightly* or *wasteful* holes to mar the writing surface. (Patented.)

$1.25 and upward

Buys a complete **"Macey" Card System.**

Shipped "On Approval," to be returned *at our expense* if not found in every way positively the best obtainable. Ask for book No. "E-5."

THE FRED MACEY CO., Grand Rapids, Mich.
Makers of Office and Library Furniture.

Please mention McClure's when you write to advertisers.

McCLURE'S MAGAZINE.

WOODS
ELECTRIC
ROAD WAGON

The lightest, smartest looking and most graceful Automobile ever built. Is a regular three-quarter size, piano box, sidebar buggy with 32-inch wheels, 60-inch box and 36-inch seat; 1⅜-inch hard rubber tires. Weight complete, 900 pounds. Speed, 12 miles per hour. Mileage capacity on one charge of the batteries, 25 miles. Will climb a 12 per cent. grade. Painted to suit purchaser. Trimmed in whipcord, dark cloth or leather, as desired. Electric lights and bell. Unexcelled for reliability, ease of management and economy. No complicated machinery, noise or jar. Always ready for immediate service. **PROMPT DELIVERY.**

On request we will send our illustrated Catalogue in colors showing many designs of Woods Carriages—all manufactured by our own skilled workmen under one roof. We equip Private or Public Stables completely.

WOODS MOTOR VEHICLE COMPANY

NEW YORK, 44th St. and Vanderbilt Ave.   CHICAGO, 545-549 Wabash Avenue

FIND OUT all about Electric Automobiles, their care, construction and operation, in a book published by Herbert S. Stone & Co., Chicago. $1.25.

Price, $1,500—No Discounts.

Auto-mobiles
for
Pleasure
Gasoline System

THE HAYNES APPERSON CO.
KOKOMO, IND., U.S.A.

THE OLDEST MANUFACTURERS IN AMERICA

Seven years' actual experience in this line will save our customers money. Write us before buying experiments. Our Carriages are substantially built, easily managed, will run any speed, good hill climbers. Anyone can use them.

Pleasure Automobiles ranging in price from $1,000 to $1,800

Booklet describing our Gasoline system, 10 cents

Descriptive Circular Free

Price, $1,600—No Discounts.

Keep Posted on Automobiles

The Hub Will Post You

THE HUB is the leading journal in the carriage and automobile trade and gives complete information on Automobiles. Don't buy an Automobile until you have read and studied THE HUB. Established 42 years.

Published monthly at $2.00 a year; single copies at news stands, 25 cents.

In order that everybody may have an opportunity to examine THE HUB, we will send it for three months for 25 cents to anyone mentioning McCLURE'S.

TRADE NEWS PUBLISHING CO., Room 8, 26 Murray St., New York

Please mention McClure's when you write to advertisers.

The Minister's Wife

FOR SEVERAL YEARS SHE WAS IN POOR HEALTH

At Last She was Completely Prostrated, and After Physicians had Failed to Relieve, Prescribes for Herself and is Cured

From the Patriot, Jackson, Mich.

Mrs. J. M. Aikin, wife of the pastor of the Free Methodist Church, of Spring Arbor, Mich., cannot say too much in praise of Dr. Williams' Pink Pills for Pale People. Mrs. Aikin has always been a hard-working woman and has reared a family of twelve children. For several years past she has been gradually running down in health, until a year ago she was completely prostrated. She tells her own story in this way:

"I was hardly able to do anything. My appetite was gone, I could not sleep, and I really believed I was slowly passing away. I had tried many physicians and taken almost all kinds of medicines, but they did me no good, and I could see plainly that I was gradually growing worse, and was completely discouraged. About this time I saw an advertisement of Dr. Williams' Pink Pills for Pale People and concluded to try them, for I believed that if they did me no good they could not make my condition worse. I sent to Webb's drug store, in Jackson, and procured two boxes. I must confess I took them with but little hope of improvement. I had not taken all of the two boxes before I began to notice a change for the better. I continued the treatment until I had taken six boxes, and I am so much better that I am now not only able to do my work, but on several occasions have assisted my neighbors. I must say I have never received so much good from so small an amount of medicine."

A young lady who is a neighbor of Mrs. Aikin, but who objects to having her name used, was troubled with spasms, and her condition became critical. Mrs. Aikin recommended Pink Pills to her. She had no faith in them, but to please her friend she sent to Webb's and procured a box. Before she had taken them a week she felt better, and after taking six boxes she is apparently a well woman.

Another young lady who declined to allow her name to be used in print was very low with Bright's disease and her life was despaired of. Upon Mrs. Aikin's recommendation she began taking Pink Pills, and after having used them but a few months, she is in better health than for years, and she gives all the credit to the wonderful curative qualities of Pink Pills.

In concluding her story Mrs. Aikin said:
"My recovery, as well as those of the two girls mentioned, has been so remarkable that I would like all the world to know what a remedy I found in Dr. Williams' Pink Pills, and if my statement will induce any sufferers to try them, I am sure they will be greatly improved, and I gladly give it."

UNSTINTED PRAISE.

From the Courier-Herald, Saginaw, Mich.

There are many ways in which people may prove benefactors to the human race. There are those who, of their abundance, spend large sums in erecting public buildings, laying out and beautifying parks, and in other ways make the cities in which they reside pleasant and attractive. Others spend their money in charitable work and in alleviating the sufferings of their less fortunate fellows, and for these acts these people are revered and honored and called blessed. The man who having obtained relief from sickness and makes public the means by which he regained his health is, while his name may not be published as extensively as is he who spends his money lavishly for the benefit of others, none the less a public benefactor.

The pretty little village of Tuscola is the oldest place in the county of the same name. It is quietly located, away from the railway, but, in spite of its quiet location, the merits of a ster-

ling remedy have become known there, and one of its citizens testifies to its efficiency. William Webb, of that village, is one of its substantial citizens, who conducts a tile yard there. A representative of the *Courier-Herald* visited Tuscola recently and hearing that Mr. Webb had been a sufferer from ill health, and had been cured by the remedy above mentioned, called on him for the purpose of ascertaining the truth of this report.

A sturdy, quiet-appearing man was pointed out to the visitor as Mr. Webb, but as he was apparently in good health (he was just then engaged in wheeling a barrow loaded with clay up a steep incline from the pit to the manufacturing department of the yard), the reporter was in doubt as to the gentleman in question being the man he was looking for, as he had expected to find a man who, at least, would not look as healthy as did the gentleman pointed out as Mr. Webb. To make sure he inquired, "Is this Mr. Webb?" and received an answer in the affirmative.

The reporter stated his errand, remarking that a man who could handle a load such as Mr. Webb had just wheeled up the incline, could not be in very poor health. To this Mr. Webb laughingly replied that he was at present enjoying very good health and had for a year or more. Continuing he said:

"About a year and a half ago I was not like this. I was not confined to my bed, but was completely worn out. I would get up in the morning feeling much more tired than when I went to bed; had no appetite for breakfast, often not being able to eat anything, and when I sat down it seemed almost like death to try to get up. I could do nothing and was badly discouraged. I took a number of remedies which I saw advertised as beneficial in cases similar to mine, but received no benefit from them.

"Finally I saw Dr. Williams' Pink Pills for Pale People advertised, and, although I had little faith in them, resolved to try them, thinking there might possibly be a chance for relief. Accordingly, I sent for six boxes and began taking them, and almost immediately commenced to feel better, and in a short time was able to resume work, and am pleased to say the old, weary feeling has not returned. I am now fifty-five years old, and am doing the work which last season I employed two men to do. I can eat and sleep well and feel excellently."

Continuing, Mr. Webb said: "These pills also helped my wife greatly. Since the birth of our last child, who is now nearly fourteen years of age, my wife has suffered from a disease which rendered her almost helpless. I do not know what the doctors called it, but I know what it was. It was a sort of paralysis, and she was unable to do any housework. We tried several doctors, but they seemed unable to give her permanent relief. I sent for five dollars' worth of Pink Pills and she commenced taking them. She improved rapidly, and the pills completely cured her. She is fifty-five years of age, the same age as myself, and is now able to do her housework without a hired girl, and these men all board with us," and he pointed to five or six men at work in the yard.

"My son's wife was also ailing, and Pink Pills made a new woman of her. I can and do recommend these pills to all who suffer as I or my wife did, as I believe they will cure them. I know of a number of people who have been benefited by them. They are a great remedy, and people who are ill should try them, as they are sure, I think, to be benefited by them. I cannot say too much for what they have done for me," and Mr. Webb resumed his work with a vigor which indicated that he was feeling quite well just at that time, at least.

Dr. Williams' Pink Pills contain all the elements necessary to give new life and richness to the blood and restore shattered nerves. They are sold in boxes (never in loose form, by the dozen or hundred) at 50 cents a box, or six boxes for $2.50, and may be had of all druggists or directly by mail from Dr. Williams' Medicine Company, Schenectady, N. Y.

Please mention McClure's when you write to advertisers.

Dedicated to Mrs. JAMES J. ARMSTRONG.

Mother Was A Lady.

or

If Jack were only here.

Words by EDW. B. MARKS.

Music by JOS. W. STERN.

1. Two drummers sat at din-ner, in a grand ho-tel one day, While
2. It's true one touch of nat-ure, it makes the whole world kin, And

din-ing they were chat-ting in a jol-ly sort of way, And
ev-ry word she ut-tered seemed to touch their hearts with-in, They

when a pret-ty wait-ress brought them a tray of food, They
sat there stunned and si-lent, un-til one cried in shame, "For-

Copyright 1896 by Jos. W. Stern & Co.
English Copyright secured.   (All Rights reserved.)

The prettiest love song in years.

"Grace O' Moore."

Now on Sale at all Music Stores.

324

spoke to her fa - mi - liar - ly in man - ner rath - er rude; At
give me Miss! I meant no harm, pray tell me what's your name?" She

first she did not no - tice them or make the least re - ply, But
told him and he cried a - gain, "I know your bro - ther too, Why

one re - mark was passed that brought the tear drops to her eye, And
we've been friends for man - y years and he of - ten speaks of you, He'll

fac - ing her tor - men - tor, with cheeks now burn - ing red, She
be so glad to see you, and if you'll on - ly wed, I'll

looked a per - fect pict - ure as ap - peal - ing - ly she said.
take you to him as my wife, for I love you since you said."

No home complete without a copy of
"KATHLEEN."
Written, composed & sung by the great "HELENE MORA."

Chorus.
Tempo di Valse.

"My mo - ther was a la-dy like yours you will al - low, And
you may have a sis-ter, who needs pro-tec-tion now I've
come to this great ci-ty to find a bro-ther dear And you
would n't dare in-sult me Sir, If Jack were on - ly here."

D.S.

Mother was a Lady - 8

Ask your music dealer to show you a copy of
HELENE MORA'S beautiful romanza.
"Loves Souvenir."

326

Since My Daughter Plays on the Typewriter.

Words and Music by
THOMAS P. GETZ.

Arranged for Piano by
GEO. W. HETZEL.

1. My daughter's as fine a young girl as you'll meet, In your trav-els day in and day
2. She'll not car-ry her lunch in a bask-et no more, And she'll not take a flask of cold
3. She says she's a reg-u-lar dai - - - sy, U-ses slang till my poor heart is

Copyright, 1889, by Thos. P. Getz.

out - - -; But she's get-ting high-ton'd and she's put-ting on airs, Since she has been work-ing a-
tay - - -; For she says that she goes out to lunch with a fish, Way down to the Bon Ton Ca-
sore - -; She now war bles snatches from op - e - ras, Where she used to sing Peg - gy O'-

- bout   When she comes home at night from her of-fice   -, She-
- fe   She says that some-times she goes out with the Boss -   -, You can
- Moore -   Sure she's gone to the dev - il en - - tire-ly   -, She 's

walks in with a swag like a fight-er   And she tells the old la - dy to
bet your sweet life he don't slight her   For she says she can give him a-
bleach'd her hair till it is light-er   And I'll dance a Can-Can on the

328

drop on her-self, Since my daughter plays on the Type - wri - ter.
- way to his wife, Since my daughter plays on the Type - wri - ter.
face of the man, That taught her to play the Type - wri - ter.

CHORUS.

She cries in her sleep your let - ter's to hand, She calls her old father es - quire - -; And the

neighbors they shout when my daughter turns out, There goes Bridget Type-wri - ter Ma - guire - - -.

Fine.

D. S.

Marching up the aisle together, As the organ pealed an air;

Telling tales of fond affection. Vowing never more to part,

Just another fatal wedding, Just another broken heart.

The fatal wedding. K —4.

THE MOST ORIGINAL OF ORIGINAL IDEAS

"WHEN YOU KNOW THE GIRL YOU LOVE, LOVES YOU"

BY THE AUTHOR AND COMPOSER OF "THE VOLUNTEER ORGANIST."

"CARRIE." "TAKE BACK THE ENGAGEMENT RING." ETC.

FOR SALE AT ALL MUSIC STORES.

"HELLO! CENTRAL, HELLO!"

Words and Music by Chas. K. Harris.
PIANO.

Arranged by F. P. Atherton.

1. One bright and pleas - ant eve - ning, While sit ting all a lone, A
2. I stood there in a - maze- ment, I knew not what to say, A
3. At last I felt quite wor - ried, I knew not what to do, My

mes sage came a ring - ing From o'er the tel - e - phone, I
voice like that I'd nev - er heard, No not for many a day, I
heart beat for that maid - en, Who felt so sad and blue, To the

Copyright 1891. by CHAS. K. HARRIS. Milwaukee, Wis.

sprang up in a hur - ry, And an - swered back hel - lo! When
an - swered back my fair one, Mis - tak - en you must be, I
'phone a - gain I an - swered, I shout - ed out hel - lo! When

soft and clear a voice so dear Came over the tel - e - phone.
nev - er said I'd meet you though Your face I'd like to see.
some one cried, I thought I'd die, Will you pay that bill you owe.

Where were you last night Har - ry, Why don't you keep your date.
I wait - ed for an an - swer, I had not long to wait.
Why don't you speak to me a - gain, Your voice I love to hear.

You prom - ised you would meet me, Down by the old gar-den gate.
An - oth - er voice then shout - ed, Are you drink-ing much of late.
When some one else then shout - ed, All right sir send down some beer.

"HELLO! CENTRAL, HELLO!" —4-3

332

I think you are a trifl - er, Then came a sob and a moan, You'd
Go sleep it off 'till morn - ing, You'll feel bet-ter when you're at home, You've
I'll meet you on the cor - ner, To be sure I'll be all a - lone, Oh!

bet - ter get an-oth-er girl. Came o - ver the tel - e - phone.
drank e - nough for twen - ty men, Came o - ver the tel - e - phone. Hel-
Har-ry my dear your act-ing so queer, Came o - ver the tel - e - phone.

lo cen - tral, hel - lo. Hel - lo! back came the an - swer to me.

Hel - lo, cen - tral, hel - lo! Hel - lo, I won - der who she can
These lines must be cross'd I
Who's the la - dy that's talk'ng to

"HELLO! CENTRAL, HELLO!" —44

be.
see.
me.

I think you're mis-tak-en, For I'm not the man, I've a
A la-dy was talk-ing A short time a-go, A man says I'm
I rang and I shout-ed, But no one re-plied. How oft'n I sob

wife and a fam-i-ly. Though I wish I could hear That sweet voice, so dear from
full as can be, Then came a re-ply, Oh Har-ry I'll die, from
and I moan, When I think of that voice, That made me re joice, From

dim . . rall. D.C.

o-ver the tel-e-phone. From o-ver the tel-e-phone.

14. Sportsmanship

Intercollegiate athletics shared in the expansion of sports audiences in the last decades of the century, and none was more popular or influential than football. Chief among the coaches who supervised the game's incredible expansion in this era was Walter Chauncey Camp (1859–1925). Camp was a Yale graduate who actually spent two years in the Yale Medical School before deciding to go into business. After several years of association with the New Haven Clock Company, Camp returned to the University and became Yale's athletic director and head football coach. He presided over the team's golden years, and his creation of the first All America teams brought him an indelible public reputation as a football mastermind. In later years Camp's interest in physical fitness would be expressed in a number of books and articles, as well as an involvement with public programs during World War I, to improve the nation's health. He was, throughout, a firm defender of the ethics of football, against attackers who were appalled by its brutality and injury rate. His personal innovations, which included the development of the scrimmage and the institutionalization of the fourth down rule, were essential elements in creating the modern game.

College Sports

WALTER CAMP

INTRODUCTION

> "Who misses or who wins the prize,
>   Go lose or conquer as you can;
> But if you fail or if you rise
>   Be each, pray God, a gentleman!"

Before taking up the direct plan of this book I want to seize upon the opportunity when, my dear sirs, I find you all together and in such good spirits that you will bear with an old preacher for sermonizing a little. I will not bore you long, but to each of you I have a word to say—to you, my boy, just home from school for the short holidays; to you, young man, whose college years are hastening by; to you, *paterfamilias*, who, relieved for a day of business or professional cares, can spare a moment to look back upon your own school and college days, over which the lapse of years has thrown a glamour that, hiding some of the hard realities, still lends a halo of romance to the incidents.

* * *

"Be each, pray God, a gentleman!" It is an easy word, and a pleasant one. I don't doubt but that you all pronounce it trippingly enough, and have each one his own high ideal of what a gentleman should be. Do you live up to it? Or are you letting it come down a little here and there; so little, perhaps, that you hardly notice it until you make comparison? A gentleman against a gentleman always plays to win. There is a tacit agreement between them that each shall do his best, and the best man shall win. A gentleman does not make his living, however, from his athletic prowess. He does not earn anything by his victories except glory and satisfaction. Perhaps the first falling off in this respect began when the laurel wreath became a mug. So long as the mug was but the emblem, and valueless otherwise, there was no harm. There is still no harm where the mug or

Walter Camp, *Walter Camp's Book of College Sports* (New York, 1893), pp. 1–9.

trophy hangs in the room of the winner is indicative of his skill; but if the silver mug becomes a silver dollar, either at the hands of the winner or the donor, let us have the laurel back again.

A gentleman never competes for money, directly or indirectly. Make no mistake about this. No matter how winding the road may be that eventually brings the sovereign into the pocket, it is the price of what should be dearer to you than anything else,—your honor. It is quite the fashion to say "sentimental bosh" to any one who preaches such an old-fashioned thing as honor; but among true gentlemen, my boy, it is just as real an article as ever, and it is one of the few things that never ring false. The man who tells you that insufferable rot about being practical and discarding sentiment, is not the man you would choose as a friend. He wouldn't stand by you in a pinch, and when we come to the reality, it is only the man who believes in such a thing as honor that is worth anything. So stick to it, my boy, and keep it bright. Carry it down into the small affairs of school and college.

If you are enough of a man to be a good athlete, and some one asks you to use that athletic ability upon their behalf, don't take money for it, or anything that amounts to pay. If you are on the school team or nine and go into training, don't break faith with your captain, yourself, and your fellows by surreptitious indulgences. This doesn't mean that if you see some other fellow smoke on the sly you are obliged to tell of it, nor does it mean that you must call him to account, unless you are the captain. If his standard is not so high as yours, that is his misfortune. If he asks your opinion, give it to him, if you like, but not in such a way as to leave the impression that you are put out by your own longing for a similar indulgence. If you are the captain and you find a man breaking training in spite of your orders, and you consider it advisable to put him off, don't be afraid to do it. Gentlemen are not cowards, mentally or physically.

If a man comes to you and endeavors to affect your choice of a college by offers of a pecuniary nature, he does not take you for a gentleman or a gentleman's son, you may be sure. Gentlemen neither offer nor take bribes.

Now, my young college friend, it is your turn. Remember it is upon you that the eyes of the preparatory school-boy are fixed, it is toward you that the younger brother looks for example, and whatever you do in your four years' course, you will see magnified by the boys who come after you. Support your class and your college in every way compatible with your position. Gentlemen are not stingy, nor are they selfish. Play if you can and your class or college needs you. Pay if you can afford it, but do not allow a false pride to lead you into subscriptions beyond your means. Don't be ashamed of enthusiasm. A man without it is a man without a purpose.

I remember a little incident of my own college course. I was a freshman, and knew almost no one in college except a certain junior. I had entered in two events in the fall athletic games, one a quarter mile, the other a hurdle race. I had run the quarter and been beaten, although I finished second. My opponents had all been upper classmen, and received no little encouragement from their friends. I felt very lonely and disgusted with myself and life in general when I got on the mark for the hurdle. I had but two competitors, and both had been cheered when they came to the scratch. Suddenly as we were getting on our marks I heard a voice half-way down the course call out, "You can do 'em," and I saw my junior friend waving his hat to me. It was not a classical remark, but it made me feel better. I was clumsy in getting off, and when we came to the sixth hurdle was nearly five yards behind the other two, but from that time on I could hear my friend roaring out, "Go in!" "You've got 'em yet!" "Now you're over," as I went up each flight. I *did* finish first, and I had hardly touched the tape before he was patting me on the back. I don't suppose it cost him much to yell for a poor freshman, but I know that I always thought of him as one of the best fellows I ever knew, and in after years I have remembered enough of the feeling that was in my heart toward him, to go out and try to make some others feel that even a freshman has friends.

Apropos of this, a word to non-contestants. In a boat-race or a foot-ball match the chances are that your own men will not hear you cheer, but the men who may try for the team or crew the next season do, and they are encouraged to better efforts by it. Now about the treatment of your rivals. A gentleman is courteous. It is not courtesy upon a ball-field to cheer an error of the opponents. If it is upon your grounds, it is the worst kind of boorishness. Moreover, if there are remarkable plays made by your rivals you yourselves should cheer; conceal any chagrin you may feel at the loss it may be to your side, but be courteous to appreciate and applaud an exceptional play by the opponents.

After winning a race or a match, there is no reason why a good, healthy lot of young men should not do plenty of cheering, but there is every reason why they should not make their enjoyment depend upon insulting those who have lost. You cannot take your hilarity off into a corner and choke it to death, and no one wants you to; but gratuitous jibes and jeers at the crestfallen mark you as a man who does not know how to bear a victory, a man whose pate is addled by the excitement or whose bringing up has been at fault.

Finally, to non-contestants, I want to say a word regarding "celebrating." Primarily, do not, I beg of you, do anything because it looks smart. Enjoy yourselves, but do not try to "show off." Don't be "tough." A little unusual hilarity, a tendency to believe that everything is expressly for the collegian, can be upon these occasions overlooked and forgiven, but be ready to appreciate the point beyond which it is carried too far; be ready to apologize quickly and instantly where offense is taken. Show that behind the jolly fun there is the instinct and cultivation of a gentleman's son, and that the ebullition of enthusiasm, although it may be a bore to those who fail to kindle at it, has nothing of the vicious element, and is thoroughly innocent of intentional offense to any one. If you find you are losing your head, go home; you will not be sorry for it.

Now for the contestants. I wish I could impress indelibly upon your minds the fact that with you rests the most enduring standard for amateur sports. With no disrespect to any class or condition—with the best regard for all strong legislation in outside athletic bodies—I say that the collegian's standard of purity in his sports should be the highest. The very fact of having the leisure to devote four years to a higher education, should be taken to involve the duty of acquiring a keener perception of right and wrong in matters where right and wrong depend upon a delicacy of honor. Gentlemen do not cheat, nor do they deceive themselves as to what cheating is. If you are elected the captain of a nine, team, or crew, read over your rules, and note exactly who are allowed as contestants by those rules, not by the custom of some predecessor, not by what you think some rival will do, but by the rules themselves. Having done that, never let a thought enter your head of making use of any man not clearly and cleanly eligible. You will save yourself many a future worry if you start fairly by looking into the record of every candidate at the outset. It is your duty to know that every one of your men is straight and square. I know what I am talking about when I say that a college captain can, in ninety-nine cases out of a hundred, become possessed of the exact truth regarding any man he thinks of trying. Don't investigate to see how much your opponent could prove, but investigate for your own satisfaction. In legislating, remember that what a gentleman wants is fair play and the best man to win. When it is possible, without losing sight of this, to legislate for improvements in method, so much the better; but primarily make every rule such that the probability of unfinished, drawn, or disputed contests is reduced to a minimum.

What if, at the time, your side may be the weaker? Don't be a coward on that account. Face it like a man, and say with your whole heart that you are on the side of the men who want no chance of retreat or escape, only a fair contest and certain victory or defeat at the end of it. To what do all the technicalities amount when compared with the sincerity of men who come together to effect that result? When the delegates earnestly desire rules that shall insure such a contest and such an issue, their work is more than half done. Don't take the coward's part and try to legislate means of avoiding the issue.

Perhaps if you, sir, the father of these boys, have had patience to listen thus far to me, you will allow me to put in a word for the love they bear these sports and the pride they take in their school and college. Talk with them about these interests. You will lose no dignity by it, and you will gain a confidence from them worth having. When you see anything in their speech or conduct that betokens a lowering of the high ideal of gentlemanliness, don't hesitate to say so. You don't want your boy "hired" by any one. If he plays, he plays as a gentleman, and not as a professional; he plays for victory, not for money; and whatever bruises he may have in the flesh, his heart is right, and he can look you in the eye as a gentleman should.

"Be each, pray God, a gentleman!"

The Moral Factors in Football
WALTER CAMP and LORIN F. DELAND

Comparison between War and Football. A comparison has often been made between the tactics of football and the theory of war. Looked at from one standpoint, the difference between the two is radical. A close study of both subjects, however, will reveal a very remarkable and inter-

Walter Camp and Lorin F. Deland, *Football* (Boston and New York, 1896), pp. 278–283.

esting likeness between the theories which underlie great battles and the miniature contests on the gridiron.

It is not strictly within the scope of this book to follow out this comparison, though it might be interesting and profitable to the football coach. But in considering the moral factors in the game of football, there is much to be gained by a reference to the moral agents in war, and the value placed upon these agents by great commanders and tacticians.

Napoleon's "Three to One" Ratio. It was a maxim of Napoleon's that in war the "moral" is to the "physical" in the ratio of three to one. This ratio of the moral and the physical is doubtless equally great in the game of football. It remains to be discovered just what these moral agents in football are, and this discovery cannot be made in any better way than by continuing the analogy a little further, and briefly enumerating the moral agents in war. McPherson, in his "Theory of War," clearly points out these moral forces, and we cannot do better than adopt his classification, referring at the same time to the parallels in the sport of football.

The Moral Agents in War. The moral agencies in war might be classed under four heads:—

(1) The Personal Qualities of the Commander-in-Chief. His knowledge of human nature; his power of influencing men through their hopes, fears, passions, interests, or prejudices; his ability to gain the love and confidence of his troops; his coolness, self-reliance, and readiness of resource in emergencies; with other qualities of a similar nature.

Coming now to the game of football, we find the correlative of these qualities in quarter-back generalship; in the influence of the captain over his men; in his reputation for coolness; in the comprehension of field tactics; in his self-reliance, and readiness of resource in all emergencies; and in the power of his last appeals to his team. These are all properly moral agents. If the captain does not possess them, the coach must do all he can to supply the deficiency both to the captain and to the team. It is better, of course, that they should be possessed by the captain himself, but in no case should they be overlooked, or their value underestimated.

The Qualifications of Generalship. On this subject let us quote the exact words of Napoleon:—

"The first quality of a general-in-chief is to have a cool head, which receives only a just impression of objects. He should not allow himself to be dazzled either by good or bad news. The sensations which he receives, successively or simultaneously, in the course of a day, should be classed in his memory so as to only occupy the just place due to each; for reason and judgment are the resultant of the correct comparison of many sensations.

There are some men who, on account of their physical and moral constitution, make a single picture for themselves out of every event; whatever knowledge, wit, courage, and other qualities they may possess, nature has not called them to the command of armies, and the direction of great military operations."

Detecting the Critical Moment. Famous generals have all shared this opinion of Napoleon's. It must not be forgotten that in every battle there is a decisive point, and a decisive moment (which, once let slip, never returns), on which, and at which, every disposable horse, man, and gun should be brought into action. The problem is to correctly appreciate that point and time, and know when it arrives. The commander who anticipates the decisive moment, and brings forward his reserves too soon, is lost. The personal qualities before enumerated are manifested in their highest degree by the faculty of correctly determining this decisive moment. The knowledge of when, where, and how to make an attack is the critical thing which distinguishes great generalship, whether in war or football.

(2) Stratagems. The object of a stratagem in war is to deceive the enemy as to your designs. To illustrate this in its simplest form, if a commander desired a general action, he would spread reports of the weakness of his army, and appear to avoid one. If, on the contrary, he did not desire a general action, he would put on a bold face and appear desirous to engage.

Strategy in war finds its parallel in football in the various plays and formations designed and employed by the team. It is not enough that a team should depend upon the simple formations already so familiar to the average opponent that he can tell, with reasonable certainty, the nature of the attack, and where it is to be made in the line. With equal certainty he has probably been coached on exactly how to repel that form of attack. To depend upon this simple form of offense is to voluntarily ignore one of the most valuable weapons in football—namely, strategy.[1]

Force of Strategy in Football. It is a great thing in football to keep your opponents guessing. Properly, they ought never to be permitted to so successfully "size up" the impending play that they are able to move headlong into the defense of their own position, without a doubt of the nature of

---

[1] The use of the word "strategy" in connection with football operations is never technically correct. Strategy can only be applied to the movements which are made when no enemy is in sight. The moment that the enemy is in sight, the proper term for such operations is "tactics." However, inasmuch as, in football, the opponents are always in sight, the use of the word "strategy" is technically impossible. It is only used in this connection by virtue of the license which it has obtained from repeated use, by other writers, in the last two or three years.

the attack. You should always work upon your opponents, not merely with muscle, but with brain. Your operations should demand of them that, at one and the same time, they exercise equally their minds and their bodies.

How difficult this may become, at critical moments, many of our readers can realize by experience. With your own players thoroughly skilled in their attack, and not needing to enter upon it with any doubt or uncertainty, but with a concentration of mind and body both upon the one desired result, they are, theoretically, in a position of distinct advantage over the opponents, whose physical movements must wait upon their mental processes. The moment that you present to your opponents a form of play so simple as to ignore the necessity of a mental impression after the attack is begun,—in other words, so simple as to make it possible for them to readily predicate what the movement is to be,—you lose the advantage just mentioned, and their defense may, without extreme risk, be fully as precipitate as your attack.

(3) The Elation or Depression of the Soldiers. This may arise from any cause—from former defeats or victories; from the health or sickness of the troops; from confidence or distrust in the commander, etc.

The correspondent of this in football is the prestige of the team, or the college which the team represents; the spirit which is infused into the players by a realization of the issue; most important of all, the attainment of a right degree of confidence which never distrusts itself or the final result, yet stops just short of that over confidence which is so harmful.

(4) Information, and the Means of Obtaining It. This would mean in war the knowledge of the country, its topography and resources, its roads and turnpikes, its rivers and railways, its storehouses and factories, its people and their temper, etc. It would also involve accurate intelligence of the enemy's movements, without which the greatest military talent is useless. The faculty of organizing a system of intelligence is a prominent quality of a great commander in war.

One may draw the parallel between this intelligence and the intelligence required in football, by pointing out to the experienced coach the necessity of a thorough apprehension of the rules by every one of his players, and the ability to act instinctively upon this information, which will only come to the player when his information is well-grounded and thoroughly assimilated by him. His knowledge of the rules must be more than skin deep. If it is a "cramming" of the last few weeks, it can profit him little in the direction which we are indicating. It is not football knowledge which is so valuable to the player as football instinct, and by this is meant the certain ability to act intuitively and automatically upon the knowledge he possesses, doing the right thing at the right time, regardless of any previous specific coaching upon the point in question. No two games of football can ever be quite alike. The situations which constantly arise cannot be entirely apprehended and provided for by the coach in his instructions. The players must meet many emergencies, armed with no other weapon than their football instinct, and this can only come by an absorption of the rules and foundation principles of the playing game.

Explanation of Many Defeats. It is these qualities, then, combined together, which represent the moral factors in football, and it is, perhaps, not conceding too much to admit that the ratio between the moral and the physical in war, as determined by Napoleon, may also be established between these moral factors in football and the mere physical factor of force or strength.

Too often the public forms its estimates of probable results from the physical factors which are visible rather than from the moral factors which are invisible. They do not see the moral forces which are being employed by the master-hand behind the scenes. This "three to one" power is responsible for many seemingly inexplicable defeats. Correspondents of the press, and the unreasoning partisans of a defeated team raise the cry of "luck" in football. Obviously there is a percentage of luck in the game, just as there is luck in any of the situations of life. But football games are not won or lost by luck, except in very rare instances. What appears to be luck is inevitably some one of the moral qualities here enumerated, which, carefully nurtured by one coach, and perhaps unapprehended or unappreciated by the opponents, proves to be the turning-point in the contest.

The two teams may have been developed along exactly similar lines; to the ordinary observer, and by the tests of ordinary comparison, they are developed to an approximately equal state of efficiency. Yet these two teams play together through a series of years with the result of one of the two teams continually winning, and the other continually losing. The public, naturally anxious to know the reason for this, is full of inquiries: *"Are they not practically the same young men, brought from the same schools? Are they not of the same age, and is it not a matter of mere chance whether they attend one college or the other?"* The answer to this question may be read between the lines of this chapter. It is not the difference in strength or the difference in skill. Neither is it by a preponderance of instruction given to one team. Frequently we find, upon examination, that the eleven best players would comprise five from one team and six from the other. It is not always the increased knowledge of the principles of team play. The difficulty lies, too often, in the moral forces here enumerated. It is for this reason that the subject has been given the importance of a separate chapter.

15. The White City

The great Columbian Exposition of 1893 dominated American magazines and newspapers for the better part of a year. Chicago had won a spirited competition against other American cities to gain Congressional approval as the site, and local boosters were intent on proving the choice to be a wise one. The hundreds of thousands of visitors seems to agree. From Henry Adams down to ordinary tourists, all acclaimed the Fair's achievement as miraculous, a tribute to native designers who had outstripped the most chauvinistic dreams.

William Dean Howells (1837–1920) joined the procession of artists and writers who toured the Exposition. Howells had left Ohio just before the Civil War to achieve literary prominence in the Northeast. As editor of the *Atlantic Monthly* in the seventies and eighties, and later as a writer for *Harper's* in New York, Howells came to represent for many Americans the best of traditional culture. Tolerant, warmhearted, generous of spirit, his novels and essays became progressively more concerned with the great social issues agitating the nation. As a spokesman for realism, influenced heavily by his understanding of Tolstoi, Howells probed the possibilities for a more equitable commonwealth, toying with idealistic and humane socialist utopias. His Altrurian traveller, as a representative of a more advanced society, pointed out to Americans some of the contradictions of their economic system, and the Fair seemed a marvelous opportunity for Howells to moralize about the social order.

The lessons which Howells drew, however, were less popular than the physical ideals the White City fed. City planning, not social engineering, was the memory most visitors took away with them. "Chicago asked in 1893 for the first time the question whether the American people knew where they were driving," Henry Adams wrote. But if Chicago asked the question, it was unable to supply an ultimately satisfying answer.

Letters of an Altrurian Traveller
WILLIAM DEAN HOWELLS

Chicago, Sept. 28, 1893.

My dear Cyril:

When I last wrote you, I thought to have settled quietly down in New York for the rest of my stay in America, and given my time wholly to the study of its life, which seemed to me typical of the life of the whole country. I do not know, even now, that I should wish altogether to revise this impression; it still appears to me just, if not so distinct and so decisive, as it appeared before I saw Chicago, or rather the World's Fair City at Chicago, which is what I want to write you of. Chicago, one might say, was after all only a Newer York, an ultimated Manhattan, the realized ideal of that largeness, loudness and fastness, which New York has persuaded the Americans is metropolitan. But after seeing the World's Fair City here, I feel as if I had caught a glimpse of the glorious capitals which will whiten the hills and shores of the east and the borderless plains of the west, when the New York and the Newer York of today shall seem to all the future Americans as impossible as they could seem to any Altrurian now.

To one of our philosophy it will not be wonderful that this Altrurian miracle should have been wrought here in the very heart, and from the very heart, of egoism seven times heated in the fiery competition hitherto the sole joy of this strange people. We know that like produces like only up to a certain point, and that then unlike comes of like since all things are of one essence; that from life comes death at last, and from death comes life again in the final issue. Yet it would be useless trying to persuade most Americans that the World's Fair City was not the effect, the fine flower, of the competition which underlies their economy, but was the first fruits of the principle of emulation which animates our happy commonwealth, and gives men, as no where else on earth, a foretaste of heaven. If I were writing to an American I should have to supply him

William Dean Howells, "Letters of an Altrurian Traveller," *The Cosmopolitan Magazine*, Vol. XVI (December, 1893), pp. 218–232.

with proofs and argue facts at every moment, which will be self-evident to you in their mere statement.

I confess that I was very loth to leave New York, which I fancied I was beginning to see whole, after my first fragmentary glimpses of it. But I perceive now that without a sight of the White City (as the Americans with their instant poetry called the official group of edifices at the great Fair) and the knowledge of its history, which I could have realized nowhere but in its presence, New York would have wanted the relief, the projection, in which I shall hereafter be able to study it. For the worst effect of sojourn in an egoistic civilization (I always use this word for lack of a closer descriptive) is that Altrurian motives and efforts become incredible, and almost inconceivable. But the Fair City is a bit of Altruria: it is as if the capital of one of our Regions had set sail and landed somehow on the shores of the vast inland sea, where the Fair City lifts its domes and columns.

Its story, which I need not rehearse to you at any length, records the first great triumph of Altrurian principles among this people in a work of peace; in their mighty civil war they were Altrurian enough; and more than once they have proved themselves capable of a magnificent self-sacrifice in bloodshed, but here for the first time in their pitiless economic struggle, their habitual warfare in which they neither give nor ask quarter, and take no prisoners, the interests submitted to the arts, and lent themselves as frankly to the work as if there had never been a question of money in the world. From the beginning it was believed that there could be no profit in the Fair; money loss was expected and accepted as a necessary part of the greater gain; and when the question passed from how much to how, in the discussion of the ways and means of creating that beauty which is the supreme use, the capitalists put themselves into the hands of the artists. They did not do it at once, and they did not all do it willingly. It is a curious trait of the American who has made money that he thinks he can make anything; and the Chicago millionaires who found themselves authorized by the nation to spend their money in the creation of the greatest marvel of the competitive world, throught themselves fully competent to work the miracle, or to choose the men who would work it according to their ideals. But their clarification, if it was not as swift as the passage of light was thorough, and I do not suppose there is now any group of rich men in Europe or America who have so luminous a sense of the true relations of the arts and the interests as they. The notion of a competition among the artists, which is the practical American's notion of the way to get the best art, was at length rejected by these most practical Americans, and one mind large enough to conceive the true means and strong enough to give its conception effect was empowered to invite the free coöperation of the arts through the foremost artists of the country. As yet the governmental function is so weak here that the national part in the work was chiefly obstructive, and finally null; and when it came to this there remained an opportunity for the arts, unlimited as to means and unhampered by conditions.

For the different buildings to be erected, different architects were chosen; and for the first time since the great ages, since the beauty of antiquity and the elegance of the renaissance, the arts were reunited. The greatest landscape gardeners, architects, sculptors and painters, gathered at Chicago for a joyous interchange of ideas and criticisms; and the miracle of beauty which they have wrought grew openly in their breath and under their hands. Each did his work and had his way with it, but in this congress of gifted minds, of sensitive spirits, each profited by the censure of all, and there were certain features of the work—as for instance, the exquisite peristyle dividing the city from the lake—which were the result of successive impulses and suggestions from so many different artists that it would be hard to divide the honor among them with exactness. No one, however, seems to have been envious of another's share, and each one gave his talent as freely as the millionaires gave their money. These great artists willingly accepted a fifth, a tenth, of the gain which they could have commanded in a private enterprise, and lavished their time upon the opportunity afforded them, for the pleasure of it, the pride of it, the pure good of it.

Of the effect, of this visible, tangible result, what better can I say, than that in its presence I felt myself again in Altruria? The tears came, and the pillared porches swam against my vision; through the hard nasal American tones, the liquid notes of our own speech stole to my inner ear; I saw under the care-worn masks of the competitive crowds, the peace, the *rest* of the dear Altrurian face; the gay tints of our own simple costumes eclipsed the different versions of the Paris fashions about me. I was at home once more, and my heart overflowed with patriotic rapture in this strange land, so remote from ours in everything, that at times Altruria really seems to me the dream which the Americans think it.

I first saw the Fair City by night, from one of the electric launches which ply upon the lagoon; and under the dimmed heaven, in the splendor of the hundred moony arc-lamps of the esplanades, and the myriad incandescent bubbles that beaded the white quays, and defined the structural lines of dome and porch and pediment, I found myself in the midst of the Court of Honor, which you will recognize on the general plan and the photographs I enclose. We fronted the beautiful Agricultural Building, which I think fitly the finest in the city, though many prefer the perfect Greek of the Art building; and on our right was the Administration building with its coroneted dome, and the magnificent sculptured fountain before it, turned silver in the radiance of the clustered electric jets at either side. On our right was the glorious peristyle, serene, pure, silent, lifting a population of statues against the night, and dividing the lagoon from the lake, whose soft moan came appealingly through the pillared spaces, and added a divine heartache to my ecstacy. Here a group of statuary showed itself prominently on quay or cornice; we caught the flamy curve of a bridge's arch; a pale column lifted its jutting prores into the light; but nothing insisted; all was harmonized to one effect of beauty, as if in symbol of the concentered impulses which had created it. For the moment I could not believe that so foul a thing as money could have been even the means of its creation. I call the effect creation because it is divinely beautiful, but no doubt suggestion would be a better word, since they have here merely sketched in stucco what we have executed in marble in each of our Regionic capitals.

In grandeur of design and freedom of expression, it is perhaps even nobler than the public edifices of some of these, as I had to acknowledge at another moment, when we rounded the shores of the Wooded Island which forms the heart of the lagoon, and the launch slowed while we got the effect of its black foliage against the vast lateral expanse of the Liberal Arts building. Then, indeed, I was reminded of our national capitol, when it shows its mighty mass above the bosks around it, on some anniversary night of our Evolution.

But the illusion of Altruria was very vivid at many moments in the Fair City, where I have spent the happiest days of my stay in America, perhaps because the place is so little American in the accepted sense. It is like our own cities in being a design, the effect of a principle, and not the straggling and shapeless accretion of accident. You will see, from the charts and views I send you, something of the design in detail, but you can form only a dim conception of the skill with which the natural advantages of the site have been turned to account, and even its disadvantages have been transmuted to the beauty which is the highest and last result of all. There was not only the great lake here, which contributes so greatly to this beauty, but there were marshes to be drained and dredged before its pure waters could be invited in. The trees which at different points offer the contrast of their foliage to the white of the edifices, remain from wilding growths which overspread the swamps and sand dunes, and which had to be destroyed in great part before these lovely groves could be evoked from them. The earth itself, which now of all the earth seems the spot best adapted to the site of such a city, had literally to be formed anew for the use it has been put to. There is now no shadow, no hint of the gigantic difficulties of the undertaking, which was carried on in the true Altrurian spirit, so far as the capitalists and artists were concerned, and with a joy like ours in seeing nature yield herself to the enlightened will of man. If I told you how time itself was overcome in this work by the swiftness of modern methods, it would be nothing new to you, for we are used to seeing the powerful machinery of our engineers change the face of the landscape, without stay for the slow processes of other days, when the ax and the saw wrought for years in the destruction of the forests that now vanish in a night. But to the Americans these things are still novel, and they boast of the speed with which the trees were dragged from the soil where they were rooted, and the morasses were effaced, and the wastes of sand made to smile with the verdure that now forms the most enchanting feature of their normal city.

They dwell upon this, and they do not seem to feel as I do the exquisite simplicity with which its life is operated, the perfection with which it is policed, and the thoroughness with which it has been dedicated to health as well as beauty. In fact, I fancy that very few out of the millions who visit this gala town realize that it has its own system of drainage, lighting and transportation, and its own government, which looks as scrupulously to the general comfort and cleanliness, as if these were the private concern of each member of the government. This is, as it is with us, military in form, and the same precision and discipline which give us the ease and freedom of our civic life, proceed here from the same spirit and the same means. The Columbian Guards, as they are called, who are here at every turn, to keep order and to care for the pleasure as well as the welfare of the people, have been trained by officers of the United States army, who still command them, and they are amenable to the rules governing the only body in America whose ideal is not interest but duty. Every night, the whole place is cleansed of the rubbish which the visitors leave behind them, as thoroughly as if it were a camp. It is merely the litter of lunch-boxes and waste paper which has to be looked after, for there is little of the filth resulting in all other American cities from the use of the horse, which is still employed in them so many centuries after it has been banished from ours. The United States mail-carts and the watering-carts are indeed anomalously drawn through the Fair City thoroughfares by horses, but wheeled chairs pushed about by a corps of high school boys and college undergraduates form the means of transportation by land for those who do not choose to walk. On the water, the electric launches are quite of our own pattern, and steam is allowed only on the boats which carry people out into the lake for a view of the peristyle. But you can get this by walking, and as in Venice, which is represented here by a fleet of gondolas, there are bridges that enable you to reach every desirable point on the lagoon.

When I have spoken of all this to my American friends they have not perceived the moral value of it, and when I have insisted upon the practical perfection of the scheme apparent in the whole, they have admitted it, but answered me that it would never do for a business city, where there was something going on besides the pleasure of the eyes and the edification of the mind. When I tell them that this is all that our Altrurian cities are for, they do not understand me; they ask where the money is made that the people live on in such play cities; and we are alike driven to despair when I try to explain that we have no money, and should think it futile and impious to have any.

I do not believe they quite appreciate the intelligence with which the Fair City proper has been separated, with a view to its value as an object lesson, from all the state and national buildings in the ground. Some of the national buildings, notably those of Germany and Sweden, are very picturesque, but the rest decline through various grades of inferiority, down to the level of the State buildings. Of these, only the California and the New York buildings have a beauty comparable to that of the Fair City: the California house, as a reminiscence of the Spanish ecclesiastical architecture in which her early history is recorded, and the New York house, as a sumptuous expression of the art which ministers to the luxury of the richest and greatest State of the Union.

By still another remove the competitive life of the present epoch is relegated to the long avenue remotest from the White City, which you will find marked as the Midway Plaisance. Even this, where a hundred shows rival one another in a furious advertisement for the favor of the passer, there is so much of a high interest that I am somewhat loth to instance it as actuated by an inferior principle; and I do so only for the sake of the contrast. In the Fair City, everything is free; in the Plaisance everything must be paid for. You strike at once here the hard level of the outside western world; and the Orient, which has mainly peopled the Plaisance, with its theaters and restaurants and shops, takes the tint of the ordinary American enterprise, and puts on somewhat the manners of the ordinary American hustler. It is not really so bad as that, but it is worse than American in some of the appeals it makes to the American public, which is decent if it is dull, and respectable if it is rapacious. The lascivious dances of the East are here, in the Persian and Turkish and Egyptian theaters, as well as the exquisite archaic drama of the Javanese and the Chinese in their village and temple. One could spend many days in the Plaisance, always entertainingly, whether profitably or unprofitably; but whether one visited the Samoan or Dahomeyan in his hut, the Bedouin and the Lap in their camps, the delicate Javanese in his bamboo cottage, or the American Indian in his tepee, one must be aware that the citizens of the Plaisance are not there for their health, as the Americans quaintly say, but for the money there is in it. Some of the reproductions of historical and foreign scenes are excellent, like the irregular square of Old Vienna, with its quaintly built and quaintly decorated shops; the German village, with its admirably realized castle and chalet; and the Cairene street, with its motley oriental life; but these are all there for the profit to be had from the pleasure of their visitors, who seem to pay as freely as they talk through their noses. The great Ferris wheel itself, with its circle revolving by night and by day in an orbit incomparably vast, is in the last analysis a money-making contrivance.

I have tried to make my American friends see the difference, as I do, between the motive that created the Fair City, and the motive that created the Plaisance, but both seem to them alike the outcome of the principle which they still believe animates their whole life. They think both an effect of the competitive conditions in which they glory not knowing that their conditions are now purely monopolistic, and not perceiving that the White City is the work of an armistice between the commercial interests ruling them. I expressed this belief to one of them, the banker, whom I met last summer in the country, and whom I ran upon one night during the first week of my visit here; and he said there could certainly be that view of it. But, like the rest, he asked where the money would have come from without the warfare of competitive conditions, and he said he could not make out how we got the money for our public works in Altruria, or, in fact, how we paid the piper. When I answered that as each one of us was secured by all against want, every one could freely give his labor, without money and without price, and the piper could play for the pure pleasure of playing, he looked stupefied and said incredulously, "Oh, come, now!"

"Why, how strange you Americans are," I could not help breaking out upon him, "with your talk about competition! There *is* no competition among you a moment longer than you can help, a moment after one proves himself stronger than another. Then you have monopoly, which even upon the limited scale it exists here is the only vital and fruitful principle, as you all see. And yet you are afraid to have it upon the largest possible scale, the national scale, the scale commensurate with the whole body politic, which implicates care for every citizen as the liege of the collectivity. When you have monopoly of such proportions money will cease to have any office among you, and such a beautiful creation as this will have effect from a consensus of the common wills and wishes."

He listened patiently, and he answered amiably: "Yes, that is what you Altrurians believe, I suppose, and certainly what you preach; and if you look at it in that light, why there certainly is no competition left, except between the monopolies. But you must allow, my dear Homos," he went on, "that at least one of the two fetishes of our barbarous worship has had something to do with the creation of all this beauty. I'll own that you have rather knocked the notion of competition on the head; the money that made this thing possible never came from competition at all; it came from some sort or shape of monopoly, as all money always does; but what do you say about individuality? You can't say that individuality has had nothing to do with it. In fact, you can't deny that it has had everything to do with it, from the individuality of the several capitalists, up or down, to the individuality of the several artists. And will you pretend in the face of all this wonderful work that individuality is a bad thing?"

"Have I misrepresented myself and country so fatally," I returned, "as to have led you to suppose that the Altrurians thought individuality a bad thing? It seems to us the most precious gift of the Deity, the dearest and holiest possession of his creatures. What I lament in America at every moment, what I lament even here, in the presence of a work so largely Altrurian in conception and execution as this, is the wholesale effacement, the heartbreaking obliteration of individuality. I know very well that you can give me the name of the munificent millionaires—large-thoughted and noble-willed men—whose largesse made this splendor possible, and the name of every artist they freed to such a glorious opportunity. Their individuality is lastingly safe in your memories; but what of the artisans of every kind and degree, whose patience and skill realized their ideals? Where will you find *their* names?"

My companion listened respectfully, but not very seriously, and in his reply he took refuge in that humor peculiar to the Americans: a sort of ether where they may draw breath for a moment free from the stifling despair which must fill every true man among them when he thinks how far short of their ideal their reality has fallen. For they were once a people with the noblest ideal; we were not mistaken about that; they did, indeed, intend the greatest good to the greatest number, and not merely the largest purse to the longest head. They are a proud people, and it is hard for them to confess that they have wandered from the right way, and fallen into a limitless bog, where they can only bemire themselves more and more till its miasms choke them or its foul waters close over them.

"My dear fellow," the banker laughed, "you are easily answered. You will find *their* names on the pay-rolls, where, I've no doubt, they preferred to have them. Why, there was an army of them; and we don't erect monuments to private soldiers, except in the lump. How would you have managed it in Altruria?"

"In Altruria," I replied, "every man who drove a nail, or stretched a line, or laid a trowel upon such a work, would have had his name somehow inscribed upon it, where he could find it, and point it out to those dear to him and proud of him. Individuality! I find no record of it here, unless it is the individuality of the few. That of the many makes no sign from the oblivion in which it is lost, either in these public works of artistic coöperation, or the exhibits of your monopolistic competition. I have wandered through these vast edifices and looked for the names of the men who wrought the marvels of ingenuity that fill them. But I have not often found the name even of a man who owns them. I have found the styles of the firms, the companies, the trusts which turn them out as impersonally as if no heart had ever ached or glowed in imagining and embodying them. This whole mighty industrial display is in so far dehumanized; and yet you talk of individuality as one of your animating principles!"

"You are hopelessly unbusinesslike, my dear Homos," said the banker, "but I like your unpracticability. There is something charming in it; there is, really; and I enjoy it particularly at this moment because it has enabled me to get back my superiority to Chicago. I am a Bostonian, you know, and I came out here with all the misgivings which a Bostonian begins to secrete as soon as he gets west of the Back Bay Fens. It is a survival of Puritanism in us. In the old times, you know, every Bostonian, no matter how he prayed and professed, felt it in his bones that he was one of the elect, and we each feel so still; only, then God elected us, and now we elect ourselves. Fancy such a man confronted with such an achievement as this, and unfriended yet by an Altrurian traveller! Why, I have gone about the last three days inwardly bowed down before Chicago in the most humiliating fashion. I've said to myself that our eastern fellows did half the thing, perhaps the best half; but then I had to own it was Chicago that imagined letting them do it, that imagined the thing as a whole, and

I had to give Chicago the glory. When I looked at it I had to forgive Chicago Chicago, but now that you've set me right about the matter, and I see that the whole thing is dehumanized, I shall feel quite easy, and I shall not give Chicago any more credit than is due."

I saw that he was joking, but I did not see how far, and I thought it best not to take him in joke at all. "Ah, I don't think you can give her too much credit, even if you take her at the worst. It seems to me, from what I have seen of your country—and, of course, I speak from a foreigner's knowledge only—that no other American city could have brought this to pass."

"You must come and stay with us a while in Boston," said the banker; and he smiled. "One other city could have done it. Boston has the public spirit and Boston has the money, but perhaps Boston has not the ambition. Perhaps we give ourselves in Boston too much to a sense of the accomplished fact. If that is a fault, it is the only fault conceivable of us. Here in Chicago they have the public spirit, and they have the money, and they are still anxious to do; they are not content as we are, simply to be. Of course, they have not so much reason! I don't know," he added thoughtfully, "but it comes in the end to what you were saying, and no other American city but Chicago *could* have brought this to pass. Leaving everything else out of the question, I doubt if any other community could have fancied the thing in its vastness; and the vastness seems an essential condition of the beauty. You couldn't possibly say it was pretty, for instance; if you admitted it was fine you would have to say it was beautiful. To be sure, if it were possible to have too much of a good thing, there are certain states of one's legs, here, when one could say there was too much of it; but that is not possible. But come, now; be honest for once, my dear fellow, and confess that you really prefer the Midway Plaisance to the Fair City!"

I looked at him with silent reproach, and he broke out laughing, and took me by the arm.

"At any rate," he said, "let us go down there, and get something to eat. 'The glory that was Greece, And the grandeur that was Rome,' here, take it out of you so that I find myself wanting lunch about every three hours. It's nearly as long as that now, since I've dined, and I feel an irresistible yearning for Old Vienna, where that pinchbeck halberdier of a watchman is just now crying the hour of nine."

"Oh, is it so late as that?" I began, for I like to keep our Altrurian hours even here, when I can, and I was going to say that I could not go with him when he continued:

"They won't turn us out, if that's what you mean. Theoretically, they do turn people out toward the small hours, but practically, one can stay here all night, I believe. That's a charming thing about the Fair, and I suppose it's rather Chicagoan; if we'd had the Fair in Boston, every soul would have had to leave before midnight. We couldn't have helped turning them out, from the mere oldmaidishness of our Puritanic tradition, and not because we really minded their staying. In New York they would have put them out from Keltic imperiousness, and locked them up in the station-house when they got them out, especially if they were sober and inoffensive."

I could not follow him in this very well, or in the playful allusiveness of his talk generally, though I have reported it, to give some notion of his manner; and so I said, by way of bringing him within easy range of my intelligence again, "I have seen no one here who showed signs of drink."

"No," he returned. "What a serious, and peaceable, and gentle crowd it is! I haven't witnessed a rudeness, or even an unkindness, since I've been here, and nobody looks as if anything stronger than apollinaris had passed his lips for a fortnight. They seem, the vast majority of them, to pass their time in the Fair City, and I wish I could flatter myself that they preferred it, as you wish me to think you do, to the Plaisance. Perhaps they are really more interested in the mechanical arts, and even the fine arts, than they are in the muscle dances, but I'm afraid it's partly because there isn't an additional charge for admission to those improving exhibits in the official buildings. Though I dare say that most of the hardhanded folks here, are really concerned in transportation and agricultural implements to a degree that it is difficult for their more cultivated fellow-countrymen to conceive of. Then, the merely instructive and historical features must have an incredible lot to say to them. We people who have had advantages, as we call them, can't begin to understand the state that most of us come here in, the state of enlightened ignorance, as one may call it, when we know how little we know, and are anxious to know more. But I congratulate you, Homos, on the opportunity you have to learn America personally, here; you won't easily have such another chance. I'm glad for your sake, too, that it (the crowd) is mainly a western and south-western crowd, a Mississippi Valley crowd. You can tell it by their accent. It's a mistake to suppose that New England has a monopoly of the habit of speaking through the nose. We may have invented it, but we have imparted it apparently to the whole west, as the Scotch-Irish of Pennsylvania have lent the twist of their 'r,' and the combined result is something frightful. But it's the only frightful thing about the westerners, as I find them here. Their fashions are not the latest, but they are not only well behaved, they are on the average pretty well dressed, as the clothing store and the paper pattern dress our people. And, they look pathetically good! When I think how hard-worked they all are, and what lonely lives most of them live on their solitary farms, I wonder they don't descend upon me with the whoop of savages. You're very fond of equality, my dear Homos! How do you like the equality of the American effect here? It's a vast level, as unbroken as the plains that seemed to widen as I came over them in the cars to Chicago, and that go widening on, I suppose, to the sunset itself. I won't speak of the people, but I *will* say the plains were dreary."

"Yes," I assented, for those plains had made me melancholy, too. They looked so habitable, and they were so solitary, though I could see that they were broken by the lines of cultivated fields, which were being plowed for wheat, or were left standing with their interminable ranks of maize. From time to time one caught sight of a forlorn farmstead, with a windmill beside it, making helpless play with its vanes as if it were vainly struggling to take flight from the monotonous landscape. There was nothing of the cheerfulness of our Altrurian farm villages; and I could understand how a dull uniformity of the human type might result from such an environment, as the banker intimated.

I have made some attempts, here, to get upon speaking terms with these average people, but I have not found them conversible. Very likely they distrusted my advances, from the warnings given them to beware of imposters and thieves at the Fair; it is one of the necessities of daily life in a competitive civilization, that you must be on your guard against strangers lest they cheat or rob you. It is hard for me to understand this, coming from a land where there is no theft and can be none, because there is no private property, and I have often bruised myself to no purpose in attempting the acquaintance of my fellow-visitors of the Fair. They never make any attempt at mine; no one has asked me a favor, here, or even a question; but each remains bent, in an intense preoccupation, upon seeing the most he can in the shortest time for the least money. Of course, there are many of the more cultivated visitors, who are more responsive, and who show themselves at least interested in me as a fellow-stranger; but these, though they are positively many, are, after all, relatively few. The vast bulk, the massed members of that immense equality which fatigued my friend, the banker, by its mere aspect, were shy of me, and I do not feel that I came to know any of them personally. They strolled singly, or in pairs, or by family groups, up and down the streets of the Fair City, or the noisy thoroughfare of the Plaisance, or through the different buildings, quiescent, patient, inoffensive, but reserved and inapproachable, as far as I was concerned. If they wished to know anything they asked the guards, who never failed in their duty of answering them fully and pleasantly.

The people from the different states visited their several State buildings, and seemed to be at home, there, with that instinctive sense of ownership which every one feels in a public edifice, and which is never tainted with the greedy wish to keep others out. They sat in long rows on the benches that lined the avenues, munching the victuals they had mostly brought with them in the lunch-boxes which strewed the place at nightfall, and were gathered up by thousands in the policing of the grounds. If they were very luxurious, they went to the tables of those eating-houses where, if they ordered a cup of tea or coffee, they could spread out the repast from their boxes and enjoy it more at their ease. But in none of these places did I see any hilarity in them, and whether they thought it unseemly or not to show any gayety, they showed none. They were peacefully content within the limits of their equality, and where it ended, as from time to time it must, they betrayed no discontent. That is what always astonishes me in America. The man of the harder lot accepts it unmurmuringly and with no apparent sense of injustice in the easier lot of another. He suffers himself, without a word, to be worse housed, worse clad, worse fed, than his merely luckier brother, who could give him no reason for his better fortune that an Altrurian would hold valid. Here, at the Fair, for example, on the days when the German village is open to the crowd without charge, the crowd streams through without an envious glance at the people dining richly and expensively at the restaurants, with no greater right than the others have to feed poorly and cheaply from their paper boxes. In the Plaisance, weary old farmwives and delicate women of the artisan class make way uncomplainingly for the ladies and gentlemen who can afford to hire wheeled chairs. As meekly and quietly they loiter by the shores of the lagoon and watch those who can pay to float upon their waters in the gondolas and electric launches. Everywhere the economic inequality is as passively accepted as if it were a natural inequality, like difference in height or strength, or as if it were something of immemorial privilege, like birth and title in the feudal countries of Europe. Yet, if one of these economically inferior Americans were told that he was not the peer of any and every other American, he would resent it as the grossest insult, such is the power of the inveterate political illusion in which the nation has been bred.

The banker and I sat long over our supper, in the graveled court of Old Vienna, talking of these things, and enjoying a bottle of delicate Rhenish wine under the mild September moon, not quite put out of countenance by the electric lamps. The gay parties about us broke up one after another, till we were left almost alone, and the watchman in his mediæval dress, with a halberd in one hand, and a lantern in the other, came round to call the hour for the last time. Then my friend beckoned to the waiter for the account, and while the man stood figuring it up, the banker said to me: "Well, you must come to Boston a hundred years hence, to the next Columbian Fair, and we will show you every body trundled about and fed at the public expense. I suppose that's what you would like to see?"

"It is what we always see in Altruria," I answered. "I haven't the least doubt it will be so with you in much less than a hundred years."

The banker was looking at the account the waiter handed him. He broke into an absent laugh, and then said to me, "I beg your pardon! You were saying?"

"Oh, nothing," I answered, and then, as he took out his pocket-book to pay, he laid the bill on the table, and I could not help seeing what our little supper had cost him. It was twelve dollars; and I was breathless; it seemed to be that two would have been richly enough.

"They give you a good meal here, don't you think?" he said. "But the worst of having dined or supped well is reflecting that if you hadn't you could have given ten or twelve fellows, who will have to go to bed supperless, a handsome surfeit; that you could have bought twenty-five hungry men a full meal each; that you could have supplied forty-eight with plenty; that you could have relieved the famine of a hundred and twenty-four. But what is the use? If you think of these things you have no peace of your life!"

I could not help answering, "We don't have to think of them in Altruria."

"Ah, I dare say," answered the banker, as he tossed the waiter a dollar, and we rose and strolled out into the Plaisance. "If all men were unselfish, I should agree with you that Altrurianism was best."

"You can't have unselfishness till you have Altrurianism," I returned. "You can't put the cart before the horse."

"Oh, yes, we can," he returned in his tone of banter. "We always put the cart before the horse in America, so that the horse can see where the cart is going."

We strolled up and down the Plaisance, where the crowd had thinned to a few stragglers like ourselves. Most of the show villages were silenced for the night. The sob of the Javanese water-wheel was hushed; even the hubbub of the Chinese theater had ceased. The Samoans slept in their stucco huts; the Bedouins were folded to slumber in their black tents. The great Ferris wheel hung motionless with its lamps like a planetary circle of fire in the sky. It was a moment that invited to musing, that made a tacit companionship precious. By an impulse to which my own feeling instantly responded, my friend passed his arm through mine.

"Don't let us go home at all! Let us go over and sleep in the peristyle. I have never slept in a peristyle, and I have a fancy for trying it. Now, don't tell me you always sleep in peristyles in Altruria!"

I answered that we did not habitually, at least, and he professed that this was some comfort to him; and then he went on to talk more seriously about the Fair, and the effect that it must have upon American civilization. He said that he hoped for an æsthetic effect from it, rather than any fresh impulse in material enterprise, which he thought the country did not need. It had inventions enough, millionaires enough, prosperity enough; the great mass of the people lived as well and travelled as swiftly as they could desire. Now what they needed was some standard of taste, and this was what the Fair City would give them. He thought that it would at once have a great influence upon architecture, and sober and refine the artists who were to house the people; and that one might expect to see every-where a return to the simplicity and beauty of the classic forms, after so much mere wandering and maundering in design, without authority or authenticity.

I heartily agreed with him in condemning the most that had yet been done in architecture in America, but I tried to make him observe that the simplicity of Greek architecture came out of the simplicity of Greek life, and the preference given in the Greek state to the intellectual over the industrial, to art over business. I pointed out that until there was some enlightened municipal or national control of the matter, no excellence of example could avail, but that the classicism of the Fair City would become, among a wilful and undisciplined people a fad with the rich and a folly with the poor, and not a real taste with either class. I explained how with us the state absolutely forbade any man to aggrieve or insult the rest by the exhibition of his ignorance in the exterior of his dwelling, and how finally architecture had become a government function, and fit dwellings were provided for all by artists who approved themselves to the public criticism. I ventured so far as to say that the whole competitive world, with the exception of a few artists, had indeed lost the sense of beauty, and I even added that the Americans as a people seemed never to have had it at all.

He was not offended, as I had feared he might be, but asked me with perfect good nature what I meant.

"Why, I mean that the Americans came into the world too late to have inherited that influence from the antique world which was lost even in Europe, when in mediæval times the picturesque barbarously substituted itself for the beautiful, and a feeling for the quaint grew up in place of love for the perfect."

"I don't understand, quite," he said, "but I'm interested. Go on!"

"Why," I went on, "I have heard people rave over the beauty of the Fair City, and then go and rave over the beauty of the German village, or of Old Vienna, in the Plaisance. They were cultivated people, too; but they did not seem to know that the reproduction of a feudal castle or of a street in the taste of the middle ages, could not be beautiful, and could at the best be only picturesque. Old Vienna is no more beautiful than the Javanese village, and the German village outrivals the Samoan village only in its greater adaptability to the purposes of the painter. There is in your modern competitive world very little beauty anywhere, but there is an abundance of picturesqueness, of forms that may be reflected upon canvas, and impart the charm of their wild irregularity to all who look at the picture, though many who enjoy it there would fail of it in a study of the original. I will go so far as to say that there are points in New York, intrinsically so hideous that it makes me shudder to recall them—"

"*Don't* recall them!" he pleaded.

"Which would be much more capable of pictorial treatment than the Fair City, here," I continued. We had in fact got back to the Court of Honor, in the course of our talk, which I have only sketched here in the meagerest abstract. The incandescent lamps had been quenched, and the arc-lights below and the moon above flooded the place with one silver, and the absence of the crowds that had earlier thronged it, left it to a solitude indescribably solemn and sweet. In that light, it was like a ghost of the antique world witnessing a loveliness lost to modern times everywhere but in our own happy country.

I felt that silence would have been a fitter tribute to it than any words of mine, but my companion prompted me with an eager, "Well!" and I went on.

"This beauty that we see there is not at all picturesque. If a painter were to attempt to treat it picturesquely, he must abandon it in despair, because the charm of the picturesque is in irregularity, and the charm of the beautiful is in symmetry, in just proportion, in equality. You Americans do not see that the work of man, who is the crown of animate life, can only be beautiful as it approaches the regularity expressive of beauty in that life. Any breathing thing that wants perfect balance of form or feature is in so far ugly; it is offensive and ridiculous, just as a perfectly balanced tree or hill would be. Nature is picturesque, but what man creates should be beautiful, or else it is inferior. Since the Greeks, no people have divined this but the Altrurians, until now; and I do not believe that you would have begun to guess at it as you certainly have here, but for the spread of our ideas among you, and I do not believe this example will have any lasting effect with you unless you become Altrurianized. The highest quality of beauty is a spiritual quality."

"I don't know precisely how far I have followed you," said my companion, who seemed struck by a novelty in truisms which are so trite with us, "but I certainly feel that there is something in what you say. You are probably right in your notion that the highest quality of beauty is a spiritual quality, and I should like very much to know what you think that spiritual quality is here."

"The quality of self-sacrifice in the capitalists who gave their money, and in the artists who gave their talent without hope of material return, but only for the pleasure of authorizing and creating beauty that shall last forever in the memory of those it has delighted."

The banker smiled compassionately.

"Ah, my dear fellow, you must realize that this was only a spurt. It could be done once, but it couldn't be kept up."

"Why not?" I asked.

"Because people have got to live, even capitalists and artists have got to live, and they couldn't live by giving away wealth and giving away work, in our conditions."

"But you will change the conditions!"

"I doubt it," said the banker with another laugh. One of the Columbian guards passed near us, and faltered a little in his walk. "Do you want us to go out?" asked my friend.

"No," the young fellow hesitated. "Oh no!" and he continued his round.

"He hadn't the heart to turn us out," said the banker, "he would hate so to be turned out himself. I wonder what will become of all the poor fellows who are concerned in the government of the Fair City when they have to return to earth! It will be rough on them." He lifted his head, and cast one long look upon the miracle about us. "Good heavens!" he broke out, "and when they shut up shop, here, will all this beauty have to be destroyed, this fabric of a vision demolished? It would be infamous, it would be sacrilegious! I have heard some talk of their burning it, as the easiest way, the only way of getting rid of it. But it mustn't be, it can't be."

"No, it can't be," I responded fervently. "It may be rapt from sight in the flames like the prophet in his chariot of fire; but it will remain still in the hearts of your great people. An immortal principle, higher than use, higher even than beauty, is expressed in it, and the time will come when they will look back upon it, and recognize in it the first embodiment of the Altrurian idea among them, and will cherish it forever in their history, as the earliest achievement of a real civic life."

I believe this, my dear Cyril, and I leave it with you as my final word concerning the great Columbian Fair.

Yours in all brotherly affection,
A. Homos.

Selected
Bibliography

The following books represent various approaches to the study of American culture in the late nineteenth century. The list is by no means exhaustive, or of uniform quality throughout. Nevertheless, almost all these works are suggestive and should be helpful to anyone concerned with this period.

Volumes with important visual materials are marked with an asterisk (*). And although original editions have been cited, where paperbacks have appeared "p" is appended (p).

(p) Beer, Thomas · *The Mauve Decade. American Life at the End of the Nineteenth Century.* New York, 1926.

Berthoff, Warner · *The Ferment of Realism. American Literature, 1884–1919.* New York and London, 1964.

(p) Bremner, Robert H. · *From the Depths. The Discovery of Poverty in the United States.* New York, 1956.

Davies, Wallace E. · *Patriotism on Parade. The Story of Veterans' and Hereditary Organizations in America 1783–1900.* Cambridge, 1955.

*(p) Giedion, Siegfried · *Mechanization Takes Command: A Contribution to Anonymous History.* New York, 1948.

(p) Hart, James D. · *The Popular Book. A History of America's Literary Taste.* New York, 1950.

(p) Higham, John · *Strangers in the Land. Patterns of American Nativism, 1860–1925.* New Brunswick, 1955.

(p) Higham, John · "The Reorientation of American Culture in the 1890s," in John Weiss, ed., *The Origins of Modern Consciousness.* Detroit, 1965.

(p) Hofstadter, Richard · *Social Darwinism in American Thought.* Philadelphia, 1944.

*(p) Kouwenhoven, John A. · *Made in America. The Arts in Modern Civilization.* New York, 1948.

Levy, Lester S. · *Grace Notes in American History, Popular Sheet Music from 1820–1900.* Norman, 1967.

McCullough, David C. · *The Johnstown Flood.* New York, 1968.

McLean, Albert F., Jr. · *American Vaudeville as Ritual.* Lexington, 1965.

*(p) Mayer, Grace M. · *Once Upon a City.* New York, 1958.

Mott, Frank Luther · *A History of American Magazine,* vols. III, IV. Cambridge, 1938, 1957.

*(p) Mumford, Lewis · *The Brown Decades. A Study of the Arts in America. 1865–1895.* New York, 1931.

*   Murrell, William · *A History of American Graphic Humor.* 2 vols. New York, 1938.

Pomeroy, Earl · *In Search of the Golden West. The Tourist in Western America.* New York, 1957.

Presbrey, Frank S. · *The History and Development of Advertising.* New York, 1929.

*   Rischin, Moses · *The Promised City. New York's Jews. 1870–1914.* Cambridge, 1962.

Rosenberg, Charles E. · *The Trial of the Assassin Guiteau.* Chicago and London, 1968.

Schlesinger, Arthur M. · *Learning How to Behave. A Historical Study of American Etiquette Books.* New York, 1946.

Schlesinger, Arthur M. · *The Rise of the City, 1877–1898.* New York, 1933.

Schwab, Arnold T. · *James Gibbons Huneker. Critic of the Seven Arts.* Stanford, 1963.

*   Taft, Pauline Dakin · *The Happy Valley. The Elegant Eighties in Upstate New York.* Syracuse, 1965.

Twyman, Robert W. · *History of Marshall Field and Co., 1852–1906.* Philadelphia, 1954.

Veysey, Laurence R. · *The Emergence of the American University.* Chicago and London, 1965.

Voigt, David Q. · *American Baseball. From Gentleman's Sport to the Commissioner System.* Norman, 1966.

Wecter, Dixon · *The Saga of American Society. A Record of Social Aspiration, 1607–1937.* New York, 1937.

(p) White, Morton G. · *Social Thought in America. The Revolt Against Formalism.* New York, 1947.

(p) Wiebe, Robert H. · *The Search for Order, 1877–1920.* New York, 1967.

Wood, James Playsted · *The Story of Advertising.* New York, 1958.

(p) Ziff, Larzer · *The American 1890s. Life and Times of a Lost Generation.* New York, 1966.